CW00551232

The Town Library of Ipswich

I. William Smarte (*detail above*) from his memorial of 1599 (*below*) in the Church of St Mary-le-Tower, Ipswich.

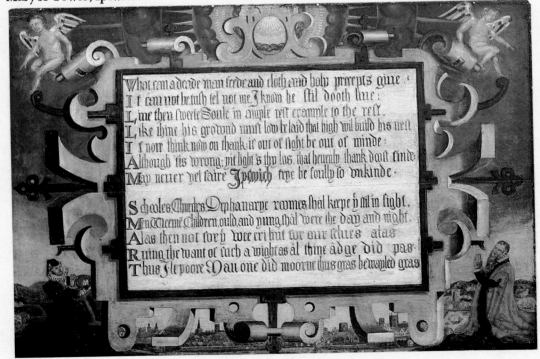

THE
TOWN LIBRARY
OF

PROVIDED FOR THE USE OF THE
TOWN PREACHERS
IN 1599

A HISTORY AND CATALOGUE

by

John Blatchly

THE BOYDELL PRESS

First published 1989 by The Boydell Press, Woodbridge

The Boydell Press is an imprint of Boydell & Brewer Ltd
PO Box 9, Woodbridge, Suffolk IP12 3DF
and of Boydell & Brewer Inc.
Wolfeboro, New Hampshire 03894–2069, USA

ISBN 0 85115 517 0

British Library Cataloguing in Publication Data
Blatchly, John
    The town library of Ipswich provided for the
    use of the town preachers in 1599 : a history
    and catalogue.
    1. Suffolk. Ipswich. Private libraries
    I. Title
    027'.1'42649
    ISBN 0–85115–517–0

Library of Congress Cataloging-in-Publication Data
Blatchly, John.
    The town library of Ipswich provided for the use of the town
    preachers in 1599 : a history and catalogue / by John Blatchly.
        p.   cm.
    Bibliography: p.
    ISBN 0851155170 (alk. paper)
    1. Libraries – England – Ipswich – History. 2. Preaching – Library
    resources – England – Ipswich – History. 3. Bibliography – Early
    printed books – Catalogs. 4. Manuscripts – Library resources –
    England – Ipswich – Catalogs. 5. Books and reading – England –
    Ipswich – History. 6. Ipswich (England) – Intellectual life.
    I. Title.
    Z791.I63B57   1989
    027.4426'49 – dc19   89–838
                                                             CIP

The paper used in this publication meets the
minimum requirements of American National Standard
for Information Sciences – Permanence of Paper for
Printed Library Materials, ANSI Z39.48–1984.

Printed in Great Britain by
St Edmundsbury Press, Bury St Edmunds, Suffolk

CONTENTS

AUTHOR CATALOGUE

Compiled from cards written and checked by Mrs A. Elisabeth Birkby, F.L.A., arranged alphabetically by authors, with a key to the abbreviations used, and followed by brief details of the manuscripts.

APPENDICES

ILLUSTRATIONS

COLOUR PLATES

FIGURES

PREFACE

The care of the precious collection which has been entrusted to me has been a labour of love, as has the writing of its history and my part in the detailed work of preparing the catalogue. At the outset I had little of the knowledge and few of the skills needed for the task, but others have been ready to inform and guide me in the paths I should take. By now I feel much better placed to appreciate the Library, and have absorbing interests in many aspects, new to me, of books, printing, the early book trade, libraries and authors. My own general education has certainly been advanced, and for that reason, if for no other, my gratitude must be expressed to all those who have helped.

First of all, Betty Birkby, also in an honorary capacity, visited the Library weekly for two years in order to prepare a catalogue card for each of the works. She has since given much time to check what I have made of her work in catalogue form. Several other professional librarians and scholars have given us their advice and support: David McKitterick at Cambridge University Library, latterly at the Wren Library at Trinity College, Paul Morgan and Henry Hallam at the Bodleian, and Suzanne Eward at Salisbury Cathedral. It is to Mirjam Foot at the British Library that we owe the notes on bindings to be found in the catalogue for any boards which merit comment. Tony Campbell and Karen Cook of the Map Library there could not have been more helpful over the identification and cataloguing of the contents of John Knight's atlases. Our County Archivist, Amanda Arrowsmith, and her colleague David Allen have helped with the transcription of handwritten additions to books, and many fellow students of Ipswich and Suffolk history have as always been most ready to help: Joan Corder, Peter Northeast, Diarmaid MacCulloch, John Webb, John Fitch, Frank Grace, Margaret Statham, and David van Zwanenburg. Norman Scarfe very generously read the History in draft, much to the advantage of later readers.

At School, David Warnes and successive generations of School archivists, particularly Sarah Waters and Anthony Howe, have done much useful work in the Library, particularly after Nicholas Pickwood, who came to instruct the team in leather and paper conservation, noticed the fore-edge shelfmarks for the first time. David also gave expert advice about layout and typography. Irvine Gray and Wallace Morfey were always prepared to help, particularly where the history of the School was concerned.

The author of such a work as this would be foolish indeed if he did not call on the wisdom of experienced antiquarian booksellers, and Paul Grinke, Tom Cook, Tony Doncaster and Len Lamb have all in different ways been of the greatest assistance; Mrs Birkby and I owe much to the latter in the collation and sure identification of the earliest books.

Several discoveries led me to be in touch with specialist historians: Andrew Watson over early owners, Glyn Parry on the Tudor historian William Harrison, and, most fruitfully of all, John Morrill at Selwyn who has since made a detailed study for eventual publication of William Dowsing's manuscript additions to his own collection of Parliamentary Sermons. His visit with Anthony Milton, Glenn Burgess and Howard Moss began the discussion of Ward's choice of books for the early Library; their individual and collective thoughts on the subject have been distilled into the final chapter here by Nicholas Cranfield and Anthony Milton.

Those who have the professional charge of the Library, Peter Labdon and Guenever Pachent, have always supported me in caring for the books, and been most enthusiastic for this publication. It has been a special pleasure to meet and discuss the collection with one who for many years had it in her care as Chief Librarian for Ipswich: Dorothy White.

The publication of such a specialised work as this would not be possible without financial assistance. First and foremost, the Governing Body of Ipswich School, and the Management Committee of the Ipswich Institute (whose own library dates from 1824) have both made generous grants-in-aid. It is especially pleasing that those who today administer the foundations or endowments of the earliest benefactors of the Library, William Smarte and Elizabeth Walter, have helped too. They are the Ipswich Foundation Street Charity Trustees who maintain the dwellings for elderly people first founded by Henry Tooley and William Smarte, and Elizabeth Walter's Charity Trustees who continue to help to maintain the fabric of the parish church of St Lawrence where she worshipped and her father John Moore has a memorial. To all these governors and trustees, and to those who have subscribed for the book before publication, I now express my gratitude.

Few people are as generous with their time and skills as Birkin Haward. He took photographs of the restored memorial to William Smarte in the Tower Church which Keith Jones has kindly allowed us to reproduce. He also made the drawings which appear as figures 1, 2 and 3. Next I acknowledge with gratitude the permission of the Curator of Ipswich Museums for the reproduction of portraits in the Borough collections as plates II and III, and that of its owner for the portrait of Hingeston in plate IV.

No-one has looked forward to the appearance of this book more than Tony Copsey, who has as usual put his unrivalled collection of Ipswich and Suffolk books at my disposal, and arranged for the colour plates to be printed by Acolortone Ltd. But only my wife Pamela knows how long it has taken to prepare copy which is truly camera-ready for Pru Harrison and the Barbers to make a volume of which we could all be proud. For all her practical help and moral support I dedicate this book to her.

John Blatchly

Ipswich School
January 1989

Watch, WARD, and keepe thy Garments tight,

For I come Thiefe-like at Midnight.

All-ſeeing, never-ſlumbring Lord;

Be thou my *Watch*, Ile be thy WARD.

Revel. 16. 15.
1. Theſ. 5. 4. 6
Pſal. 121. 4.

THE GOVERNMENT OF IPSWICH
IN THE 16TH, 17TH AND 18TH CENTURIES

First in seniority came 12 PORTMEN (The Twelve), self replacing, and elected for life, from whose number the Great Court usually elected annually two BAILIFFS (joint Mayors and Chief Magistrates) and four other Justices.

Next there were 24 COMMON COUNCILMEN (The Twenty Four), self replacing and for life, from whose ranks the Town Treasurer, Coroners, Clavigers and other officers were usually elected annually.

The Portmen and Common Council Men met as the ASSEMBLY to discuss town affairs, but officially decisions were to be voted on at GREAT COURTS.

The CORPORATION included also a larger and variable number of FREE BURGESSES (free by birth, servitude, or occasionally by payment), and met at GREAT COURTS to vote on all corporate matters and in elections to borough office. Most important of all, the Corporation voted to send two Burgesses to Parliament.

NOTE: When in the History the words School and Library are given capital letters they refer to the Grammar School of Ipswich and the Town Library. By the Book is meant the Benefactors' Book which is described in Chapter II.

The Assembly Books (C6/1/3–9) and Great Court Books (C5/14/3–10) of the Corporation which cover the period up to Municipal Reform may be consulted at the Suffolk Record Office in Ipswich. Nathaniel Bacon made extracts from them up to 1649 in his Annals of Ipswiche, of which an edited version by W.H. Richardson was published in 1884. W.E. Layton published later extracts up to 1672 in *East Anglian Notes & Queries*, (N.S.) I to VIII between 1885 and 1900. Many facts in the following history (particularly those for which dates are stated) will be found in these sources. Dated payments, unless otherwise stated, are taken from the Town Treasurers' or Chamberlains' account books, also available at the Ipswich office. Venn's *Alumni Cantabrigienses* is another source frequently quoted without special indication.

WILLIAM SMARTE 'FIRST BENEFACTOR TO THIS LIBRARY'

'Mr William Smarte, *Portman, may be consider'd as the accidental Founder of the publick Library; for it appears from a Memorandum in the Library, that his* Latin *Books were not disposed of as directed in his Will, Clause E, but were kept in a Chest, 'till the Year 1612, when they were deposited in that spacious room in Christ's Hospital where they now are: And tho' the Value of these Books and Manuscripts was not great, this Legacy seems to have put the Corporation upon erecting a publick Library, which otherwise perhaps they might not have done.'*

Richard Canning in *Ipswich Gifts and Legacies,* 1747.[1]

Ipswich in the sixteenth century had two great merchant benefactors, Henry Tooley and William Smarte. *Great Tooley of Ipswich*[2] tells the life of the first who died in 1552, but of Smarte little has been written. Half a century separated their deaths, but the names Tooley and Smarte are joined still in the almshouses they founded which, rebuilt in 1845, stand close to the original site in Foundation Street. The younger man, William Smarte, draper, Portman and Burgess to Parliament for the borough, added to Tooley's foundation in 1591, and between then and his death in 1599 made plans which justify this line on his memorial in the civic church of St Mary-le-Tower:

Schooles, churches, orphanarye roomes shal keepe ye stil in sight.

This can be read in the acrostic on his name on the curious painted wooden panel which combines portraits of Smarte and his wife Alice with the earliest known panoramic view of the town (*pl. I*). Smarte endowed scholarships for boys of the Grammar School going up to Pembroke Hall at Cambridge together with a fellowship, often held later by those same scholars. For the better instruction of the ministers of the town, particularly the common preachers, the clause E of the will[3] mentioned by Canning made provision as follows:

my latten printed bookes and writen bookes in volume and p'chmente... I gyve towardes one librarye safelie to be keepte in the vestrye of the parishe church of St. Mary Tower in Ipswich aforesayde, & the doore to have two sufficiente lockes and keyes th'one to remayne in the custodye of the minister of the parishe for the time beinge and the other to be kepte by the Churchwardens of the sayde p'ishe for the tyme beinge to be used ther by the com'on preacher of the sayd Towne for the tyme beinge or any other pre'cher mynded to preache in the saide p'ishe church...

William Smarte was the eldest son of Richard Smarte and Katherine Went his wife. Richard was himself a draper of the Tower parish and held the office of Bailiff, the highest in the borough, more than once. He was twice elected Burgess to Parliament, in 1545 and 1555, and died in 1560 leaving four manors in Essex and Suffolk to William and other lands and property to four younger sons and daughters, as well as a particularly fine collection of plate.[4]

---

[1] [R. Canning], *An Account of the Gifts and Legacies that have been given and bequeathed to Charitable Uses in the Town of Ipswich; with Some Account of the Present State and Management, and Some Proposals for the future Regulation of them.* (Ipswich 1747), pp.140–150 deal with the Library.

[2] J.G. Webb, *Great Tooley of Ipswich: Portrait of an early Tudor merchant.* (Ipswich, for the Suffolk Records Society 1962).

[3] PCC 90 Kidd (1599).

[4] PCC 48 Mellersh, and J.G. Webb, *Suffolk Review,* I (1958), 166.

Richard Smarte is twice portrayed by John Foxe in his *Actes and Monuments*[5] as a persecutor of Puritans in Marian times. Bishop Hopton at his episcopal visitation in July 1556 was on the point of releasing an Ipswich tailor and versifier called Peter Moone, having accepted his affirmation, when Richard Smarte pressed him to send for Moone's wife, 'a perillous woman' and far more likely to prove stubborn and incriminate both. Smarte did worse in November 1558 when, with Sir Henry Doyle the High Sheriff, he presided at the burning of Alice Driver and Alexander Gouche on the Cornhill. The condemned pair asked leave to say their prayers beforehand, but Smarte replied "On, on, have done. Make an end, naile them to the stake." When notwithstanding they continued in prayer he cried "Come off, have them to the fire." Foxe enjoyed a digression during the Moone narrative to tell of Smarte's change of heart in the next reign:

> He was an earnest member of their Romish law, doing of a very conscience that he did, who after the death of Queen Mary [just thirteen days after the Cornhill burning] lived not many yeeres, but rendred his life in godly repentance, protesting that if God should suffer him to live, he would never be the man he had bin before, what lawes soever should come againe: so that before the time of his sicknes he frequenting earnestly ye sermons in the same town made by divers godly learned men, wood weep as it had been a child, being notwithstanding of courage as stout a man as any was in Ipswich.

Where his son William stood in religion we must enquire. His first appearance in office was as Treasurer in 1560–1, then in 1562 Coroner and Claviger. Elected Portman in 1565, he became Bailiff five times between 1569 and 1594. In May 1586 he showed himself prepared to submit to imprisonment in the Marshalsea for the action he took to prevent the export of Suffolk bacon to the Earl of Leicester's garrison in the Low Countries. Assembling the people by proclamation, he took them on board a ship belonging to one Thomas Bennett, and sold and distributed the food as he saw fit. In this he had the backing of the Corporation, for the Town Clerk and others took letters to the Privy Council at the town's expense 'for the better clering of the said Mr Smart'.[6] His defence would have lain in the Act requiring magistrates to keep markets open; but here he was not acting against a local monopoly, but preventing supplies reaching the forces of the Crown defending Protestantism against the Spaniards. If this was less than patriotic, Smarte lost nothing in the eyes of his fellow townsmen. That September he became Bailiff for the fourth time, and in October 1588 was elected to represent them in Parliament, now styled 'gentleman'. He seems to have remained an active magistrate at least until September 1598, and was nearly seventy years old when he died a year later. His wife Alice somewhat hastily married Ralph Scrivener of Belstead, but this was almost suggested in Smarte's will:

> Item I gyve to Raffe Scryvener gent. fyve poundes to be payde within one moneth after my decease prayinge him to give favo'r, furtherance and continuance to the just causes of my sayde wief myne executrix...

Alice died in October 1600, but in the following year Ralph Scrivener founded four more scholarships to Pembroke as she had requested. Ipswich and Pembroke Hall's good fortune arose from the fact that William and Alice Smarte were childless.

William's complicated and elaborately worded will was made 8 January 1598/9 and proved 2 November following. His grey stone ledger slab, now mural on the west wall of the Tower church near the painted memorial, bears the inscription: 'Guilielmus Smart, integerrimae pietatis justitiaeque Senator defunctus est 23 Septembris 1599.' Between that January and September one significant change took place in Smarte's intention to found a Library at Ipswich. No mention is made in the will of any gift to Pembroke Hall, yet the library there includes over one hundred manuscript volumes of his, most of which formerly belonged to the great Abbey of Bury St. Edmunds.[7] They apparently went

5   J. Foxe, *Acts and Monuments*, ed. S.R.C. Cattley and G. Townsend. (8 vols., 1837–41), VIII, 101, 223, 496, 598.
6   *Acts of the Privy Council of England*, XIV, pp.128–9, 134, 160.
7   M.R. James, *On the Abbey of St Edmund at Bury: i: The Library* (Cambridge Antiquarian Society 8vo. Publ. no.

to Cambridge in 1599. This left just eight manuscripts for Ipswich, four (in three volumes) certainly from Bury, as well as some 26 printed books.

By some means Smarte had become the owner of a large number of Bury manuscripts; at the Dissolution there in 1539 he could hardly have been of an age to do so, but his father Richard would have been glad enough to save them from destruction. It may be significant that many of them bear or bore the pressmark B, that is, the books were near neighbours on the shelves of the Abbey library, and were perhaps sold or just taken away as a lot on that basis. It is also of interest that a smaller batch of manuscripts (seven allowed by Ker to be of Bury origin) were in Suffolk until 1634, when their owner Jeremiah Holt, rector of Stonham Aspal, presented them to his Cambridge college, St John's. The elder Smarte's will makes no mention of books of any kind, but he or another of his generation must have acquired them soon after 1539 or they would have become dispersed. In a list of Pembroke library manuscripts made by Thomas James, Bodley's Librarian, and published in his *Ecloga Oxonio-Cantabrigiensis* in 1600, the Smarte volumes are introduced as follows:

> Gulielmus Smart Aldermannus Gypovicensis, vir piissimae memoriae, qui placide in domino obdormivit an. superiori 1599 dedit aulae Penbrochianae hos omnes libros qui sequuntur, ex procuratione Magistri Buckenhamij huius Col. socij.

Matthew Wren, later successively Bishop of Norwich and of Ely, went into rather more detail in his Register of Benefactors to the College Library. What follows is Dr M.R. James's translation of Wren's Latin:

> All these came from the Monastery of S. Edmund in Suffolk, and were given to us in the year 1599 by the means of Mr. Richard Buckenham, Fellow. Had he left us a Catalogue of his gift, he would have rendered us a great service: for besides the books here named, he [Smarte] gave no doubt a considerable number which are now, alas! wanting. I have consulted the Catalogue by James of Oxford. Hardly a year had elapsed since the gift was made when he catalogued the books; and he reckons 191 volumes. No confidence, however, can be placed in him; for he has frequently included the gifts of others. Yet it is certain that of those in his list about thirty are missing.

Richard Buckenham was the second son of William Buckenham, a wealthy Ipswich mercer who had held Corporation office from 1563 to his death in 1595. The Buckenhams and Smartes were neighbours in the Tower parish and, whereas William Smarte was a supervisor of William Buckenham's will,[8] Edward Buckenham, the third son, was witness to William Smarte's. Richard must have been born in the late 1560s as he matriculated at Pembroke at Easter 1584 and became a Fellow about 1588. He was rector of Great Bromley in Essex from 1600 to 1612, proceeded to D.D. in 1615 and died in 1628 having been a Prebendary of Chichester since 1609 and Archdeacon of Lewes. From his will [9] we learn of a large family and an eldest son Richard at Christ's College for whom he left his own books; they could be sold if necessary to keep him there. The only mention of Ipswich in the will is of three tenements with gardens there; Pembroke Hall is forgotten too. By persuading Smarte to give manuscripts and endowments to the college however Buckenham had established the main route by which able Ipswichians have proceeded to Cambridge ever since. He did remember Samuel Harsnett, whose library now belongs to Colchester, but not with books. Harsnett was Buckenham's senior by nearly twenty years, his patron through Cambridge and in the Chichester diocese. Young Richard had been sent to Chigwell School, Harsnett's own foundation, and Buckenham wrote in his will: 'to Samuel, Bishop of Norwich, in token of my thankfull hart for all his goodnes to me, 40s. to make a gold ring.'

The elder Buckenham's intervention in Smarte's testamentary affairs is now seen to have been a

28, 1895) and *English Historical Review*, XLI (1926), 251–260, and N.R. Ker, *Medieval Libraries of Great Britain, a list of surviving books*. (Royal Hist. Soc., 2nd. ed., 1964), 16–22. and A.G. Watson's *Supplement*, (London 1987).
[8] PCC 35 Scott (1595).
[9] PCC 82 Barrington (1628).

shrewd move at a critical point in the young cleric's career. He must have helped Smarte to change his mind about the manuscripts at some time between January 1598/9 and the following September, for Thomas James implies and Wren states that the manuscripts arrived in Cambridge in 1599. Like Wren, we find ourselves regretting that Buckenham left no record of the transfer, but if, as seems likely, he had diverted from Ipswich the greater part of the founding bequest to the Library, the less he said or wrote about it the better. It could be that the Protestant burgesses of the town preferred to see this mass of pre-Reformation theology go elsewhere; fortunately Launcelot Andrewes, Master at Pembroke Hall, was a man with the breadth of vision to take it into safe keeping.

From the clear italic inscription on fo.ii^v of Ipswich ms 8 we must infer that an earlier attempt had been made to secure some of Smarte's books for a Cambridge college. The vital word is erased:

20 Julii 1596
Collegium
Ex dono Gulielmi Smarte

Similar but undated and unmutilated inscriptions in Pembroke MS 29 and 41 in the same hand have 'Collegium Magdalense'. Under ultra-violet light, traces of ink from the erased word are seen to be consistent with the same name. Although obviously the three manuscripts thus inscribed never did go to Magdalene College, it is interesting to search for links between that college and Ipswich, and one does not have to look far. The first town preacher of Ipswich from 1560 to his death in 1575 was the overtly Protestant Roger Kelke, Master of Magdalene, and his deputy from 1571, Alexander Keyes, one of the Fellows. Probably as a result, three ushers of the Grammar School were Magdalene men, two of them educated at the School and sent up with exhibitions by the town.[10] James Leman, at school until 1576, Usher from 1594 until 1604, and then Master until he fell foul of the Corporation in 1608, might well have wished that Smarte would give some or all of his books to his college, the one with which for several decades the School had had its strongest links.

The eight manuscripts which did come to the Ipswich Library from Smarte are still in the collection, and both M.R. James and N.R. Ker have published descriptions of them.[11] We, like them, will use the numbers applied in gilt to their Victorian bindings in about 1864 by Sterling Westhorp. It is worth noting here that Ker was in error when he stated that the earliest list by Samuel Ward in the Benefactors' Book of 1615 has the manuscripts in the order 4, 6, 1, 5, 7, 3, 8, 2. In fact, Ward's order is 3, 8, 6, 1, 4, 2, 5, 7. A Vulgate of about 1230 (ms 9) is not one of Smarte's gifts, and its marginalia of 1570 to 1710 are of sufficient local interest to be described more fully. The 'Withipoll' Book of Hours (ms 7), though evidently given by Smarte, is not of Bury origin, nor, according to Ker, are mss 1,3 and 5, and ms 2 may not be. The Book of Hours, the Vulgate and the 17th century ms 10 will be the subjects of Chapter XIII.

The reader may at this stage find it useful to have for reference a transcript of the only surviving detailed record of Smarte's bequest, Ward's list on page B3 of the Benefactors' Book. Westhorp's numbers for manuscripts and John King's (of 1799) for books are added in the left-hand column. Ward's flourish γ seems to cover a multitude of Latin endings.

	Mr Smart late portman, besides many other good deeds
ms	gave to ye use of a Librarie these bookes following vz
3,8,6	vetera manuscripta octo 1us in Exod. 2us in Jud. & Psal. 3us
1,4	miscellan. ex Cyrillo & Gregorio 4us Concordanti bibl. 5us
2	Mariale St. Edm^d in laudem beata Maria 6us Beda in Evang. Lucae:
5,7	7us Opuscule anony. imperfec 8us precationis summula:

[10] I.E. Gray and W.E. Potter, *Ipswich School 1400–1950*. (Ipswich 1950), 45.

[11] M.R. James, 'Description of the Ancient MSS in the Ipswich Public Library' in *Proc. Suffolk Inst. Arch.*, XXII (1934), 86–103, and N.R. Ker, *Medieval Manuscripts in British Libraries*. (Oxford 1977) II, 990–3.

King

–		Biblia ex editione Hieronymi cu' glossa 1 vol. (extracted)
4(4), 133		Lyra glossa in 4 Vols. Hieronym. biblia l vol.
3		Aquinas in ep'las Pauli:
182		Destructorium vitiorum [*sic*]
199(1&2)		Brigittae revelationes in 2 vol:
122		Brunfelsi ƒ in nov. testam. & Zacha: in harmon. evang. 1 vol.
lost		Bartolome ƒ de p'prietatio rerum
698		Egisipp ƒ de excidio Hierosol: in Theodereto in ep'las pauli l vol.
5		Richard ƒ de media villa
189		Johannes de Bassolis Justiniae in 4^{or} sentent. l vol.
185		Johannes Maior in sentent. 2 vol
'705'		Salemonis eccl'iae constant: epi' glossa
207		Sermones Meffreth sive hortul ƒ Reginae
71		Lyndwoodi provincialis
–	(x)	⎰ Polychronicon mega Lateratu' in fol. magno. ⎱ (x extracted
–	(x)	⎱ Hugonis Cardinalis 2 vol: (obsele:) both rent
lost		Erasmi annot: in novu' testamentu' in peeces)
lost		Ch^{r}ysosto: Homilis quaedam graecolat: in 8°
lost		Historia Petri Comestoris & Bedae in l vol.
lost		Speculu' morale Vincentii

The above is in Samuel Ward's hand (his later additions in brackets); what follows is in another:

Memorandum. These bookes beeing bequeathed to a librarie were reserved by the Towne in an old chest untill this was founded a° 1612.

It will be seen that 17 of Smarte's printed books remain today, including *Destructorium viciorum* which, though missing in 1630 and replaced then by John Allen, minister of St Mary Quay, was found later, so that there are now two almost identical copies. Of five books lost, the Erasmus was replaced about 1615 by Ward's close friend and colleague John Carter, the celebrated minister of Bramford, later of Belstead. Four other books were extracted by Ward, either because of their condition or because a better edition had been acquired. The *Polychronicon* of Higden may have been a Caxton. Coincidentally, Sir Charles Sherrington presented a single leaf from the 1482 edition to Ipswich in 1935, and this is in the Library. In the replacement Latin Bible with commentary by Hugo de S. Charo (6 vols., Basel 1504 King 8), Ward wrote 'vetera praetererunt nova facta sunt omnia'.

The memorandum at the foot of the list, not in Ward's hand, but probably in that of the donor of the new Hugo, John Cottesford (alternately Master, Usher, Master and Usher of the School between 1611 and 1618), tells us what in fact happened to Smarte's books in the decade following his death. This gave rise to Canning's remark quoted at the head of the Chapter: the 'Books were not disposed of as he directed...'. It is easy to see why a chest rather than a room was appropriate. Buckenham's intervention had reduced the collection from well over a hundred to just 34 volumes, and a secure chest was ideal, presumably kept in the vestry of St. Mary-le-Tower. Incidentally there is no chest of appropriate size and age in the church today.

Much of interest can be gathered from manuscript inscriptions in the printed books which Smarte gave. Although labels were specially printed for some 34 later donors, none were provided for Smarte's books, but his name appears in most, in some in what must be his own hand, but in a variety of styles. In five (King 3, 4(1), 5, 182, and '705') 'W^{s} Smarte Gippi'' is written on the title page in a minute but stylish secretary hand:

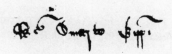

and in three (King 3, 182 and 199(1)) are Black-letter statements of recommendation or ownership:

Gulielm⁹ Smarte mei

verus possessor est⸫⸪

Gulielmus Smarte me vendicat⸓

iste liber spectat ad Gulielmū Smarte⸓

Six have Black-letter fore-edge titles, but the edges of the remainder have been trimmed with the book-ploughs of Victorian binders with total loss of markings.

The most interesting inscription is to be found on the title page of Meffreth's *Sermones* (King 207) in a clear italic hand but roughly deleted:

Willielmus [*sic*] Smart hunc possedet libru' teste Willielmus groume amen so
be yt mi sister Elsibet and my brother Rychard and my brother Thomas whan I dye
praye for me ye all goode sister and brothr praye for me & all men goode lord.

None but William Smarte can have written this, and he can hardly have expected the sentiments expressed to appeal to the Puritan ministers who were to have the book in their library. One of them, probably Ward, seeing this request to one living sister and one or two dead brothers to pray for Smarte, struck it through with over a score of thick pen strokes. It seems as though towards the end of his life William was turning again to the faith which earned his father notoriety in Foxe's writings. It is perhaps significant that the only legacy left by Richard or William Smarte to the ministers of the town was a collection of pre-Reformation books and manuscripts. The William Groome who was witness was a fellow clothier of Smarte's, son of William Groome of Lavenham and of Margaret, daughter of Robert Daundy, like Richard Smarte a Bailiff of Ipswich in Marian times. [12]

On the title page of Meffreth there is also written 'Mr Toley', surely not an indication that the great Henry himself owned it. In that book and several others the neat italic hand of William Blower is to be found. He was minister at Claydon from 1587 until 1602 when he died. At Bishop Redman's visitation in 1597 it was reported that he only 'sometymes weareth the surplesse in reading dyvyne service', and had not made a perambulation of his parish that year. [13] In King 185 at the *incipit* we read 'Mr Blower 21 Ap'lis 1598' and in King 112 on the woodcut frontispiece 'Mr Blower 30 Marcij 1599'. Blower certainly had access to the books 18 months before Smarte died, and evidently felt free to write in them. In two books, (a John Major, King 185 and a Richard of Middleton, King 5) there are on the titles 'liber doctor' astewyck' and, most interesting of all, in the second volume of Nicholas de Lyra's *Textus Bibliae* (King 4(2)) on the verso of the last folio 'From Jeffry Astwicke by I. Leugar 3 Junij 1597'. Jeffery Astwicke was born in 1562 the son of Thomas Astwicke, tailor of St. Lawrence parish, and Maryon his wife; further details about the man and his doctorate have not been found despite careful searches. John Lewgar was Beadle at Christ's Hospital several times

[12] F.W. Steer, 'The Dandy Pedigree' in *Proc. Suff. Inst. Arch.*, XXVII (1957), 143, No.102.
[13] J.F. Williams (ed.) *Bishop Redman's Visitation 1597.* (Norfolk Record Society. Norwich 1946), 147.

between 1584 and 1592, but does not thereafter appear to have been in the service of the town. One Edmund Wilson was Sexton at the Tower Church from 1596 to 1603 and would presumably have taken charge of the books had they gone there.[14] The Astwicke-Lewgar inscription quoted above does imply that in 1597, well in advance of the eventual bequest, the former poor-house Beadle was responsible for receiving returned volumes on loan; it is hardly likely that he would have other business with works of advanced theology.

What emerges from the dated inscriptions associated with Blower and Astwicke is that the volumes were available for their use at least two years or more before Smarte died. Perhaps on hearing of the similar foundation at St James's church in Bury St Edmunds in 1595, Smarte lost no time in putting the nucleus of a Library into the principal church of Ipswich.

The last question to be asked about Smarte's printed books concerns their provenance, for most of them had earlier owners. Two seem to have belonged at one time to the elusive Dr Astwicke, himself an early user of others of the books. The majority were published before the Dissolution, and could have come from Bury with the manuscripts. One, Lyndewode's *Super Constitutiones Provinciales Angliae,* 1505 (King 71) has many interesting and amusing manuscript additions, most of them by John Thetford when, before 1519, he was a canon of Butley Priory. They have been described in some detail by Professor Dickens,[15] but on the last leaf a stanza in Thetford's hand has charm enough to make it worth quoting:

> And a man wytt what that were
> comyng for to see and here
> he woold not mysspend an owr
> for of all treasure yt beryth ye flow'r.

Thetford went on to be the last Prior of Christ Church (or Holy Trinity Priory) in Ipswich at its suppression in 1536; the book may or may not have come to Ipswich with him. There is in the margin of fo. xii the impression of a wood-block stamp whose design is a florid crowned 'R' (possibly with a 'T' implied). Sir Thomas Rush was one of the commissioners at the Dissolution of both Butley and Christchurch, and it has been suggested that the mark is his. The Royal crown was his badge of office as serjeant-at-arms to both Henries; he also used it to decorate the bressumer beam on the Brook Street frontage of his mansion in St Stephen's parish in Ipswich.[16]

Several earlier owners of books had inscribed their names in them; most notably Richard Nix, Bishop of Norwich who owned the Aquinas (King 3) in 1506. The Latin Bible of 1514 (King 133) cost an early owner, Thomas Topcliff, Doctor of Canon Law, six shillings. On the flyleaves he wrote amongst other things a cure for 'towthe achys' and a recipe for 'A Lax: Pygge Potage'. The book was already in Suffolk by 1570, for in that year Christopher Broke wrote on the last leaf his complaint against the parson of Westhorpe who had given him but two of the twelve shillings he had promised him for serving from Palm Sunday through all the holy days. One of the same name was minister in Ipswich at St Peter in 1579 and St Stephen in 1581. V.B. Redstone quotes an entry in the Chamberlains' Accounts of the time: 'Paid to Christopher Brookes for a French testament 6d.'[17] Could this connect with Broke the minister, and was the purchase towards the Library? It is certainly frustrating that diligent searches have failed to locate the original extract.

It would be good to think that in time more will be discovered about Smarte's true intentions, and about the earliest arrangements made for the books and their first users. From what has been

---

[14] St Lawrence registers and Town Treasurers' and Chamberlains' accounts give this information about Astwicke, Lewgar and Wilson.

[15] A.G. Dickens, *The Register or Chronicle of Butley Priory, 1510–1535.* (Winchester 1951), 79.

[16] D.N.J. MacCulloch and J.M. Blatchly, 'Recent Discoveries at St Stephen's Church, Ipswich' in *Proc. Suff. Inst. Arch. & History,* XXXVI (1986), 113.

[17] V.B. Redstone, *Ipswich Borough Records.* (Extracts, first publ. in *East Anglian Daily Times,* Ipswich 1926–38) No. 12: Schools and Books, 5.

found so far, the impression is gained that Smarte may not have been too concerned to provide the preachers of Ipswich with the texts they would have chosen for themselves. Had he really wished to, a bequest of money to buy books would have been more appropriate. As will next become clear, Canning's suggestion that Smarte's legacy 'put the Corporation upon erecting a Publick library' does not bear examination, for nothing further was done for the next ten years.

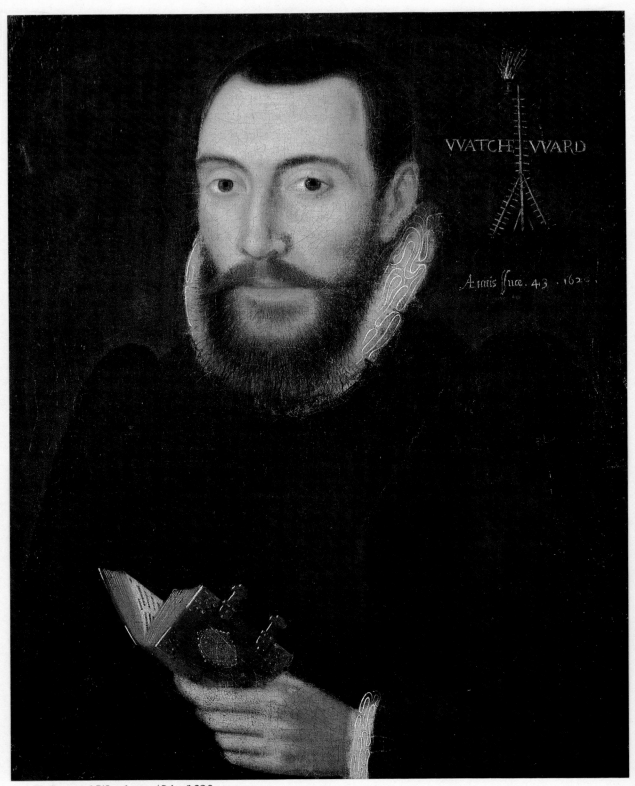

II. Samuel Ward *aet.* 43 in 1620.

II

THE LIBRARY HOUSED FOR SAMUEL WARD 1611–1618

> *'And whereas yt hath pleased God to put into the harte of Mr Ward our preacher, to stirre up this Corporacon, for the erecting of a Librarie, wch beeing furnished with all kinde of bookes can not but grately further the advancement of God's Glorie, his worshippe and religion amongst us. I doe will and bequeath fower pounds of lawfull English monie to bee paid within one yeare next after my decease ov'r and above the xx.[s] I have allreadye payd towardes the supplie of that good worke begunne.'*

From the Will of George Raymond the elder, grocer of Ipswich, 1617.[18]

We have no means of telling what use successive town preachers and others made of Smarte's books and manuscripts while they remained in the 'old chest', nor the length of time they would have lain there had Samuel Ward not been appointed to the preachership on 1 November 1605.[19]

Samuel Ward was born about 1577, the son of John Ward, preacher of Haverhill, and Susanna his wife. He went up to St John's College, Cambridge in 1594 and after taking his B.A. became a founder Fellow of Sidney Sussex College in 1599. Ordained in 1601, he was for a time preacher at Haverhill, but an annual salary of 100 marks with ten more with which to rent a house brought him to Ipswich at All Saints-tide in 1605, and for this stipend he was to preach three times weekly to the assembled Corporation in the Tower church, supplying deputies during allowed absences of up to 20 days a year. After two years in the post he was elected for life (should he wish to stay) and his salary was raised by ten marks. In 1608 he added a B.D. degree to his M.A., the fees paid by the town, and the following year the Corporation bought the house which is now 19 and 21 Lower Brook Street for him and his wife Deborah at a cost of £120, for which a rent of 10 marks was retained. He continued to please the burgesses, for in 1610 his salary became £90, and in 1616, £100 a year. All expenses of the Preacher's house were remitted, and he was by far the highest paid office holder in the town; for comparison the Grammar School Master received £24 6s 8d and the Usher £13 6s 8d. It would be interesting to know whether the portrait painted in 1620 (*pl. II*) was commissioned by the Corporation or by Ward himself, and through whose hands it came into the collection of 'that crabby bookseller' John Raw soon after 1800.

Not only was Ward more highly paid than the schoolmasters, his was a position of some authority in the School and over other town charities. Ten months after his appointment as preacher he was the junior of three divines appointed to examine the Master, James Leman, to establish 'whether he be worthy and sufficient for the place'; the others were doctors of divinity, one the celebrated William Jones of East Bergholt whose work on Philemon and Hebrews was later given to the Library (King 176). Leman was violently opposed, rightly, to borough moves to divert the revenues of Richard Felaw's 15th century gift from the Grammar School to the founding of a new charity school, and his removal from the Mastership seems to have been vindictive. He fought on through the courts at every level for 17 years before he was awarded a pension for life by order of the Archbishop of Canterbury and the Bishop of London in 1622. Ward's ready and immediate espousal of radical Corporation policy was to stand him in good stead. In October 1613 when Alexander Read, Fellow of Pembroke Hall, had vacated the Mastership of the School after little more than a year in the post, it was Ward who was asked to go over to Cambridge 'abowt the obteyninge of Mr Stoker or some other sufficient man' for a Master. His college connections fitted him well for the task.

[18] SRO Ipswich: IC/AA1/50/292 (1617).
[19] Great Court Book 4 November 1605. (Richardson, 424).

Two years earlier than this, on 19 February 1610/1, the Assembly had 'agreed that Mr Ward, Mr Carter, Mr Garthwayte and Mr Roe [minister at the Tower church] shall examine the Schollers of the Grammar Schole whether there be any fitt to be sent to Cambridge or not and to certify which of them (whose parents shall be willing to sende thither) they shall find fittest to be sent for the obteyning of a schollersheppe in Pembroke Hall according to Mr Smarte his gifte'. This task had been Ward's once already in 1610, but at the same Assembly, Ward and his colleagues, all ministers, were also 'appoynted to vew the house for the scolemaster of the Grammar Schole' and 'make view in the hospitall for some convenient Romes there for the placing of a librarie'.

This is the first recorded mention of the setting up of a library in a room of a publicly owned building. By 'hospitall' was meant the claustral buildings of the former Dominican Friary in St Edmund Pountney Lane, later Foundation Street. The four clerics chose the northern half of the 100 foot long first floor room in the north-east range which had been the dormitory of the friars. The southern half, partitioned off, was leased to the Taylors' Guild for their hall. Although the date at which the room was set up is given as 1612 on page B2 of the Benefactors' Book, the fact that it was not until January 1613/4 that the Assembly gave orders for the main work of preparation to be done must make 1614 more likely. Coincidentally the City Library at Norwich was in 1608 set up in a part of the former Blackfriars there.[20]

That some donors gave books as early as February and August 1613 we learn from the gift labels which Ward had printed to record benefactions permanently, but it is most unlikely that there were presses ready to receive the books for another year at least. It has been suggested that the labels would have been printed in Cambridge, but Paul Morgan, who listed them for the Addenda of the revised *S.T.C.*, feels that they may have been produced locally using a limited assortment of types in a binder's pallet – presumably the pallet of William Saires (*vide infra*). The labels are listed and illustrated at appendix C.

Although the Library was to be closely associated with the School for most of its active existence, there were good reasons why the burden fell at first on Ward rather than on the masters. The whole project was Ward's initiative in any case, a working Library for him and other preachers, and the School was in process of moving to a new site. Between 1612 and 1614 plans were afoot and building work was in progress for establishing the former frater of the friars as the Schoolroom. The frater is shown in front of the dorter range in Joshua Kirby's engraving of 1748 entitled 'The West View of Christ's Hospital in Ipswich'. Although its main axis ran north-south, it has often been referred to as the friars' 'chapel', but the late Roy Gilyard-Beer set that matter right once and for all.[21] When precisely the School moved across the road from Felaw's House (the 1483 School) it is not known, but the refurbished frater was certainly in use by Michaelmas 1614. Between 1611 and 1616 the School had four Masters and four Ushers, but as John Cottesford held both offices twice each only five men were involved. This being so, it is quite surprising that in such unsettled times Ward obtained gifts of books from all but one of them, and that John Coney, Usher from 1613 to 1616, could give Ward the assistance he did.

John Coney was the son of Robert Connye of Newbury, Fellow of King's and in 1577 Lady Margaret Preacher. The elder Connye was rector of the Wrethams in Norfolk, where his son joined him as curate after graduating from King's and being deaconed at Norwich, aged 24, in 1607. John Coney came to Ipswich when his father died in 1613 and as Usher was given a 'backhouse' adjoining the refectory Schoolroom. Probably because of his extra duties in the Library, Coney's Usher's stipend was increased by the Great Court to £20 in August 1614. Even so, his work in School and Library seems to have left Ward and the Corporation in his debt, for in the Assembly Book for May 1618, some time after Coney's death, aged 34 at most, it was agreed 'that Mrs Conye to have payde to her for her husbond's paynestaking in his lyfetime about the settling of the bokes in the librarie and for other his paynes taken about the bokes and Librarie – xl.ˢ'.

Coney's painstaking is still to be seen, first in the inscriptions he wrote in his own and others' gifts

20 G.A. Stephen, *Three Centuries of a City Library.* (Norwich 1917), 4 and frontispiece.
21 R. Gilyard Beer, 'Ipswich Blackfriars' in *Proc. Suff. Inst. Arch. & History* XXXIV (1977), 15–23.

to the Library but for which Ward had not afforded printed labels. He was the master of formal Roman and of a polished Italic, both in good imitation of print. His 'Tuccius *In Cantica Cat: Solo: Lugd. 1606*', yet to be identified, was lost very early on, but he wrote in Vitalis' *Speculum Morale*:

Apr: 20 . 1615 .
Alterum donum Iohannis Conei in Ludo Regio
Pædagogi & Librarij Gyppenwicensis .

in the gift of the short-term Master he served:

August 1613 The gift of Alex: Read Fellowe
of Pembrook hall in Camb:

for a recent Bailiff, Burgess to Parliament for the borough from 1614 to 1627, whose 12 volumes of Calvin's works surely deserved printed labels:

tunc the first) The gift of Mr Robert Snelling :
Portman of Ipswich. 1615 .

and for the minister at St Mary-le-Tower, soon to depart for Saxmundham:

Donum Nuttall ministri
Marianæ Ecclesiæ Gyp:

The Library Room

It was on 7 January 1613/4, three years after Ward's committee of ministers had chosen the room, that the assembly ordered 'that the Chamber at the North End of Taylors Hall be glassed fitting for a Library to lay and bestow books safely there'. In the Treasurer's Accounts for April 1614, Robert Windes was paid £1 7s 3d for 'Glazing The Librare Chamber', and on 30 August, Pumfrey the joyner £6 11s 5d 'for two presses for the Librarie and for lyneing the windows and mending the dore that shutts between the Librarie and the Taylors' Hall'. John Coney meanwhile received 11s 4d 'for money laid out about the Librare for the presses as by his bill'. The Taylors' Guild continued to hire the south chamber until 1617.

The appearance of the room is known in some detail, despite its demolition in the early 1850s, for Fred Russel and Wat Hagreen published an etching in 1845 of the northern end, [22] and Jabez Hare in 1830 [23] and Henry Davy in 1846 [24] both produced drawings and prints looking south. In Hare's engraving, made when the Grammar School was still in occupation, two large double-fronted cupboards can be seen, standing at that time with their backs to the south wall. One appears to be more elaborate than the other (which probably belonged to the School), and both were kept at the

[22] Etching: 'Interior of the Grammar School', drawn by F.B. Russel and etched by W. Hagreen and published in their *Picturesque Antiquities of Ipswich,* (Ipswich 1845).
[23] G.R. Clarke, *The History and Description of the Town and Borough of Ipswich.* (Ipswich 1830). The engraving: 'Interior of the Grammar School, Ipswich', drawn by Jabez Hare and engraved by J.F. Lambert, faces p. 281.
[24] Etching by H. Davy 'Interior of the Old Grammar School...' and published by him (Ipswich 1846). The original drawings are in BL Add. MS 19,179, fo.122.

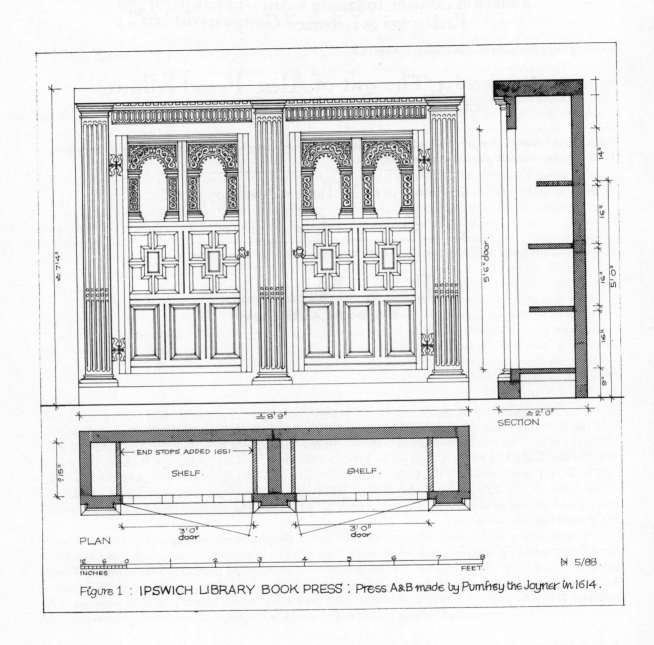

SECTION

PLAN

END STOPS ADDED 1651

SHELF.

SHELF.

3'0" door

3'0" door

INCHES

FEET.

⋈ 5/88.

Figure 1 : IPSWICH LIBRARY BOOK PRESS : Press A&B made by Pumfrey the Joyner in 1614.

12

far end of the Schoolroom built specially, but used only from 1842 to 1851, behind the Master's House (Ward's preacher's house formerly) in Brook Street. Of this scene the School possesses schoolboy drawings made by the future P.R.A., Edward Poynter, in 1851. The two cupboards went there with the School in 1842, but were not, as far as can be ascertained, sent up to Henley Road in 1851. By great good fortune the Ipswich architect Richard Phipson made a measured drawing of one of them,[25] the grander obviously, and thus we have some idea of the trouble the joyner Pumfrey took to decorate the first presses (*fig. 1*). Evidence will be given in Chapter VI for presses A and B having four shelves each; it has been demonstrated by measuring the books themselves that the cupboard Phipson drew would just accommodate the books in Coney's early A and B shelf lists on eight shelves. Pumfrey was paid for two presses; whether Phipson's cupboard counted as two, or whether two 'double' presses AB and CD were made for the money is not clear, but probably the latter to cope with the flood of book gifts coming in to the new foundation.

On 18 May 1618 the Assembly decided that 'Whereas Mr Ward hathe layde out x.^{li} vii.^{s} aboute the settinge uppe of presses in the Library for the bestowing of the bokes there and other things nedeful to be used there It is Agreed that the sd. x.^{li} vii.^{s} be paid unto him by the treasurer of this towne'. With this sum Ward probably provided presses EF and GH, for by then they would certainly have been needed. Evidence that eventually seven double presses furnished the room can be obtained from the manuscript catalogue made by Robert Coningsby in 1705.

In choosing to line the walls of the Library with presses (admittedly free-standing ones) Ward was following the very latest fashion, set as recently as 1610 in the Arts end of Bodley's Library. Wall-cases at the Escorial (1567) and in the Vatican Library (1587) had led the way on the continent, but in England some libraries, particularly at Oxford colleges, were planned on the stall system well into the 18th century.[26] The decision not to chain the books was also a departure from tradition. As recently as 1598, Francis Trigge had chosen to chain his new library at Grantham.

As for glazing, it is worth commenting on the factors which may have influenced the choice of frater for Schoolroom and dorter for Library. The frater had large 13th and 14th century windows, closely spaced, and needed only to be 'planchered' over worn medieval tiles and ventilated with three roof 'pentices' to become a fine light teaching space. The northern end of the dorter was comparatively poorly lit, with only two useful six-light mullioned windows facing west; the two on the east, one of two and the other of eight lights, but neither tall enough to give much light,[27] were blocked internally with brick and the first presses were probably set up against the blank wall so created. A tall six-light window with transoms was put into the north wall to give extra light to the Library, a wall which must have been blank when it did double duty as the south wall of the friars' chancel. The church of the Ipswich Blackfriars was the only building taken down at the Dissolution, so that the claustral ranges were left virtually entire; precisely the reverse happened at Norwich.

The reconstruction and plan (*figs. 2 and 3*) showing the most probable layout for presses A to O is based on consideration of the initial alterations to fenestration, the order in which presses were filled and a knowledge of those unfilled in 1650 and 1705.

---

[25] Ipswich Museums and Galleries: R.M. Phipson's first album, illustration 24a.
[26] N. Pevsner, *A History of Building Types*. (1976), 96–7.
[27] Pencil and wash drawings by H. Davy in BL Add. MS 19,179, fo. 122.

Figure 2 : Library in former Dormitory of Blackfriars c1614 to 1767. PN 5/88.

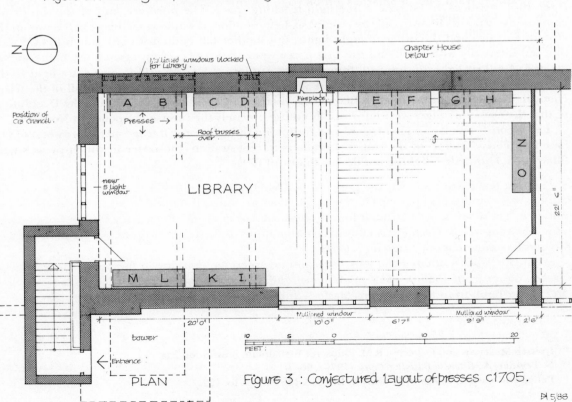

Figure 3 : Conjectured Layout of presses c1705.

PN 5/88

14

'which Vellum Book is very indifferently wrote & without method'

Samuel Pickering, Notary Publick. [28]

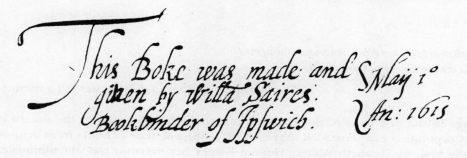

This inscription in John Coney's hand is written on the paper flyleaf of the full calf-bound book which contains 26 vellum leaves. J.B. Oldham found the same two roll stamps used together on the wooden boards on books of 1562 and 1581 in other libraries.[29] This suggests either that Saires re-used boards from an older book, and one with clasps (the marks are there), or that he acquired and used tools long obselete in London. Saires sold books to the churchwardens of St Peter's church in 1617, [30] and was therefore bookseller as well as binder. The William Sayer who borrowed £10 'of Mr Gooding's gift' in 1638 was probably a son whose work in the Library in 1651 is detailed below. The Book came rather late in the order of events for establishing the Library, and this may account in part for the lack of chronological order in the lists of donors and books. Coney started the book at both ends, with shelf lists for presses A and B in the front on pages A3 to A7. The book is paginated rather than foliated, the A pages in Coningsby's hand and the B in Ward's. At the other end of the Book is Samuel Ward's list of Smarte's gift on page B3; this has been transcribed in Chapter I. Next follow two pages, mainly in Coney's italic, listing what was purchased with £50 granted by the Corporation from legacies Mrs. Elizabeth Walter left to the town in 1588. Lists in four categories come next, all headed 'An: 1615'.

Page	Category		Numbers of donors	Number for whom labels were printed
B6	Bayliffs & Portmen	BP	17 to 1630	9
B7	Knights and Gentlemen	KG	15 to 1630	4
B8	Ministers & Schollers	MS	50 to 1650	1
B9	Burgesses & Townesmen	BT	42 to 1650	20

The first few entries in each category are by Coney and it is difficult to tell precisely where his hand gave way to others'; perhaps it deteriorated before his early demise, or others made efforts to imitate it. There are some signs that John Cottesford, Usher again after Coney's death for a year or so, was helping Ward. His hand is known from signatures in the books he gave, the six-volume Latin Bible with commentary by Hugo de S. Charo.

Eventually Ward's untidy italic took over, and he entered everything in the book before William Clarke, Master from 1630 to 1645, made entries in 1636. With two exceptions, all those recording gifts in the Book from then on were Masters, and attempts to categorise donors were given up in

---

[28] SRO Ipswich: C13/3/1, fo. 85.

[29] J.B. Oldham, *English Blind-Stamped Bindings.* (Cambridge 1952) Rolls FB.b(3) and TC.a(5) on pp. 46 and 56 respectively.

[30] BL Add. MS 25,344, fo.57.ᵛ Of these Churchwardens' accounts for St Peter's Ipswich, 1563–1664, there is a microfilm copy in SRO Ipswich: JC1/1/4.

1650. At about the same date the cost of books accessioned ceased to be noted; instead the date of presentation was given. Wherever in this account handwriting is attributed it is by comparison with autograph or otherwise authenticated specimens.

Mrs Walter's gift

At some stage in the first years of the Library's existence, though strangely the record does not survive, the Corporation was persuaded to grant £50 for the purchase of books from bequests made in 1588 to the town by Elizabeth Walter. Thomas Kempe her executor was still administering the estate in 1598; it could be that Ward was able to apply directly to him. Mrs Walter was the widow of Richard Walter, a London girdler, and daughter of John Moore, a wealthy Ipswich merchant and Portman, once M.P. for the borough, and 'a wise and religious man'. Moore had died a year before his daughter and his epitaph in 6 Latin verses on brass in St Lawrence church was written by the then town preacher, Robert Wright. When Elizabeth made her will[31] she was 'of Christ Church next unto Aldgate in the city of London' and although she left £50 for 'the maintenance of a godly learned preacher in St Lawrence', and £300 for 'the relief of virtuous preachers who may be in need'; there is no mention of books for their use. The money left to be applied in Ipswich did not become available immediately, and in September 1594 there was 'a treaty appointed with the Lo: Maior and his brethren by suche as mr. Bayliffs shall appoint concerning Mrs Walter's gift, and recovery of the same to this Towne'.[32]

Ward seems to have spent the princely sum he was allowed over a period, stopping just 4s 2d short of the total and adding about 40 folios and a dozen smaller volumes to the shelves, only eight of which have been lost or superseded. A full transcript of the list of purchases on pages B4 and B5 in the Benefactors' Book is given in appendix D. Details of most of the books purchased were entered there by Coney, whose fore-edge titles on the books themselves remain beautifully clear today. It is particularly fortunate, as we shall see, that he wrote down the prices paid. The four dozen or so gift labels which were printed ran out when the books listed on B4 had been shelved, so that manuscript inscriptions were needed in the remainder, mostly in Coney's careful and varied scripts.

Four items are listed by Ward himself, obtained after Coney's death in 1617 or 1618. They include two books published in the latter year, and a pair of globes, terrestrial and celestial, which cost £4 10s. Unfortunately the globes have not been heard of since a post-war clear-out of the Town Hall in 1946. They are likely to have been printed either by Hondius from plates by Molyneux, or by Bleau. The price is reasonable; for a gilded pair Sir Thomas Bodley paid almost £20 in 1601.

Only four of the volumes Ward bought with the Walter money show signs of having had previous owners: the pair of Duns Scotus volumes (Venice 1497 and 1506) and works by Gesner and Besodner. The last two are marked in the list 'oxon: bibliothecae' – had Ward bought some Bodleian duplicates? The indications are that at least the first three dozen purchases on B4 were from the same bookseller, as on the title pages of six of the works are what have been identified as coded prices in the same hand. More than thirty other works given to the Library before 1630 bear marks in the same code, but the importance of their occurrence in the Walter list is that the prices asked and paid can be directly compared, showing that the code is the simplest possible: a = 1, b = 2, to t = 19, omitting i.

---

[31] PCC 15 Leicester (1588).
[32] Great Court Book 19 July 1594 (Richardson, 377).

King no.	Publ.	Author	Code =	Price asked £	s	d	Price paid £	s	d
67	1567	St Ambrose 2 vols.	a.k.	1	10	0	1	5	0
505	1566	St Cyril of Alexandria	a.f.h.	1	6	8	1	5	0
456	1572	St Gregory the great 2v.	a.k.	1	10	0	1	5	8
108	1554	St Justin Martyr	j.f.		9	6		7	6
72	1570	St Irenaeus	f.		6	0		5	6
598	1608	Bp Theodoret	a.h.d.	1	8	4	1	6	6
			Totals: £6		10	6	£5	15	2

From these six purchases it appears that Ward was being allowed a discount of half a crown in the pound. A fuller survey of these interesting price marks has already appeared in *The Book Collector*. [33] The subject is further discussed in the next two chapters.

[33] J.M. Blatchly, 'Ipswich Town Library' in *The Book Collector* 35 (1986), 191–8.

III

EARLY DONORS AND THEIR GIFTS 1613–1618

'It is great pity y^t The Benefactors' names are not written either in fair Text or Sett Romaine Hand for ye more clerer memoriall of such generous persons.'

Joseph Waite, Minister of St Margaret's, 1651 to 1657
(Benefactors' Book p.B1)

The numbers of donors in each of the four categories listed in the Book have been given in the previous chapter. The order itself is telling: bailiffs, and the portmen from whose ranks the former were chosen, appear above knights and gentlemen, and ministers and scholars before the free burgesses and other townsfolk, even though on promotion to the Twelve from the Twenty-four those in the fourth list could and did jump to the first.

Waite's complaint quoted above is well justified by the scrawled, faint and smudged entries made by Ward when for some twenty years he alone made entries in the Book. The order in which names occur is sometimes confusing. For example, Nicholas Easton was Master from 1616 to 1630, and William Clarke his successor until 1645, yet they are 41st and 39th respectively in the list of ministers and scholars. Again, James Tomson gave by will in 1615,[34] but his name was not recorded until about 1636; his executrix, also a donor,[35] does not appear at all. In the lists in appendix B the donors in each category are numbered serially in the order in which their names appear in the Book, omitting duplicate entries.

Bayliffs and Portmen (to BP 14)

In September each year the Great Court elected two Bailiffs from the twelve Portmen to be joint heads of the Corporation and Chief Magistrates for the following twelve months. It was not uncommon for a man to serve as Bailiff several times, but rarely in successive years. The 17 donors in the first list include all but eight of those holding the principal office between the death of Smarte in 1599 and September 1630. Members of the otherwise prominent Gooding family are conspicuous by their failure to contribute. No Bailiffs elected for the first time in the 1630s gave books or money, but in the early days of the Library Ward enjoyed the almost total support of the senior members of the Corporation. The gift labels of Portmen had 'Master' before their names, a title to which Common Councilmen and free burgesses did not aspire.

Robert Cutler heads the list with a gift of £10. Son of another Robert, merchant and Portman of St Nicholas, the younger Robert was six times Bailiff, and, granted arms in 1612, moved to Sproughton. At least one of the eleven Walther works he paid for had had an earlier owner. On the last leaf of the *Homilies on Mark's Gospel* (King 97) is a scribbled account for harrowing in 1588 (on glebe land perhaps?), and an antidote in case 'thou beest poysoned'. Matthew Brownrigg's Lorinus (King 453 and 484) and Valentia (King 533) seem to have been his own, as his merchant's mark is on the reverse of the title page in four volumes; the crucifix in the woodcut printer's device has in several been crudely excised. Thomas Sicklemore gave Nauclerus' *Chronica* (1544, King 10) with William Cecil's characteristic italic 'Gulielmus Cecilius' on the title page and many marginal notes in the same hand, two of which are especially revealing, as Dr Glyn Parry has remarked. One is Cecil's

[34] SRO Ipswich: Archdeaconry of Suffolk Wills IC/AA2 48/236 (1615).
[35] SRO Ipswich: IC/AA2 48/158 (1615).

note that Constantine the Great had conferred the right to wear the Imperial diadem on the Kings of England; his sketch of an appropriate crown is in the margin. The other is his evident interest in the confrontation between the emperor Theodosius and Saint Ambrose, which had contemporary relevance in the debate between Elizabeth, as Supreme Head of the Church, and her bishops. An incunable Sicklemore gave, the *Epistolae Familiares* of Pope Pius II (1481, King 130) bears the signature of Richard Bryngkeley, Franciscan Prior Provincial in 1518; it belonged to the library of the Cambridge Greyfriars (See appendix G). Robert Snelling's £10 provided Calvin's works in 12 volumes, all bought new, two of them marked with the simple coded prices 'a.' and 'k.'.

The Actons, father and son, most generously gave £10 each, but for neither were labels provided. William Acton was of the Elms parish, but his son John, who was High Sheriff of the County in 1617, established the family at Bramford. It is written in the Book that, presumably at his father's death in 1616, he [John] 'added to his father's gyfte these', and no fewer than 30 works were listed, which must have cost far more than £10. Amongst them, at least twelve European histories were second-hand, and bear the marks of ownership of William Harrison the topographer and historian, author of *The Description of England* (1577), who sometimes signed himself 'FitzHenry'. In this and in his unpublished universal history, 'The Great English Chronology' Harrison quotes from most of them. At his death in 1593 his Puritan preacher son Edmund inherited his large library, and, before leaving for a preachership in Derry in 1617 (his brother-in-law George Downham was Bishop there), disposed of the books that Acton or Ward acquired for Ipswich. The Derry and Raphoe Diocesan Library still has about 150 books from Harrison's collection, and two others are at Trinity College, Dublin, among Archbishop Ussher's books, so that Ipswich has the second largest holding of this Tudor scholar's books.[36] Of those still in the original boards, five are identically blind stamped with a large central boss, showing that at some time in the early 17th century, probably immediately before coming to Ipswich they were rebound; they mostly also have a coded mark on the title page of a type commonest in the Bury St James library (and for that reason named 'Bury' marks). They have not yet been elucidated, but consist of what may be al or a Greek letter α or τ followed by a number between 3 and 90, sometimes followed by .1 or .2. In several books William Harrison noted the prices he paid for them, uncoded, always less than a pound. No doubt Agricola's *De re metallica* ([1556] King 136) would have cost him more than six shillings had the title page been present. The doggerel verse in ms on the last leaf of this book is poignant:

> I lyve in hope
> for hope I not
> or hope I ill
> ye gallows will
> my goodness spyll.

Knights and Gentlemen (to KG 7)

It is no new phenomenon that those whose circumstances permit move out of Ipswich; the only knight in the list, Sir Edmund Withipoll, was resident in the borough, but his house on the site of Christchurch Priory stood outside the ramparts. Withipoll's gifts are of the greatest interest: a book bought by his great grandfather Paul Withipoll in Sevile for 11 shillings in about 1500 (King 253), a copy of Gratian's *Decretals* formerly the property of Hugo Fraunce, a monk of the fashionable Syon monastery (1490, King 460), those of Gregory IX printed in 1519 by Rembolt's widow (King 461) and a Clein printing of 1517, part of the *Historiale* of St Antoninus, Archbishop of Florence. For some reason William Blower (see Chapter I) wrote his name and the date '4 M^ar^tii 1597' on the title page of this book, as has already been remarked that he did in two of Smarte's books in 1598 and

---

[36] Dr G.J.R. Parry confirmed William Harrison's hand in these books, gave information about Edmund Harrison, and commented on the notes in Cecil's Nauclerus.

1599. Was Withipoll giving a book to the Library which he had borrowed from Smarte and failed to return? Sir Edmund's great grandmother Anne Withipoll's Book of Hours (ms 7) apparently came to the Library in the Smarte gift. Books given by Sir Isaac Jermy and Sir Clypesby Gaudy arrived in the 1620s; these worthies lived at Stutton and Wenham parva respectively, near enough to Ipswich for Ward's appeal to them to succeed.

Thomas Cornwallis of Earl Soham married a Grimston; her family had strong Puritan connections and a house in Tower Street which later became the Edgar home. Two gentleman married close relatives of Portmen donors and doubtless gave at their suggestion. One was Nicholas Revett of Brandeston who married Mary, daughter of Thomas Sicklemore. The other was Francis Brewster of Wrentham, an active parliamentarian and a J.P., whose wife Elizabeth was sister of Robert Snelling. The first attempt at a printed label for Brewster did not do; 'Esquire' was not enough, and 'Master' had to be added, the mark of his degree from Pembroke Hall. This seems a great deal of trouble to label a single volume to the giver's liking.

Edward Bacon of Shrubland was third son of the Lord Keeper of the Great Seal by his first wife, and half-brother to Francis Bacon, Baron Verulam. After his death his widow Helen gave to the Library a book he had greatly treasured, 'the French bible of Mr Bezae's gyft to him'. On a blank leaf she wrote:

> This book was given to Edward Bacon, Esquire, by Theodore Beza, in whose house he had lived diverse years in Geneva, as a monument of their Christian acquaintance; recorded by Lambert Duncan in an epistle dedicatorie to the sayde gentleman, intended by him in his lifetime to be placed in this Library; and now by Mrs Helena Bacon, his wife and sole executrix, given to the same use A° D'ni 1618. Septemb^r 25th.

Bacon, like another half-brother Anthony, younger by ten years, had been a pupil of Beza's, and a letter from the latter had accompanied the gift. Unfortunately both letter and inscribed leaf were removed from the Bible at some time in the middle of the last century.[37]

Among other gentlemen, John Lany was Recorder, and Leonard Caston, who lived in Archdeacon Pykenham's House in Northgate Street, was a considerable benefactor to the Tower parish and to the town. Some names are harder to identify, and two, Thomas Ungle and Jeremy Hubbard, appear twice, once here (added much later) and again in their proper place in the list of Burgesses and Townsmen.

Ministers and Schollers (to MS 24)

It was entirely consistent with Ward's standing in the town that he should have been the only cleric whose gifts to the Library had printed labels, and that his name should head the third list in Coney's best script:

	£	s
M^r Sa: Ward publike preacher of Ipswich		
the workes of Pareus in vol. 9	2	10

Why nine volumes is not clear: Coney's first shelf list shows only six of the seven which remain, two more having been given in about 1618, and one of those lost between 1650 and 1705. It was left to Ward himself to insert, above his own name, the books costing £3 given by Dr John Burges 'late preacher to ye towne'. Burges served from 1591 to 1602, but the fact that one of his gifts was not published until 1617 shows that he was probably still living locally then. Few clerics gave more to the foundation than these town preachers. The next names on the list are those of Ward's closest colleagues: John Carter and Thomas Scott (who later through his *Vox Populi* added insult to the

[37] S. Westhorp, 'On the Library of the Town of Ipswich' in *Journal of the British Archaeological Association* (1865), 65–75 (Beza Bible 67–8).

injury of Ward's celebrated 'Double Deliveraunce' engraving). Then follow the majority of the parochial clergy of Ipswich from 1612 to 1640, the year in which Ward died. From lists of the incumbents of the twelve Ipswich parishes during those years it appears that well over half gave money or books to the Library, and no doubt all but the least learned made use of it in their studies. Amongst the names in this list are those of several Masters and Ushers of the school, and at least three medical men, all M.D. Not all donors were Puritan to the core: John Watson of Woolpit, for example, was ejected by the Committee for Scandalous Ministers in 1643, but the use of false witness against him is suspected.[38] Coincidentally another of Watson's own books came to the Library, bought with Dorothy Seckford's bequest in the 1670s (Stucki King 602).

Ralph Brownrigg, nephew of Matthew Brownrigg, then a Fellow of Pembroke Hall, but later Vice-Chancellor, and Bishop of Exeter, gave a Hebrew Lexicon (King 693), now lost. Thomas Draxe of Harwich gave 'his owne workes in 2 vol.', both lost, but how many of the ten he published we shall never know.

A little after 1618, Alexander Rainold 'preacher of Tattingstone' presented Forster's Hebrew-Latin Dictionary (King 620) somewhat enigmatically inscribed in Latin and Hebrew, and including the lines: 'Gyppovico saluberrimum consilium nec minus Raynoldo. Quis iste occultans consilium.'

With few exceptions, the books given by clerical donors were theological, and usually from their own shelves; the collection thus built up will have served them well. Each church needed only the prescribed works in addition, and the opportunity was taken in 1985 to add those mustered annually by the churchwardens of St Stephen's to the Town Library. They are: Erasmus' *Paraphrases* 1548 and 1549, Jewel 1611 and the *Homilies* 1635. Of these works only Jewel has a duplicate in the Library.

Burgesses and Townesmen (to BT 29)

In many cases the trades of these donors are entered in the Book and shown on their printed gift labels, so that we have a grocer, a draper, a mercer and a glover, a tanner, a dyer and a shearman, and, as befits the town on the Orwell, a merchant, a mariner and a shipcarpenter. The labels for this fourth category must have been ordered separately, for why else were they set in Great Primer (18 pt.) while those for the more senior Portmen were in English (14 pt.)?

A few puzzling features of the labelling of gifts must be considered. The relabelling of Henry Buckenham's five volumes of Binius for John Hodges will be dealt with in the next chapter. There is a discrepancy between the label in the Selneccer (King 93): 'The gift of George Coppin, free Burgesse of Ipswich ' and the entry in the Book: M[r] Ste: Coppin: Selneccerus in Ep'las Pauli £1'. The will of George Coppin, draper,[39] reveals that Stephen Copping his brother was named his executor and there is this clause: 'I gyve toward the Lybrarye of the Towne of Ipswich Twenty shillings'. For the fact that beneath Copping's label there is another for 'Peter Cole Grocer' there is no explanation. Cole clearly objected to a label on which his trade seemed to have become part of his name, for other slips for his gifts were reprinted without 'Grocer' and in 14 pt.

Some other bequests of this period throw interesting light on the affairs of the Library, most notably that of George Raymond quoted at the head of the second chapter. James Tomson, a glover of Carr Street, died in the autumn of 1615 leaving Mabel Clemetson, spinster, his executrix to enjoy the greater part of his estate for the year she survived him. Both of their wills mention the Library, his [34] as follows:,

> I give and bequeath fortie shillings towards the byinge of Bookes for the librarie of Ipswich, to be payd unto Thomas Carter and Edmond Day and be bestowed according to their discretion.

[38] C. Holmes (ed.) *The Suffolk Committees for Scandalous Ministers 1644–1646.* (Suffolk Records Society XIII 1970), 29.

[39] SRO Ipswich: IC/AA2 47/14 (1614).

Thomas Carter, minister of St Margaret's from 1603 to 1624 (and St Helen's from 1611) was to preach Tomson's funeral sermon, and is a surprising absentee from the list of minister donors. Edmund Day, dyer, gave £4 for books in February 1613. When in October 1622 Day [40] was given £15 to 'ride to London on the business of the Town Lector', was he buying books for the Library? Mistress Clemetson's[35] will *states merely:*

> I give towards the Library in Ipswiche Twentie Shillings to be paid within six monthes after my decease.

The Tomson and Clemetson gifts were in the event combined to buy the six volumes of the 1525 edition of the works of Jerome (King 477) and, appropriately, four were labelled from Tomson and two from his executrix, their labels set apart from all the others in the Library by having factotums, decorative devices from the same blocks as on the labels of gifts of Sir John Suckling in 1618 to an unidentified library.[41] The Suckling, Tomson and Clemetson labels are all tentatively assigned to John Bill of London, himself a donor to this Library, in the Bookplates section of the revised *S.T.C.*

One more will reveals an otherwise unrecorded donor and a book lost before 1705 when Coningsby listed it among those 'Desunt'. Bezaleel Sherman, grocer of St Lawrence parish, who died in 1618 gave 'To the Librarye of Ipswich a book called Speed's Chronicle'.[42] His second wife who died in 1624 was a daughter of Dr John Burges the town preacher; his first was a Copping. Support for the Library came from a very small circle of people many of whom were related to one another.

Robert Benham was the first donor to have 'IPSWICH' gilt-stamped on the boards of his gifts. The varied lettering styles used for this purpose over the next 150 years (*fig. 4*) make an interesting series.

Thomas Eldred appears first as a Burgess and later as a Portman donor, because he was only a Common Council-Man when in about 1614 he gave some theological works. Elected a Portman in 1620, he was Bailiff in 1621–2. Born in 1561, son of another Thomas, tallow chandler, he sailed on board the *Desire* with Thomas Cavendish, circumnavigating the globe between 1586 and 1588. His will, made and proved in 1624,[43] includes bequests of £10 to Samuel Ward, and £5 to the Library, and with this were added Lorinus on the Psalms in three volumes (King 469) and a very fine 1551 edition of Gesner's Bestiary (4 vols. in three, King 465 and 466) with the woodcuts of the animals hand-coloured. It seems very likely that these books were originally Eldred's, a powerful reminder of sights he had seen on his travels. I suggest that Ward would have been able and willing to take them in lieu of money from the estate.

Ward's position as executor in another man's will may explain why the Library contains a two-volume Latin Bible edited by Augustin Marlorat which had belonged to Thomas Reddrich, described in the Burial register at St Margaret's in 1617 as 'ane ould minester of the word of God'. Reddrich had inscribed his name in English and Greek characters on the title page, and made many marginal notes as well. The gift label is for John Randes, whose £2 is recorded in the Book. Ward probably put the money into the estate of the deceased minister, and took the books for the Library. Reddrich, a considerable benefactor to the town and to the parish of his burial, did not give to the Library directly.[44]

Thomas Lane is listed only because, as the principal Ipswich carrier of the time, he 'gave ye caraidge of most of ye bookes'. He certainly operated a London service; whether a Cambridge one also is not recorded. The Book puts no figure on the value of this useful service.

[40] SRO Ipswich: HD 36/2781/15.
[41] B. North Lee, *Early Printed Book Labels.* (London 1976), 54.
[42] PCC 127 Meade (1617).
[43] PCC 53 Byrde (1620).
[44] PCC 93 Weldon (1617).

a. *c.* 1615

c. 1651

b. *c.* 1635

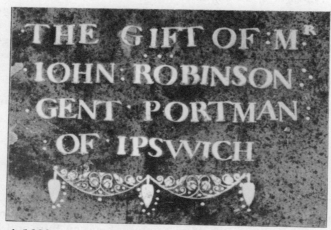

d. 1666

e. 1681

Figure 4a–e. Ipswich gilt-stamps on boards of books given 1615–1756

The collective generosity of the four groups of benefactors up to the year 1618 may be briefly summarised:

		£	s	
14	Bayliffs & Portmen	78	16	disregarding Smarte
7	Knights & Gentlemen	12	10	
24	Ministers & Schollers	31	0	
29	Burgesses & Townesmen	82	0	omitting Mrs. Walter

Ungle and Hubbard have been counted in the fourth (BT) category only. The Twelve can be seen from this to have given a fine lead to which the other burgesses responded well, many clergy giving within their limited means.

Sources of supply for the books

The existence of the *Catalogue of the Suffolk Parochial Libraries*[45] and the recent publication of a detailed catalogue of the Grantham Chained Library[46] allow a comparison of the contents of libraries set up at the turn of the sixteenth century in three towns in eastern England. Books were bought for St James's Church at Bury St Edmunds from 1595, by Francis Trigge for Grantham from 1598, and Samuel Ward here in Ipswich from about 1613 onwards. The comparisons are summarised below:

Approx. number of works held by 1640		Works held in common with Ipswich	% of own stock	Editions in common with Ipswich	% of own stock	Incidence of	
						simple code	Bury marks
Bury St James	350	127	36	48	14	1	21
Grantham	350	111	31	43	12	35	0
Ipswich	650					39	12

Perhaps, in view of the universal importance and popularity of certain works, it is not surprising that such high percentages of titles are held in common between Bury and Ipswich, and between Grantham and Ipswich. The availability of identical editions, particularly unusual ones, to Ward when almost two decades had elapsed since the other libraries had been stocked does perhaps indicate a common source of supply, and Cambridge was the most accessible centre for all three towns. The simple code, quite common at Grantham, was obviously in use at least twenty years before Ward was buying for Ipswich. The comparative incidences of the simple code and the Bury marks could be significant, particularly the absence of the former at Bury and of the latter at Grantham.

Of course, purchases for all three of the libraries could have been made both in Cambridge and in London, and Ward, like the churchwardens of St Peter's, could have patronised William Sayer in Ipswich also. How convenient it would be if it could be shown that the simple code had its origin in one place (say London), and the Bury marks in another (perhaps Cambridge). The speculation continues in the next chapter, but there is more to be done before any definite conclusions can be drawn from the evidence.

Examples of simple coded prices:

Latin Bible 1608–9	King 73	*a rf*
Justin Martyr 1554	King 108	*Jf.*
Cyril Alex. 1566	King 505	*a. f. k,*

Examples of Bury marks:

Appian Alex. 1554	King 146	*al.12*
Maffeius 1559	King 132	*2 i3.*
Pistorius 1582	King 549	*e 3 4 2*

[45] J.A. Fitch and A.E. Birkby, *Suffolk Parochial Libraries. A Catalogue.* (London 1977).
[46] J. Glenn and D. Walsh, *Catalogue of the Francis Trigge Chained Library.* (Cambridge 1988).

IV

THE PREACHERS' LIBRARY IN USE 1619–1636

'One halfe of the Scriptures I have handled among you, and endeavoured to acquaint you with the whole Councell of God.'

Samuel Ward in the Preface to *"The Happiness of Practice"*,
dedicated to the Worshipfull the Bailiffes, Burgers
and Commonalties of the Town of Ipswich, 1621.

We have seen that Samuel Ward was the true founder of the Ipswich Library. At Leicester, the town preacher John Angell did the same, but not before 1632. The good use Ward made of his Library may be judged from the works he makes reference to in his printed *Sermons and Treatises*, nine of which were published in one volume in 1627/8 and again in 1636. The majority of the sources he quotes are in the Library; for example, of 38 named in the sermon *Christ is All in All*, 1622, 24 are recognisably titles in the collection.

This is not the place for a full account of Ward's career in the ministry, but a brief outline is needed. He gave the last 34 years of his life to the service of the people of Ipswich, and was a powerful influence without parochial bounds. In *The Religion of Protestants,* Patrick Collinson [47] points out that no fewer than ten ministers had held the post of town preacher in the preceeding 34 years. No wonder that Ward was well paid and housed in some style, provided with a fine Library and given strong backing when, as often happened, he ran into conflict with the ecclesiastical authorities. As Professor Collinson says of him, 'he was embattled against the corrupt innovations of the Court', but the wiser prelates who came to know him recognised in him 'much readiness to serve the Church of England'. This did not save him from punishment and even imprisonment when he was particularly provocative or foolhardy, but on every occasion he enjoyed the confidence and support of the Corporation. After his last permanent removal from the pulpit by Laud in 1635 the Ipswich burgesses were prepared to go without their regular weekly lectures rather than appoint a successor. Bishop Wren, who spent much of his short episcopate, when not at Court, in Suffolk in order to monitor the activities of preaching ministers like Ward, must have been astonished at the riots on the streets of Ipswich which followed Ward's final ban, and at the apparent unconcern of the town's leaders.[48] These incidents in early 1636 led to the entire Assembly facing charges in the Star Chamber, but that only strengthened resolves to support the man who had preached the gospel in Ipswich for more than half a lifetime. For two three-year periods during that time, no doubt when preachers without livings were under fire, Ward was given the extra security of the incumbency of the Tower church as well as the preachership, and in April 1638 it was arranged for him to purchase the Preacher's House for £140. He was wealthy enough by 1632 to own a piece of land near Christ's Hospital worth £1000; for one Jeffery Kerby of London left his Company, the Grocers, £2000 to buy it and to erect on it a second hospital in Ipswich. For some reason the Company did nothing about it.[48a] Ward was far from penniless at his death on 8 March 1639/40; nevertheless the Corporation saw to it that his wife and son Samuel (who was probably handicapped) were allowed a pension of £25 a quarter for the rest of their lives.

It does not appear that Ward took much further trouble over the Library after 1635, for without

[47] P. Collinson, *The Religion of Protestants.* (Oxford 1982), 177–8.
[48] W.E. Layton, 'Ecclesiastical Disturbances in Ipswich' in *E.A.N. & Q.* (N.S.) II (1887–8), 209, 257, 315, 373, 405.
[48a] PCC 127 Awdley (1632), and Guildhall Library MS 11,616, fo. 232 and 11,588, pp. 507, 540.

his preaching its main use to him was at an end. Until then he was certainly busy there, as we see from entries in the Book, and from his own jottings on its endpapers. These show a good deal of activity around the year 1630, and, as Ward seems to have started writing his memoranda at the top of the left hand page and worked his way down to foot of the page to record gifts which are known to have been received about 1635, approximate dating in between is possible. The notes are often repetitive, and those on the right hand page generally duplicate those on the left.

From the earliest of these rough 'housekeeping notes' we learn that in the late 1620s Ward was owed £4 12s for work 'layd out on the chamber', a figure offset by the gift of £3 from John Carnaby, Portman, and one of the Governors of Christ's Hospital, 'wherewithall the chamber adjoining to the Librarie was in part repayred'. The remaining 32s came from John Webbe, minister of Falkenham, who also gave nine works still in the collection. Three, as we read on the right hand page, were not paid for promptly. The Taylors' Guild had vacated the southern half of the dorter in 1617, since when the Library could, presumably, have expanded, but this seems not to have happened. The fact that Ward was prepared to refurbish the chamber must indicate that it now had some projected use in connection with the Library next door, perhaps additional working space or a room for meetings of ministers.

It is not clear whether the £4 12s included the sums 'for presses, windowes & [word deleted] w'ch ye towne owes me', but 'on ye new Chamb.' the three tradesmen's bills came to £2 3s (joyner, mason and glazier) with more due to Smyth the locksmith. It is likely that presses IK and LM were provided at this time.

Ward had to note that various donors owed him sums they had promised: Jonathan Skinner, at the Tower Church from 1627 to 1630, Nicholas Beard at St Peter's, and 'the scholeme.ʳ' – Nicholas Easton up to 1630 – owing one of 'divers halfe £4'. Easton did indeed give £2 eventually, but he may have defaulted until after Clarke, his successor, had subscribed, which would explain their reverse order in the Book. John Fenton of St Lawrence had given, as had George Turnbull of St Margaret's, the latter 'his father's workes'. They are long lost, so that we can only guess at the identity of their author. Richard Turnbull, an Oxford graduate of Lincolnshire origin whose *Expositions* on St James, St Jude and Psalm 15 were published in 1591 and 1606 seems most likely; he died in 1593.

The note 'Mr Hodges books not yet assigned but in the library' is a most interesting one, with which it would help to link the first on the page: 'Mr Webbe mony for Councells. 5l.' John Hodges of London appears in the list of Knights and Gentlemen for books totalling £10 given in the late 1620s:

> Mr Hodges of London. Councells of Binius his edition
> 5 vol: Banez 2 vol. Ripa 1 vol. Durand 1 vol.
> Nugnus 1 vol. Rada vols. 2.

Most of these books have coded prices on their title pages, the same simple code found in books purchased 15 years earlier with the Walter money, and at the turn of the century at Grantham. Two of them have also, in the same hand, what look like further bookseller's marks, perhaps location codes to room and shelf in the stock, since each contains an R and an N of sorts. Other examples have been found in the early libraries at Guildford, Norwich, Beccles and Leicester; the R numbers seem to run from 1 to 6, and the N from 0 to 13.

King	Publ.	Author	Vols.	'Stock mark'	Code	Price asked £	s	d
96	1609	Ripa	1	R5 N12 [deleted] R4	a.	1	0	0
124	1612	Nugnus	1	R6 NO	a.k.	1	10	0
299	1620	Rada	2		q.i.		16	9
446	1606	Binius	5		e.	5	0	0
54	1615	Banez	2		–	1	0	0
525	1595	Durandus	1		–	1	10	0

[The last two prices asked are estimates] Total £10 16 9

There is much confusion over the donor of the five-volume set of the Councils of Binius, for in each volume, under the calligraphic labels inscribed 'The gift of John Hodges', are printed labels of February 1613 for 'Henry Buckenham, Mercer, and one of the Common Counsell of Ipswich'. Henry Buckenham is listed under Burgesses and Townsmen as giving £5 for this work, as is John Hodges some 15 years later, though the edition pre-dates both gifts. For some reason Hodges' claim to have presented them takes precedence, but only by pasting over the labels of the first giver. Presumably Buckenham's money was diverted to other purposes. So why did Ward need £5 for the 'Councells' from John Webbe also?

One possible explanation for the very large gift from London was that it came directly or indirectly from one of the main suppliers of books to the Library. Was John Hodges connected with George Hodges of Little Britain [49] who dealt mainly in theological books from 1621 to 1632? If so, we may have identified a London user of the simple code. Hodges' gift may then have been just another form of discount. Against this suggestion, it must be admitted that when two other booksellers presented books of their own production, John Bill at the outset, and Christopher Meredith in about 1640, they were not listed in the Book at all, and no codes or marks are to be found in their gifts, but once more London is indicated as a source of books. In fact John Hodges was married to Abigail Bloyse, daughter of another Portman donor, William Bloyse; he was Captain and later Colonel under her brother William whose Roundhead Foot Regiment was at the siege of Colchester. Appointed Deputy Lieutenant of the County in 1645, Hodges lived at the house now called Woodbridge Abbey, later, until his death in 1651, at Layham.

The dated entry which comes below the notes already discussed is most illuminating: 'These Books wanting y^t have bene taken out of ye librarie since ye founding, & this present day & yeere Feb 8th 1630 missing.' Several titles follow, most eventually deleted with the addition 'Restored by Mr –'s gyft'. The fact that there had been losses from the Library in the first 15 years implies that others than Ward had been borrowing books, but we have no real evidence. There must have been little adequate supervision, and apart from gift labels, and manuscript inscriptions which rarely mention Ipswich, there was nothing to show that books belonged to the collection. The interesting thing is that Ward was actively seeking fresh benefactions to replace missing works, showing that he needed and used every book in the Library, consisting, as it did, almost entirely of theology. The following table summarises the losses and Ward's progress towards replacement:

Author and title of lost work		Original donor	Replaced by	King
Polanus	Syntagma Theologiae	Robert Cole, Portman	Jude Allen	580
Bucanus	Loci Communes	John Sherwood, M.D.	–	–
Vermigli	Loci Communes	Edmund Day, dyer	John Webbe	634
Babington	Opera	Wm. Smith of Freston	John Catcher	64
John Boys	Anglic. Homiliae	John Burrell	'to gett'	–
Perkins	'2da pars wanting'	Roger Cutler [gave 2 v.]	3rd is there	29
Alex. Carp.	Dest. Viciorum	Wm. Smarte (found later)	John Allen	182
Bartholomaeus	De ppriet rerum	Wm. Smarte	–	–
Chrysostom	Homiliis Gk.Lat.	Wm. Smarte	–	–

Most of the remaining notes on the left hand page concern the drive to collect a set of the works of Lorinus. Ward needed a newer edition of Lorinus on the Psalms and Ecclesiastes than the one-volume version of 1606 which Matthew Brownrigg gave (and which was kept on shelf A2 according to Coney's first lists). Ward sold the old edition (apparently for the large sum of £5) after Thomas Eldred and another had given four volumes covering the commentaries concerned; with the proceeds he intended to buy Rivet on the Psalms and Ludolph of Saxony on the Evangelists. Other donors were found for these (They are King 296 and 36 respectively) and the money was

[49] H.G. Aldis et al., *Dictionary of Printers and Booksellers in England... 1557–1640.* (1910), 138.

presumably applied elsewhere. Three more benefactors, Messrs Reignolds, Cleere and Warner, added to the Lorinus set and in all eight folios remain today.

Not many secular works came to the Library in Ward's time, but there are a few notable exceptions. One such is from Mr John Causton, minister of Otley and Clopton, who, according to the Book 'gave by will a deske Ortelius 1 vol. Raynerii Pantheologia 2 vols: but his executors never delivered yé 2° pt of Rayneri?'. Causton died in 1631 and his will[50] was noncupative. In that case, Ward was lucky that the Ortelius (King 434) and one volume of the *Pantheologia* had been given in Causton's lifetime, as both have especially interesting features. The maps in the atlas are hinged on paper guards from two sources: a printed astrological calendar, and a manuscript 'List of Skevell [shovel] men and Laborers prestid to Callis... out of Essex as also... Kent for the Kynges Maiesties affares... 20 May to 5 June.' The year of the King's great expedition, 1545, is the most likely, especially as on the 5 June the Privy Council ordered the pensioners at Dover to be sent home.[51] The Rainer is the largest and the earliest book in the Library, a Koberger of 1474 (King '706'). This has an inscription on the last leaf: 'M^d q' hoc volumen pertinet conve'tu' Cantab'ggie per p^{ro}curacion' frat'is Galfrid' Jullys. Geoffrey Jullys, B.Th. of Cambridge, was Prior of the Cambridge Dominicans in 1507, still there 1510, and Prior of the Sudbury house in 1530.[52]

Another secular donation, by John Catcher, 'vintener', was Raleigh's *History of the World* 1628 (King 158). Catcher and John Smythier, merchant, who gave four volumes of Samuel Purchas' works (King 89 and 159); for some reason each reserved one volume of their gift 'for life in his owne custody', but if necessary their respective executors saw to it that the books concerned came to the Library in due course. John Smythier and Thomas Foster, minister at St Matthew's, whose own donations are lost, were both witnesses for the defence at Ward's final appearance in the Court of High Commission.[53]

Robert Leman of Brightwell, Fishmonger, High Sheriff of London and son of a Lord Mayor, gave 10 volumes of the works of Francis Suarez, on the first of which the town's name is stamped in a most decorative cartouche (*fig. 4b*). Leman's links with St Stephen's parish led eventually to his monument by the Christmas brothers being placed in the chancel there.

At Ward's death his own books were left to his preacher sons Nathaniel and Joseph who were his executors, and not (as has often been written following statements in the official lists of benefactions to the town) to the Library.[54] Ward did not add a collection of his own published works, but that is hardly surprising in the light of his own avowed opposition to their being printed at all. His black marble graveslab lies now in the north chancel aisle of the Tower church with the simple but worn legend 'Watch Ward for yet a little while and He that shall come will come'. He enjoyed plays on his own name, as further exemplified by the verse to be found set between woodcuts of lighted beacons in the 1636 collected edition of the *Sermons*:

> *Watch*, WARD, and keepe thy Garments tight,
> For I come Thiefe-like at Midnight.
> All-seeing, never slumb'ring Lord;
> Be thou my *Watch*, Ile be thy WARD.

[50] NCC 172 Purgall (1631).
[51] *Letters and Papers.* Vol. 20, Part 1, No. 872, p. 438, and *Acts of the Privy Council,* 1545, p.181.
[52] Prof. A.G. Watson identified Jullys whose acquisition for the Cambridge Blackfriars will be listed in the next supplement to Ker's *Medieval Libraries.*
[53] *State Papers Domestic Series,* CCLXI, fos. 105, 259.
[54] PCC 47 Coventry (1640), and SRO Ipswich: C13/3/1, fo. 85 and GA402/1, 344.

V

MASTER AND MINISTERS TAKE CHARGE 1636–1650

'You have heard much of Faith in my reverend predecessor's time, as appeareth by what is left on record; and God has directed me to strike upon the same nail, I may say, as many years together as I intended days at the first.'

Matthew Lawrence refers to Ward in the epilogue
of his *Use and Practice of Faith*, 1657.

The end of Ward's active ministry brought the flow of gifts to the Library almost to a halt. The next hand in the Book is that of William Clarke, Master from 1630 to 1645, and his first entry is a surprising one. Benjamin Cutler, Gentleman, well known as an Arminian High churchman, later fought for the King at Newark.[55] He gave seven volumes of theology in 1636, and Ward may well have been pleased that someone else should accession them. Clarke is thought to have been educated at Westminster and Trinity College, Cambridge. His own gifts came to the Library earlier, and he recorded those of two others after Cutler, both incumbents of St Peter's: Jeremy Cateline the elder who was there from 1617 to 1636, and Peter Witham from 1639; his gift was dated 26 October 1641. This, as we shall see, was not Clarke's last service to the Library.

The next entry, of the much earlier gift of James Tomson, appears to be in the hand of Nathaniel Smart, Ward's successor as town preacher at the age of 22, son of another Nathaniel who gave books in about 1632. Both Nathaniels were perpetual curates of St Nicholas in their time; they were unrelated to the family of Portmen. The younger Smart was married to William Clarke's daughter Ruth.[56]

Two unlisted benefactors around 1640 are worth mention. Christopher Meredith, stationer of London, who by then may have become a supplier to the Library, gave a copy of Spelman's *Concilia* of his own printing. John Blomefeild the elder, ironmonger of the Quay parish, left £3 to the Library and smaller bequests to Ward and three other Ipswich ministers. By the time his will[57] was proved in November 1640, Ward was dead, and if the gift ever came to the Library there is no evidence of its application.

From time to time Treasurer's accounts of the Corporation were kept in sufficient detail to show what was being done for the fabric of the Library. In 1639 to 1640, 28 new quarrels (small panes) for the window cost 2s 4d, and in 1641 to 1642 £8 2s was spent on more expensive works. The windows seemed to need replacement very frequently. In 1645 to 1646 Matthew Windes replaced 195 quarrels, and mended the 'window at the north end', the whole costing £1 8s 2d.

Matthew Lawrence came from Lincolnshire to succeed Smart as town preacher in August 1643, but, perhaps because he only 'intended [to stay] days at the first', his 'Bookes and household stuffe' did not follow him until in April 1647 the Corporation increased his annual salary to £120 and added £20 as 'a Gratuitie from the Towne towards the better furnishinge of his howse and Librarye'. Lawrence's hand is to be found nowhere in the Town Library. Instead, we find that of his son-in-law Joseph Waite, who assisted him in caring for it from about 1647 onwards, perhaps because Lawrence's health was not good; he certainly complained of finding his preaching duties demanding.[58] Waite's mother was sister to Samuel Ward, so that his Puritan credentials were impeccable; he was minister at St Margaret's from 1651 until at least 1655 when he obtained the living of

---

[55] ex inf. Dr B.G. Blackwood, and *E.A.N & Q.* (N.S.) I (1886–7), 166, 199.
[56] PCC 375 Brent (1653).
[57] SRO Ipswich: Archdeaconry of Suffolk wills IC/AA1/78/22.
[58] A. Everitt, *Suffolk in the Great Rebellion 1640–1660*, Suffolk Records Society III (1960), 111–3.

Sproughton which he held for the remaining 15 years of his ministry and his life. His memorial there recalls Ward's in the punning inscription:

Behold I come
Rev. 16. 15
I. Waite
Job 14. 14

Waite's hand is the most stylish in the Book apart from Coney's, and he inscribed the title pages of the gifts of five donors, two by wills of 1647 and 1649/50. This last was that of Nicholas Stanton, Waite's predecessor at St Margaret's, and one of the five Ipswich clerics named in November 1645 when a proposal was made to divide the Province of Suffolk into fourteen Classical Presbyteries.[59] The second Precinct or Division, based on Ipswich, would be led by William Bloyse and Nathaniel Bacon, Esquires, the then Bailiffs. Lawrence naturally headed the list of ministers of this *Classis*, followed by John Ward, usually stated to be Samuel's brother, at St Clement's, Robert Stansby of St Helen's, John Fuller of St Peter's, and Stanton. Glascock the Master was one of the 'others to be joyned to the Ministers'. Stanton's will,[60] witnessed by Lawrence and Ward, gives a clear hint that the *Classis* was running the Library.

I give to the Library in Ipswich aforesaid to bee laid out in bookes according to the direction of the ministers thereof or the maior part of them the sume of Five pounds.

Two years earlier, when Mistress Susan Penning, spinster, fourth daughter of Anthony Penning, Esq. of St Matthew's parish, made her will[61] she asked that Lawrence should preach her funeral sermon (presumably at Sternfield where she was buried), or failing him, John Fuller. She next made bequests to them and to the other three members of the *Classis*, adding Nathaniel Smart and William Fincham (of the Tower church in 1649) and then followed the Library gift with an even clearer instruction about its application:

I give twentie pownds to buy books for the Librarie in Ipswich, accordinge to the discretion of the afore menconed minesters or the greatest pt. of them.

Here then is the evidence that, apart from their more important business, the *Classis* ministers were managing the Library, with Joseph Waite, somewhat their junior, carrying out routine tasks allotted to him by a committee whose chairman was his father-in-law. The Library would have afforded them a suitable place to meet, particularly if there had to be informed discussion before majority decisions could be taken over the application of larger gifts or bequests. At Norwich the eight ministers running the library there in the mid-1650s kept minutes of the meetings they held in the room.[62]

The books bought with the Penning and Stanton bequests included some recently published commentaries by Leigh, Usher, de Groot and Estius. These and other donations of the time were shelved together: quartos on E.2 and G.2, folios to fill up K.3 and the whole of K.4; the remainder were the first books to go into press I, on shelves 4 and 5. This we know because they were still together there when Coningsby made his catalogue in 1705.

Most of Waite's accessions have IPSWICH and 1651 gilt-stamped near the top of the front board, the first serious attempt on the part of those caring for the books to indicate ownership by the town. Waite also penned fore-edge titles on the books, and for Mrs Penning's set of the works of Sanctius in 9 volumes he made fold-out fore-edge flaps. Those for the 2nd and 6th volumes only have been

[59] J. Browne, *History of Congregationalism in Norfolk and Suffolk.* (1877), 608 for Classis lists dated 5 November 1645.
[60] PCC 31 Pembroke (1649).
[61] SRO Ipswich: IC/AA1/85/84 (1647).
[62] G.A. Stephen, *op. cit.*, 6.

found folded into the pages. There are also fragments of a fore-edge label remaining in the first of the 13 volumes of Tostado (King 443) to buy which William Cutler had given Ward £10.

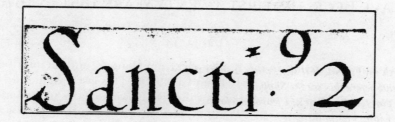

Lawrence died in March 1651/2 (a date universally misquoted from the error on his Tower church memorial). In the will which his widow Judith proved in May 1652 [63] he left £2 to the Library without guidance as to its application. Lawrence had already given the *Opera Collecta* of John Cameron, 1642 (King 622) and the book has 1651 gilt-stamped on the cover. For some reason Waite omitted to record as donors either Lawrence or the younger Cateline, minister of St Peter's from 1636 to 1639 and then of Barham, though he did inscribe their gifts, and after the death of the former there are no further entries in the Book until the 1660s when books bought with four large gifts are listed by Cave Beck, the polymath with a flair for invention who arrived as Master in September 1650.

[63] PCC 118 Bowyer (1652).

VI

CAVE BECK: HIS FIRST TWENTY YEARS 1651 to 1670

> *'Launch forth my Friend. But stay, make a short stop,*
> *Let me be dead before this see the Shop,*
> *Should thy plot take, my* Beck, *I fear henceforth,*
> *To loose my Library as nothing worth.*
>
> *To my intimate and ingenious Friend, Mr* BECK,
> *upon his* UNIVERSAL CHARACTER, *serving all Languages,*
> *Jo. Waite, M.A.'*

When Cave Beck, at 27, came to Ipswich in September 1650, a most unusual young man became Master of the Grammar School. [64] He was the complete all-rounder: lawyer, divine, mathematician and linguist, a man happy to be by turns courtier, schoolmaster, incumbent, tutor, chaplain or writer. His predecessor Glascock had left for Felsted after only five years at Ipswich. Beck served the School for seven, and for a further six months during a later interregnum, but stayed in the town until his death in 1706, enjoying two town livings, St Margaret's and St Helen's, as well as Monk Soham and another in Worcestershire, each of them for more than thirty years. In 1657 his attempt at a universal language, *The Universal Character*, was published simultaneously in French and English. Based as it was on groups of Arabic numerals with prefixed letters or syllables, it was hardly likely to prove useful in practice, despite its author's belief that a child of ten could learn the whole system in four months.

Beck was Royalist enough to have received an Oxford M.A. as a member of the first Charles' court there, and to have accompanied his patron Viscount Hereford when he was one of the six peers who brought Charles II home from Holland, but was evidently acceptable too to the strongly Puritan Bacons, Nathaniel and Francis, for to them he dedicated his book. The former town preacher Nathaniel Smart and Joseph Waite each wrote introductory verse eulogies of the author and his book; it is the last four lines of the latter's offering that are quoted above.

For all the diversity of Beck's interests and of the posts he held, one ambition eluded him: Fellowship of the Royal Society. The nearest he came to it was as correspondent on matters of scientific interest occurring in the county, and then only on the second application of Dr Nathaniel Fairfax of Woodbridge to the Secretary, Henry Oldenburg. Beck was an assiduous correspondent, as Oldenburg discovered, and there was interest at the Society in comparing Beck's language with another scheme of John Wilkins, Warden of Wadham. Fairfax's words in recommendation of Beck to Oldenburg are an apt preface to an account of his contribution to the Town Library: 'a Divine of steddy reasonings, shrewd reaches, narrow searchings, mathematically given', and in a second letter: 'of steddy and wary reasonings, shrewd fetches, of a genius made for new works'.

Beck found the ailing Lawrence nominally directing the affairs of the Library through Joseph Waite, with the former Master, William Clarke, also an old man, but now perpetual curate of St Nicholas until his death in 1653, prepared to supervise work on the furnishings of the room. The collection of rather more than 600 volumes, mostly theological, was shelved in five and a half of the six double presses. Most of the books had been the choice of Samuel Ward, the most recent of Lawrence and his *Classis* companions. Donations were few during the years of the Civil War and the Commonwealth, but Beck probably foresaw better times to come. Ward's Library was of limited

---

[64] V. Salmon, 'Cave Beck: a seventeenth century Ipswich schoolmaster and his Universal Character' in *Proc. Suff. Inst. Arch.* XXXIII (1975), 285–298.

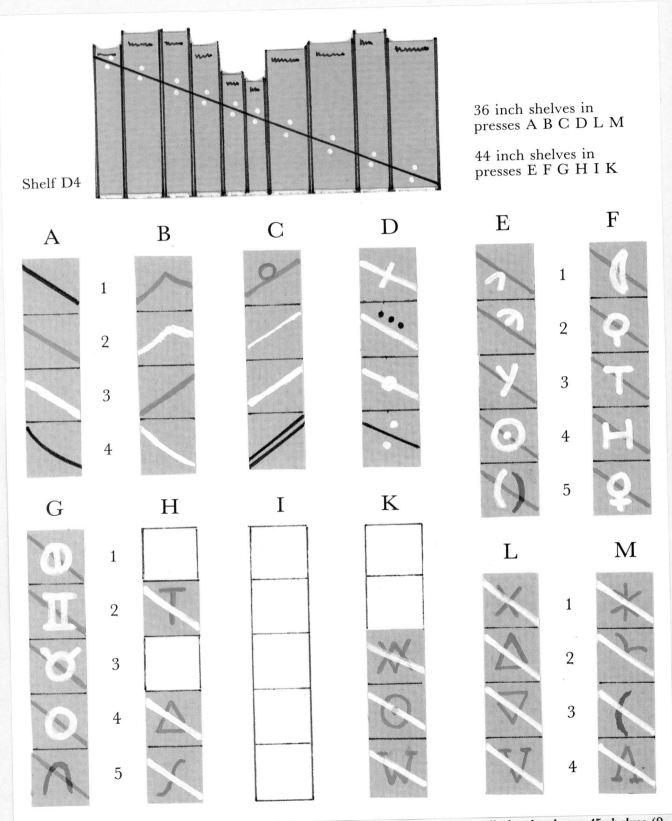

Shelf D4

36 inch shelves in presses A B C D L M

44 inch shelves in presses E F G H I K

III. The arrangement of the Library in 1651: the fore-edge shelfmark system applied to books on 45 shelves (9 others empty) in six double presses.

interest and value to Beck; the most important thing was that it should be easy to check to see that all the books were in their places, and to this end he turned his 'genius for new works' and set about devising a system that made this possible.

The books of the Library were at the time, as elsewhere, kept fore-edge outwards and most of the shelves were full. It is hardly surprising that by 1650 Coney's early shelf lists for Presses A and B no longer applied, for at some stage the need to impose a system on the collection had led to the following far from rigid arrangements:

Presses	
A and B	Works of the Fathers
C, D and E	Protestant theology and Bible commentaries
F and G	Catholic and Protestant theology mixed
H.5	Ecclesiastical history
M	History: 1, European; 2, British; 3 and 4, Church history

If Beck had rearranged the Library before applying his new system, the recently accessioned books he left together on shelves E.2 and G.2 and in presses I and K would have been distributed to their proper classes. Beck now had diagonal lines drawn in white, green or black paint across the fore-edges of the books on each shelf. The lines ran from top left to bottom right, or *vice versa* on 36 inch shelves; on 44 inch shelves, they ran down to the middle and up again on the right. The lines on books in Presses A and B were plain, but from C onwards distinctive marks were applied to the fore-edge of each book in one of the three colours or in red, the same symbol for all the volumes on one shelf. The unfaded green colour can best be seen on the vellum covered boards of Brightman's *Apocalypse* (King 680). Beck's symbols were chosen from the alphabet and from those currently used in alchemy and astronomy. E.4 and E.5, for example, had ☉ and ☽, *aurum* and *argentum*, F.2. and F.5 ♀ and ♀, *nox* and *cuprum*.

G.1	☿	nitre	L.2	△	ignis
G.2	♊	gemini	L.3	▽	aqua
G.3	♉	taurus	L.4	⋁	vin

The complete system is illustrated in *plate III*.

Waite's fore-edge flaps, so recently provided, were in the way of the new marks and had to be torn off, or, as in the case of two volumes only, tucked into the pages. The advantage of the new system was that the books could be mustered at a glance, even by an illiterate. From Beck's point of view it was an ideal system for a closed collection of books in which he had less interest than his predecessors.

All this is confirmed by a remarkable survival: one of the Chamberlains' warrants for work in the Library in April 1651 which was supervised by William Clarke. This, mainly in Clarke's hand, is included in a collection 65 made by the 19th century Ipswich postmaster and antiquary W.S.Fitch as a result of his being given almost unlimited access to the Borough archives by William Batley in the 1820s. In the transcript which follows it can be seen that one Basil Breame was paid three shillings for putting the lines on the books. It can hardly be coincidental that one of the same name, probably the son born in 1652 to Bezaleel (Basil) and Hellin Breame of St Nicholas parish, is named as tenant of one of Cave Beck's three tenements in that parish in his will of 1706. [66] The original warrant measures no more than six inches by four:

[65] SRO Ipswich: HD 88/3/5.
[66] NCC 6 Allexander (1706).

Layd out about the Library as followeth

	s	d
Imp. to Willia' Day the Joyner, for 3 pare of Joynts	3	6
It. for buttons for the doorse, Iron hookes, nayles & worke	2	0
It. afterward for altering the shelves in one deske for making the books stand tite & keeping them fro' falling in at the ends of all or most of the shelves	4	4
It. for 4 staves wch we' wanted for two of the tables for brass & Iron nayles & red Incle to nayle upon the velume	1	7
It. for his worke	0	8
It. to Basil Breame for making the lines on the bookes	3	0
It. to Mr Sayer for 3 skins of velume	6	0
It. for 6 sheets of paper for the doorse	0	6
It. to Mr Thorp for writing the papers upon the 11 doorse	11	0
It. for writing the 3 tables	16	0
It. for writing the little table	0	4

In the hand of William Dey, Town Clerk:

We requier you to paie unto Mr William Clarke the severall sumes above specified amounting to xlviii.^{s} xi.^{d} and by him disbursed for the causes aforesaid And this shall be yor warrant given under o.^{r} hands this xiith day of Aprill 1651

Nicholas Sicklemore & Thomas Griggs
Chamberlains of Ipswich

Peter Fisher
Ro: Dunkon
(Bailiffs)

William Day was not paid much for his work of making three stools, providing handles and hook-and-eye fastenings for the twelve doors, modifying most of the 54 shelves (there were 45 in use) to make the books 'stand tite', mending tables, presumably by replacing broken foot-rails, and inlaying the tops of three of them with vellum edged with red linen tape and brass headed nails. On the plan section of the scale drawing of a double press (*fig. 1*) the end stops he added to the shelves have been shown shaded. Without them, two or three books at each end of a shelf would have been hidden by the wide pilasters at either side of the press doors, and it would have been pointless to add the fore-edge shelf marks. Mr Sayer was probably the son and namesake of the man who made and gave the Book to the new Library in 1615. Later a Portman, he occupied property in the Tower and St Lawrence parishes, and at his death in 1680 left £100 to provide bread for the poor.[67]

No books received into the Library after 1651 were given fore-edge marks, nor even fore-edge titles, and they must therefore have been shelved in the modern way, spine outwards. New acquisitions were not numerous, and Beck could easily keep a check on the books he had chosen and therefore valued and used most. The limiting inflexibility of Beck's system for expanding classes of books must have been another reason for treating new books differently from the existing stock.

Mr Thorp the scribe was paid at handsome rates for the lists he wrote for the eleven press doors, that number confirming that Press I was still almost empty at the time. The three 'tables' and a 'little table' were, I suggest, benefactors' lists fit to be framed and hung in the room. At Norwich in 1656 the ministers had two frames made for the Orders for the regulation of the Library,[68] and at King's Lynn, as early as 1638, the 'makeing and wrighting of a Table' cost 20s.[69] To compress the four benefactors' lists of the Book into three, it would have been possible to put Portmen and Gentlemen together; just such a composite list has been written on the front cover of Coningsby's 1705

---

[67] [R. Canning], *op. cit.*, 156.

[68] G. A. Stephen, *op. cit.*, 6.

[69] T.E. Maw, 'The Church Libraries of King's Lynn' in *The Antiquary* 40 (1904), 235–240.

catalogue by someone who may have copied it from Thorp's first table. It is a careful amalgamation of the donors in the senior categories complete up to 1650 and with one addition of the 1660s. It is unlikely that anyone fifty years later could have thus assembled the names of all the Portmen, included those promoted after they had been listed as Burgesses and Townesmen. Thorp's three tables will have had comparable numbers on each; Ministers and Schollers, and Burgesses and Townesmen on the second and third respectively. How fine the room must have looked after this modest expenditure on improvements and embellishments, and how lucky we are to have the details with which to furnish it in the imagination.

With the deaths of Lawrence and Clarke in 1651/2 and 1653 respectively, Beck's charge of the Library must have become complete even if it were not already so, for the next town preacherships were of short duration. In turn the Corporation pursued two well-known ministers whose initials are enshrined for ever in the joint pseudonym 'Smectymnuus' on the pamphlet they published with Calamy, Young and Spurstowe in 1641. Stephen Marshall held the post from May 1653 to his death in November 1655 and left the Library £5 in his will,[70] yet no books bear his name today. Matthew Newcomen, lecturer at Dedham, vacillated from the following February until July 1656 before refusing, for he was not prepared to leave his Essex flock less than adequately provided for. There are works by all five 'Smectymnuus' divines in the six volumes of Parliamentary sermons, King 654.

Beck then was in charge, but surely he needed and had the help of Waite for much of the next 20 years, for although that cleric moved to Sproughton in 1655, he continued to keep the Registers at St Margaret's for Beck until his death in 1670.[71] Beck succeeded him there in 1657 but did no more than sign each year's entries 'Cave Beck curate' or 'minister'. Waite must have been assistant to Beck, or at the least Register clerk. 1657 was also the year that Waite's eulogy appeared in Beck's treatise, and another book came from the same press and publisher with Waite as co-editor of Nathaniel Smart and John Ward. This was the posthumous edition of *The Use and Practice of Faith* by Waite's father-in-law Matthew Lawrence. Waite does emerge as a man readily prepared to serve others, first Lawrence and the *Classis*, and then his 'intimate and ingenious friend' Beck.

The London publishers of the Beck and Lawrence books printed them for William Weekley, bookseller, 'to be sold at his shop at Ipswich'. From 1650 to 1660 Weekley commissioned the printing of eleven works, all but one theological, several by Ipswich clerics who are likely to have used the Library in their work: Stanton of the *Classis*, Newcomen visiting from Dedham, and Benjamin Bruning, town preacher from 1656 to 1663.[72]

In 1655 Henry Davis 'Masson' and his man charged £1 3s 4d for 7 days' work at the Library. Three years later further moves were made to attend to the fabric of the room. In the Assembly Book for 23 August it was 'ordered that the Tresurer do forthw'th Repayer the Librarie'. On 16 December, presumably because nothing had been done, the order was given again to 'Repaire, Tile and glase the Librarie belonginge to this Towne'. At the same Assembly there was a disturbing report of books being taken from the Library and sold:

> It is Ordered That the Twoe books That is to saye Speeds Cronologie & Bishupp Andrews Workes Formerlie Taken out of the Librarie of this Towne by Samuell Inglethorpe And by him sold For one & Thirtie shillings to Mr. Anthony Applewhite. It is ordered that the p'sent Chamberlins shall paie Mr. Applewhite the sd. One & Thirtie Shillings & see the bookes placed in the Librarie againe.

Neither book is in the Library today, as the Speed was lost again by 1705, and a newer edition of Bishop Andrewes' *Works* was given by Edward Reynolds at his first episcopal visitation of Ipswich in

---

[70] PCC 1656, fo.40.

[71] Detailed extracts from the registers were edited by C.H. Evelyn White in *E.A.N. & Q.* (N.S.) X (1903–4), 147, 173, 190, 201.

[72] N. Stanton, *The Good Masters Plea against the Evill Servants Cavill.* (1650); M. Newcomen, *A Sermon preached at the funeral of Samuel Collins.* (1658); B. Bruning *[Greek], or, The Best Wisdome.* (1660).

1662. Oddly enough, the flyleaf of the original copy was preserved, pasted into the Bishop's gift, showing that Beck had not yet forgiven Inglethorpe. It bears the note:

> Least by Mr Samuell Inglethorpe in
> consederation of xvi.^{s} as appears by my book
> Samuel Inglethorpe

Applewhite, a haberdasher, who presumably bought the books in good faith, became one of the Twenty Four in 1662; Samuell Inglethorpe's name does not recur in Corporation records.

Beck made no entries himself in the Book before 1662, but, starting on 31 August 1668, filled four pages in a large version of his somewhat ungainly hand, listing the gifts of four donors who gave books or money to provide them in 1668, 1668. 1666 and 1662 respectively. Beck could hardly spend the money Bishop Edward Reynolds gave on secular works, nor prevent John Colman from presenting works of theology. One of these was a collection of Reynolds' sermons, including the one he delivered from the Tower church pulpit, newly furnished with 'velvet cloth and cushion at the expense of the town', at the Visitation of October 1662. But when it came to spending the £20 bequest of John Robinson (on whose mural monument in the Tower church the legacy is mentioned) and the gift of Nicholas Phillips, Portmen both, Beck chose Mathematics, science, history, law, topography and some of the earliest publications of the Royal Society. Beck was determined to provide the burgesses of Ipswich with the materials of the new learning, and though from time to time between preacherships he was responsible for giving the now weekly lectures before the Corporation in the Tower church, he clearly felt the Library to be already more than adequately provided with *Theologica*.

As has been shown, entries in the Book at this period are so few and so disorganised that one is inclined to believe that Beck and Waite had commenced a separate record now lost. It is impossible to estimate the total numbers of unlisted benefactors, particularly those whose gifts themselves are gone, but of those we can identify, only four went unnamed in the whole of Ward's time, and four out of eleven in Lawrence's, but from Beck's taking charge up to 1670 only four are listed out of seventeen that are known to have given. Some other donors' names can be found in the books they gave, or from wills, and one from an entry in the Great Court Book for 6 November 1661:

> Wheras Sr Henrie Felton, Barronett, have given to this towne to be bestowed uppon the Librarie of this town the Bible in sev'all Languages contayninge six sev'all Volumes. It is agreed that there shalbe thankes Returned him fro' the towne And that Mr Recorder & Mr Phillipps be desired to Return the sd. thanckes And it is allsoe agreed that Sr Henrie Felton's name shalbe writte uppon Ev'rie of the said books & the same bookes shalbe delivered in to the sd Librarie.

Accordingly, enormous labels were lettered in gold and pasted into each volume, showing in what reverence Sir Henry, of Playford, Portman, Bailiff in 1685, and Deputy Lieutenant of the County from 1660, was held by the town. The cost 'for portridge' and for 'wrighting his name in gold' in the books was 10s 10d.

Although the Restoration of the Monarchy was not greeted with universal approbation in the town,[73] it did create an atmosphere in which stock could be taken of the state of town buildings and property. In September 1663, Henry Gosnold, the town Treasurer, made inventories of the furnishings in the Gaol, Lecturer's House and School House (Felaw's House), together with notes on measures to improve their security.[74] No list was made in the Library, but accounts for the year include:

It. paid Holloway for 4 kees for the Libary	00 04 00
and for Alteringe the Lock & setinge in	00 01 02

---

[73] A. Everitt, *op. cit.*, 125.
[74] Appendix to Accoumpt of Henry Gosnold, Treasurer 1663–4, SRO Ipswich: C9/20/80, pp.20–1.

The four keys would have gone to the Bailiffs, Beck and probably to Waite.

Five years later there were ambitious plans afoot to raise money for what must have been major works in the Library when the Assembly agreed:

> that Mr Robert Sparrowe, Mr John Wright & Mr Gilbert Lindfeild shall doe their best Endeavour to sell the house called old Junes by the towne pounde for the best price and to take the money & dispose of itt for the best advantage For the Repairinge & beautifieinge of the library.

Perhaps 'old Junes' proved unsaleable, for in April 1669 an even more radical idea was agreed:

> that the Mony Raised for the Beere Lycences this year shalbe laid out about the Repaire of the Librarie, & Mr Sparrowe, Mr Wright, Mr Towne Clerke & Mr Feast are desired to take care about itt. Mr Feast to be Receiver & Expenditor.

The ale-house keepers' beer licences produced about £30 *per annum* at this time. William Feast was one of the borough coroners; he would not have spent such a large sum in a hurry. By May 1671 he seems not even to have started:

> Agreed that Mr Bailiffe John Wright, Mr Lindfeild, Mr Clarke & John Sawyer shall take care for the Repaier of the Roome called Marchant Taylors' Hall & the Library as farr as the mony Received of the Alehouse Kepers for their Licenses Shall Amount unto.

Over the next few years the Treasurers' accounts show a few entries for work at the Library. For example, in 1672–3, £1 17s to John Skidmore and Joseph Page; in 1674–5, £4 18s 6d (but some of that for the School), and another 3s 2d for glazing in 1680–1. Were the boys of the Grammar School vandals? Their own building needed a very great deal of new glazing almost every year.

One luxury which the new source of income permitted was the cleaning and sweeping of the Library, for which an annual amount of one pound appears in the Chamberlains' accounts from 1668. The same sum had been paid at St James's church in Bury St Edmunds each year since 1619 when it was first paid to Roberte Studd 'for aydeing and wypinge the books in the library'.[75] For the first 26 years of the new arrangement in Ipswich, the payment went to Sarah Hubbard or her husband Samuel. Sarah was in 1675 'Goody Hubbard' and from 1682 onwards 'Widow'. Hubbard was the resident Guider of Christ's Hospital, responsible for the supervision of the young, the sick and the elderly sheltered there.

[75] SRO Bury: HD1150/2 in the account of Thomas Bright for the year ending 16 January 1619/20.

VII

DISTINGUISHED PATRONS
1670–1705

'This volume no erratas has
The whole may for erratas pas
If to correct them you intend
You'l find it Labour without end
Tis therefore better let them go
God only 'tis, knows who getts who.'

Verse by John Knight on fly leaf of the first volume of
his copy of Dugdale's *Baronage* in Caius Library.[76]

For the whole of this long period in the history of the Library it is difficult to establish with certainty who was in charge. The Masters who succeeded Beck did not, so far as can be seen, have any hand in it, probably because Beck was still active and influential in the town and better placed to attract the interest and gifts of the well known and the wealthy. He may also have become somewhat possessive, as will be discussed in Chapter VIII. It would help if there were more entries in the Book, but only two of the eighteen known donors' names are to be found there, the first in the hand of Robert Clark, Town Clerk from 1661 to 1697, and the second in what appears to be a large and florid version of Cave Beck's:

6 ° May 1675 S. ʳ Andrewe Hackett gave to the Library
A Century of Sermons Preached by John
Hackett Lord Bishopp of Lichfield & Coventry
father to the sd. Andrewe

August 1 ° 1695 Capt Deverux Edgar gave to this Library
Cambdens Britannia
newly translated into English
with Large Additions

Hackett, a Master in Chancery, had Suffolk links through his mother, a Stebbing of Earl Soham; her mother was an Edgar. Between Devereux Edgar of Grimstone House in Tower Street and Robert Clark, there was 'nigh neighbourhood and friendship'.[77] Both were dominant figures in the political life of the town and in the two parishes. At a time when party factions began to divide the Corporation, both were staunch Tories, as generally were the Masters and the senior local incumbents, particularly Cave Beck at St Margaret's. Joseph Cutlove, minister at the Tower church from 1677 to 1707/8, seems to have been an exception, at least in his voting in the 1705 Poll for Knights of the Shire. Edgar's five sons went to the Grammar School under Robert Coningsby, Master from 1696 to 1712, and Robert Edgar the eldest gave another copy of the 1695 Britannia to the School library when he left for Queens' in 1700. 1695 was the year that Devereux Edgar paid for the painting of the roof panels at St Margaret's in memory of his mother who died that year. Five years

---

[76] E.M. and R.T.C. Calvert, *Serjeant Surgeon: John Knight, Surgeon General 1664–1680.* (1939).
[77] Manuscript plan entitled 'The Forme Frame or Manner of the North Isle of Sᶜᵗ Mary le Tower Church Ipswich etc. Private Possession.

later he and Cave Beck devised a display of family heraldry on shields on the hammerbeam ends which included their own coats, in Beck's case, predictably, an invention.[78]

These then are the men who had some part in the running of the Library at this time. Robert Clark kept an official record of all Town benefactors, but did not take much trouble over gifts to the Library. His book [79] has just one page of them, mostly in the hand of his clerk or deputy. Dates are not given, but eight donors are named who gave between 1661 and 1687, two of them unrecorded elsewhere: Sir Nicholas Bacon, K.B. of Shrubland Hall, and Captain Nicholas Kerrington of Wapping, both of whom died in 1687, the latter bequeathing £100 to the town.[80] Clark's own hand adds to the list the gifts of Sir John Barker, M.P. for Ipswich from 1685 to 1689, and inscribes the flyleaf of the book given by John Lambe, Esq. of Barham, whose brother-in-law Nathaniel Acton, Esq. of Bramford gave *The Works of King Charles the Martyr* (King 547) in 1690. This book, and the 1649 edition of the *Eikon Basilike* (King 262), will have been of great interest and use to Cave Beck, who, always an ardent Royalist, had a strong interest in the authorship of the *Eikon*. When Dr Richard Hollingworth had prepared his written case for the book being the defeated King's own work, he received a letter from Beck which was printed at the end of his tract.[81] First Beck gave the assurances he had received from Major Robert Huntington at Ipswich (who read the manuscript after Naseby and began to change his loyalty to the King's side thereafter) and, in 1660 in Holland, from Dr John Earle, the translator of the book into Latin. He then finished his account in fine style:

> For my part, I am apt to believe no Person was able to frame that Book, but a Suffering King, and no Suffering King, but King Charles the Martyr.

One more interesting fact comes from Clark's record of gifts to the town. Mrs Dorothy Seckford of Seckford Hall at Bealings was the widow of Henry Seckford Esq. who died in 1638. In her will made in 1672 and proved the next year, she left 'for the benefitt of the Library of Ipswich... £20 to be paid by mine executor [Sir Henry North, Bt.] for books of that value to remain and be left in the sd. Library for ever.' Clark added a note 'The Bookes were bought by Mr Cutlove Minister & some small some [sum] added to the 20 ^{li} & put into the Library.' This indicates that even if the bequest was received earlier it was not spent until Cutlove, a former Grammar School pupil here, arrived as Tower church minister in 1677. Indeed one work chosen, Cudworth's *Intellectual System of the Universe* (King 218) was not published until 1678. The two-volume Dionysius of 1634 (King 498) has the ownership inscriptions of two Bishops of Salisbury, John Davenant and Humphrey Henchman. Henchman married Davenant's neice, and the *D.N.B.* records that the former bishop had bequeathed him 'a good serviceable gelding, a great Concordance of the New Testament, and Dionysius the Areopagite'. It was Cutlove who inscribed all the Seckford books and the Chateillon of 1573 (King 514) given by Dr John Eachard, the Suffolk man who became Master of Catherine Hall in 1675.

The main interest of this period is in the quite notable people who gave books. The antiquary Silas Taylor presented a copy of his *History of Gavelkind* in 1668. He was Keeper of the King's Stores at Harwich, where he made collections for a history not published until Samuel Dale incorporated them into his *History and Antiquities of Harwich and Dovercourt* in 1730. Taylor was well known to Dr John Knight, Surgeon-General to the forces, himself in 1680 a major donor. In Minsheu's *Ductor in Linguas* 1617 (King 473) Taylor wrote in the gap after 'And are to be sold at' on the title page to the

---

[78] J.K. Corder and J.M. Blatchly, 'Notes on the series of coats of arms below the roof of St Margaret's Church, Ipswich' in *The Blazon* 36 (Suffolk Heraldry Society 1986).
[79] SRO Ipswich: C13/1, a manuscript Account of Ipswich Charities which Robert Clarke was ordered by the Great Court to make in September 1657. The list of Library donors is at fo. 133.[v]
[80] [R. Canning], *op. cit.*, 199.
[81] R. Hollingworth, *The Character of Charles I...* (1692), 27–8. Huntington paid Hearth Tax at Battisford in 1640 (source in footnote 132); his Civil War career under Fairfax is well documented, e.g. P. Young, *Naseby 1645, the Campaign and the Battle.* (1985), 162–3 and passim.

Spanish section: 'the Devil's Arse at Peak'. This must refer to the Derbyshire cave renamed 'the Devil's Hole' by Sir Walter Scott, but the allusion is obscure unless Taylor, a former Roundhead commander, retained his distaste for all things Spanish.

Sir Manuell Sorrell, knighted as Senior Bailiff at the Restoration, left £100 to the town in his will.[82] He died early in 1669/70 and the bequest, which was to be lent in sums of £25 at a time to grocers needing financial assistance, was not received until 1673. At an Assembly held on 6 May 1673, it was reported that 'Mr Nathaniell Sorrell hath p'mised to give to the benefitt of the library six pounds in regard to the £100 of his father was not payd in soo soone itt should have bin although paid as soon itt was received.' Nathaniell Sorrell was the second son of Sir Manuell; Andrew the eldest might have been expected to arrange the payment, but was within only months of his own end. If books were bought with the money there is no record of them.

Samuel Butler, Usher from 1668 to 1672 when he became Rector of Nacton, gave several volumes, and Dr John Wallace, M.D., of St Nicholas parish gave others, mostly small and showing marks of personal ownership and use. Son of another Doctor John (who examined the ailing and complaining Lawrence for the Corporation in 1646[83]), he graduated from St John's College, Cambridge and practised in Ipswich throughout the last quarter of the century. Apart from Burnet's *History of the Reformation* (King 614) the books he gave were Venetian printings of a century earlier and included Baldessare Castiglione's classic *Il Cortegiano* (King 341) and Sansovino's *Del Secretario* (King 353). The former had belonged to Sir Henry Glemham, M.P. for Suffolk, Ipswich and Aldeburgh from 1601 to 1620. Wallace certainly had a marked interest in Italian matters; and in the library of the Royal College of Physicians is the forged illuminated certificate which purports to confer the degree of M.D. from the University of Padua on his father. One glaring error is that its date is 1628, ten years late for the Doge named in the document. Seven internationally famous doctors' signatures are forged in the younger Wallace's hand using different styles and pens.

The largest gift to the Library after Ward's time was that of Dr John Knight, whose topographical books and atlases were, as their labels state 'delivered into this Library February 1680', three months after his death at the age of eighty. Dr John Knight was married in St Matthew's Church, Ipswich, but lived mainly in London, moving to King's Lynn in the interregnum, and then serving the future Charles II in exile and travelling home with him in 1660. He was appointed Serjeant Surgeon to the King in 1661. His duties as Surgeon General to the Forces brought him to Suffolk and Essex in the Dutch Wars, to Southwold, Ipswich and Harwich in 1666. He received the honorary freedom of Ipswich in September 1673, and when making his will in October 1680 directed that his collection of 66 heraldic manuscripts should go to his old College, Caius, and his printed books to Ipswich Library. Almost every book illustration is hand-coloured by Knight himself, who, in a discourse on flags written at Pepys' request in 1678, referred to his 'revered father Thomas' as the Arms-Painter who painted the banners and streamers required in 1623 for the fleet bringing Prince Charles and the Duke of Buckingham home from Spain. The colouring of the heraldry, notably in Thoroton's *Nottinghamshire* (King 644) is particularly fine. It seems very probable, particularly in view of his being in possession of so rich a collection of Ordinaries and Visitations, some in their hands, that he was also related to Thomas Knight, Chester Herald (d. 1618), and his father Edmund Knight, Norroy King of Arms (d. 1593, who is said, with others, to have plundered the Heralds' College collections in 1588).[84]

The will clause concerning manuscripts and books refers to a 'schedule... hereunto annexed'

[82] PCC 84 Penn (1670).

[83] Assembly Book 23 July 1646 (Richardson, 544). The bogus degree certificate is in the library of the Royal College of Surgeons, but aphotographic copy is held at SRO Ipswich: JA1/42/1.

[84] PCC 138 Bath (1680). Knight's 'discourse' for Pepys is in P.L. 2877, pp. 404–36. I am grateful to Dr Richard Luckett for confirming that John Knight does call his father Thomas on p. 417, since the Calverts repeatedly name him John, Herald Painter to Charles I. For the Tudor theft see A. Wagner, *Heralds of England*. (London 1967), 220.

which, though signed, was neither witnessed nor dated, but his executors nevertheless followed the instructions it gave to the letter:

> Item I give & bequeath to the Library of the College of Gonvile and Caius in Cambridge al my manuscripts & Heraldry being about fifty folios & ten quartos as also Dugdale's two volumes of the Baronage to which are by myself added most of the armes, desiring the Master and fellows of the said College, they accepting mine with these essential adornments, that they would let the town of Ipswich have theirs they now have or refusing this; my wil is that the town of Ipswich have myne...

> Item I give & bequeath to the Library of the town of Ipswich the Monasticon Anglicanum in 3 volums. Lazius de gentium migrationibus; Sanson's mapps in two large volumes; Dugdales Warwickshire, Burton's Leicestershire, Thoroton's Nottingham, Carew's Cornwal, Lambert's Perambulation of Kent, Philpott's Kent, Survey of Cheshire by Smith and Webb and one other volume of Cheshire by Leicester, Burton's Comentari on Antoninus, 3 fol: Scriptorum Germanicorum; Broald [*sic*] chronicum Scriptura; Helvicus his chronology; Ashmole's history of the Garter; Segars, Honours Military & Civil; Milles [Glover's] de Nobilitate, Plot's Natural History.

> John Knight

Just three of these works are now lost, the *Survey of Cheshire,* the *Perambulation of Kent* and the Segar. Apart from their hand colouring, Knight's books have three characteristics where they survive: marbled edges, a circular blind-stamped coat of arms of Knight with the motto *'Suivant Sainct Pierre'* on the centre of the front board, and large calligraphic gift labels (*fig. 5*). The first of the two volumes of the *Baronage of England* (King 503) has a more modest inscription in the hand of Clark's assistant, having come from Caius as Knight requested. Before sending the duplicate set to Ipswich, the Librarian there cut out the original gift inscription and pasted it into Knight's copy.

Knight's two-volume atlas of nearly 200 maps by the principal French court cartographers Sanson and Duval is of the greatest interest. He must have acquired the volumes sometime after 1671, the latest date appearing on any map. As recently as 1984 (see appendix H) Mme Mireille Pastoureau of the Bibliothque Nationale listed the contents of many atlases by these mapmakers, yet we have maps by both Sanson and Duval which are new to her. A few early Italian maps have been included, some folded as though they had been posted. The arrangement of the maps (for example ancient beside modern for the same nation, and Tartary beside Little Tartary) indicates the hand of an amateur: if it is Knight's, he was no geographer.

One further matter connected with John Knight is relevant. His royal appointment and historical interests brought him into contact with men like Pepys, Evelyn and the grandly-designated Cosmographer Royal, John Ogilby. In the 1670s, Ogilby was preparing his three-part survey of Britain: town plans, county maps and, for the first time ever, maps of the post-roads. In the bitter winter of 1673/4 he sent Gregory King and Robert Felgate to Ipswich to prepare the large plan of the town, publication of which was delayed until 1698. In 1675 the first edition of *Britannia, Volume the First* appeared with 100 double-leaf maps of roads interleaved with letterpress descriptions of the routes. That Ogilby chose to publish a plan of Ipswich on nine double-leaf sheets must have been at the instigation of Knight, who personally persuaded the Corporation to assist with the project in various ways. First, the Great Court agreed on 14 April 1674:

> that the Impressions or Effigies of the Common Seale & Admirall Seale belonging to this towne with the draft of the towne Armes shall be by Mr Brame att the charge of the towne made & sent to Mr Ogelby.

This Brame was probably John rather than Basil. Next on 17 June 1674:

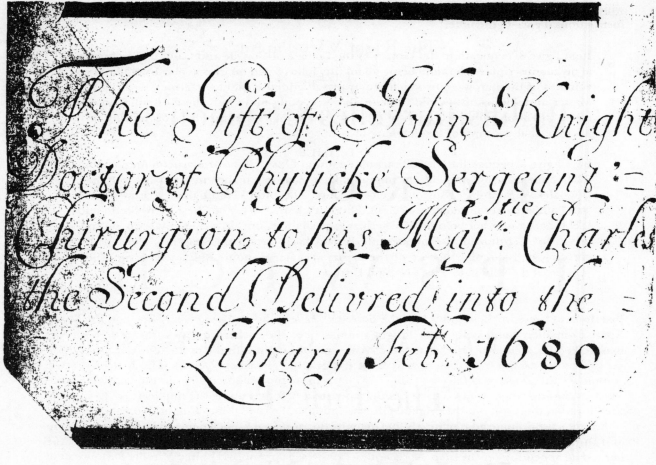

Figure 5. The calligraphic gift label in Dr John Knight's Philipot.

Considering the great charge Mr Ogilby is and will be at in carrying on his Britannia it is ordered that 30 guineas be paid to Mr Serjeant Knight to be delivered to Mr Ogilby as from this town.

and the receipt, somewhat defective, is pasted into John Wodderspoon's grangerised copy of his own *Memorials of the Ancient Town of Ipswich,* 1850: [85]

1674
[Recd.] then of J° Knight
[P]rincipal chirurgeon
[to his] Matie thirty guinnies   g
[bei]ng a gratuity from   30:0
the Worshipful the Bayliffs
& Corporation Of Ipswich
I say received
John Ogilby

This corporate generosity had its reward in a copy of the 1675 road atlas, with no inscription, but a specially printed dedication leaf inserted to face the address to the King (*fig. 6*). Members of the

[85] SRO Ipswich: HD495.

TO

The Right VVorſhipful

THE

Bailiffs, Burgeſſes & Comonalty,

OF THE

BOROUGH

OF

IPSVVICH:

THIS

ROYAL VOLUME,

BEING

The Firſt Part

OF HIS

BRITANNIA,

IS MOST

HUMBLY PRESENTED

AND

DEDICATED

BY HIS

MAJESTY'S

Coſmographer,

JOHN OGILBY.

Figure 6. Dedication leaf from *Britannia Volume the First*, 1675.

Corporation would have been less flattered had they realised how difficult Ogilby found it to sell the work; it is known that many copies were disposed of as lottery prizes after Ogilby's death.[86] The book makes the first published reference to the Library at page 108, but Ogilby, presumably misled by Knight, links School and Library in the description of Ipswich: 'a Free School with a fair Library'. Bishop Gibson picked this up when writing the additions for Suffolk in his 1695 edition of Camden: 'a *Free-school*.. having also the conveniency of a very good *Library*'. Later editions elaborated the account, adding: 'stored with Bookes of various kinds, for the benefit of the *Inhabitants* and *Strangers*'.

Little is known about the users and readers of the Town Library once it ceased to be almost entirely the preserve of the preaching ministers. One man, however, left a remarkable record of his use, for on the tenth page of most books published and given before 1630 he wrote the initials 'B.G.' in the upper margin. When he came to the Hebrew Concordance printed by Ambrose Froben in 1581 (King 455) he must have turned it upside down in his confusion, for his 'B.G.' appears inverted at the foot of the seventh folio!

$$\mathcal{B} \; \mathcal{G}$$

10

Had B.G. applied the early 17th century booksellers' price code to his own initials he might have chosen to write them on the ninth page (two plus seven) rather than the tenth. The most puzzling thing about these marks is that they were made only in works which were published and donated to the Library half a century or more before B.G. went to work on them. The man who in the later 1680s had the opportunity for all this browsing was Balthazar Gardemau, and a comparison of hands confirms that he was responsible.[87] A Huguenot born about 1656, who graduated as a minister at the Protestant Academy of Saumur, he came to England and was in September 1682 licensed as stipendary curate at St. Mary Elms, with the special duty of catechizing the boys. His work included a ministry among his fellow refugees, and he taught their children English in succession to Monsieur Caesar de Beaulieu, who in April 1682 had been allowed 'a chamber in the Usher's house' (Felaw's House) for the purpose. It seems likely that Gardemau moved his charges to the room next to the Library (the former Taylors' Hall), for how could he read and mark over 350 volumes without constant and ready access to them? To return to the puzzle: the most modern book he initialled was published in 1628, the year that the Huguenot fortress at La Rochelle was reduced. This date will have had renewed significance for Gardemau and his compatriots when in 1685 the Edict of Nantes was finally revoked. A more straightforward notion would be that he was preparing a catalogue of the Library in chronological order, and had not taken (or did not wish to take) it further than 1628 when in March 1689/90 he moved to Coddenham. There he eventually married Lady Catherine Bacon, widow of his patron Nicholas Bacon, Esq., thus becoming master of Shrubland Hall himself. His own library, left for the use of his successors in the living, is an unusually interesting example of a parochial library; it includes some books he purchased and provided for the 'Cleydon Society', perhaps for the clergy of that Deanery. The elegant mural monument set up for Gardemau in the chancel at Coddenham by his widow has piles of five marble books at each end of the pediment, ten in all – his number again perhaps?[88]

[86] 'Ogilby's Heir' in *John Ogilby Cosmographer Royal: Catalogue of a Commemorative Exhibition held at Guildhall Art Gallery, 1976–7.*

[87] The initials are to be found in several of the Coddenham Library books, at present stored at Ipswich Library in Northgate Street; for example, in J. Bingham's *The French Churches Apology for the Church of England.* (1706).

[88] J.A. Fitch, 'Balthazar Gardemau, a Huguenot Squarson and his Library' in *Huguenot Society of London Proceedings* 20 (1968), 241–272.

The Treasurer's accounts periodically show work going on at the Library: in 1689–90, £1 8s 11d for roofing and guttering, 12s for some plastering (including 4 bushels of hair for the purpose) and 8s 11d for materials required for these jobs; in 1698–9 work at the Library and the Lecturer's House which cannot be differentiated; and in 1699–1700 several tradesmen including a mason and an accomptant (quantity surveyor) charged £10 1s 10d. In 1694 John Wade, the new Guider, took over the Library cleaning and so added a pound a year to his salary.

VIII

ROBERT CONINGSBY, MASTER
THE FIRST CATALOGUE AND A SECOND LIBRARY FOR THE SCHOOL
1705–1712

The first Oxford graduate to be elected Master of the Grammar School for well over a century was a St John's man who came to Ipswich from Merchant Taylors' School where he had been Under Master for five years. His belongings arrived from London by sea after him in October 1695, one of the few details of his 17-year tenure of the Mastership which have come down to us other than his involvement in libraries.[89] It is true that Masters and ex-Masters had run the Library continuously since 1636, but since Beck left the School in 1657 none of his successors seems to have been allowed to. The fact that Robert Woodside, who followed Beck, saw the immediate need to persuade the Corporation to provide other books for school use surely indicates that the Town Library was not available to him or to his Usher in their teaching, particularly since some of the first books they collected for the School were already in the town collection. At the very first Assembly after Woodside's appointment it was agreed:

> that thes bookes Followinge That is to saie, Scapula, Erasmus Adagies, twoe Dictionaries
> & a Bible shallbe bought att the Charge of the Towne & sent to the schoole to be used As
> Common bookes And that the Master be desired to buy the Same.[90]

For these the Chamberlains paid £2 17s. When Woodside died only two years later, his widow had to be compensated, amongst other things, for presses he had provided for the School in the meantime. Already then, the School and the town had separate libraries, but the indications are that the new collection grew most rapidly in the early years of Coningsby's Mastership. Fewer than 30 volumes belonging to the School collection remain today, but in 1877 Dr Holden's son Edward, a sixth former and Library Prefect, made a detailed catalogue of the 157 works in more than 200 volumes then extant.[91] In about 1800 there had been over 400. Luckily, the young Holden recorded the owners' and donors' inscriptions which he found in many of the books now lost, and from these a good deal can still be deduced. The 1604 Scapula and the 1629 Erasmus bought in 1657 were still there in 1877, the former duplicating the Town Library copy presented to the town by Nicholas Easton, Master from 1616 to 1630.

From 1697, perhaps because Coningsby despaired of Beck's ever relinquishing charge of the Town Library, he established a tradition of leavers and former members presenting books to the school. Joseph Cutlove led the way and we know of a dozen more donations in the next eight years, the last the first of several by John Gaudy the Usher, an Ipswichian himself. These books, including the *Opera* of Lucian which Coningsby himself presented in 1702, were inscribed by the latter:

Ex Libb:
Scholae publicae Gippovicensis

whereas those he accessioned for the Town Library from 1705 onwards had on their title pages:

Ex Libb:
Bibl: Ipsvic:

[89] V.B. Redstone, *Ipswich Borough Records* No.16, Fluctuations, 6 (see footnote 17 above).
[90] Assembly Book 26 May 1657.
[91] E.A.L. Holden's manuscript Catalogue of the School Library is in the Archive Collections of the School.

One very interesting gift to the school in 1701, Calepinus' *Dictionarium octolingue* seems to have come from one John Beck, probably son of the former Master. Beck had been given it in 1666 by a grateful and admiring school contemporary Cornelius Hoogenbrich, presumably a connection of the Huguenot immigrants who in 1662 set up a fulling mill and woollen manufactory in the town,[92] and possibly related to Cornelius Hubright, made a Freeman of the borough in 1604.[93] The dedicatory inscription reads as follows:

1666
Optimi indolis atque spei adolescenti
Johanni beckio postquam per annum hospitio
parentium usus esset idiscedens hunc librum
in remuneration' beneficiorum decrevit
pax optima rerum
Cornelius Hoogenbrich

It seem likely that both boys had attended the Grammar School in Robert Stephenson's time as Master, and that John Beck had died by 1701 when his father passed the book to Coningsby for the School. The Town Library already possessed the eleven-language version (King 481), a gift of the Master Nicholas Easton, indicating that in his day the shared use of books needed for both town and School was accepted. The registers of St Margaret's were kept irregularly around 1700, so that John Beck's burial is not to be found there; in his will of 1706 Cave Beck mentions no offspring, only his second wife Sarah.[64]

It was in 1705 that Coningsby at last turned his attention to the Town Library; to judge from the care he took there he did so officially. First he made a list of missing books on page A1 of the Book. This could have been done very quickly using Beck's fore-edge shelfmarks unless the books had already been reshelved spine outwards in the presses.

Desunt 1705

B.2.	Optatus
C.1.	Unum ex Calvini volum.
E.2.	Zepperi tria volum.
E.3.	Unum ex D. Parei volum.
F.2.	Unum ex Riveti vol.
+H.2.	Besodneri Biblioth. Theol.
I.3.	Cotton's Concordance
M.2.	Speed's Chronicle
+	Unum ex Pelargi vol.
+	Unum ex Tostati

+ These three lines deleted as the books were not lost.

The shelf numbers in this list are the only ones of the 1651 arrangements to appear in the Book. Had the catalogue Coningsby now set out to make been lost, the key to Beck's marks would have been lost too, except in so far as most of the marks themselves are still clearly legible. Coningsby thriftily appropriated a boy's partly-used Geometry notebook for his catalogue and it has been preserved among the borough records.[94] It has some fifty paper leaves bound into slightly stouter covers covered with thin vellum. The lists, alphabetical by author, are neatly written by Coningsby, the first letter of each author's name in red, and a shelf number given for every book. Hands other

[92] V.B. Redstone, 'The Dutch and Huguenot Settlements of Ipswich' in *Huguenot Society of London Proceedings* 12 (1921), 183–204.
[93] Great Court Book 3 March 1604 (Richardson, 418).
[94] SRO Ipswich: C2/16 (deposited with the Town Library by courtesy of the Chief Executive of the Borough and the County Archivist).

than Coningsby's occur in the later entries: Hingeston the Master, then King and someone working for him when in 1798 he was preparing his lists for publication the following year. His *Alphabetical Catalogue* is based on this earlier manuscript version almost entirely. King merely dropped Beck's shelf numbers which by then no longer applied. Using the manuscript catalogue it is possible to reconstruct the shelving arrangements of the Library at various dates: in 1651 when the shelf marks were applied, in 1712 when Coningsby died, and 1767, just before the Library was moved to another room in the Blackfriars. In 1712, for example, the shelves filled wholly or partially since 1651 were: H.3, I.2 to I.5, K.1 and K.2, the four shelves of N, and O.2 and O.3. This left H.1, I.1, O.1 and O.4, more than enough room for the gifts of the next (and last) fifty years.

Coningsby did not receive many gifts for the Library; just an eight- volume set of *Bibliotheca Patrum Concionatoria* from Joseph Cutlove, and two books from Miles Wallis, Portman and Bailiff, who inscribed a most elegant label for one of them (at least - the other is lost) himself. The fate of this book in the 19th century is described in Chapter XI.

It was also in 1705 that the Great Court formalized the responsibility of the Guider of Christ's Hospital for the cleaning of the room. In the Order for the Guider we read: '9thly He shall have Twenty Shillings yearly pd. him by the Chamberlains for cleaning the Library.' In 1711 John Wade was succeeded by John Jermyn who stayed five years in the post. On 23 October 1710 the Assembly took action on the alarming news that 'Whereas some part of the Library house is fallen downe. It is ordered that the same, be forthwith rebuilt by the Towne Trea'rer, at the charge of this Corporation.' The relevant accounts do not exist to show what was done and at what cost.

In 1712 Robert Coningsby died in office, holding also the rectories of Woolverstone and Trimley. He penned his own will in 1709, naming as his executors Major Devereux Edgar and Dr John Dade.[95] Ignoring all possible claims of the Town Library he wrote:

> I give and bequeath to ye Press [*sic*] in ye Gram'ar School of Ipswich these following books at my Study *viz.* Ptolemeus Bertij, Constantini Lex. graec; Hesychij Lex graec; Spelmanni glossarum, Leigh's Critica Sacra.

It seems that the books did come to the School, but of the five listed only two (Constantine and Hesychius) were there to be catalogued by Edward Holden in 1877. Leigh's *Critica Sacra*, inscribed 'Ex.Libb: Rob't Coningsby 1704' is extant, catalogued and kept with the Town Library by John King who mistakenly thought that Stanton's bequest in 1649 must have provided two copies of Leigh's book. King ought to have noticed 'Scholae Gippovicensis' in large letters in Coningsby's hand on the top-edge, and been alerted by the absence of Hingeston's usual 'Ipswich Library' on the title page. The presence of the top-edge inscription does suggest that the gift of books to the School was made in the Master's lifetime, and not left for Dade and Edgar to arrange.

Robert Coningsby seems to have felt that the School had a greater need of books than the town. To his successors he passed a useful collection of texts, ancient and modern, to form the nucleus of a school library, and an orderly Town Library with, at last, a proper author catalogue in manuscript.

---

[95] SRO Ipswich: IC/AA1/142/51 (1712).

IV. The Revd. Richard Canning, by Thomas Gainsborough.

IX

POLITICAL CONTROVERSY
AND THE COLLECTION CLOSED
1712–1766

'But some men, as it seems, will neither do good themselves, nor suffer it to be done by others.'

Richard Canning [96]

For the next 25 years Edward Leedes was Master and *de facto* custodian of the Library. His father, another Edward, was Master of Bury School, and the younger man came to Ipswich with five years' experience as Under-master to his late father's successor there. Leedes wrote and published several classical schoolbooks and, following a Bury School tradition, had printed in Ipswich in 1722 a *Catechesis Ecclesiae Anglicanae ... in usum Scholae Regis Henrici ejus nominis Octavi in Burgo Gippovicensi.* In view of this interest in books it is surprising that so little happened to the Library in Leedes' time. John Gaudy, Coningsby's last Usher, left after only a term. In 1721 Robert Hingeston, another Ipswich and Pembroke man, arrived as Usher, and stayed until his death in 1766, holding the Mastership from 1743. Leedes gave at least 18 books to the School library (according to Holden's catalogue of 1877); Hingeston gave some as Usher and others as Master. Leedes was never a donor to the Town Library.

The most important gift accessioned by Leedes was the collection of 171 sermons preached before Parliament between 1640 and 1646, (King 654) much annotated, and bound in six volumes in reversed calf gilt-stamped 'W.D.' by their first owner, William Dowsing. These were given by William Matthews, minister of St Margaret's, in 1725, the year he moved to St Lawrence. Matthews may have bought them at the sale of the library of Dowsing's eldest son Samuel in 1704. Any doubts about whether the first owner of the sermons and the despoiler of East Anglian churches in the 1640s with a commission from the Earl of Manchester were the same person are dispelled when the marginal additions are studied. Dowsing collected and glossed other sermons than these; his autograph annotations are to be found in earlier works in the Folger Library in Washington [97] and the University Library at Cambridge. [98] The signatures on each folio of the will of William Dowsing 'the elder' of Stratford St Mary, made 21 August 1667 and proved 21 September 1668, are in the hand of the sermon reader, showing once and for all that none of the William Dowsings buried at Laxfield at various dates in the 1660s and 1670s can be the iconoclast. [99] The notorious Dowsing was, as Matthias Candler wrote in about 1655, 'of Coddenham, since of Stratford'. [100] If further proof were needed there is written on the back of the second sermon in the sixth volume the draft of a letter dated 6 March 1642/3 to Matthew Newcomen at Dedham in which the writer suggests that the time is ripe to begin the work of destruction of all 'reliques of popery' in Cambridge. The draft is initialled 'W.D.'

In the first edition of *The Suffolk Traveller* (1735), the author John Kirby, who was both schoolmaster and surveyor by profession, noted under Ipswich 'a large publick Library, where is a good

---

[96] [R. Canning], *op. cit.*, 145.

[97] J. Fit John, *A Diamonde most Precious.* (1577) STC 10929, the Folger Library copy.

[98] W. Tyndale, *Obedience of a Christian Man.* (1548?) STC 10929, the Cambridge University Library copy (Syn.8.54.172) lacks title page. Two other books with Dowsing's notes were owned by C. Deedes of Chichester when he described them in *East Anglian Notes and Queries* (N.S.): Quarles' *Divine Fancies* (1632) in VII, 17, and *Eikon Alethine* (1649) in XI, 33.

[99] SRO Ipswich IC/AA1/98/149 (1668).

[100] BL Harl. MS 6,071, fo. 358.

Collection of the Fathers, Schoolmen, Commentators &c.' Was this Leedes' description or Kirby's observation?

When Hingeston succeeded to the Mastership, the Corporation was well into a 30-year period when the Whig party was in power. Masters of the Grammar School were on the whole of the other persuasion, but so long as they continued to accept the nominees of the burgesses to Foundation places, and to accept with fair grace the misapplication of the revenue from Felaw's endowments, things went smoothly enough.

In October 1743, just a few days after Hingeston's election, the Corporation appointed a committee to enquire into borough charities. No notice was taken of the Library, but Samuel Pickering, Notary Publick, (not one of the committee) made some notes of his own in his MS Collections for Ipswich in 1744.[101] His record is not always accurate, for example: 'Mr Samuel Ward Lecturer of this Town about the year 1645 gave his whole Library to the use of the Town of Ipswich...' is wholly misleading. After summarising the donations of over 20 benefactors from William Smarte to Dr Thomas Bishop, minister at the Tower church until 1737, he concludes:

> It seem necessary for the Library to be review'd by some judicious person & an exact Index or Catalogue to be taken of the Books & MSS therein that a fair Transcript thereof, together with an account of the Benefactors Names, sums given &c. might be entred in a Book (to be bo.^t) for that purpose. When a Book is lent out it seem reasonable a Deposit sho.^d be made to answer its return. It would seem a reasonable Charity to supply ye Library with those Books wch are (at p'sent) wanting.

Some of these points are noted by Pickering on pages B1 and B2 in the Book. He cannot have seen Coningsby's perfectly adequate manuscript catalogue.

The activities of the charity committee caused a great stir in the town, in some quarters real anxiety, and when the report made to the Corporation in September 1744 was not published, the Revd. Richard Canning, perpetual curate of St Lawrence from 1734 to 1775, and an outspoken opponent of the ruling party in the town, set about writing, under a thin veil of anonymity, his own *Account of the Gifts and Legacies,* etc. This book reached subscribers in 1747, and its imminent appearance did not rule out Canning as a member of another official committee charged with the examination of the rules and regulations of the Grammar School. It did, however, mar an initiative he took over the Library that same year, 1746, as he relates wistfully in the chapter of his *Account* which deals with the 'Publick Library'. He uses the third person to conceal his part as principal in the affair; either John Margerum or John Cornelius must be the Senior Bailiff in question.

> A Clergyman of this Town, who had taken the Trouble of examining every Book in the Library, observed that tho' the Name of the Person who gave each Book, is written upon the Title-Page of more than three-fourths of them, yet *when the Books are* out of the Library, and *in the Possession of a private Person,* there is nothing to shew, to what Place they belong, nor to what Use they were given. For tho' a Book is said to be the Gift of *John a Nokes,* it might as well be given by him to the Person in whose Possession it is, as to the *Ipswich-Library.* He perceived likewise, that the Books were very likely to come into the Hands of private Persons; for tho' the Keys are commonly lodg'd with the Master of the Free-School, they are often in the Possession of *the Guide* of *Christ's Hospital,* who has twenty Shillings a Year for cleaning the Room. Therefore as one probable Means of preventing any further Embezzlement of the Books, this Clergyman, at his own Expence, provided a decent Copper-Plate, and caused a thousand Copies to be taken off, one of which he intended to have cleav'd upon the Back of the Title-Page of each Book, that every one might know to what Place it belong'd, and to what Use it was given. These Prints, and the Plate were intended by him as a small Gift to the Library, and an Earnest

[101] S. Pickering, Manuscript Collections for Ipswich Vol. III, (1744) fos. 61–2 in private possession, but copied by D.E. Davy in BL Add. MS 19,093, fo. 145.^v

of more; he not in the least doubting, but every Member of the Corporation would readily permit any other Person to take Care of the Library, tho' he might take no Care of it himself. But some men, as it seems, will neither do good themselves, nor suffer it to be done by others; For Intelligence being given of this mischievous Design, when the Person employ'd to paste on the Prints came at the Time previously agreed upon with the *Rev. Mr. Hingeston* the School-Master, The *Senior Bailiff*, who never had them before, had the Keys in his keeping; and the Answer was, "That he would not part with them, *'till he had consulted with some of the Heads of the Corporation.*" '

So the Library was *inspected*, and a Consultation held, and the *wise* Result of this was, *that the Print should not be used*; for all the Members of this *Inspection*, either concurr'd in Opinion with the Leader of it, or else acquiesced with what they had not power to prevent. If the Donor of this Plate had added another Label to it, and said in Words at length, *this Plate was given by——— A.D.* 1746, all Pretence for objecting to it, had been prevented; for this is no more than what is done to three-fourths of the Gifts to the Library: But he thought it would be a modester Way of privately expressing that, if his Arms were in *Miniature*, added by *Way of Embellishment to the Plate*; and well knowing that such Sort of Embellishments were *by no Means unusual in Things of this Nature*, he had not the least Suspicion that any Person, let him be never so perverse, could be offended at it.

But as it is difficult exactly to know what Conclusions may be made by the Perverseness of Man, if Care be not taken to prevent it; it happens luckily in the present Case, that all Possibility of any such Danger as *the Inspectors* would be thought to discover, is effectually prevented by the Label at the Bottom of the Print; the Blank Part of which was evidently intended to be filled up *with the Name of the person who gave each particular Book.*

As these Reasons then are so *childish and ridiculous*, that they could not influence any sensible Man, no nor (to use the polite Language of the *Ipswich*-Levee) *the greatest Fool that ever lived*; and *as the consulted Head* that uttered them, is known not to want common Understanding; the Reader is left to judge whether these were the *real Reasons*, or whether they were only *the weak and lame Pretence for insulting this Clergyman*, either *because he was suppos'd to have some Concern in publishing this Account of these Charities*, or for some other Reasons of *too Personal a Nature* to be here mentioned.

In other parts of the same chapter, Canning confirms that one or two presses were then still unfilled, that the room to the south of the Library, once in part repaired with John Carnaby's gift, 'is in so ruinous a Condition at present that there is not the least Appearance, that any Thing had ever been laid out upon it', that there had been no losses of books in the last forty years (that is, since Coningsby's *Desunt* in 1705), and that almost the only book of value missing was Calvin's *Institutions*. Coincidentally this book, as an inscription on the title page tells, was returned the following May: 'The Revd. Mr Folkard Rector of Clopton return'd to this Library Calvin's *Institutions* which he bought many years since not knowing that it was not the Property of the Person that sold it to him. At the same time he gave to the town Dr Stebbing's *Polemical Tracts*.' Francis Folkard was a subscriber to the *Gifts and Legacies*, and read there, no doubt, what Canning had written about the missing Calvin.

Canning ended his account of the Library by proposing eight draft regulations aimed at making the books more easily available to 'all proper persons' without the 'public suffering by their embezzlement', so that 'the Library would flourish and soon receive sufficient Encouragement from the Publick, if Gentlemen were to see their Gifts were properly disposed of, and a proper Care were taken of them'. Had his advice been heeded, the bookplate (*fig.* 7) would have been only the first of many of his own gifts to the Library. His rules follow:

1. That a Lock be provided for every Press, so that the Room may be clean'd by the Servants of the Hospital, without their being allow'd to come at the Books.

Figure 7. The Revd. Richard Canning's bookplate, 1746.

2. That an exact Catalogue be taken of all the Books, and a Duplicate taken of it, one to be kept in the Treasury, the other in the Library.

3. That a proper Person be appointed by the Corporation to be a Library-Keeper, who should give Security for the Books entrusted to him, and be answerable for any Deficiency. And it is presum'd. that any Person who shall be thought a proper Master of the Grammar School, will always be a proper Person to be entrusted with the Care of the Library.

4. That the Library-Keeper be empower'd to lend any of the Books to any Person that he shall think proper, at his Discretion; but that he should be answerable for all the Books so lent by him.

5. That either of the Bailiffs, any Portman, or Common-Council-Man, be authorised to take any Book for his own Use; and to order the Delivery of any Book or Books, to such Person or Persons as he shall think proper, by Warrant under his Hand to the Library-Keeper, which Warrant should be a Discharge for those Books, and the Person by whom the Warrant is drawn should be answerable for the Books delivered by Virtue of the said Warrant, until they be returned.

6. That every Person taking, or borrowing any Book, should give the Library-Keeper a Receipt for it, which Receipt should be deliver'd upon the Return of the Book.

7. That the Library-Keeper should keep a Book, in which he should enter an Account of all Books, lent by him, taken by any of the Bailiffs, Portmen, or Common-Council-Men, or delivered by their Warrants, specifying the Time when, and the Person to whom each Book is delivered, and the Time when it is returned.

8. That a small annual Salary be appointed to the Library-Keeper, for his Trouble, (five or six Pounds might be sufficient) which Salary might be paid out of the Profits of *Mr. Smart's* Estate, or *Tooley's*.

Little of profit came from Canning's concern; his complaint and his suggestions were ignored by the Corporation. Rather than waste the rejected bookplates, Canning had one bound into every copy of his *Gifts and Legacies*. No doubt at Canning's persuasion, Robert Hingeston wrote 'Ipswich Library' on the title page of all the books not otherwise clearly identified with the town. Robert and his brother Peter, perpetual curate at St Peter's, continued to be generous donors to the Library, as were John Tanner, son of the bishop whose works were received from him, and Joshua Kirby, who presented his own *Treatise on Perspective* (King 320), on the title page of which Hingeston wrote 'Ipswich Library The Gift of the ingenious Author'.

Henry Hubbard, Ipswichian and Fellow of Emanuel, and Thomas Stisted of Caius gave too. They and all the others who cared for or gave to the Library in the 1750s had another interest in common. With Joseph Gibbs the Borough Organist and Thomas Gainsborough (whose Foundation Street garden abutted Hingeston's) they met weekly for music-making, and most of them sat to the great artist in the days before his fame spread. The portraits he painted of Richard Canning and Robert Hingeston are reproduced as *plates IV and V* respectively. It would be interesting to know where the Music Club met, and whether on occasion a literary mood took the members to the Library. Something of the kind must have happened to account for the late flowering of gifts to the Library in Hingeston's time, a shower compared with the trickle during the two previous Masterships when the School library had benefitted instead. Evidence of an otherwise unrecorded 'Ipswich Society' of the time, with literary interests, is to be found in the Library. The titlepage of each of the three volumes of Dr Middleton's *Life of Cicero* 1741 (King 422) is inscribed 'Ipswich Socy. No.17'. Identification of so short a written passage is difficult, but the hand resembles that of Thomas Bishop junior, who succeeded his father at his death in 1737, so that between them they served 60 years in the cure. What does seem surprising is that only one work from the Society's stock should have been added to the Town Library when, presumably, it ceased to function, but perhaps it came with Thomas Hewett's bequest in 1773, having been acquired by him earlier.

Hingeston's last entries in the Book are dated 1759; he seems to be the first custodian who entered every book he received, but with him the collection virtually closed. He did have one more important task to oversee, that of moving the School to new quarters, a move that led eventually to the resiting of the Library also.

Altogether the Library had three separate homes in the Blackfriars buildings, and their relative situations can be best illustrated by adapting the plan published in 1748 by Joshua Kirby to accompany his account and engraving of 'The West View of Christ's Hospital in Ipswich'.[102] In *fig. 8*, the lettering of the relevant spaces has been modified for easy reference, and a first floor plan of the former dormitory has been inset.

From 1612 to 1764 the School was in the former frater (E) and the Library in (F). Until 1617 the chamber (H) was hired by the Taylors' Guild, and before 1764 seems to have been used as a dormitory for Christ's Hospital boys. The room next to the Library (G) has not previously been referred to. Its alarming use from 1619 is learnt from the account given by Edward Wade, Guide at the Hospital from 1805 to 1818 at least, to William Batley, Town Clerk and five times Bailiff at various dates between 1784 and 1823.[103] Wade had served his apprenticeship under Thomas Truelove, Guide and Bridewell Keeper from 1744 to 1766. Sarah Truelove his wife cleaned the Library from 1763 to 1768.

> Over the Bridewell there was a large room (F and H) parted off, one part lodging room for the Hospital boys (H), the other for the Library (F), and on the Grammar School (E) being taken down, part of the present schoolroom was fitted up for the purpose of a School (H) and the Library continued at the other part untill the increase of scholars required the use of the whole Room, when the Library was moved to a room under it (A). That on the East side of the large Room abovemen.^d, next the Library end, was another Room (G) used as a Store room, & the present Guide (Edward Wade) recollects nearly two loads of touch rope, several coats of Mail, iron Helmets, & other warlike stores being left therein about the year 1760 when his apprenticeship expired. This probably was the place which appears by an original Letter lately found, and dated 1619, was provided as a depot for Gunpowder, Matches, *etc*, for in 1635 the Trained Bands being ordered to attend the Lord Keeper of England were directed to take a certain quantity of Gunpowder out of the Hospital and in 1646 the ordinance and Ammunition of the castle of Cambridge, in consequence of the vote of the Committee of Parliament, was ordered to be received by this Town and laid up in part of the Hospital.

A letter dated 18 December 1619 [104] in the borough archives, is addressed to the Bailiffs from Sir Henry Glemham and Sir Lionell Tallmach asking that some other place than the Hospital should be 'appoynted... for the stowage of powder and match' so that 'Mr George Parkhurst (one of the Governors of the Hospital) maie be freed of the Danger thereof'. Far from removing the 'warlike stores' then, some of them were still there in 1760, possibly for much longer, as we shall see.

The passage quoted is far more informative than any references to the rooms in the official borough records of the period. All that is to be found in them towards the end of Hingeston's time is the setting up of a committee on 18 November 1763 'to sell the Grammar School of this Corporation and to fix upon a proper place for a new School'.

On 1 December, Richard Revett and others surveyed the northern half of the Hospital buildings

---

[102] Joshua Kirby, *Historical Account of the Twelve Prints... in... Suffolk.* (Ipswich 1748), 7–12 and Plate 1.
[103] W. Batley, Manuscript Account of the Ipswich Charities copied by Davy in BL Add. MS 19,094, fo. 223^V. SRO Ipswich: C13/5 is Batley's draft for GA402/1, and when he had written a fair copy of a subject in the latter, he tore the section out of the former. Luckily, Davy copied much useful material from the draft (e.g. p. 160 in this instance) before the dismemberment had taken place.
[104] SRO Ipswich: HD 36/2781/2.

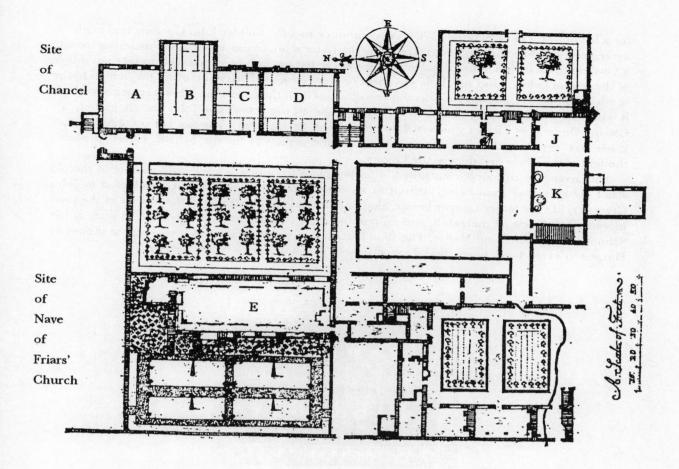

Site
of
Chancel

A B C D

J

K

Site
of
Nave
of
Friars'
Church

E

North-East range: A to G

| A | *Sacristy* |
| | LIBRARY 1767–1820 |

| B | *Chapter House* |
| | Hospital Chapel |

| CD | Bridwell |
| C | Powder store 1767– |

| FGH | *Dormitory* |

F	LIBRARY 1612–1767
G	'Warlike stores' 1619–1767
H	Taylors' Hall –1617
	Gardemau's Writing School c.1685
	Hospital Boys' Dormitory –1763
	Grammer School 1763–7

| FGH | Grammar School 1767–1842 |

| E | *Refectory* |
| | Grammar School 1612–1763 |

| J | Hospital Governors' Room |
| | where LIBRARY housed 1820–1832 |

| K | Christ's Hospital Kitchen |

FIRST FLOOR

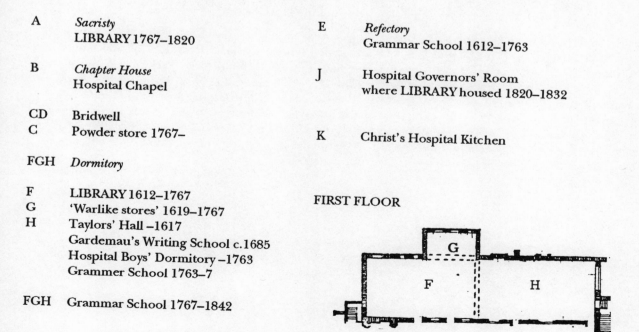

G

F   H

Figure 8. Plan of former Blackfriars made 1748, adapted to show room uses.

for a fee of £12. On 22 February 1764, the committee met the builder John Gooding and made an agreement with him that he would take down the frater schoolroom and sort the materials for sale according to his instructions. The demolition was carried out in July, presumably to take advantage of the school holiday, and very little was spent on new work or repairs in moving the School to the south chamber (H), a room considerably less spacious than the frater, the Library remaining where it was. John Gooding charged £3 1s 6d 'To work done att the Lybry', and John Forsett, glazier, 'To Glazing Done at ye Library now ye Grammar School, £2 15s 5½d'. The last bill is confusing, but Wade was very clear that the Library did not at first make way for the School. Forsett probably thought of the whole first floor as the Library.

This arrangement hardly constituted 'a proper place for a new School', and the site of the old schoolroom, rather than being allowed as an extension to the playground, was leased to John Gravenor, like his father Cooper before him, one of the least admirable of the leaders of the town hierarchy. This was all makeshift, and an unsatisfactory conclusion to Hingeston's 55 years at the School as boy, Usher and Master. The Blue Party was in power again; was it shortage of money or Hingeston's reluctance to see the Library displaced which delayed a better solution?

Figure 4f. Ipswich gilt-stamp on board of book given 1756.

V. The Revd. Robert Hingeston, Usher 1721–1743; Master 1743–1766, by Thomas Gainsborough.

X

JOHN KING
1767–1799

*'We ask pardon of the Reader for detaining him so long about
so trifling a concern, and proceed in our Undertaking.'*

Richard Canning[105]

When John King, a former fellow of Peterhouse, came to Ipswich from Newcastle-upon-Tyne where
for seven years he had been undermaster at the Grammar School, he seems, like many a new broom,
to have been able and willing to sweep clean. The same Great Court which appointed him on 13
February 1767 ordered 'necessary and proper Repairs to the House lately in the occupation of the
Revd. Mr Hingeston', also 'the Library and School to be fitted up in a proper manner and that it be
done at the expense of the Corporation.' The work began immediately, as we shall see.

The Grammar School was now enabled to expand from the south chamber (*fig. 8*, H) into the
former Library (F) and into the 'warlike store'-room (G) whose contents went down to (C), a fact we
know from W.S. Fitch's tales of his schooldays in about 1805.[106] The partition between the two large
rooms was removed to make a suitably large schoolroom for the arrangement of all the forms
according to the fashion which prevailed down to about 1880. The Library came off badly in these
changes, as it was consigned to the ground floor former sacristy of the friars (A), a room only half
the size of the chamber above which had been its home for 155 years. Not only was there a lack of
space, but, by all accounts, the room was damp. In the east wall were four arched openings blocked
with brickwork, two doors and two windows. The ceiling was raftered and the only remaining door
opened directly onto the elements from the west. At least the room with the 'warlike stores' was at
one remove beyond the former chapter house, then a chapel.

Fortunately the original Treasurer's vouchers for 1767 survive, and are amply revealing about the
relative amounts spent on the Lecturer's House (still so-called though it had been the Master's since
1712), and on the Grammar School and the Library. Altogether the Corporation paid Samuel Lane
£34 for work on the house, and £85 to various contractors for enlarging the school and moving the
Library. Edward Betts was the main contractor, and his men were engaged there from 23 February
to 27 June; John Forsett was the glazier who fitted glass supplied by Daniel Morgan, and John Martin
provided the ironmongery. Only two items are specifically identified with the Library. Betts paid a
mere 6d. to 'a Labourer for Helpeing to remove the Presses' on 30 April, and on 18 May used '40
foot of old [oak?] for studs at Library' worth 5s.

The main work complete, Samuel Lane on 10 August charged 'for job at the Grammar School-
Wall and Library':

	£	s	d
For a trowel and Lab.ʳ 3 Days and half	0	12	9
for plastering in the Liberry half a day	0	1	10
for hanging copper stove & mending the grate	0	6	6
Total	£1	1	1

[105] [R. Canning], *op. cit.*, 148.
[106] *A pilgrymage to Ippsewyche beynge Master Naso hys deazel.* A manuscript account of a visit and tour of the
town (conducted by Fitch) in 1850, written and presented by Theodosius Purland to his host T.B. Ross, then
Mayor.

The last two items give some idea of the standards of comfort which Library users may have enjoyed in the cheerless room below the Grammar School. Not all the presses could be fitted around its walls and at least one was left upstairs, eventually to be moved with the School to its temporary great schoolroom in Lower Brook Street in 1842. This is the press Phipson drew there, the one to be seen in the copper engraving by Jabez Hare of the dormitory schoolroom in Clarke's *History of Ipswich* and in Poynter's schoolboy drawing made about 1850.[107] To some extent at least the books of the Library were split up after 1767, a fact which may account for later losses.

Kirby's plan of 1748 has been used to explain the occupation of spaces in the north-east claustral range at different dates (*fig. 8*). In 1976 it was found to be remarkably accurate in helping to fix points for trial excavations on the site.[108] Since then, in 1984 and 1985, the whole site has been dug exhaustively, the nave and chancel of the friars' church have been laid bare (the wall on the left of Kirby's plan and engraving is the nave south wall), and it is planned for the ruins of the church, sacristy (A) and chapter house (B) to become a permanent monument, an open space between the former Unicorn brewery and the proposed development to the south. The most complete survival today is the sacristy, home of the Library from 1767 to 1820, for three of its walls stand to a few feet, and that on the east, with its four blocked openings, to rafter height. The room gives no impression of having made a suitable home for the books even in the drawings made by John Wodderspoon and Henry Davy before the almost total demolition of 1851.[109]

One gift came to the Library in the year of the move, 1767. It was Dr Thomas Bishop's *Church Catechism* (1736, King 417) presented by the author's son and namesake, and his successor at the Tower church. The book came *via* the Revd. Thomas Hewett, Rector of Bucklesham, a more considerable benefactor himself later on, and it contains on the flyleaf a brief eulogy of Dr Bishop by Hewett. The elder Bishop obviously had his detractors in the town, for it ends 'It is Pity the People of Ipswich thro' their Prejudices are so Little Acquainted with This Book. I mind not the envy of some of the Clergy who knew him.' When Hewett died six years later he left his own library jointly to St Mary's, Woodbridge and Ipswich Library, stipulating that 'the Fathers and that sort of Learning' should go to Woodbridge with the old bookcases, but that some books, particularly duplicates, should come to Ipswich. 'Smaller Books' should not be lent out; 'larger Books to be lent', but only on leaving a deposit.[110] His wishes must have gone unheeded, for of 59 works which then came to the Library, 27, an unusually high proportion, are missing. This is hardly surprising since no list was prepared, and the books were not marked in any way. By the time that King came to catalogue the Library, he could only identify about of the third of the works as Hewett gifts with certainty. What he did not realise was that they had been put in groups together on empty shelves and are the only books in the collection to lack Hingeston's 'Ipswich Library' on the title page. In appendix E an attempt has been made to list them all. Some of the losses are grievous, for the Aldine Pausanias and first edition of Spenser's *Faerie Queen* (King 243) would be prize possessions today, as would Sir William Petty's *Political Arithmetick* (1691, King 402), and Bacon's *De Augmentaris Scientarum* (1662, King 398). These all disappeared in the 19th century, the first after 1860. Thus it was that the collection which grew from Smarte's bequest in 1599 closed with Hewett's 173 years later.

Contrary to many accounts which state that most Town Preachers after Ward were also Masters of the Grammar School, King was the first to hold both offices. This he did from 1768 to 1791 when on 29 September 'the warm thanks of this Court to the Revd. Mr King for his long and faithfull services as Lecturer to this Corporation' were expressed on his resignation. Seven years later he resigned as Master, but before he could retire to his living at Witnesham he was given one last task. On the day that the new Master was chosen, 20 July 1798, the Great Court ordered 'that the Reverend John King

---

[107] Poynter's drawing reproduced in W.M. Morfey, *A Brief View of the History of Ipswich School* (1984).

[108] K. Wade and J. Blatchly, 'Excavations at Ipswich Blackfriars in 1898 and 1976' in *Proc. Suff. Inst. Arch. & History*, XXXIV (1977), 25.

[109] Wodderspoon's drawing is in SRO Ipswich: HD495/2. Henry Davy's are in BL Add. MS 19,179, fos. 126 and 127.

[110] J.A. Fitch and A.E. Birkby, *op. cit.*, xvi.

do cause a correct Catalogue of the contents of the Library to be made out and signed by himself to be delivered to the Bailiffs previous to their confiding it to the care of his successor'. Who this successor was it is not clear; there are no signs that Ingram, Master for only two years, took a hand in the care of the books. Is there a hint here that the Corporation suspected that the Library was not in good order? It had been inadequately housed for over thirty years, but, either because it had been little used, or because King had been vigilant, he must have been pleased to have to list only two books as missing: a *Suffolk Traveller* of 1764 (King 429), and Sir John Narborough's *Voyages* (King 428), both Hewett gifts. King listed but failed to number four oversize works (now '701' to '704') and completely overlooked two others ('705' and '706'), all of which are still in the collection.

King, without making a very great labour of the task, did in one respect more than he was ordered; he prepared two lists rather than one for publication together by the unsuccessful printer William Burrell in 1799. Burrell's only other project, *The Ipswich Magazine* began that February and ended the next. The title pages of both lists confirm that the 'Books of the Town Library' were now 'under the Public Grammar=School'. The second, the *Alphabetical Catalogue*, was based with necessary additions on Coningsby's manuscript lists. The other, the *Numerical Catalogue*, was numbered in the order the books were arranged in their presses at the time, the only system being that only books of the same format were shelved together. This supposition is encouraged by finding long sequences of folios succeeded by quartos together, then octavos and so on. A single sheet in King's hand tucked into the back of Coningsby's reused geometry notebook catalogue is headed 'Books in the Press at the entrance into the School', i.e. near the door into the dormitory schoolroom above the sacristy. The books listed by King are numbered from 395 to 423, and then from 697 to 700, these the last four titles in the *Numerical Catalogue*. Among the first sequence, 417 is one of Mrs Walter's gifts to the Library, renumbered 696 by King in his *Catalogue*, but the remaining 27 titles are School library books, showing that there were at least 422 books in that collection at the time of King's retirement. As had been said, Holden's son Edward found just 157 works in 1877, ten of them printed after 1799, and we have only twenty today, two of them unknown to Holden because they were lost by the School earlier in the 19th century but restored to it in recent years.

King had no thought of acknowledging Coningsby's work which must have made his job so very much easier. He did not even trouble to interpolate titles added after Coningsby's time in their proper order. The lists are full of errors which could have been eliminated by proof reading; and where volumes contain several works bound together only the first is listed. Few Suffolk books are rarer than King's little volume, a quarto of 62pp. in sugar paper wrappers, for the edition was a small one and not many owners took the trouble to have copies bound. William Batley, Town clerk at the time, noted in about 1820 that there were still then several copies in the town treasury, and Burrell kept a good number himself. They came in handy to him in 1832 when he, near destitute, distributed copies to all members of the newly formed Ipswich Literary Institution with his application to be their first Librarian.[111] This he did to show himself capable in the field he aspired to enter. No doubt most of the recipients discarded the unsolicited trifle. There is one copy in the Library today, three in the collections of the Suffolk Record Office, and others in the copyright libraries. None are known of in private hands. As early as 1830 David Elisha Davy was driven to the lengths of copying the whole by hand into his Manuscript Collections for Ipswich, though he did eventually obtain a copy for his own library. Lord John Hervey, President of the Suffolk Institute of Archaeology from 1870 to 1886, was reduced to the same expedient, and his carefully written copy has come to the Library.

King's last service to the Library was no doubt a cause of considerable satisfaction to him. Using Canning's original copper plate from which the date 1746 and the arms had been erased, he had bookplates printed for both libraries, Town and School (*fig. 9*). King and Canning would have known one another, for King arrived in Ipswich eight years before the other died. The donors' names on the lower scrolls are inserted in King's hand, with which he also adapted the bookplates

---

[111] Ipswich Literary Institution Minute Book 1832–1851 in SRO Ipswich K13/1/3.1. Burrell's letters to Committee members are dated 19 April 1832.

Figure 9. The Revd. John King's version of Canning's
bookplate, 1799

for School use by adding the words 'School Classical' between 'Ipswich' and 'Library' beside the upper scroll. He pasted the labels inside the front boards, not, as Canning had intended, on the reverse of the title pages. Most books arrived back after their most recent restoration with the wrong labels inserted with a latex-based adhesive. The tedious work of removing several hundred wrongly placed labels was accomplished by a team of ten Ipswichians on a single day in June 1988. Their correct replacement took just a few hours.

John King died at Witnesham in 1822. His portrait, stipple-engraved from a miniature (*fig. 10*), was published privately for the benefit of many who wished to remember the man who had served the School long and well, and with remarkable success.

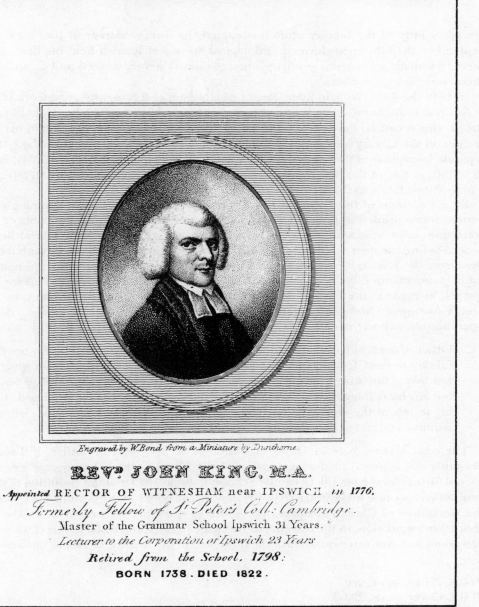

Engraved by W. Bond from a Miniature by Dunthorne.

REV⁹ JOHN KING, M.A.

Appointed RECTOR OF WITNESHAM near IPSWICH *in 1776.*
*Formerly Fellow of S*ᵗ *Peter's Coll: Cambridge.*
Master of the Grammar School Ipswich 31 Years.
Lecturer to the Corporation of Ipswich 23 Years
Retired from the School, 1798:
BORN 1738 . DIED 1822 .

Figure 10.

XI

THE NINETEENTH CENTURY
FIVE MOVES FOR THE LIBRARY

'...our worthy burgesses, we suppose, are engaged in commerce rather than in literature; for the books are but little used or regarded.'

G.R. Clarke[112]

We know little of the Library while it occupied the former sacristy of the friars, save that on 30 September 1818 the newly-formed Philological Society of Ipswich held the first of many meetings there.[113] Initially six or seven gentlemen met to discuss literary subjects and compose essays; by 1830 there were twenty members.

In 1819 the Revd. William Edge, Rector of Hollesley and Naughton, and from 1822 of Rushmere St Andrew, brought out a new edition of *Ipswich Gifts and Legacies.* The book did not cause much of a stir on this occasion; nevertheless the author thought it prudent to maintain his anonymity. The section on the Library is mistitled 'Public Library'. Since 1791, as Edge described, there had been a separate institution of that name, not to mention the Ipswich Book Club (1764), Book Societies of the 1790s at two of the dissenting chapels, the Book and Pamphlet Club (1808) and the Ipswich Union Public Library (1817).

Edge's account of the Town Library is a greatly abridged version of Canning's, with the list of benefactors reprinted without alteration. Edge did add a list of the most valuable of the works in the collection, most unwise unless security could be guaranteed. Certainly several items listed disappeared before the next careful check was made in 1860, including the autograph letter of Theodore Beza from the French Bible he had given to Edward Bacon.[37] William Batley annotated a copy of the list of donors from Edge's book and pasted it into the manuscript Collections for the Charities of Ipswich he made in the 1820s.[114] Most of his additions came from the Benefactors' Book, and from King's *Numerical Catalogue,* and not all are reliable. Batley went on to state the rules then in operation about borrowing:

> Either of the Bailiffs, a Portman or a Common Council Man may take any book out of the Library to read, leaving an acknowledgement thereof in the place from which the book was taken, but any other person must have an authority from the Bailiffs and in taking out any book must leave a receipt for it with the Guide of the Hospital and an undertaking to return the same within a reasonable time, and this receipt to be delivered to the Bailiffs to be laid in the place from whence the book was taken.

The next Master, William Howorth, although he also held the office of Town Lecturer, was obviously not involved in the supervision of the Library, which in any case was during his time moved further away from the Grammar School. It was in 1820 that the condition of the sacristy room gave sufficient cause for concern to justify moving the books to the ground floor committee room of the Governors of Christ's Hospital. The room in question was next door to the kitchen of that charitable foundation, in the extreme south range of the former Blackfriars claustral buildings. The new room had only three-quarters of the floor area of the sacristy, but there was a pleasant view from

[112] G.R. Clarke, *op. cit.,* 280.
[113] G.R. Clarke, *op. cit.,* 292–3.
[114] W. Batley, SRO Ipswich GA 402/1, 345 (move to Governors' Room); 346 (Rules); Appendix, 32–36 (Donors lists).

an east window on to the garden or yard of the Governors and another on the south side into Shire Hall Yard. Presumably the Philological Society moved there too. Batley commented that this was where the books would be kept 'until a more suitable place was provided.

In view of Clarke's comment at the head of the chapter it is perhaps surprising that the next move was not long coming; in January 1832 the Ipswich Literary Institution was set up with rooms in the Palladian Town Hall building designed and built by Benjamin Batley Catt in 1818. The Great Court ordered on the 17 September following 'that the Corporation Library be removed from its present situation to the new Rooms in the Hall and be placed under the care of the Committee of the Ipswich Literary Institution under the same restrictions as to the lending of the books as now exist.' Details of the new accommodation appear in the draft Prospectus of the Institution: 'they [the members] will also have the use of the Committee Room of the Institution, a room about 16 feet square which also will be well warmed and lighted, in which it is proposed to place the valuable library of the Corporation of Ipswich and such other miscellaneous collection of books as may be put under the care of or presented to the Institution.'[111] The main Reading Room, we are told, measured 30 feet by 55.

The first librarian was appointed in September 1832 from a large field of applicants which included one former and one future Ipswich printer and publisher: William Burrell who printed King's *Catalogue*, and Joseph Mumford Burton, 'destitute three years'. Henry Tracey was successful; his referees included John Eddowes Sparrowe, Town Clerk, and the schoolmaster Robert Burcham Clamp, sure signs that 'Blue' influence was at work. Tracey, himself 'sometime master of a respectable School in this town', assured the committee that he would 'be adopting an uniform, attentive and industrious line of conduct', in order to earn his £40 salary (the Town Lecturer had only £50 at this time), with half a crown allowed weekly for cleaning the books and furniture. Despite his assurances, in less than three years Tracey was 'dismissed for irregular conduct' of a financial nature. He left little in the books of the Town Library beyond a few fly-leaf transcriptions in books whose Latin titles seemed to him to need elucidation. These he initialled, and if his successor felt his efforts needed amendment we have his initials too, or at least, two of them: N.L. His full name was Horatio Nelson Trafalgar Levett, and he too had run a school, in Carr Street, and was appointed at £52 a year. Effectively he was paid in arrears, as he was required to deposit £50 as security.

One young Ipswichian, Edward Byles Cowell, later Professor of Sanskrit at Cambridge, and friend of FitzGerald for whom he translated *Omar Khayham*, owed much to Levett and the Library, which he visited regularly from the age of fourteen.[115] For about eight years all went well with Levett's librarianship, but then he seems to have become irregular in his attendance, and, worse, neglected his duties so far as *to play chess with the members*. After several warnings he resigned, leaving his recently appointed co-librarian William Mills in charge. Levett did leave one particularly disagreeable legacy in many of the books. Fearful that collectors would purloin engraved title pages or portraits, he set out to write the name of the Institution on their versos. This was too laborious; instead he had made a one-inch square woodblock bearing the town arms in a gothic border. This he applied as an ink stamp, too often on the face of the engraving itself; the Ortelius atlas suffered particularly from this appalling treatment. The later and smaller oval stamp with 'Literary Institution' and the Town arms was applied only to certain fore-edges, e.g. those of the the 13-volume Tostado.

One visitor to the Library in 1847 was Francis Capper Brooke of Ufford. A notable collector of books, he was quick to pick out and list the twenty most remarkable works for inclusion in his friend D.E. Davy's Ipswich Manuscript Collections.[116] The next year the first Ipswich Museum opened in the street which still bears its name, and over the next decade there were plans, which did not materialise, to accommodate the Library there. The membership and income of the Literary Institution were flagging when the only surviving minute book was closed in 1851, but with Edward Giles as

[115] G. Cowell, *The Life and Letters of Edward Byles Cowell.* (1904) 7.
[116] BL Add. MS 19,093, fo. 145.r–v

librarian activities continued until in 1862 all the books which belonged to the then defunct body were sold at auction.

In January 1859, Councillor John Tracy, a dentist of St Stephen's parish, tried to stir the Town Council to do something for the Library. He felt it 'a pity to see such books' (including 'a bible worth from 60 to 70 guineas') 'covered with old newspapers and dust'. Eventually a committee was set up consisting of Tracy and two other Liberal council members, W.H. Alexander and T.S. Gowing, to investigate the state of the collection. Impatient for the outcome, the leader writer of the radical *Suffolk Chronicle* made a passing reference on 3 December to the Library 'lying idly by, in dull seclusion amid dirt and dust'; this was immediately refuted in ironic fashion. On 10 December a second leader appeared, full of sarcasm and headed 'The Corporation Library' from which two passages of interest must be quoted:

> Last week we referred to the books in general terms – this week we can be a little more precise. The Library was examined a few months ago, by Mr W.P.Hunt, solicitor, of St Matthew's, a gentleman well known for his industry and zeal in collecting valuable records, and as a connisseur of literary curiosities; and he has assured us that he found the books in a very dirty condition, decidedly unfit for public use. Walton's *Polyglot Bible*, a magnificent work, worth at the present time about twenty guineas, was found, after a long search, covered up with old paper, in a rubbish closet, where, likewise, were some valuable MSS.

> Is this all? Are no books missing? Nay, how many are missing? That is a question we can only partly answer. During the week, a gentleman, entirely unsolicited on our part, has shown me a volume, belonging to the Corporation Library. There is no mistake about this. On the inside of one cover are the Ipswich arms – on the other, in large letters, the name of the donor and the date of the gift,– Miles Wallis, one of the Bailiffs of Ipswich, who presented it to the Corporation in 1706. The book was recently purchased at a bookstall in this town for eighteenpence!

It is fortunate that the buyer was prepared for his purchase to be returned to the collection. It was William Lloyd's *Historical Account of Church Government* (1684 King 374), and the donor's fine penmanship on the gift label is thus preserved in the book. The leader writer continued:

> 'It must not be a matter of surprise, if any gentleman on visiting the Library finds things a little changed. On Wednesday last – (we made our complaint on Saturday) – one of the Town servants was set to work to clean the books. We did not see him, but have been informed that ere he had half finished his work, he looked very much like an amateur chimney-sweep.'

The three-man Committee worked speedily after this to produce a brief factual report which would set the record straight. When, thirty years previously, the books had gone to the Town Hall no inventory had been taken; the Committee had to use King's *Catalogue.* They appended a list of 66 works missing, but it was totally misleading, including as it did 33 which are in the Library today. When presenting their report to the Council on 25 January, Thomas Shave Gowing went on to make one interesting comment which went some way towards explaining how 422 works of the School library became 147 in 1877: 'In several of the books we found written "Given to the Library of the Ipswich Grammar School" '. Dr H.A. Holden, the Headmaster, was asked whether, conversely, missing Town Library books has found their way to the School, but the answer was that that had not happened.

At the same meeting there was some debate about the likely causes of the 32 losses since 1799. One statistic seems significant. In the short sequence King 398 to 432, twenty works had disappeared (all from Hewett), indication surely (since the subjects varied widely) that they had been removed from a press which was for some reason more easily accessible than the others; because they were unmarked they were not identifiable with the Library.

Alderman S.H. Cowell, founder of the printing firm of Cowell's, suggested 'whether it might not be desirable to sell these books, which, he understood, presented a most uninviting appearance, and buy some modern books, which might be added to the Mechanics Institution Library or be the foundation of a public free library. He believed they were generally most uninteresting books and such as would never be used. Some were of considerable value, but the larger number were good for nothing but waste paper... and [since 1835] not twenty people had looked at them.' Mr Thomas Conder, junior, and Mr Gowing were quick to oppose the suggestion, pointing out the need in a provincial town for more books of reference rather than fewer, and that more use would be made of the books if more were aware of the existence of the collection.

Following the meeting Alderman Alexander arranged for many of the books to be repaired or rebound, presumably by Phillips and Taylor, whose binder's label is common. In September 1863 it was reported that the books now needed to be re-arranged and numbered. The Town Clerk could organise access to them on request. They were to go to the newly enlarged Museum since a new Town Hall was to replace the old; in the longer term the Town Library should become part of a County Reference Library in the town. The following year, Alexander died, and the council paid a bill for £34 outstanding for binding work. For two years, Alexander had spent several hours every day checking the books and the catalogue, and arranging for repairs.

Richard Gowing wrote in his 1864 *Descriptive Handbook of Ipswich*: 'When the new Town Hall is built, it is intended to afford accommodation, under the same roof, for a Town Library, and for the Museum... With regard to the Town Library... these books have just been put into complete repair.' This was not to be, however, and later that year the collection was transferred to a room in the Museum in time for the British Archaeological Association visit to Ipswich, to which body on 10 August 1864 Mr Sterling Westhorp read a long paper on the Library. When printed in the *Journal* the talk took up ten pages.[37] Westhorp had himself prepared a manuscript catalogue of the collection in which a new numbering system of his own was employed. Those books which have not since then been re-spined bear his gilt-stamped numbers today. The paper itself, consisting as it does mainly of descriptions of books which most interested the author, adds little to our knowledge of the Library; Westhorp, on his own admission, drew only on the fruits of a few weeks' study.

In the years before the new Town Hall opened in 1870, public debate about the next move for the Library continued. Should it go to the fine first-floor library planned for the head of the grand staircase, should extra accommodation be found at the Museum, or should a new reference library be built elsewhere to incorporate it? It was argued that more use had been made of the books since they had been at the Museum than for centuries before. As late as July 1869 it seemed that the Town Hall library would be the place chosen for the much-travelled collection, for the Museum was to house the books of a proposed free library.

Five years later nothing had been done, and in the *East Anglian Daily Times* for 30 January 1875 a writer who signed himself 'Slingsby' gave a lengthy eye-witness account of the room used by the Town Library during the previous ten years in an article entitled 'Sauntering in Ipswich Museum'. 'A mere glance at its ponderous tomes is enough to make the mouth of any Dryasdust water', wrote 'Slingsby'. He went on to doubt whether the collection was properly appreciated, and pointed out that within the preceding three years there had been talk of it 'occupying space which might well be devoted to works of more general interest'.

At last the pressure on space in the Museum became too great, and in 1877 the Council rented a small house next to it in which evening classes could be held, the upper rooms of which were fitted with cases to take the Library. This did not suit 'A Ratepayer' whose letter entitled 'A plea for our Town Library' was published in the *Suffolk Chronicle* for 25 October 1879. He informed his readers that 'it will be found in a back room at our Museum. It formerly occupied a noble room at the Town Hall. When that building was pulled down it was removed to the ground floor [of the Museum], and some years ago had to make way for some stuffed birds. It has never been heard of since.'

In July 1881 the town held grand celebrations for the opening in High Street of a new Museum, School of Science and Art, and part of what in 1888 became the Victoria Free Library. All this was under one roof and cost £7000. Dr J.E. Taylor had been Curator since 1872 and was largely instrumental in bringing this plan about. The Library was newly housed in the room occupied today by the Curator of Ipswich Museums. Alderman Westhorp was the Chairman of the Building Committee and of the School of Art, but Dr Holden was chairman of the Museum Committee. A truly great Classical scholar, unappreciated by his governors, he left Ipswich after 25 years as Headmaster to teach at University. His speech, one of over twenty at the Mayor's *Dejeuner* which followed the opening,[117] has one interesting reference to the Town Library:

> The old musty tomes of one of the three oldest libraries in existence [*sic*] are now made accessible to the public, clothed anew and not ashamed to show their faces, as they have been for many a year. There would also be found there priceless MSS, which, until a few days since, were entirely unknown to me; and have been unearthed on this occasion and brought to light, henceforth to find a fitter home.

The 'henceforth to find' is an odd phrase to use at a grand opening; Dr Holden could hardly have foreseen the place to which the Library would come a century later. It was in November 1982 that the Library came to Holden's own memorial, the room in Fleury's 1851 Ipswich School which Holden's old pupils had furnished with bookcases to serve as a memorial to him and the School library after his death in 1896. He would no doubt approve of their presence there, and perhaps be not a little envious of his successors who carry out their custody of the collection by using the room as a study.

[117] Opening of the New Lock... Post Office... Museum, Free Library and School of Art at Ipswich. (Reprinted from the *East Anglian Daily Times* for 27 and 28 July 1881), 22–3.

XII

THE PRESENT CENTURY

'And it is presum'd that any Person who shall be thought a proper Master of the Grammar School, will always be a proper Person to be entrusted with the Care of the Library.'

Richard Canning [118]

It only remains briefly to trace the progress of the Library through the last 90 years. Dr Taylor died in 1895 and was succeeded as Curator by Mr Frank Woolnough. In 1901 Henry Ogle arrived as Librarian and immediately took great pride in his special charge of the Town Library. By December 1903 he had prepared a schedule of works lost since the 1799 *Lists* were printed. Six had gone from the collection since the report to the Town Council in 1860. Ogle used Westhorp's article in the *Journal of the British Archaeological Association*, [37] an indication that the manuscript catalogue of 1864 had been mislaid.

Mr Ogle wrote an article on the Library for the August 1904 edition of *The Library Assistant* [119] in which he claimed second place for Ipswich in the order of foundation of town libraries: Norwich 1608, Ipswich 1612 and Bristol 1613, remarking that all three were at the time important trading ports. Foreign trade, he suggested, bred an interest in literature and made people aware of the the literary treasures already established in continental cities. Ogle assumed, wrongly, that Grantham was a parochial library because its home was the parvise chamber of the church; it was in fact in the control of the borough there from its formation in 1598. [46]

Ipswich stands third then as a town library, but it could be argued that Smarte intended a parochial collection, and for parish libraries there is a different order: Leicester 1586, Bury St. Edmunds 1595, Newcastle 1597 and Ipswich 1599. [120] From both lists Bishop Parkhurst's library at Guildford Royal Grammar School (1573) has been omitted on the grounds that it was neither parochial nor a town library (though some evidence runs counter to the latter conclusion).

Henry Ogle was the first to appreciate and publicise the significance of the collection of Parliamentary Sermons annotated by William Dowsing (King 654). How unfortunate it was that he spent £3 on rebinding the six volumes in vellum, and that he discarded the old reversed calf boards with the initials 'W.D.' gilt-stamped on them in 'quaintly shaped seventeenth century letters'. The Library Committee had in fact stipulated 'suitable and thorough binding of the volumes in keeping with their present appearance'. At the time, W. Phillips and E.W. Scopes shared the work of rebinding for Ipswich Library equally. [121]

It was in 1914 that Alderman William Paul gave a site in Northgate Street for a new Borough Library. Ogle worked tirelessly on the design which took ten years to come to fruition, but after the eventual move from High Street he ceased to be Chief Librarian and continued in a supernumerary capacity until his retirement in 1932. This at least gave him the opportunity to devote time to the Town library, for which he almost completed a detailed sheaf catalogue. There were no losses from the collection in his time, nor have there been any since.

Mr Leonard Chubb's arrival as Chief Librarian from Birmingham in 1931 saw developments in making the Library in Northgate Street the official county depository for manorial records. Over the next two years the strong room in the basement in which the Town Library had been housed was

---

[118] [R. Canning], *op. cit.*, 149.
[119] H.G. Ogle, 'An Old Town Library' in *The Library Assistant* for August 1904, 141–5.
[120] *The Parochial Libraries of the Church of England.* (London 1959), 16 and 42.
[121] Ipswich Library Subcommittee minute 700 for 5 January 1904.

fitted with steel shelving and a grille door for day-time ventilation. Deposits soon overfilled the room, and it was not until the records departed for the cellars of the Town Hall in 1947 that the books of the Library could again be satisfactorily examined.

In February 1931 the nine medieval manuscripts of the collection were sent to Eton for the Provost, Dr James to prepare detailed descriptions for publication in the Suffolk Institute's *Proceedings*.[11] They were not new to James, who had seen them nearly forty years previously when he had visited Ipswich Museum in search of manuscripts of Bury Abbey origin for the study he was writing for the Cambridge Antiquarian Society.[7] The notes he took on 27 December 1893 are preserved in the Library still.

From 1924 to 1982 the Library remained in its basement store, where a small but steady stream of scholars sought it. The only illumination until the mid-1970s was from a single light bulb on a long lead. Rebinding and repair was carried out periodically as and when funds were available. More than 100 volumes were sent to Dunn and Wilson at a total cost of £385 (which included the cost of the cardboard boxes in which they were stored on their return). This was done between 1954 and 1959 in Miss D.M. White's time as Chief Librarian.

As recently as the late 1970s, 500 volumes were rebound with a gift to the town by the USAF at Bentwaters to mark the Silver Jubilee of Her Majesty the Queen, and a larger grant from the British Library. A good working handlist was prepared at the same time by Sir John Fiennes and Mr R.P. Collett, Adult Studies Librarian until 1982.

Articles on the collection have appeared from time to time, in *Book Auction Records* 1914, *The East Anglian Magazine* 1954 and *The Times Literary Supplement* for 18 August 1950.[122] None of them breaks new ground over earlier accounts. Several books and manuscripts have been exhibited on various occasions from 1936 onwards, more recently at the Caxton Quatercentenary in 1976, and at the 1980 Arts Festival, both in the Corn Exchange, and in 'Suffolk Church Treasures' at Christchurch Mansion in 1984.

At the reorganisation of local government in 1974, libraries became a county responsibility, and in June 1982 the Libraries, Museums, Records and Amenities Committee of Suffolk County Council accepted the suggestion of the County Librarian, Mr Peter Labdon, that the Town Library should henceforth be housed at Ipswich School. The Holden Library, replaced by a new school library in 1981, was temporarily empty of books. The transfer took place on 22 November 1982 in two full loads of the Mobile Library, processions of boys carrying the books from van to Library in little more than an hour. An official opening was held on 19 January 1983, since when many groups and individuals have visited the Library by prior arrangement, over 300 people in the first year alone.

The Holden memorial bookcases form eleven bays with from four to seven shelves in each. The bays are numbered and the shelves lettered. In the catalogue, Beck's and Coningsby's press and shelfmarks (e.g. M2) are preserved, followed by King's Catalogue numbers. Lastly the modern shelf numbers (e.g. 7G) are added.

[122] T. Edwards-Jones, 'Ipswich Libraries and Book Clubs' in *Book Auction Records* 1914, xxxvii–xli; P. Hepworth,

XIII

MANUSCRIPTS WITH IPSWICH ASSOCIATIONS

'Note – There is in this Library the old and new Testaments wrote in vellum remarkably small, so that with my Eyes I can read no more than the Titles to the Several Books.'

Samuel Pickering
Notary Publick 1744 [101]

Two of the medieval manuscripts on vellum described by M.R. James and N.R. Ker,[11] and one of the 17th century on paper, not previously examined, deserve special mention for the light they throw on 16th and 17th century Ipswich.

The Withipoll Book of Hours

This volume (ms 7) consists of two early 16th century books of devotions bound together. Both are dateable to the first decade of the century from internal evidence. At fo. 97 begins the 'Hore beate virginis marie secundum usum Sarum' and at its foot is the inscription 'Anne Wythypoll owth thys boke'.

Anne, daughter of Robert Curson of Brightwell, already twice widowed, married Paul, son of John Withipoll, a Bristol shipowner and merchant in woollen cloth, in 1510. The first prayer in the book mentions Paul, but the name is written over an erasure: 'Deus pater pacem et veram concordiam ac verum amorem inter me et maritum meum Paulum constante [*sic*] et pacifica diem istum et ceteros dies vite nostre...'. The word *Paulum* is spread out to fill the space left by a longer name. Anne's previous husbands had been William Freville and William Reede. There is room for *Gulielmum* (or *Wilhelmum*) and traces of ink remain where the lower left hand part of the initial G or W would have been.

There is also a printed book in the Library which once belonged to Paul Withipoll. It was given by his great grandson, Sir Edmund Withipoll, the first donor in the list of Knights and Gentlemen. Published in Lyons in 1500 it is *Postilla sive expositio epistolarum et evangeliorum dominicalium* by William of Auvergne, (King 253) and on its fly leaf is written 'Thys boke is Powle Wythypoll's bowght in Sevyl in Almoneda for 11s.' If Paul Withipoll bought the book when it was newly published, he, aged about 20, must have travelled on his father's business, trading mainly in cloth, but also in wine, oil, honey, salt, cork and iron with ports in Portugal, Spain, Castile and Bordeaux. It must have been on another expedition to Italy in 1514 that Paul commissioned Antonio de Solario to portray him praying to the Virgin and Child in what is now known as the Withipoll triptych in Bristol City Art Gallery. Paul eventually became Master of the Merchant Taylors Company, and just before his death in 1547 bought the site of Holy Trinity Priory in Ipswich where over the next three years his son Edmund built Christchurch.[123]

All that is known of Paul and Anne Withipoll suggests that they were pious and cultured people. The Book of Hours did not come to the Library through Sir Edmund, but, according to Samuel Ward who listed it as 'precationis summula', it was one of Smarte's manuscript gifts. After the book left Withipoll ownership it suffered savage treatment; nearly all the English rubrics were scratched out in ink. For whoever did this, the word 'Pope' had to be erased totally; deletion was not enough. No Smarte would have done this, any more than a Withipoll, and suspicion must therefore fall upon

[123] G.C. Moore-Smith, *The Withypoll Family.* (Walthamstow Antiquarian Society Publ. 34 1936), Chapter I.

Ward, for none had stronger motive and better opportunity. Comparison of the rubric deletions and his untidy crossings-out in the back of the Benefactors' Book only strengthens the case against Ward.

How fortunate that a book with such interesting Ipswich links did not go with the hundred other Smarte manuscripts to Pembroke Hall; this was probably no coincidence. Robert Hingeston accepted that Smarte gave it to the Library, and so inscribed it in about 1750. The fore-edge title 'ORATIONES' in Roman capitals an inch high looks much earlier.

The thirteenth century Vulgate

Of ms 9 James wrote: 'Biblia. Vellum 8 by 5 [inches]. ff. 1 + 355, double columns of 55 line. Cent. XIII in a very fine close hand. Binding Modern.' After the collation: 'Apparently another gift of Smart. A large number of names of the 16th and 17th centuries are scribbled on fly leaf and margins, which are hardly worth copying.'

The Provost of Eton was mistaken in two respects. From Smarte came only eight manuscripts, and no Bible is among them. A more convincing provenance can be suggested. No other book in the Library has anywhere near as many manuscript additions, many of which bear dates which are spread fairly evenly from 1584 to 1711, The book was only added to the Library after this later date, and the marginalia are of considerable interest to anyone interested in the history of Ipswich.

The first, on the first folio, is only legible with the aid of ultra-violet light, and is the key to all the others:

> Donum thesaurae Villae
> Cognomine Roberti Salowse

Two lines below in the same hand are only partly decipherable; they begin 'Trust in the Lord...' and 'But trust not ...' Robert Sallowes, yeoman, was Treasurer to the Corporation from 1564 to 1568, and his gift to the town was not to a library, but for more mundane use, as appears on fo.35^v:

> Hic liber ad Consules Gippi' pro tempore existente
> pertinet tamen utitur in C[onsiliis?]

The hand is Christopher Ballard's, Chamberlain in 1595 and Claviger from 1597 to his death in 1615. This is one of nine dated entries he made in the Bible between 1588 and 1609. Only the egregious William Sidey, who wrote his name (only) 19 times, exceeded Ballard's total.

Sallowes' presentation was used in the courts of Ipswich for nearly 150 years, as a bible on which to swear oaths on appointment to office in the borough or before giving evidence. Seven chamberlains and seven Attorneys at Small Pleas wrote their names here, as well as a handful of Town Clerks, but by far the most regular users of the margins of this 13th century treasure were Serjeants at the Mace, of whom there were always four. Of the 59 men to hold this office between 1564 and 1715, 31 at least are here, so that to sign on election must have been customary. What is perhaps surprising is the high standard of literacy of the majority of these men, an indication perhaps that the sons of ten of them who won places on the foundation at the Grammer School would have been capable of benefiting by their time there. There are no lapses in decancy in what was written, whether or not an entry was signed. Women are not represented, save for two patriotic mentions of Queen Anne. The slogan which was painted in letter of gold on the wall above the Corporation Pew in the Tower church was copied by Chessingham Gaudy, Serjeant from 1697:

> Feare God and the King
> and Medle not with them
> that are given to Change
> C   1700   G

There is wry humour in lines written in 1684, probably also by Gaudy:

> Poor men Labour
> Rich men Grind
> Knaves divise
> and foles belive

and the four Serjeants in 1595 appear in nickname on the first leaf below Sallowes' donation inscription:

John Puddinge	(for Gooding
John Fishmonger	for Fisher
John Hearnsaie	for Herne – a gossip?
Dick Baldepate	for Beaumont)
Seriantes	

and below, in the same hand, probably that of Christopher Tolson, former gaoler, and Serjeant from 1592 to 1594: 'Steale Curlls John Fysher', an allusion which defies explanation.

Quotations from scripture are common: 'J.Miles *mercator Stultus*' wrote the opening to the 18th Psalm in 10 Latin verses; others chose proverbs and maxims of every kind in English, French, Italian and Latin. A few examples will suffice to show the range:

fo.3^r   *Ung homme sans foy*
       n'a soucy du Loy   Thomas Salter

fo.5^r   *felix quem faciunt Aliena pericula Cautem* J.F.

fo.132^r   *Non minor est virtus quam quaerere parta tueri*

fo.180^r   *Dives divitias non congregat absque labori*
       non tenet absque mihi, non Desevit absque dolore
             John Sicklemor (thrice Bailiff and
                 father of John, Recorder and M.P.)

fo.181^v   *Hic liber, hae literae simul hec coelestia dicta*
       Aetherio, tollunt, saepe, prosque, polo
           Christopher Ballard, junior 1609

fo.198^r   swete is the sowre that dw'th in ye bud
       but soure is the swete that deceith in the blossom

fo.310^v   *Qui ante non dabet peste dolebatt*

fo.354^v   he that hath faulsed his faith has lost his reputation
       Edmund Lambe, who wrote this in Italian and English

In legal Latin there are draft openings to deeds, likely enough in a book so long used in court. On the last folio the Chamberlains signed a statement on 5 October 1602 to the effect that '18d. ys the Just Summe of the rentes Bellonginge to the Towne of Ipswiche *per me* Christopher Cardinall & Jo. Flick.'

Two more pieces are worth quoting, one on the favourite theme of mortality:

fo.346^r   Frinds I am gone soone thou shalt follow
         perhaps today perhaps tomorrow –
      thy time uncertain spend it well
         remember heaven think on hell
      make sure thy pardon leave thy sin
        wch contience saith thou livest in
            I–G

The other elegantly conceals the name of Leonard Woolley, Attorney in the Court of Small Pleas from November 1625. His admission to the office was noted in Bacon's *Annals*, as was his dismissal for non-attendance.[124] Woolley wrote his name openly on two other margins in the book.

fo.353[r]

> Whome Romans call the awfull king of beasts
> the pretious unguent w[ch] Christ's head anoynted
> the coat wherew[th] kind nature sheepe invests
> the word whereat in anger swords are poynted
>> Describes his name that here amongst his betters
>> Durst not record it in more p'per letters

Shortly after 1710 the book was rebound, elaborately if the blue gauffered edges are an indication; 1711 was the date in the last dated marginal graffito. The binder trimmed something like half an inch from the outside margins with resulting loss to many of the additions. Were the margins complete it seems likely that most if not all the Serjeants' names would be found there. Altogether over 120 names are here preserved, mostly autograph. Several members of the same family, for example the Ballards, Coppings and Wilkinsons, chose to write their names on the same page. Soon after 1711, then, the book was recognised as of too good for its legal and ceremonial employment, and it was taken to the Library for safer keeping. Perhaps John Gaudy, Usher since 1705, whose own name invades a margin, alerted Edward Leedes, newly arrived Master in 1712, to the plight of a finely written Vulgate. Leedes, an author himself, was to take good care of both Town and School Libraries, and would have been quick to charge of the book.

About Sallowes himself there hangs something of a mystery. From Chamberlain in 1556, one of the 24-men in 1559 and Treasurer in the mid-1560s, he became one of the four Wardens of the Henry Tooley Foundation in 1575–7, and succeeded William Smarte as Overseer of the Tallow Chandlers who worked there. In 1574 he was assessed for poor rate at threepence a week in St Stephen's parish, while William Smarte in Tower parish paid tenpence, and at this point he cannot have been far from holding some of the highest offices in the Corporation. Instead, however, he seems to have suffered a sharp decline, forced to leave his town house before 1582 and in 1588 admitted to the Foundation, and as one of the fifty poor inmates allowed one shilling a week. According to the Ordinance Book of Tooley's Charity for the 15 May 1589 he was allocated a further shilling a week because of 'his age and extreme Payne and povertie that hee endureth'. There is a marginal entry: 'One of the 24 relieved. No state so sure but may fall.' It would be interesting to know the cause of Sallowes' decline; he was not long resident at the Hospital before he died in February 1589/90. He continued to receive 2s. a week until the end, when the last entry in the Foundation Accounts concerning him reads 'Paid for the buryenge of oulde Sallowes xxij[d].' He was 75 years of age.[125]

It would be of the greatest interest to discover something of the provenance of the manuscript, particularly if its likely local origin could be confirmed. Mr Nicholas Rogers dates it to the late 1220s or 1230s, noting certain similarities of draughtsmanship and technique with the obituary roll of Lucy de Vere, Prioress of Hedingham, which dates from after 1226.[126] There is nothing in the manuscript to argue against an East Anglian provenance, and there is a similarity between the hand which penned a chronological note above the contents list on the verso of the first leaf, and that of the 13th century list of donors and books belonging to a Franciscan house, deduced to be that of Ipswich, which survives as a vellum fly leaf to an early 15th century manuscript in the Suffolk Record Office.[127] In the book list there is a reference to 'a Bible in one volume, which same Bible was

[124] Great Court Book 7 November 1625 and 17 April 1640 (Richardson, 486 and 524).

[125] J.G. Webb, *Poor Relief in Elizabethan Ipswich*. (Suffolk Records Society IX 1966), 22, 30, 84, 99, and 141, Foundation Accounts 1589–90 (BL Add. MS 25,343, fos. 133[r] and 134[v]), Ipswich Depositions Book 15–27 Eliz., 87, (SRO Ipswich) and many refs. in Richardson.

[126] BL Egerton MS 2,849.

[127] Albertus de Saxonia, Sophismata; MS in SRO Ipswich HD1043/1. [D.M. White], 'A mediaeval manuscript of Ipswich interest', in *Ipswich Library Journal* 46 (January 1939), 14–17 and N.R. Ker, *op. cit.* (1977), 993.

distributed to the separate rooms of the friars'. William, 'formerly rector of Hecham' [Higham] was the donor. The suppression inventory of 1537 at Ipswich Greyfriars mentions 'xx books, good and ill' in the choir. It is interesting to speculate on the possible link, and to note that, according to M.R. James, another Suffolk corporation used a book from a former monastic establishment locally as one to swear oaths upon. At Eye, the famous Red Book mustered at the Dissolution of Eye Priory was so employed during the 17th and 18th centuries, but then unfortunately mislaid or destroyed by some who were ignorant of its Anglo-Saxon dating and importance to the history of Christianity in East Anglia.[128]

Catechisms in four languages

The third manuscript, on paper, conveniently numbered ms 10 (though King counted it 355 among the printed books) is entitled 'Catecheticae Versiones Variae'. The Catechism is written in four columns across facing pages in English, Latin, Greek and Hebrew. The entry on page 55: 'Jan: 26 1637 Permitto ut ista versio catechismi imprimatur. Johan Oliver' shows that the manuscript was prepared for printing and officially read by John Oliver, later President of Magdalen College, Oxford. This is the earliest known example of Oliver's work as licenser for the press.[129] Five copies of the rare octavo volume printed in 1638 without alteration or addition from the first 55 pages of the manuscript by M. F[lesher] for the Company of Stationers (STC.4806) are recorded in the revised *S.T.C.*, the only clue to authorship the initials G. S. after the Preface, as on the title page of ms 10. In the Guildhall Library copy is written the entirely reasonable suggestion that G. S. was George Sandys, poet and traveller, who published similar books at about the same time, one other over initials only.[130]

The manuscript continues after the published portion with several graces in English and Hebrew, and then on page 71 Oliver writes: 'of this catechisme thus turnd into meeter'. Latin and Greek verse versions follow, giving support to the idea that the poet Sandys was responsible. After graces in verse in Latin and Greek, and the catechism in English and Hebrew verse, the work ends with versions of the Decalogue, the Creed, the Commandments and the Lord's Prayer in the four languages, mostly in verse. On page 178 the name 'R. Hur' is written in a fresh hand, with the date 'die S Sep 15 An [16]69'. This gave J. Cordy Jeaffreson the idea that the manuscript was written then.[131] His comment 'An eccentric performance, of little merit' now needs re-evaluation.

It is difficult to link Sandys with Ipswich, but his brother and nephew, both Sir Miles Sandys, lived near Cambridge where the donor John Wallace may have bought books secondhand. He also gave six works, mostly Venetian printings, as already mentioned in Chapter VII. Wallace's hand is to be found on the last two leaves of the little book, on the first just: 'Thatch.ˢ 49s. 17 days – 3s. per day' and 'choose you this day', and, on the second, a list of names with the flavour of St Nicholas parish of which he was a leading member from about 1675 until the early years of the 18th century. He lived in the fine dwelling which John Cutler bequeathed to the parish in 1657; and which stood at the corner of King Street and Cutler Street.

N[icholas?]

Nich: Haly	Wil: Spanton
Fra: Cole	Tho: Osbourn g:
Sim: Buttrum	Ben: Norman
Will Herbert	Rich: Barker

[128] M.R. James, *Suffolk and Norfolk.* (1930), 12.
[129] W.W. Greg, *Licensers for the Press, etc. to 1640.* Oxford Bibliographical Society 1962), 73.
[130] For example, STC.21724, published in 1636. The Guildhall Library copy of the printed *Catecheticae* belonged to the Ashburnham Library.
[131] *Royal Commission on Historical Manuscripts, 9th Report*, Part I, (1883), 257b.

Edm. Tye
Wid: Mayhew
Ric: Cook Sr R Br:
Jo: Rands Sr R Br: & Baldeston
Jo: Fyn Howse & Land
Jo: Hodg. Esq Sorrell
Jo: Baldeston his house
Wid: Gerling Jo Sterling
Rob: Gross
Geor: Sippings Mr Baly
Wid. Mayhew sen. Jo Sterling
Jo: Sterling
Wil: Meadows Sr R: Br:
Jo: Gerling & Fillgate
Miller, Sr R: Br:

Wid: Brown
Tho: Smith Sr R Br:
Jo. Gosling Sr Rob Br
Rob: Hallybread owse & Ld
Wil: Hallybread
Ric: Burrell . Baldeston
Tho: Osborn jn: Baldeston
Hen: Warner
Ph: Cohen . Brand
Wid. Chambers
Jo. Rands Hallybread
Wid: Man
Catchpole
Wil: Cole – wid Major

One possibility is that this is a list of residents in part of the parish with owners or former owners named also where relevant. Sir Robert Broke was Recorder in 1685 and Bailiff the following year, dying without issue in 1693/4. Comparison with the Hearth Tax lists of 1674 [132] and those of 1689 in *Ipswich 200 Years Ago* [133] throws no further light on Wallace's list, but it looks as though the doctor took some interest, perhaps a speculative one, in the ownership of property in his locality.

[132] S.H.A. Hervey (Ed.) *Suffolk in 1674: being the Hearth Tax returns.* (Suffolk Green Book 11, Woodbridge 1905).
[133] H. Chamberlain, *Ipswich 200 years ago.* (Ipswich 1889).

XIV

THE PREACHER'S CHOICE OF BOOKS

by Nicholas Cranfield and Anthony Milton

'Such as reade the Bible by fits upon rainy dayes, not eating the booke with John, *but tasting onely with the tippe of the tongue: Such as meditate by snatches, never chewing the cud and digesting their meat, they may happely get a smackering for discourse and table talke; but not enough to keepe soule & life together, much lesse for strengthe and vigour.'* [134]

In this rather scornful way Ward chastised his fellow clergy at a Visitation sermon in Ipswich: the Word of God was not to be taken lightly or without pain. There could be no higher task for the minister than the able exposition of the Bible to the benefit of all hearers. As he later reminded those who heard or read his sermon, *The Happinesse of Practice*, the true joy for the husbandman lay not in the sowing and the planting but in the reaping and gathering to fill the barns:

> One halfe of the Scriptures I have handled among you, endeavoured to acquaint you with the whole Counsell of God: and what is now the top of all my ambition, but to make you Doers, of what you have beene Hearers? [135]

Such a high calling and such demanding work required extensive use, and critical appreciation, of the Bible. It was a proper understanding of the Scriptures,

> that maketh ministers to be fruitfull preachers: that maketh private persons to be profitable hearers: that yeeldeth matter of wholesome meditation to the minde: that putteth vigour of good affections in the heart.[136]

In a sermon preached in London thirty years before he became a bishop, Thomas Westfield urged that a dutiful minister must not only study the Bible proficiently but,

> next therunto the writings of the auncient, & most learned fathers of the primitive churche, before those of latter times, they being not so subject to error, as some of them are.[137]

By the early seventeenth century a wide range of exegetical and hermeneutical volumes was readily accessible. Foremost among these remained, as Westfield hoped, the Fathers of the Church whose scholarship was fired in part by the need to define and to establish the canonicity of the Scriptures. Origen, Basil, Athanasius, Gregory Nazianzen, Cyril of Alexandria and John Chrysostom among the Greeks and Ambrose, Jerome, Augustine and Gregory the Great for the Latins. Thereafter, despite the work of Oecumenius, few Byzantines had contributed much to the tradition of exposition and in the medieval period it had been habitual to favour the compilations of *catenae*.[138]

It was not until the coming of the European renaissance that more rigorous work could be

---

[134] S. Ward, *A coal from the Altar, to kindle the holy fire of* Zeale. (London 1615), p.57.

[135] S. Ward, *The Happinesse of Practice.* (London 1621), Sigs. A3,ᵛ A4.ʳ

[136] R. Cleaver, *A Briefe explanation of the Whole Booke of the Proverbs of Salomon.* (London 1615), Sig. A3.ᵛ

[137] BL Egerton MS 2,877, fo. 64.

[138] An individual study of medieval methods may be found in, H. Caplan, 'Four senses of Scriptural Interpretation' in *Speculum*, IV (1929), 282–290.

undertaken on the Bible, both literary and critical in nature. The recovery of Hebrew [139] and the increasing dexterity with which scholars handled the original texts [140] made possible the Reformers' enthusiastic use of the Bible as a preaching source. In turn the appearance of the Bible in the vernacular required of its expositors a degree of scholarship similar to that exercised by the Fathers of the Church.

How much such exegetical work prompted, or was prompted by, the invention of the printing press and of moveable type cannot easily be accounted.[141] But in the wake of printing and the increasingly rapid dissemination of learning it was possible to claim that the English Reformation had, on God's behalf, restored 'the cleare and sunne-shine light of His glorious Gospell.' God had not lacked for 'golden trumpets' or for 'golden candlesticks' when it came to spreading His message: Luther, Melancthon, Bucer, Oecolampadius, Calvin, Bullinger, Zwingli, Peter Marytr Vermigli and Zanchius were among the authors who informed and shaped the mind of the Elizabethan and early Stuart Church in England.[142] Although it was not until later in the seventeenth century that institutional libraries acceded expository works and commentaries in English – in 1598 the notable Puritan foundation of Emmanuel College in Ward's own university held only one English commentary, a translation of Calvin on the Prophets [143] – the Library of Ward of Ipswich shows the range of titles to hand for a town preacher.

As one might expect of a collection founded to serve the needs of a noted preacher, the majority of the books are concerned with biblical exegesis rather than with systematic and doctrinal exposition. There are few works of controversy despite the tenor of the age:[144] this is in direct contrast to the nearby library at Colchester, given to the city by Bishop Samuel Harsnett, who prosecuted Ward for non-conformity in 1622.[145] Indeed in several instances the more obscure exegetical works of an author are included in the absence of the doctrinal writings for which they were better known. A typical example of this is Andreas Osiander, whose *Harmony on the Gospels* is included but not his most important theological contribution, *De Justificatione*. Grotius is represented by his least important biblical annotations, added in the decade following Ward's death, and only *De Arte Grammatica* ensures that Vossius is recorded in the Library at all.

The controversies taking place during Ward's ministry and lifetime are overlooked; the issue over order and function debated at the 1604 Hampton Court Conference and again, for the benefit of the Scots, in 1606 and two years later in Scotland, the heated exchanges in the 1620s following the publication of Richard Montagu's *Appello Caesarem*, and the altar controversy of the 1630s which flared in the wake of the Metropolitical Visitation of 1634 and as part of the continuing argument over the 'beauty of holiness'. Cave Beck's enthusiasm for the antiquarian did not bring in John

[139] G. Lloyd Jones, *The discovery of Hebrew in Tudor England; a third language*. (Manchester 1983).

[140] In 1577 John Rainolds, later President of Corpus Christi College, Oxford, drew his pupils' attention to the importance to be attached to the reading of both Greek and Hebrew. J. Rainolds, *Motives to Godly Knowledge*. (London 1613), Sig. A5.

[141] A good local study may be had from M.V. Chrisman, *Lay Culture, Learned Culture, Books and Social Change in Strasbourg, 1480–1599*. (Yale 1982).

[142] W. Perkins, *A godlie and learned exposition upon the whole epistle of Jude*. (London 1601), 'To the Christian Reader.' (unpaginated).

[143] For instance the following may be consulted: J.F. Fuggles, 'A history of the library of S. John's College, Oxford, from the foundation of the College to 1660', unpublished B. Litt. thesis, Oxford University (1975) J.R. Liddell, 'The Library of Corpus Christi College, Oxford', unpublished B. Litt. thesis, Oxford University (1933) S. John's College, Cambridge MS U.5. This manuscript lists the substantial donation in 1632 of some six hundred books to his former college by John Williams, the disgraced bishop of Lincoln. S. Bush and G. Ramussen, 'Emmanuel College Library's First Inventory' in *Transactions of the Cambridge Bibliographical Society*, VIII, v (1985), 514–556.

[144] Dr John Morrill has pointed out that the library includes the writing of no archbishops down to 1688 even though much of their work was non-polemical. Francis White's *Replie to Fisher the Jesuit* is included but not Laud's.

[145] G. Goodwin, *Catalogue of the Harsnett Library at Colchester*. (London 1888.) Harsnett's library contained very few works of commentary, only one of which is in English.

Selden's *History of Tithes* and the collection has no pieces on Sabbatarianism. Nor are there works on the three much disputed ceremonies, of the cross at Baptism, of the ring at Marriage and of kneeling at the Holy Name. Although two of the many pieces Thomas Morton wrote against Rome are included his *Defence of the Innocencie of Three Ceremonies* is not. Perhaps more surprisingly, in the debates with Rome, there are no writings on either side in the Oath of Allegiance controversy, except for King James' own writings available from the 1616 edition of his works: absent are Becanus, Du Perron and Parsons on the one side and Barclay, Buckeridge, Gordon, Harris or Andrewes for the other on this matter. As will be seen the representation of anti-Roman writings is far from being comprehensive. Taken into consideration alongside the conscious exclusion of works concerning disputes which must have been of major interest at the time it must be argued that such writings were not thought relevant or fitting for the preacher's Library. Private use might be had of such pieces – although this begs the question of their availability; would grave divines own their own copies of scurrilous, ephemeral works of topical contention? – while the purpose of the Town Library was to provide the preacher with the key volumes of exegesis that he might preach the gospel boldly.

The collection is broadly that of an industrious, perhaps laboured, preacher. Samuel Ward himself chose to make the bedrock that of Patristics when he administered the £50 gift from Mrs Walter to the town. In appendix D will be found John Coney's listing of the entire purchase. If there is a preference it is towards the works of the Latin Fathers rather than those of the Greek.[146] Beyond the safety of Patristic authorship the Library holds a wide collection of near contemporary biblical commentaries and hermeneutical works, both Reformed and Catholic.

The champions of the continental Reformation, lauded by Perkins, continued to exert a powerful influence over the thinking of all those engaged in theological discourse and preaching in England; Calvin is well represented and there are works by both Theodore Beza and Danaeus as well as the complete works of both Girolamo Zanchius, who died in 1590, and his fellow faculty member at Heidelberg, Zacharias Ursinus (d. 1583). Most popular among the works of Ursinus was his commentary on the catechism, *The summe of christian religion*, which ran to several editions between 1587 and 1633 while Perkins himself undertook to popularise Zanchius.[147] The influence of Geneva and Heidelberg is not, however, overwhelming and it is the work of other Swiss Reformed writers, notably those of Zurich, with Henry Bullinger,[148] Gualter, Lavater and Peter Martyr Vermigli, which provides the core of foreign Reformed thinking in the Library. Wolfgang Musculus, who had himself visited England in 1548, fifteen years before his death, and Conrad Pellicanus are also well represented although it may be noted that the contribution of Musculus was restricted to his biblical works: his more famous and most important work, *Loci Communes*, is not to be found.

Despite the size of the Library's holding of Reformed writings there are few general theological works dealing specifically with doctrines of predestination and grace, although both English and Continental authors addressed these matters frequently, especially after the Arminian disputes in the United Provinces and at the Synod of Dort. While Bradwardine's *De Causa Dei* and the *Acts of the Synod of Dort* certainly bear witness to an interest in the Arminian upheavals, there is no evidence that Ward ever attempted a systematic policy of acquisition of works dealing exclusively with these areas of theology. Indeed none of the anti-Arminian treatises composed in England or abroad, was acquired at the time. It was not until the 1660s that the works of Jacob Arminius and of his follower

---

[146] Dr Morrill has suggested to us that this is to be expected as Calvinist thinkers preferred the austerity of the Latin while 'liberal' Anglicans, like Archbishop Laud, tended to hold an affinity with the Greek Fathers. This may in part be true but it may also be a question of education: Robert Browne derided the use of Greek (and indeed of Hebrew) in the pulpit as the 'maidens of the bishops'. *The Writings of Robert Harrison & Robert Browne.* eds. A. Peel and L.H. Carlson, (London 1953), p.173.

[147] W. Perkins, 'A Briefe Discourse taken out of the writings of H. Zanchius' in W. Perkins, *A Case of Conscience.* (Cambridge 1595).

[148] It has been pointed out that Bullinger's influence in England waned as the writings of Perkins became more widespread. R.T. Kendall, *Calvin and English Calvinism to 1649.* (Oxford 1979), p. 4n.

Petrus Bertius were entered,[149] by which time they were probably being given a sympathetic reading, rather than being exploited for Calvinist polemical purposes.

At Geneva Theodore Beza, Calvin's successor, had been the first thinker to make the issue of limited atonement central to his perspective of theology; basing his enquiry around the Letter to the Romans,[150] Beza constructed a programme which later became known as supralapsarianism. These ideas of predestination differed greatly from those of Calvin and influenced Perkins, Zanchius and Ursinus, whose works, as seen above, are to met with in the Library; surprisingly such volumes do not enjoy a monopoly. More moderate expositions of predestinarian doctrines may be found in many of the Protestant authors in the collection; it is interesting to note, for example, the inclusion of the works of the Danish anti-Calvinist Niels Hemmingsen, who had influenced Lancelot Andrewes, William Barlow and John Overall in their consideration of the 1595 Lambeth Articles,[151] and the biblical commentaries of the German, Matthias Martinus, who had taught at Herborn and was one of the moderate Bremen delegates at the Synod of Dort. With the exception of the Cambridge Richard Greenham, there is also a notable lack of any of the native 'experimental predestinarian' devotional treatises which became so popular in the period: Dod and Cleaver's *Plaine and Familiar Exposition of the Ten Commandements* which ran to no fewer than nineteen editions between 1603 and 1635, and is arguably the most influential single commentary in seventeenth century England for the Protestant discussion of personal and social ethics, is not to be found. Absent too are works by William Bradshaw and by Richard Rogers, who compiled more than one hundred sermons on Judges into a substantial volume dedicated to Sir Edward Coke. In part the reliance upon Perkins and on Peter Martyr Vermigli made these works expressive of more extreme predestinarian ideas. In this same tradition the works of Preston and Sibbs were not acquired until the 1660s. Overall, Dr Morrill has noted that the Library lacks works directed at the theological and pastoral self-improvement of the laity.

Alongside these Protestant writings is a wealth of works by Papist writers, including the most famous of Romanist exegetes such as Joannes Maldonatus, Arias Montanus and Cornelius à Lapide, a Flemish Jesuit who taught at both Louvain and Rome. Other Catholic writers found favour for works close to a Protestant regard: thus the Valencian Jesuit Benedict Pererius is included for his work on Romans but not for his commentary on Genesis, which was the most popular European writing on the first book of the Pentateuch.[152] The commentaries added even included those of notorious Tridentine Catholics, such as Alphonsus Salmeron and Joannes de Pineda, the latter a member of the Inquisition.

As has been noticed there were few works pertinent to the Arminian debates and their effect on the Church in England, but the Library houses several works which derived from another contemporary theological discussion; the conflict between the Dominicans and the Jesuits in matters of grace, free will and predestination. Almost all the works in this collection which bear on this dispute are the anti-Molinist writings of rigid Dominicans, which would appeal to Calvinist sensibilities and views on the nature of grace. Thus the important commentaries on Aquinas by the principal anti-Molinists Domingo Banez and Bartolomaeus de Medina are included as are Didacus Alvares' *De auxiliis divinae gratiae* and the complete works of Franciscus Suarez. The Jesuit side in the controversy is scarcely indicated at all: the *Concordia* of Ludovicus Molina is absent and the only treatise by Leonardus Lessius is a lesser work acquired after the Restoration. At Oxford in the 1610s when disputes arose between the anti-Calvinists and the traditionalists,[153] the library of the leading anti-

---

[149] The later publications of Simon Episcopius and of the ambivalent John Cameron, both associated with Arminian views, were also brought in at the Restoration.

[150] In particular Beza concerned himself with Romans ix, 23.

[151] N.R.N. Tyacke, *Anti-Calvinists. The rise of English Arminianism c.1590–1640.* (Oxford 1987), p.20.

[152] A. Williams, *The Common Expositor. An account of the commentaries on Genesis 1527–1633.* (Chapel Hill 1948), p.8. Using the hermeneutical writings on Genesis, Williams cogently explores the question of their 17th century usage. *Ibid.*, pp. 26 ff.

[153] See for instance, C.M. Dent, *Protestant Reformers in Elizabethan Oxford.* (Oxford 1983). N.R.N. Tyacke, *op. cit.*

Calvinist at Corpus Christi contained suspect works by Molina and Lessius, as well as Arminius.[154] The only prominent pro-Molinist writing in the collection is the eight volume commentary on Aquinas by Gabriel Vazquez.

In possessing the works of Caesar Baronius, Robert Bellarmine, Vazquez and Suarez, the Library is well-equipped with the major anti-Protestants of the day. Somewhat surprisingly, there are few of the Protestant rebuttals to the claims advanced by the Romanists. David Paraeus against Bellarmine came in 1636, as the gift of a minister recently ejected from his Ipswich living by Bishop Wren. The Magdeburg Centuries balance the excesses of the *Annals* of Baronius but the Library does not hold the writings of either Richard Montagu or of Isaac Casaubon who so fully corrected the errors in the historical claims initiated by Baronius. Two of the many curiosities to be encountered among the later acquisitions of Romanist books are Melchior Hittorpius' printing of an ancient Roman Ordinal, one volume of a two volume set purchased from the Walter money: *Auctarium bibliothecae patrum et auctorum ecclesiasticorum* of 1610, and a copy of Franciscus Sancta Clara's *Deus, Natura, Gratia*, which was published in the 1630s to reconcile the Church of England to Rome. In its appendix the work attempts to interpret the Thirty Nine Articles in the light of the Council of Trent. The piece caused great fear of crypto-papism when it appeared in 1634 and it is difficult to understand how Ipswich sanctioned its purchase in 1662 with part of Bishop Reynolds' gift to the Library unless there was a serious interest in earlier irenicist views.

The noted absence of English responses to the claims of Rome and the seeming indifference to local issues of controversy explain the paucity of writings by English theologians in the Library. In England the tradition of biblical exegesis cannot be said to replace the 'Latin culture' until the 1620s and 1630s so that there were few English exegetes to rival those of continental Europe, whether Reformed or Roman, until the decade of the Civil Wars. Rather unexpectedly there are few volumes written in defence of the Church of England, against Puritans or foreign catholics. Hooker, arguably the chief publicist and defender of the English Settlement of religion, Thomas Bilson, John Whitgift and William Chillingworth are absent, as are the writers who defended *iure divino* episcopal government: Bridges, Carleton, George Downame and Saravia. The writers who are represented in defence of the Church of England are those whose classical works were primarily directed across the Channel; indeed the Library possesses the 1625 Latin translation, undertaken by Sir Nathaniel Brent at Archbishop Abbot's specific request, of Francis Mason's 1614 work. Where Hooker is missing, Richard Field's 1606 *Of the Church* is included as are the monumental defences of Bishop John Jewel in his complete works. The English writers absorbed into the collection during Ward's lifetime are either moderate Puritans, such as Babington, Becon, Foxe, Fulke, Rainolds and Willett – all of them standard authors – early Reformers (Barnes, Frith and Tyndale) or orthodox English Calvinists, like Robert Abbot, elder brother to the Archbishop of Canterbury, Thomas Morton, Joseph Hall and John Davenant, none of whose views were not compromised by accepting bishoprics.

To turn to the Lutheran works in the Library which were available to the preacher, the breadth of interest seems to be broader than the works of Calvinists or Romanists. The works of Luther, Melancthon and of Brentius are to be expected. The *Examen* of Chemnitius on the Council of Trent was widely popular but for a Library which elsewhere eschewed the purchase of doctrinal systematics it is strange that his rarely read *Loci Theologici* should find shelf space. Also included are some of the co-authors of the Lutheran's uncompromising *Formula Concordiae*, Chytraeus and Selneccer, for once less than hostile to all-comers. Aegidius Hunnius, who like Chytraeus and Selneccer is not known for his ability to compromise, is represented only by a non-controversial text of homiletics. Since few Lutheran writings composed after the *Formula Concordiae* were known in England and of them Johann Gerhard was best known for works of popular piety (his *Meditationes Sacrae ad veram pietatem excitandam*) it is remarkable that the town preachers had available to them, by the singular

'John Howson's Answers to Archbishop Abbot's Accusations at his 'Trial' before James I at Greenwich, 10 June 1615.' *eds.* N.W.S. Cranfield and K.C. Fincham, in *Camden Miscellany*, xxix. (1987), pp. 319–341.
[154] Bodley Library, Oxford, O.U. Arch., Hyp. B. 20, fos. 18.[r–v] This listing of 1613 has been recently discussed by Dr Tyacke, *op. cit.* pp. 65–6.

generosity of John Webbe of Falkenham, several of Gerhard's doctrinal works. His *Loca Theologica*, of which the Library has all but the second volume, defended the Lutheran doctrines of consubstantiation and of ubiquitarianism.

Beyond the theological concerns of the age the Library is well stocked for books which were historical or antiquarian in their scope. The Magdeburg Centuries, and the works of Foxe, Sleidan and Beroaldus, allowed the reader to investigate recent history within the tradition of apocalyptic writing although it is not likely that the donors to the collection intended to make an apocalyptic historiography possible: the important works of Abbot, Bale, Broughton, Bullinger, Patrick Forbes, Fulke, Napier or Rainolds on this subject are all unrepresented. Of the commentaries on the Revelation to St. John the Divine the Library held those of David Paraeus and of Thomas Brightman, making up for the gaps of Broughton and Forbes.

Ward once averred of his age,

> What times can tell of the like light, learning, preaching, knowledge? Oh that I could say practice and thankefulnesse answerable.[155]

He could remain sure that the Library which he first oversaw was likely to enable successive preachers to withstand the future risk of ignorance which remains the greatest enemy to the study of the Bible.

---

[155] S. Ward, *A peace offering to God for the blessings we enjoy under his Maiesties reigne, with a Thanksgiving for the princes safe return...* (London 1624), p. 39.

AUTHOR CATALOGUE

Key to abbreviations in the order they appear at the end of each entry

BINDING:

Place of binding and period (cy = contemporary, within 5 years of publication)

A	Armorial
B	Blind
G	Gilt
E	Edged
F	Framed
R	Ruled
S	Stamped
O:	References to illustrations in Oldham (see below)
L	Leather and calf
V	Vellum
Reb.	Rebound
Rep.	Repaired

SIZE: Height of book in centimetres

CATALOGUE NUMBERS: from STC, Wing, Goff and Adams (see below).

DEFECTS

INSCRIPTIONS

p:	Price if stated plainly
cp:	Coded price (Main code with stops after each letter – see Chapters II and III; others transcribed as they appear. A dash between letters indicates that they are placed at either end of the place of publication. For the 'dot' code see example below.)
bm	'Bury' mark (see Ch. III)
ms	Manuscript additions, those of ownership before others
½t	Half title
tp	Title page .i. would be shown .i./m
fp	Frontispiece m
fl	Flyleaf
bg	Initials of Balthazar Gardemau on p.10 or fo.10 (See Chapter VII)

DONORS

BP, KG, MS, BT, UL, LP	Abbreviations for donor categories in Appendix B.
	(date of gift where specified in donation inscription or label)
DU	Donor unknown
	(date of gift if on tp)
PGL	Printed gift label numbers (See Appendix C.)

EDGE MARKINGS

AE	All edges
FE	Fore-edge
TE	Top-edge
g	gilt
m	marbled
p	ploughed with loss of markings, if any
t	manuscript title
BLt	Black letter ms title

LOCATIONS Old and New and Numbering

Letter and number: Press and shelf number when the fore-edge shelfmarks
were applied in April 1651.

[Letter and number]: Press and shelf number for books added (on HI, H3, all of I, K1
and 2, all N and O), between 1651 and entry in Coningsby's
MS catalogue of 1705.

King numbers from printed *Catalogue* of 1799.

Number and letter: Bookcase and shelf in Holden Library at Ipswich School in 1989.

REFERENCES

O: J.B. Oldham: *English blind-stamped bindings.* (Cambridge 1952), and *Blind panels of English binders.* (Cambridge 1958).

STC: A.W. Pollard and G.R. Redgrave: *A short-title catalogue of books printed in England, Scotland and Ireland and of English books printed abroad 1475–1640.* (Oxford 1926).

STC^2: *Second edition*, revised and enlarged by W.A. Jackson and F.S. Ferguson, completed by C.F. Pantzer. 2 vols. (London 1976–86).

Wing: Donald Wing, *Short-title catalogue of books printed in England, etc. 1641–1700.* 3 vols. (New York 1957).

Wing^2: *Second edition, revised and enlarged.* 2 vols. of three only published. (New York 1972–82).

Goff: F.R. Goff, *Incunabula in American Libraries.* (New York 1964).

Adams: H.M. Adams, *Catalogue of books printed on the continent of Europe 1501–1600 in Cambridge libraries.* 2 vols. (Cambridge 1967).

ABBOT (Robert), *Bp.* A defence of the reformed Catholicke of M.W. Perkins ...against the bastard Counter-catholicke of D. Bishop. (3 parts in two vols.)
London, impensis Thomae Adams, 1611 – Pts.1 & 2; Impensis G. Bishop, 1609 – Pt.3. Rep. 18.5cm.
STC.48.5, 50 and 50.5.   bg   KG4   FEt   G1
King 227 and 228 10B

AENEAS SYLVIUS *Piccolomini.*   *See* PIUS II, *Pope.*

AGRICOLA (Georg), *elder.*   De re metallica libri XII. Eiusdem De animantibus subterraneis liber, ab autore recognitus.
Basileae, apud Hieron. Frobenium et Nicolaum Episcopium, 1556. Reb. 31cm.
Adams A.349   lacks tp   ms owner & p: Wm. Harrison vi^s verse and several names on last leaf
bg   BP13   FEt   M1
King 136 4A

AINSWORTH (Henry).   Annotations upon the five bookes of Moses, the booke of the Psalmes, and the Song of Songs.
London, printed for John Bellamie (by Miles Fletcher and John Haviland), 1627. Reb. 32cm.
STC.219   bg   MS32   FEt   F3
King 66 10C

ALCIATUS (Andreas).   Emblemata: cum Claudii Minois ad eadem commentariis... Editio quarta.
Lugduni Batavorum, ex officina Plantiniana, apud Franciscum Raphelengium, 1591. L reb. 16cm.
Adams A.612   cp: + over B of Batavorum   ms end fl   probably LP12
King 403 7A

ALEXANDER *Carpentarius.*   Destructorium viciorum. Venundantur Parrhisiis in edibus Claudii Chevalon.
Lutecie, impensis Egidii Gormontii et Claudii Chevalloni, 1516. Reb. 28cm.
Adams D.374   ms owners: Thos. Denton, John Allen.   ms additions   bg   MS37   FEBLt   H4
King 182(1) 1B

————Destructorium viciorum.   Venundantur Parrhisiis... in edibus Egidii de Gourmont... correctum ac venundatum per Jacobum Ferrebouc.
Parisius, impensis Johannis Parvi, Egidii de Gourmont, & Francisci Regnault, 1521. London 1522–3
O:1053 and FCb(2)623 BS rep. 28cm.
not in Adams   ms owner: W^s Smarte Gippi' BL inscr. & additions   bg   BP0   FEBLt   H4
King 182(2) 3A

ALEXANDER *of Hales.*   Clavis Theologie: Pars secunda summe theologice *preceded by* Tabula alphabetica in summam, (by Peter Keschinger), *Lugduni, per Jacobum Myt,* 1517 (2 parts in one vol.)
Lugduni, impensis Antonii Koburger, 1516. ?Netherlandish cy BS rep. 32cm.
Adams A.696 (part only)   ms owner & p: Gardner 6s 8d   bg   MS23   FEBLt   H5
King 652 1B

ALLEN (Robert).   The doctrine of the Gospel. By a plaine and familiar interpretation of the particular points or Articles thereof:... divided into three bookes. (3 vols. in one)
London, Thomas Creede, 1606. English cy. Royal AGS Reb. 29cm.
STC.364   (Dedication to KG3 *inter alia*)   bg   MS22   FEt   F2
King 195 1C

ALSTED (Johann Heinrich).   [Encyclopaedia, septem tomis distincta.] (Tom. 1–3: lib. I–XX) *and* Tomus quartus encyclopaediae (Tom. 4–7: lib. XXI–XXXV) (7 vols. in two)
Herbornae Nassoviorum, [s.n.], 1630. Reb. 34cm.
lacks general title   BT35   FEt   F3
King 557 10D

———— Methodus sacrosanctae theologiae octo libris tradita, in quorum: (I Praecognita, etc.) (2 books in one vol.)
Hanoviae, prostat apud Conradum Eifridum, 1623. Reb. 20cm.

BT35   FEt   F2   King 660 10B

———— Theologia catachetica, exhibens sacratissimam novitiolorum Christianorum Scholam,... ex Bibliis... exponitur:
Hanoviae, apud Conradum Eifridum, 1622. Rep. 20cm.

BT35   FEt   F2   King 666 10B

———— Theologia didactica, exhibens locos communes theologicos methodo scholastica, quatuor in partes tributa. (4 parts in one vol.)
Hanoviae, sumptibus Conradi Eifridi, 1627. Reb. 20cm.

BT35   FEt   F2   King 247 10B

———— Theologia naturalis exhibens augustissimam naturae scholam;... adversos atheos, epicureos, et sophistas huius temporis, duobus libris pertractata. (2 parts in one vol.)
Hanoviae, sumptibus Conradi Eyfridii, 1623. Reb. 20cm.

BT35   FEt   F2   King 246 10B

———— Theologia polemica, exhibens praecipuas huius aevi in religionis negatio controversis... Editio secunda.
Hanoviae, sumptibus Conradi Eifridi, 1627. Reb. 20cm.

BT35   FEt   F2   King 239 10B

ALUNNO (Francesco).   Della fabrica del mondo,... libri dieci... le voci di Dante del Petrarca... & d'altri buoni autthori. Con un nuovo Vocabulario in fine, aggiunto da Thomaso Porcacchi. (2 vols. in one)
In Venetia, appresso Gio. Battista Uscio, 1588. Reb. 29cm.

not in Adams   DU   FEp   [I4]   King 609 1B

ALVARES (Didacus), *Abp.*   De auxiliis divinae gratiae et humani arbitrii viribus, et libertate,... concordia, libri duodecim. Editio postrema ab ipso auctore recognita.
Lugduni, sumptibus Jacobi Cardon & Petri Cavellat, 1620. Rep. 33cm.

bg   BT19   FEt   L1   King 19 4D

ALVERNUS (Gulielmus).   *See* WILLIAM OF AUVERGNE.

AMBROSE, *Bp., Saint.*   Omnia quotquot extant... opera, primum per Des. Erasmum, mox per Sig. Gelenium deinde per alios eruditos viros diligenter castigata. (5 vols. in two)
Basileae, per Eusebius Episcopium & Nicolai Episcopii haeredes, 1567. Rep. 33cm.

Adams A.942   cp: a.k.   bg   BT1   PGL32   FEt   B2   King 67 11D

AMMIANUS MARCELLINUS.   *See* MARCELLINUS, A.

ANDREWES (Lancelot), *Bp.*   The morall law expounded,... upon the ten commandments: being his lectures... whereunto is annexed... nineteen sermons upon prayer;
London, printed for Michael Sparke, Robert Milbourne, Richard Cotes, and Andrew Crooke, 1642. Rep. 28cm.

Wing A.3140   LP4   FEt   [I3]   King 172 6B

———— Opuscula quaedam posthuma. *with his* Stricturae: or, a briefe answer... to Cardinal Perron. *also includes his* Tortura torti, 1609. (3 vols. in one)

Londini, excudebat Felix Kyngston pro R. B. & Andraea Hebb, 1629. Reb. 21cm.

STC.602 & 625   BT34   FEt   G2

King 300 7D

——— XCVI sermons. The second edition. (3 parts in one vol.)
London, printed by R. Badger, 1631. Rep. 32cm.

STC.607   fl from earlier copy (see Ch. VI)   LP4   [I4]

King 151 11D

——— Tortura torti: sive, ad Matthaei Torti librum responsio... pro juramento fidelitatis. *bound with his* Opuscula quaedam posthuma, 1629. (One of 3 vols.)
Londini, excudebat Rogerus Barkerus, 1609. Reb. 21cm.

STC.626   BT34   FEt   G2

King 300 7D

ANNILO (Orosius), *pseudonym.   See* BERING, V.

ANSELM, *Abp., Saint.*   Opera omnia... hac ultima editione praeter tomi quarti accessionem... aliquot novis opusculis aucta. Studio Joannis Picardi... (4 vols. in one)
Coloniae Agrippinae, ex officina Cholin. sumptibus Petri Cholini, 1612. Rep. 33cm.

bg   BT1   PGL32   FEt   B3

King 31 10D

ANTONINUS, *Abp. of Florence, Saint.*   Historiarum... tribus tomis discretarum solertiorique studio recognitarum pars prima cum gemino eiusdem indice. (First of three parts)
[Lugduni], Joannis Clein, 1517. Reb. 29cm.

Adams A.1209(1)   ms on tp: Mr Blower 4 m'tii 1597   bg   KG1   FEp   M1

King 95 6B

APPIAN *of Alexandria.*   Romanorum historiarum, de bellis Punicis... omnia per Sigismundum Gelenium Latine reddita... de bellis Hispanicis... Illyricis.
Basileae, per Hier. Frobenium, et Nic. Episcopium, 1554. BS rep. 30cm.

Adams A.1347   ms owner & p: Wm Harrison vi^s viii^d   bm: al 12   bg   BP13   FEt   M1

King 146 4A

ARCHIMEDES.   [Greek.] Opera quae extant. Novis demonstrationibus commentariisque illustrata. Per Davidem Rivaltum...
Parisiis, apud Claudium Morellum, 1615. Reb. 34cm.

LP3   FEp   [O2]

King 538 7E

ARETIUS (Benedictus).   Commentarii in... Novum Testamentum [attrib. title]: Commentarii in Evangeliam, Commentarii in sacram Actuum Apostolicorum historiam, *and* Commentarii... in omnes Epistolas D.Pauli et canonicas, Itemque in Apocalypsin D.Joannis... Editio postrema... emendatior. (3 vols. in one)
Bernae Helvetiorum, excudebat Joannes le Preux, 1606–08. Reb. 32cm.

lacks first title   bg   BP9   FEt   C2

King 208 11C

——— S.S.Theologiae problemata hoc est: loci communes Christianae religionis, methodice explicati... editio nova, superioribus emendiator.
Bernae Helvetiorum, excudebat Joannes le Preux, 1603. Rep. 32cm.

bg   BP9   PGL14 over PGL10 (defective)   FEt   C2

King 635 11C

ARIAS MONTANO (Benedito).   Commentaria in duodecim Prophetas: nunc tandem ab ipso auctore recognita. *Antverpiae, ex officina Christophori Plantini*, 1583. Reb. 24cm.

Adams M.1633   lacks all before p. 31   BT1   FEp   G2

King 301 8B

———— *See also* BIBLE – Polyglot, 1599, *and* O.T. – Hebrew, 1571.

ARISTOTLE. [Greek.] Operum... nova editio, Graece & Latine... ex bibliotheca Isaaci Casauboni. Accesserunt ex libris Aristotelis, fragmenta quaedam. (2 vols.) *Lugduni, apud Guillelmum Laemarium,* 1590. Reb. 36cm.

Adams A.1736   ms owner: John Watson and Gk.inscr. bm: α 90   bg   MS24   FEp   H5
King 468 11E

ARMINIUS (Jacobus).   Opera theologica... nunc denuo coniunctim recusa. *[Frankfurt], prostant apud Guilielmum Fizterum Anglum,* 1631. L reb. 21cm.

BP13 [I2]
King 662 9B

———— *See also* TWISSE, W.

ARNOBIUS.   Disputationum adversus gentes libri VII. (edited by Gebhart Elmenhorst) *bound with* MINUCIUS FELIX Octavius, 1612. (2 vols in one) *Hamburgi, [s.n.]* 1610.

bg   BT1   FEt   A4
King 39 9D

ARROWSMITH (John).   Tactica sacra, sive de milite spirituali pugnante, vincente, & triumphante dissertatio, tribus libris comprehensa:... accesserunt eiusdem orationes. *Cantabrigiae, excudebat Joannes Field, impensis Joannis Rothwell, Londini,* 1657. Rep. 20cm.

Wing A.3777   LP1   [I2]
King 249 10B

———— *See also* Parliamentary Sermons.

ASHE (Simeon).   *See* Parliamentary Sermons.

ASHMOLE (Elias).   The institution, laws & ceremonies of the most noble Order of the Garter collected and digested into one body. *London, printed for J. Macock, for Nathanael Brooke,* 1672. Rep. 39cm.

Wing A.3983   UL24   msGL   AEm   [N4]
King 441 7G

ATHANASIUS, *Abp., Saint.*   [Greek.] Opera quae reperiuntur omnia, in duos tomos tributa... cum interpretatione Latine Petri Nannii, & aliorum ubi illa desiderabatur. (3 vols. in one) *Heidelberg, ex officina Commeliniana,* 1601. Rep. 34cm.

bg   BT1   PGL32   FEt   A2
King 13 10D

———— Sanctissima, eloquentissimaque opera... que omnia olimi'a Latina facta... interpretibus, una cum doctissima Erasmi Roterodani ad pium lectorem paraclesi. *Parisiis, venundantur ab Joanne Paruo,* 1519. Reb. 32cm.

not in Adams but in BLSTC p.33   ms additions & pilcrows   UL7   (1644)   FEp   A2
King 7 10D

ATHENAEUS *of Naucratis.*   [Greek.] Deipnosophistarum libri quindecim,... cum Jacobi Dalechampii Latina versione:... Editio postrema. Juxta Isaaci Casauboni recensionem, adornata... *bound with* CASAUBON, I. Animadversionum, 1664. (2 vols. in one)
 Lugduni, sumptibus Joannis Antonii Huguetan, & Marci Antonii Ravaud, 1657. Rep. 34cm.

UL22   FEt   [O2]
King 487 11E

ATTERSOLL (William).   A commentarie upon the fourth booke of Moses, called Numbers. Containing the foundation of the Church and Common-wealth of the Israelites,... more than five hundred theologicall questions, decided and determined. *London, printed by William Jaggard, 1618.* Rep. 33cm.

STC.893   bg   MS37   FEt   K3

King 134 10D

AUCTARIUM BIBLIOTHECAE PATRUM.   De divinis Catholicae Ecclesiae officiis et mysteriis, varii vetustorum aliquot ecclesiae patrum ac scriptorum ecclesiasticorum libri;... partim editi partim repurgati per Melchiorem Hittorpium... [tomus primus] Nunc primum auctarii loco caeteris Bibliothecae Veterum Patrum tomis adjuncti. *Parisiis, [Grand Navire], 1610.* Reb. 36cm.

bg   BT1   PGL32   FEt   A3

King 475(1) 1A

———— Auctarii Bibliothecae Patrum et Auctorum Ecclesiasticorum, Tomus Secundus... Commentarios, Liturgias & Epistolas... partim ex antiquioribus editionibus, partim ex... Codicibus manuscriptis.
Parisiis, [Grand Navire], 1610. Reb. 36cm.

bg   BT1   PGL32   FEt   A3

King 475(2) 1A

AUGUSTINE, *Bp., Saint.*   Omnium operum primus (-decimus) tomus summa vigilantia... Des. Erasmum Roterodamum. (Index & 10 vols. in nine) *Basileae, [apud Jo. Frobenium], 1528–29.* English *c.1530–45* O:FPb(2)666 BS rep. 38cm.

Adams A.2157   bg   BP1   PGL19   FEt   B4

King 464 8F

AVENTINUS (Johannes).   Annalium Boiorum libri VII ex autenticis manuscriptis recogniti... Nic. Cisneri. *Basileae, ad Pernaem Lecythum, 1580.* Rep. 32cm.

Adams A.2309   bg   BP3   FEt   M1

King 109 4A

AZPILCUETA NAVARRE (Martin de).   Consiliorum sive responsorum (-volumen secundum) iuxta ordinem Decretalium dispositi... Nunc tertio typis mandati (-in lucem editum) (2 vols.) *Antverpiae, apud Petrum & Joannem Belleros, 1619.* Reb. 24cm.

p:15s   MS44   FEt   AE banded colouring   H2

King 267 8B

BABINGTON (Gervase) *Bp.*   The workes... containing comfortable notes upon the five bookes of Moses... as also an exposition... with a conference and three sermons. (3 vols. in one)
London, printed by G. Eld and M. Flesher; sold by John Parker (for Henry Featherstone), 1622. Rep. 32cm.

STC.1079   BT34   FEt   F3

King 64 6C

BACON (Francis).   Sylva sylvarum: or a naturall historie. In ten centuries... Published after the authors death, by William Rawley. *includes his* New Atlantis... A worke unfinished. (2 parts in one vol.)
London, printed by J. H. for William Lee, 1627. Rep. 28cm.

STC.1169   bg   MS39   FEt   H5

King 183 6B

BAILLIE (Robert).   *See* Parliamentary Sermons.

BAKER (*Sir* Richard).   A chronicle of the kings of England,... unto the death of King James... with a continuation in this fourth edition... to His Majesties most happy and wonderful restauration...
London, pr. by E. Cotes for G. Saubridg, and T. Williams, 1665. Reb. 32cm.

Wing B.505   LP1   FEp   [N1]

King 52 6C

BALDUIN (Friedrich).   Tractatus luculentus, posthumus... De materiâ rarissime antehac

87

enucleatâ, casibus nimirum conscientiae, summo studio elaboratus a Friderico Balduino et iam...
post... authoris mortem in lucem editus.
Wittenbergae, impensis Pauli Helwigii, 1628. Rep. 20cm.

bg   MS30   FEt   F1   King 658 8A

BALDUIN (Petrus).   *See* CICERO, M.T.

BANEZ (Domingo).   Scholastica commentaria in primum partem Thomae usque ad LXIIII quaes-
tionem... Nunc post omnes omnium editiones... summa theologorum Duacensium recogniti. (4 vols
in two)
Duaci, ex typographia Petri Borremans, 1614–15. Rep. 36cm.

bg   KG14   FEt   L1   King 54 4D

BARNES (Robert).   *See* TYNDALE, W. *etc.*

BARON (Robert), *of Aberdeen.*   ...Metaphysica generalis. Accedunt nunc primum... ex parte speciali-
li... ad usum theologiae accommodata. Opus postumum.
Londini, ex officina R. Danielis, & vaeneunt apud Th. Robinson & Ri. Davis ... Oxonienses, [1658]. Rep.
15cm.

Wing B.883   cp: g–m   DU   [K2]   King 350 7A

BARONIUS (Cesare).   Annales ecclesiastici...editio novissima ab ipsomet aucta & recognita *with*
BZOVIUS, A. Annalium ecclesiasticarum Tomus XIV, 1618. (14 vols. and supplt. in eight)
Coloniae Agrippinae, sumptibus Joannis Gymnici & Antonii Hierati, 1609–16. Rep. 36cm.

bg   BP11   FEt   M4   King 447 9F

BARTHOLOME DE MEDINA.   *See* MEDINA, B.

BASIL, 'the Great', *Saint.*   Opera Omnia: Iam recens per Wolfgangum Musculum partim locis
aliquot castigata, partim... aucta. (3 vols. in one)
Basileae, per Joan. Oporinum et haeredes Joannis Hervagii, 1565. Rep. 32cm.

Adams B.341   bg   BT1   PGL32   FEt   A2   King 119 8C

————— Opera omnia, quae reperiri potuerunt. Nunc primum Graece & Latine coniunctim edita...
Accessit appendix conciones a Symeone Magistro excerptas, & notas continet. (3 vols in two)
Parisiis, apud Michaelem Sonnium, 1618. Rep. 34cm.

bg   BT1   FEt   A2   King 544 10E

BASIRE (Isaac).   Deo & ecclesiae sacrum. Sacriledge arraigned and condemned by Saint Paul...
published first in 1646... The second edition corrected, and enlarged.
London, printed by W. G. for W. Wells, and R. Scot, 1668. L reb. 17cm.

Wing B.1033   DU   FEt   [I2]   King 327 7B

BASSOLIS (Joannes de).   Opera. In quatuor sententiarum. (first two of four parts)
Sumpt. universitatis Parisiensis, Francisci Regnault & Joannis Frellon, [1516–17]. Reb. 28cm.

Adams B.372(1–2)   lacks tp   ms: Mr Blower 21 ap'lis 1598   bg   BP0   FEp   H4   King 189 3A

BAYLE (Pierre).   The dictionary historical and critical of Mr Peter Bayle... second edition... to
which is prefixed, the life of the author, revised, corrected, and enlarged, by Mr. Des Maizeaux. (5
vols.)

London, printed for J. J. and P. Knapton et al., 1734–38. Rep. 35cm.
probably LP12

King 509 2D

———— *See also* MORERI, L.

BECON (Thomas).   [The worckes]: The seconde part of the bokes, which Thomas Beacon hath made & published, diligently perused and corrected, and now newely set forth, *with* The thyrd parte of the bookes,... nowe first of all published and set forth in printe. (2 vols. in one)
London, [John Day], 1560–63. Reb. 29cm.
STC.1710 (lacking Vol. 1)   ms owner: John Gibbon whose verse on Becon's portrait is on tp verso
Vol.3   LP2   [I3]

King 181 8C

BEDE,'The Venerable', *Saint.*   Opera quotquot reperiri potuerunt omnia hac ultima impressione ornatius in lucem edita. (8 vols. in three)
Coloniae Agrippinae, sumpt. Anton. Hierati & Joan. Gymnici, 1612. Rep. 37cm.
bg   BT21   PGL1   FEt   B3

King 479 5G

BELL (Robert).   *See* SPAIN – History.

BELLARMINE (Robert), *Abp., Saint.*   Disputationes... de controversiis Christianae fidei, adversus huius temporis haereticos, quatuor tomis comprehensae... Editio aucta et emendata... ab auctore vulgato Romae. (4 vols. in three)
Parisiis, ex officinis Tri-Adelphorum, 1613. Prob. London GS cy rep. 34cm.
bg   KG5   FEt   L2

King 543 8E

———— *See also* BRIGHTMAN, T. *and* PAREUS, D.

BERING (Vitus).   Orosii Annilonis dissertatio de bello Dano-Anglico... dissensionum inter geminos populos, contentionumq; causis... de iniquitate Anglici scripti...
*Ad exemplum Parisiis impressum, [s.n.,*1665]. L reb. 19cm.
½t only   LP1   FEt   [I2]

King 248 7B

BERNARD, *Saint.*   ...Opera omnia... diligentissime nunc primum recognita, ... accesserunt... episto-lae... editae, & notae Jo. Picardi.
Antverpiae, apud Joannem Keerbergium, 1609. Rep. 34cm.
bg   BT1   PGL32   FEt   B3

King 50 3E

BEROALDUS (Matthaeus).   Chronicon, scripturae sacrae autoritate constitutum. (5 parts in one vol.)
[Geneva], apud Anton. Chuppinum, 1575. donor's ABS rep. 30cm.
Adams B.757   ms owner & additions: John Hollins   UL24   FEm   [N2]

King 205 2B

BERTIUS (Petrus).   Scripta adversaria collationis Hagiensis habitae anno 1611... De divina prae-destinatione & capitibus ei adnexis, quae... Latina fecit. (2 parts in one vol.)
Lugduni Batavorum, excudit Joannes Patius, 1615. Rep. 20cm.
LP4   FEt   [H3]

King 252 10B

BESODNERUS (Petrus), *ed.*   Bibliotheca theologica, hoc est, index bibliorum praecipuorum, eo-rundemq;... D. Christophori Pelargi inprimis ex bibliotheca eius instructissima... concinnavit.
Francofurti Marchionum, sumtibus Johannis Thymii, excudebat Johann. Eichorn, 1608. L reb. 18cm.
BT1   FEp   H2

King 263 9B

BESSE (Pierre de).   Conciones, sive conceptus theologici ac praedicabiles ... habitae... interprete Matthia Martinetz... Editio quinta... Tomus tertius(-quartus). (2 vols. of four)
Coloniae Agrippinae, sumptibus Joannis Kinchii, 1629. Reb. 21cm.

LP4   [I2]   King 664 11B

BEVERIDGE (William), *Bp.*   Codex canonum Ecclesiae primitivae vindicatus ac illustratus.
Londini, typis S. Roycroft. Prostant apud Robertum Scott, 1678. Donor's GS (1681) rep. 24cm.

Wing B.2090   UL26   AEm   [N2]   King 285 9B

————— *ed.* [Greek.] sive Pandectae canonum SS. Apostolorum et conciliorum ab Ecclesia Graeca receptorum;... quorum plurima e Bibliothecae Bodleianae aliarumque MSS codicibus nunc primum edita:... in duos tomos. (2 vols.)
Oxonii, e theatro Sheldoniano, sumptibus Guilielmi Wells & Roberti Scott Lond., 1672. Reb. 43cm.

Wing B.2115   UL26   AEm   [N2]   King 436 1E

BEZA (Theodore).   Icones, id est verae imagines virorum doctrina simul et pietate illustrium... additis... vitae & operae descriptionibus...
[Geneva], apud Joannem Laonium, 1580. V 24cm.

Adams B.915   lacks Cij and Dj   ms donor's signature   MS45   FEp   [I3]   King 286 9B

————— Volumen primum (alterum-tertium) tractationum theologicarum in quibus pleraque Christianae religionis dogmata adversus haereses... defenduntur. Editio secunda ab auctore recognita. (3 vols. in one)
Genevae, excudebat Eustathius Vignon, 1582. Reb. 33cm.

Adams B.955, 958 & 959   bg   BP8   PGL12   FEt   D3   King 137 9D

————— *See also* BIBLE – French, 1588; BIBLE – Latin, 1603; BIBLE – N.T. Greek, 1598; CALVIN, J., 1593 *and* MERCER, J.

BIBLE – English.   [The Byble in Englyshe. A version of the seventh Great Bible, but containing some leaves from the fifth. *London, printed by Rycharde Grafton*, December 1541.] BS rep. 38cm.

STC.2076   many defects: lacks all tp and 6 prelim. leaves. Starts: A descripcyon and successe... 1 fo., then Cranmer's preface, 3 fos. Biblical text complete in 5 parts, but Nn6–8 lacking at end   graffiti in many hands UL7 (1644)   FEt   K5   King 161 1E

BIBLE – French.   La Bible, qui est toute la saincte escriture du vieil & du nouveau Testament:... le tout reveu... par les Pasteurs & Professeurs de l'Eglise de Geneve.
A Geneve, [s.n.], 1588. Prob. London early 17th cent. GS rep. 41cm.

Adams B.1153   bg   widow of KG3 (label and letter from Beza lost)   FEt   K5   King 472 7G

BIBLE – Hebrew.   Biblia Hebraica, without points. [Old Testament] *with* Novum Testamentum Syriacum literis chaldaicis excusum. (2 parts in one vol.) *bound with* STERNHOLD, T. and HOPKINS, J. The whole booke of psalmes..., 1633. Rep. 16cm
[Amsterdam, printed by Christopher Plantin, 1574.]

Adams B.1801 and B.1233   O.T. lacks tp and begins at p. 17 of Genesis   ms additions by donor and others on all blanks   UL19   [K2]   King 332 5A

BIBLE – Latin.   Prima(-sexta) pars huius operis: contine's textum Biblie cu' postilla Hugonis Cardinalis... (6 vols.)
[Basel], Johannes Amerbach et al., [1504]. Reb. 32cm.

Adams B.984   ms donor's autographs; Samuel Ward inscr. on tp vol.5   bg   MS6   FEp   G5

King 8 11D

———— Biblia cu' pleno apparatu summariorum co'cordantiarum ... distinctio'e Basilee nuper impressa. Additi sunt Eusebii Pamphili... decem canones;...
Basilea, [per J. Froben], 1514. Reb. 32cm.

Adams B.992   ms owner, p & additions: Thomas Toppclyff D.C.L. 6s   bg   BP0   FEp   A4

King 133=506 3A

———— Veteri Testamenti cum catholica expositione Ecclesiastica *and* Novi Testamenti catholica expositio Ecclesiastica id est Ex universis probatis theologis... excerpta ab Augustino Marlorato. Editio secunda. (5 vols. in two)
Genevae, excudebat Henricus Stephanus, Huldrichi Fuggeri typographus, 1562–64.   London cy O: HMa(6)
BS wooden bds. rep. 40cm.

Adams M.618   ms owner & additions: Thos. Reddrich   bg   BT24   PGL30   FEt   C3

King 452 11E

———— Biblia sacra ex Sebastiani Castalionis postrema recognitione... Cum annotationibus eiusdem,... (2 vols. in one)
Basileae, per Petrum Pernam, 1573. Prob. London late 17th cent. GR rep. 35cm.

Adams B.1083   UL23   [N2]

King 514 8D

———— Testamenti veteris Biblia Sacra, sive libri canonici... Latini recens ex Hebraeo facti,... ab Immanuele Tremellio, & Franscisco Junio... Novi Testamenti... ex Graeco a Theodoro Beza in Latinum versos notisque itidem illustratos. *Hanoviae, typis Wechelianis, apud Claudium Marnium & haeredes Joannis Aubrii*, 1603. Rep. 35cm.

bg   BT22   FEt   K3

King 491 3C

———— Sacrorum bibliorum pars I.-III. Secundum veterem seu vulgatam translationem, ad fontes Hebraici textus emendata:...editio ultima. (3 vols.)
[Frankfurt], ex officina typographica Matthiae Beckeri [Joannis Saurii] sumptibus Joannis Berneri, 1608–9. Reb. 34cm.

cp: a.r.f.   bg   BT18   PGL25   FEt   E5

King 73 3C

———— *See also* NICHOLAS *of Lyra.*

BIBLE – Polyglot.   Sacra Biblia, Hebraice, Graece, et Latine. Cum annotationibus Francisci Vatabli... Omnia cum editione Complutensi diligenter collata. Editio postrema... Novum Testamentum Graecolatinum Ben. Ariae Montani (2 vols.)
[Heidelberg], ex officina Commeliniana, 1599. Rep. 38cm.

Adams B.975   BP12   PGL26   FEt   K5

King 459 10F

———— Sacra Biblia polyglotta, complectentia textus originales Hebraicum... in sex tomos... edidit Brianus Waltonus. (6 vols.)
Londini, imprimebat Thomas Roycroft, 1655–57. Rep. 45cm.

Wing B.2797   UL17 (1661)   gilt-msGL   AEm   [N3]

King 433 1E

BIBLE – O.T. – Greek.   Septuaginta interpretum Tomus I–III, & tomus ultima... summa cura edidit. [by J.E. Grabe] (4 vols. in eight)
Oxonii, e theatro Sheldoniano, 1707. GRL rep. 20cm.

probably LP12

King 424 7B

BIBLE – O.T. – Hebrew. Biblia Hebraica. (4 parts in two vols.) *Parisiis, ex officina Roberti Stephani,* 1539–44. GR rep. 26cm.

Adams B.1221   ms owner and copious additions: Baroniah Dowe   bg   MS20   FEt   A1

King 284 6A

———— Biblia Hebraica. Eorundum Latina interpretatio Xantis Pagnini Lucensis, Benedicti Ariae Montani... & quorundam aliorum collato studio,... (2 vols. in one)
[Antwerp], ab Christophoro Plantino, 1571. Reb. 38cm.

Adams B.970   cp: .xu.   BP3   FEt   K5

King 471 10F

BIBLE – O.T. – Latin Textus Biblie cum glossa ordinaria Nicholai de lyra postilla moralitatibus eiusdem, Pauli Burgensis additionibus, Matthie Thoring replicis. Prima pars.
Basilea, Johann Petri & J. Froben, [1506]. prob. Cambridge (not the Heavy Binder) BS rep. 36cm.

Adams B.985(1)   ms owner: Wˢ Smarte Gippi' p (possibly for three vols.): £4 2s   bg   BP0   FEt
G5

King 4(1) 3A

———— Biblia latina cum postillis Nicolai de Lyra et quaestionibus eiusdem contra judaicum perfidiam et additionibus Pauli Burgensis (Second and third of 4 vols.)
Strasburg, [Jean Grüniger], 1492. Cambridge (Heavy Binder, 1485–1505) BS rep. 30cm.

Goff B.617(2 & 3)   vol. 3 lacks first fo.   ms inscr. on last leaf of vol. 2: 'from Jeffry Astwicke by I.
Leugar 3 Junii 1597'   woodcuts in vol. 3   bg   BP0   FEBLt   G5   King 4(2 & 3) 3A

BIBLE – N.T. – English.   The text of the New Testament translated out of the vulgar Latine by the Papists... at Rhemes, thereunto is added the translation used in the Church of England. The whole worke, perused... more amply than in the former edition... by W. Fulke.
Londini, impensis G. B., 1601. Prob. London cy GS rep. 33cm.

STC.2900   bg   BT13   [PGL27]   FEt   F3

King 561 8D

BIBLE – N.T. – Greek and Latin.   Novum Testamentum... eiusdem Th. Bezae annotationes,... quasi brevi commentario explicatur. (2 parts in one vol.)
[Geneva, Stephanus], 1598 L reb. 35cm.

Adams B.1715   bg   MS12   FEt   K3

King 548 6D

———— *See also* WALAEUS, B.

BIBLE – N.T. – Latin.   Novum Testamentum annotationibus eruditis & piis iam primum explicatum et illustratum, per Lucam Lossium. (4 vols. in three)
Francoforti, apud haeredes Christiani Egenolphi, 1558–62. German cy BS V rep. 32cm.

Adams L.1527   cp: g (in 567)   BT40 (1636)   FEt   E5

King 565, 566 & 567 9D

———— *See also* NICHOLAS *of Lyra.*

BIBLE – Concordance – Greek, Hebrew and Latin.   KIRCHER (Conrad). Concordantiae veteris Testamenti Graecae, Ebraeis vocibus respondentes... lexicon Ebraicolatinum... (2 vols.)
Francofurti, apud Claudium Marnium, & heredes Johannis Aubrii, 1607. BS cy Royal Arms and GS IPSWICH 1651 rep. 26cm.

BT43   FEt   K3

King 279 5D

BIBLE – Concordance – Greek and Latin.   STEPHANUS (Henricus). Concordantiae Graecolatinae Testamenti Novi, nunc primum plenae editae... Accessit huic editioni supplementum eorum omnium quae hactenus desiderabantur. (2 parts in one vol.)

[Geneva], Oliva Pauli Stephani, 1600. L reb. 32cm.

Adams S.1758   bg   BT2   PGL16   FEt   K5

King 203 1B

——— Concordantiae Graecolatinae Testamenti Novi. Hac editione pleniores et uberiores editae... Editio secunda.
[Geneva], ex typographia Petri & Jacobi Chouet, 1624. Rep. 34cm.

DU   FEt   K5

King 630 1B

BIBLE – Concordance – Hebrew.   Concordantias Hebraicas.
[Basel, Ambrose Froben, 1581.] Reb. 37cm.

Adams B.1954   bg   BT9   PGL lost   FEt   K5

King 455 5G

BIBLE – Concordance – Latin.   Concordantiae Bibliorum id est, Dictiones omnes quae in vulgata editione Latina librorum veteris & novi testamenti leguntur.
[Frankfurt], apud Andreae Wecheli haeredes, Claudium Marnium & Joannem Aubrium, 1600. Rep. 40cm.

Adams B.1962   bg   DU   PGL lost   FEt   K5

King 470 7G

BIBLIANDER (Theodor).   Temporum a condito mundo usque ad ultimam ipsius aetatem supputatio partitio que exactior... quam scribebat Theodorus Bibliander... bound with MULERIUS, N., Judaeorum annus, 1630.
Basileae, per Joannem Oporinum, 1588. BS rep. 30cm.

cp: d.   DU   FEt   [I3]

King 126 11C

BIBLIOTHECA FRATRUM POLONORUM. See CRELLIUS, J.; SOZZINI, F.P.; SZLICHTING, J.; WOLZOGEN, J.L.

BIBLIOTHECA VETERUM PATRUM.   See LA BIGNE, M. de.

BINIUS (Severinus).   Concilia generalia, et provincialia, quaecunque reperiri potuerunt: item epistolae decretales et Romanor. pontific. vitae...in tomus quatuor distributa. (4 vols. in five)
Coloniae Agrippinae, apud Joan. Gymnicum, & Ant. Hierat., 1606. Rep. 39cm.

KG14   PGL10 under ms donor label   FEt   A3

King 446 1D

BIRCKBEK (Simon).   The Protestants evidence, taken out of good records;... distributed into severall centuries, and opened. (2 parts in one vol.)
London, printed for Robert Milbourne, 1635. Rep. 21cm.

STC.3083   ms owner: John Burro[ugh]   cp: j-n ad.   LP4   H3

King 297 7D

BISHOP (Thomas), of Ipswich.   The errors and absurdities of the Arian and Seminarian schemes,... represented in eight sermons preach'd at... St. Paul's... in... 1724, and 1725. (Lady Moyer Lectures) to which is added Concio ad Clerum in... Ecclesia Cantabrigiensi..., 1725.
London, printed for Bernard Lintot, 1726. (2 vols. in one) GR rep. 20cm.

LP10

King 418 7C

——— A plain and practical exposition of the catechism of the Church of England.
London, printed for M. Downing and T. Longman, 1736. Rep. 21cm.

ms inscr. by LP12   UL36

King 417 7C

BOCKSTADIUS (Johannes).   See SCULTETUS, A. and BOCKSTADIUS, J.

BOLTON (Samuel).   The dead saint speaking, to saints and sinners, living:... in severall treatises... never before published.
London, printed by Robert Ibbitson, for Thomas Parkhurst, 1657. Rep. 28cm.

Wing B.3518   LP1   FEt   [I3]   King 167 6A

——— *See also* Parliamentary Sermons.

BONAVENTURE, 'Doctor Seraphicus', *Saint.*   Opera Sixti V. Pont, Max. iussu diligentissime emendata...nunc primum in Germania post Roman. Vaticanam editionem prodeunt in lucem. (7 vols. in four)
Moguntiae, sumptibus Antonii Hierati, 1609. Rep. 36cm.

bg   BT27   FEt   L4   King 457 5G

BOND (John).   *See* Parliamentary Sermons.

BORRHAUS (Martin).   In sancti viri Jobi historiam salutari de mysterio crucis et de lege atque evangelio doctrina refertam... commentarii. Eiusdem in Salomonis... Ecclesiastes... annotationes. (2 vols. in one)
Basileae, per Petrum Pernam, 1564. Rep. 30cm.

Adams B.2509   bg   BT1   FEt   D2   King 105 4C

BOWLES (Oliver).   *See* Parliamentary Sermons.

BOXHORN (Marcus Zuerius).   Historia universalis sacra et profana, a Christo nato ad annum usque (1650). In qua... variae mutationes in ecclesia et republica... hactenus ineditis monumentis traduntur. (2 parts in one vol.)
Lugduni Batavorum, ex officina Petri Leffen, 1652. Rep. 20cm.

UL22   FEt   [I2]   King 357 11B

BOYLE (Robert).   A defence of the doctrine touching the spring and weight of the air, propos'd... against the objections of Franciscus Linus. *and his* An examen of Mr T. Hobbes his dialogus physicus De natura aeris as far as it concerns Mr R. Boyle's book of new experiments... *bound with his* New experiments. Oxford, 1662. (3 vols. in one)
London, printed by J. G., for Thomas Robinson in Oxon., 1662. Rep. 20cm.

Wing B.3941   LP1   FEt   [H3]   King 254 5B

——— Experiments and considerations touching colours... The beginning of an experimental history of colours. *with his* Short account of some observations... about a diamond that shines in the dark. (2 parts in one vol.)
London, printed for Henry Herringman, 1664. Reb. 18cm.

Wing B.3967   LP1   FEt   [H3]   King 378 5B

——— New experiments physico-mechanical, touching the spring of the air, and its effects, (...a new pneumatical engine) written by way of a letter. [Second edition.] Whereunto is added A defence of the experiments... against the objections of Franciscus Linus and Thomas Hobbes. (3 vols. in one)
Oxford, printed by H. Hall, for Tho: Robinson, 1662. Rep. 20cm.

Wing B.3999   LP1   FEt   [H3]   King 254 5B

——— The origine of formes and qualities, (According to the corpuscular philosophy) illustrated by considerations and experiments... Second edition. (3 parts in one vol.)
Oxford, printed by H. Hall, for Ric: Davis, 1667. Rep. 19cm.

Wing B.4015   LP1   FEt   [H3]   King 330 5B

————— Some considerations touching the usefulnesse of experimental naturall philosophy, propos'd in a familiar discourse to a friend,... Second edition. (2 parts in one vol.)
Oxford, printed by Hen: Hall, for Ric: Davis, 1664. Rep. 20cm.

Wing B.4030　LP1　FEt　[H3]

King 692 5C

BOYS (Edward).　Sixteen sermons, preached upon several occasions.
London, pr. by Richard Hodgkinson, for William Oliver, in Norwich, 1672. Reb. 22cm.

Wing B.4065　probably LP12　FEt

King 697 7D

BRADWARDINE (Thomas), *Abp.*　...De causa Dei, contra Pelagium et De virtute causarum... libri
tres:... opera et studio Henrici Savilii... Ex scriptis codicibus nunc primum editi.
Londini, ex officina Nortoniana, apud Joannem Billium, 1618. Rep. 34cm.

STC.3534　bg not on p.10　BT1　FEt　E5

King 594 9D

BREEN (Daniel van). ...Opera theologica... De tractatu... Operum Episcopii secundae parti inserto,
exhibet. (3 parts in one vol.)
Amstelaedami, sumptibus Francisci Cuperi, (Henrici Dendrini for Part 3), 1664–66. Rep. 32cm.

UL22　[O2]

King 615 1B

BRENZ (Johann).　Operum... Tomus septimus... commentarii in Acta Apostolorum... Epistolas
Pauli ad Romanos, Galatas, Philippenses, Philemonem. (Seventh of 8 vol. set: 1578–90)
Tubingae, excudebat Georgius Gruppenbachius, 1588. Chain mark rep. 32cm.

Adams B.2749　bg　BT6　PGL9　FEt　E5

King 593 9C

————— Esias propheta, commentariis explicatus. *Francoforti ad Moenum apud haeredes Petri Brubachii,*
1570. Rep. 32cm.

not in Adams　bm: τ.15.　bg　BT6　PGL9　FEt　E5

King 647 9C

————— Evangelion quod inscribitur, secundum Joannem, usque ad historiam de Lazaro...octuaginta
duabus homiliis explicatum.
Halae Suevorum, excudebant Petrus Frentz & Petrus Brubacchius, 1545 (1548). Rep. 30cm.

Adams B.2796　ms owner's signature on tp deleted　bm: τ.10.2　marginalia in 2 hands　bg　BT6
　PGL9　FEt　E5

King 646 9C

————— In Evangelion... secundum Lucam, duodecim priora capita, Homiliae centum & decem,...
octaginta in duodecim posteriora capita, ac in historiam Passionis & Resurrectionis Christi. (2 vols.)
Francoforti per Petrum Brubachium, 1563. Rep. 32cm.

Adams B.2793　bm: τ.12 (both vols.)　bg　BT6　PGL9　FEt　E5

King 590 & 628 9C

BRIDGE (William).　*See* Parliamentary Sermons.

BRIDGES (Walter).　*See* Parliamentary Sermons.

BRIDGET *of Sweden, Saint.*　Revelationes celestes beate Birgitte vidue: de regno Suecie: octo libris
divise. Adiungit etiam in fine librorum Tabula. (2 parts in one vol.)
Nurenbergensis, impensis Joannis Koberger, in officina Federici Peypus, 1517. Prob. Netherlandish cy BS
wooden boards rep. 31cm.

Adams B.2834　lacks fo.2　ms Latin donor's BL inscr. and 'opus dabet fidem verbis'　bg　BP0
FEBLt　H4

King 199(1) 3A

————Another copy. Reb. 31cm.

Adams B.2834   ms marginalia some woodcut inits. & many pilcrows hand coloured   bg   BP0
FEp   H4   King 199(2) 3A

BRIGHTMAN (Thomas).   Apocalypsis apocalypseos. Id est, Apocalypsis D. Johannis analysi et
scholiis illustrata;... & refutatio Rob. Bellarmini de Antichriste. (2 parts in one vol.)
Francofurti, prostat apud viduam Levini Hulsii, 1609. V rep. 20cm.

bg   BT25   FEt   G2   King 680 7D

BROWN (Edward), *comp.*   *See* GRATIUS, O.

BROWNE (*Sir* Thomas).   Posthumous works of the learned... late of Norwich. Printed from his
original manuscripts... to which is prefix'd his life. (8 parts in one vol.)
London, printed for W. Mears, and J. Hooke, 1723. Reb. 20cm.

lacks portrait   LP12   King 416 7C

BRUNFELS (Otto).   Annotationes... in quatuor Evangelia & Acta apostolorum, ... ex scriptoribus
congestae... divinarum rerum candidatis, usui futurae. *bound with* ZACHARIAS, Bp., De concordia,
1535.
Argentorati, Georgio Ulrichero, 1535. English cy O: ANj(1)568 BS (claspmarks) rep. 32cm.

Adams B.1813   ms 'Mr Blower 31 maij 1599' and annotations, drawings and pilcrows in the same
hand in both vols.   bg   BP0   FEt   D2   King 112 4C

BUCER (Martin).   Metaphrasis et enarratio in Epistola ad Romanos. *with his* In Epistolam ad
Ephesios,... [M.B.] habitae Cantabrigiae in Anglia, Anno MDL & LI... nunc primum in lucem
editae... Immanuelis Tremelii. (2 vols. in one)
Basileae, apud Petrum Pernam, 1562. Reb. 32cm.

Adams B.3044   bg   BT6   PGL9   FEt   C4   King 642 10C

———— In sacra quatuor Evangelia, enarrationes perpetuae, secundum & postremum recognitae.
with Psalmorum libri quinque ad Hebraicam veritatem traducti, et... enarrati. Eiusdem commentarii
in librum Judicum & in Sophoniam Prophetam. (2 vols. in one)
[Geneva], Oliva Roberti Stephani, 1553–54. L reb. 34cm.

Adams B.3041   bg   BT6   PGL9   FEt   C4   King 550 10D

———— Scripta Anglicana fere omnia... a Con. Huberto... singulari fide collecta... Adiuncta est
historia de obitu Buceri... illi & Paulo Fagio... digna contigere.
Basileae, ex Petri Pernae officina, 1577. Rep. 32cm.

Adams B.3049   bg   BT6   PGL9   FEt   C4   King 636 10C

BUCHMAN (Theodor), *comp.*   *See* BIBLIANDER, T.

BULLINGER (Johann Heinrich).   Commentarii in omnes Pauli Apostoli Epistolas, atque etiam in
Epistolam ad Hebraeos. Adiunximus eiusdem authoris Commentarios in omnes Epistolas Canoni-
cas.
Tiguri, apud Christophorum Froschoverum, 1582. Rep. 31cm.

Adams B.3241   bg   BT6   PGL9   FEt   C4   King 633 10C

———— Daniel sapientissimus Dei Propheta,... expositus homilis LXVI... Accessit... Epitome temporum et rerum ab orbe condito ad excidium... (2 parts in one vol.)

Tiguri, excudebat C. Froschoverus, 1576. Rep. 31cm.

Adams B.3218   bg   BT6   PGL9   FEt   C4

King 211 10C

———— In sacrosanctum Evangelium... secundum Marcum, commentariorum lib.VI... *with* In Acta Apostolorum commentariorum libri VI, ab authore recogniti... *and with* In Apocalypsim... revelatam quidem per angelum Domini, ... conscriptam a Johanne... conciones centum. (3 vols. in one)
Tiguri, apud Frosch., in officina Froschoviana, 1554–84–90. Rep. 31cm.

Adams B.3224 & 3236   1590 later edition of Adams B.3250   bg   BT6   PGL9   FEt   C4

King 648 10C

———— Isais excellentissimus Dei Propheta,... expositus homiliis CXC.
Tiguri, excudebat Christophorus Froschoverus, 1567. Rep. 31cm.

Adams B.3213   bg   BT6   PGL9   FEt   C4

King 637 10C

BURCHARD, *Abbot of Ursperg.*   ...Chronicum absolutissimum a Nino Assyriorum rege usque ad tempora Friderici II... usque ad Carolum V. Augustum,... collecta.
Basileae, apud Petrum Pernam, 1569. V 31cm.

Adams C.2520   bg   BP3   FEp   M3

King 120 1C

BURGESS (Anthony).   *See* Parliamentary Sermons.

BURGESS (Cornelius).   *See* Parliamentary Sermons.

BURNET (Gilbert), *Bp.*   The history of the Reformation of the Church of England. In two parts... The second edition, corrected. (2 vols.)
London, printed by T. H. for Richard Chiswell, 1681. L reb. 31cm.

Wing B.5798   LP7   AEm   [N2]

King 614 6B

BURNET (Thomas).   The theory of the earth: containing an account of the original of the earth, and of all the general changes... till the consummation of all things. The two first books concerning the deluge, and... paradise.
London, printed by R. Norton, for Walter Kettilby, 1684. Rep. 30cm.

Wing B.5950   LP7   [N2]

King 204 6B

BURROUGHES (Jeremiah).   *See* Parliamentary Sermons.

BURTON (William).   A commentary on Antoninus his itinerary, or journies of the Romane empire, so far as it concerneth Britain:... with a chorographicall map...
London, printed by Tho. Roycroft; and to be sold by Henry Twyford, and T. Twyford, 1658. L reb. 28cm.

Wing B.6185   UL24   msGL   FEt   [N1]

King 78 6A

———— The description of Leicester Shire; containing matters of antiquitye, historye, armorye, and genealogy...
London, printed for W. Jaggard for J. White, 1622. Reb. 27cm.

STC.4179   lacks tp   UL24   msGL   FEp   [N2]

King 168 6A

BUXTORF (Johannes).   Lexicon Hebraicum et Chaldaicum:... accessere huic editioni radices Ebraicae cum versione Belgica. (2 parts in one vol.)
Amstelodami, sumptibus Johannis Jansonii Junioris, 1654–55. Reb. 18cm.

additional hand coloured engr. illus. title (1655) 'Germanica' under pasted correction label 'Belgica'   UL19   FEt   [K1]

King 387 7C

———— Thesaurus grammaticus linguae sanctae Hebraeae, duobus libris methodice propositus...
editio sexta, recognita a Johanne Buxtorfio, filio.
Basileae, impensis Johannis Buxtorfi junioris, typis Joh. Jacobi Deckeri, 1663. Reb. 18cm.

cp: 3q 4 (m over 3)　UL19　FEt　[K1]　　　　　　　　　　　　　　　　　King 375 7C

BYFIELD (Richard).　*See* Parliamentary Sermons.

BZOVIUS (Abraham).　Annalium ecclesiasticorum post... Caesarem Baronium, Tomus XIV. Opus
nunc primum in lucem editum. (8th vol. of set)
Coloniae Agrippinae, apud Antonium Boetzerum, 1618. Rep. 36cm.

bg　BP11　FEt　M4　　　　　　　　　　　　　　　　　　　　　　　　King 447 9F

CALAMY (Edmund), *the elder.*　*See* Parliamentary Sermons.

CALEPINUS (Ambrosius).　Dictionarium undecim linguarum,... respondent autem Latinis voca-
bulis Hebraica, Graeca, Gallica, Italica, Germanica, Belgica, Hispanica, Polonica, Ungarica, Anglica... *and* Onomasticum vero a Conrado Gesnero... (2 parts in one vol.)
Basileae, per Sebastianum Henricpetri, 1605. Reb. 36cm.

bg　MS41　FEt　K5　　　　　　　　　　　　　　　　　　　　　　　　King 481 10F

CALVIN (Jean).　Commentarii in Isaiam prophetam. Primum collecti opera... N. Gallasii:... nunc
postremo aliquot locis ex autographo ipsius authoris restituti.
Genevae, apud Eustathium Vignon, 1583. Rep. 31cm.

Adams B.1585　bg　BP4　msGL　FEt　C1　　　　　　　　　　　　　King 113 4B

———— Commentarii in omnes Pauli Apostoli Epistolas, atque etiam in Epistolam ad Hebraeos.
Adiunximus... Commentarios in omnes Epistolas Canonicas. (2 vols. in one)
Genevae, apud haeredes Eustathii Vignon, 1600. Rep. 34cm.

Adams C.324　bg　BP4　msGL　FEt　C1　　　　　　　　　　　　　King 28 4B

———— Commentarius in librum Psalmorum. In hac postrema editione praeter multos locos...
emendatos... representavimus...
Genevae, apud Joannem Vignon, 1610. Rep. 32cm.

bg　BP4　msGL　FEt　C1　　　　　　　　　　　　　　　　　　　King 122 4B

———— Harmonia ex Evangelistis tribus composita, Matthaeo, Marco, & Luca, commentariis... expo-
sita:... eiusdem in Johannem evangelistam commentarius. *with his* Commentarii integri in Acta
Apostolorum. (2 vols. in one)
Genevae, excudebat Joannes Vignon, 1609–14. Rep. 34cm.

bg　BP4　msGL　FEt　C1　　　　　　　　　　　　　　　　　　　King 45 4B

———— Homiliae in I. librum Samuelis. Ex Gallicis Latinae factae & nunc primum in lucem editae.
Genevae, excudebat Gabriel Carterius, 1614. Rep. 33cm.

cp: k.　bg　BP4　msGL　FEt　C1　　　　　　　　　　　　　　　　King 46 4B

———— Institutio Christianae religionis.
Genevae, apud Johannem le Preux, 1609. Rep. 32cm.

Hingeston note of 19 May 1748 return　bg　BP4　msGL　FEt　C1　　　　King 47 4B

———— In librum Jobi conciones. Ab ipsius concionantis ore fideliter... nunc vero primum Latina
editae... cum praefatione Theodori Bezae.

Genevae, apud haeredes Eustathii Vignon, 1593. Rep. 34cm.

Adams C.285   bg   BP4   msGL   FEt   C1

King 43 4B

———— In quinque libros Mosis commentarii... in librum Josue commentarius. (2 vols. in one)
[Geneva], in officina Sanctandreana, 1595. Rep. 30cm.

Adams C.278   bg   BP4   msGL   FEt   C1

King 213 4B

———— Praelectiones, in duodecim Prophetas (quos vocant) minores...
Genevae, apud Joannem Vignon, 1610. Rep. 31cm.

bg   BP4   msGL   FEt   C1

King 104 4B

———— Praelectiones in Ezechielis prophetae viginti capita priora,... J. Budae & C. Jonuilaeo labore & industria excerptae. *bound with his* Epistolae et responsa. (2 vols. in one)
Genevae, apud Johannem Vignon, Petrum & Jacobum Chouet, 1616. Reb. 34cm.

cp: a.   bg   BP4   msGL   FEt   C1

King 572 4B

———— Praelectiones in librum prophetiarum Jeremiae, et lamentationes Joannis Budaei & Caroli Jonuillaei labore & industria exceptae... Tertia editio.
Genevae, apud haered. Eustath. Vignon, 1589. Rep. 30cm.

Adams C.298   bg   BP4   msGL   FEt   C1

King 601 4B

———— Tractatus theologici omnes, in unum volumen certis classibus congesti:... Tertia editio... cui accesserunt... in libros Senecae de Clementia commentarii. (2 vols. in one)
Genevae, ex typographia Jacobi Stoer, 1611. Reb. 34cm.

bg   BP4   msGL   FEt   C1

King 616 4B

CAMDEN (William).   Anglica, Normannica, Hibernica, Cambrica, a veteribus scripta: ... nunc primum in lucem editi, ex Bibliotheca Guilielmi Camdeni.
Francofurti, impensis Claudii Marnii & haeredum Johannis Aubrii, 1603. L reb. 36cm.

bg   BP13   FEt   M2

King 49 7E

———— (Gibson, Edmund, *ed.*) Camden's Britannia, newly translated into English: with large additions...
London, printed by F. Collins, for A. Swalle, and A. & J. Churchil, 1695. Reb. 37cm.

Wing C.359   lacks map of Cornwall   LP6   [N4]

King 76 7G

CAMERARIUS (Philippus).   Operae horarum subcisivarum sive meditationes historicae auctiores quam antea editae... Centuria prima, 1615. *also includes* Centuria altera, 1620. *and* Centuria tertia, 1618. (3 vols. in one)
Francofurti, typis Egenolphi Emmelii, [Nicholai Hoffmani], impensis Petri Kopffii, 1615–20. Reb. 21cm.

MS30   FEt   H2

King 266 7D

CAMERON (John).   [Greek.] Opera partim ab auctore ipso edita... e Gallico nunc primum in Latinam linguam translata.
Genevae, in officina Jacobi Chouet, 1642. IPSWICH 1651 GS rep. 32cm.

UL9   FEt   K4

King 622 8D

CAREW (Richard).   The survey of Cornwall. Written by Richard Carew of Antonie, Esquire. (2 books in one vol.)
London, printed by S. S[tafford] for John Jaggard, 1602. Rep. 19cm.

STC.4615   ms owners: Robert Carew, Andrew Lenn (1636) and other names: Ralph May, Wm. Rawe and ms notes   UL24   msGL   [N2]

King 678 7C

CARTER (Thomas).   *See* Parliamentary Sermons.

CARTER (William).   *See* Parliamentary Sermons.

CARTWRIGHT (Thomas).   Commentarii succincti & dilucidi in proverbia Salomonis... praefatio... Johannis Polyandri.
Lugduni Batavorum, apud Guilielmum Brewsterum, 1617. Rep. 20cm.

bg   MS25   FEt   G2   King 223 7C

————— A confutation of the Rhemists translation, glosses, and annotations on the New Testament,... by occasion whereof the true sence, scope and doctrine... by them abused, is now given.
Printed in the year 1618 at Leiden by W. Brewster. Reb. 29cm.

STC.4709   bg   MS35   FEt   F3   King 198 6B

CARYL (Joseph).   *See* Parliamentary Sermons.

CASAUBON (Isaac).   Animadversionum in Athenaei Deipnosophistas. Editio postrema, authoris cura. *bound with* ATHENAEUS, Deipnosophistarum libri XV, 1657. (2 vols. in one)
Lugduni, sumptibus Joannis-Antonii Huguetan & Marci-Antonii Ravaud, 1664. Rep. 34cm.

UL22   FEt   [O2]   King 487 11E

————— *See also* ARISTOTLE.

CASE (Thomas).   *See* Parliamentary Sermons.

CASSIODORUS (Flavius Magnus Aurelius).   *See* NICEPHORUS CALLISTUS *and* DIODORUS, S.

CASTELL (Edmund).   Lexicon heptaglotton. (1 vol. in two)
Londini, imprimebat Thomas Roycroft, 1669. Rep. 41cm.

Wing C.1224   DU   AEm   [N3]   King 435 1E

CASTELLIO (Sebastian).   *See* BIBLE – Latin, 1573.

CASTIGLIONE (Baldassare).   Il cortegiano... nuovamente stampato, & con somma diligentia riveduto. (4 books in one vol.)
Vinegia, per Domenico Giglio, 1587. prob. English BS reb. 13cm.

Adams C.941   ms owners: Henry Glemham, John Wallace   cp: a.f.   p: 2s 6d   UL32   [N2]
King 341 5A

CAWDREY (Daniel).   *See* Parliamentary Sermons.

CHAMBERS (Humphry).   *See* Parliamentary Sermons.

CHAMIER (Daniel).   [Hebrew.] Panstratiae Catholicae, sive controversiarum de religione adversus pontificios corpus. Tomis quatuor distributum. (4 vols. in two)
Francofurti, apud Egenolphum Emmelium, 1627. IPSWICH GS (now vol. 2 only) rep. 37cm.

bg   KG8   FEt   D4   King 463 4E

CHARLES I. Basilika.   The works of King Charles the martyr:... with the history of his life; as also of his tryal and martyrdome. Second edition. *London, printed for Ric. Chiswell,* 1687. Rep. 38cm.

Wing C.2076   UL31   FEt   [O2]   King 547 6D

———— *See also* EIKON BASILIKE, 1649.

CHATEILLON (Sebastien). *See* BIBLE - Latin, 1573.

CHEKE (*Sir* John). De pronuntiatione Graecae potissimum linguae disputationes cum Stephano Wintonensi Episcopo, septem contrariis epistolis comprehensae, magna quadam & elegantia & eruditione refertae.
Basileae, per Nicol. Episcopium juniorem, 1555. Early 17th cent. GS rep. 17cm.
Adams C.1432   ms Latin inscription dated 1564   p: xviii^d   probably LP12   King 404 11A

CHEMNITZ (Martin). Examinis Concilii Tridentini... opus integrum, quatuor partes... uno volumine complectens. (4 parts in one vol.) *Genevae, excudebat Stephanus Gamonetus,* 1614. IPSWICH GS rep. 32cm.
bg   BT10   FEt   E4
                King 9 8D

———— Harmoniae Evangelicae... primum inchoatae, & per Polycarpum Lyserum continuatae, libri quinque,... uno hoc volumine... emendatiores editi. (2 parts in one vol.)
[Geneva], excudebat Petrus Aubertus, 1615. IPSWICH GS rep. 33cm.
bg   BT10   FEt   E4
                King 37 8D

———— Loci theologici... editi opera & studio Polycarpi Lyseri. Editio nova, emaculata: cui nunc recens accesserunt fundamenta sanae doctrina de vera... Item: Libellus de duabus naturis in Christo.. (5 parts in one vol.)
Witebergae, typis Martini Henckelii [Johannis Gormanni], impensis Clementis Bergeri & Zachariae Schreri, 1610. IPSWICH GS rep. 32cm.
bg   BT10   FEt   E4
                King 35 8D

CHEYNELL (Francis). *See* Parliamentary Sermons.

CHILD (*Sir* Josiah). A new discourse of trade, wherein is recommended several weighty points relating to companies of merchants. The Act of navigation. Naturalization of strangers. And our woollen manufactures... and the nature of plantations.
London, printed, and sold by Sam. Crouch, Tho. Horne, and Jos. Hindmarsh, 1694.   L reb.   16cm.
Wing C.3861   probably LP12
                King 406 7A

CHILLINGWORTH (William). The religion of Protestants a safe way to salvation. Or, an answer to a book... which pretends to prove the contrary. To which is added in this third impression The apostolical institution of Episcopacy... As also, IX sermons. (3 vols. in one)
London, printed by E. Cotes, for J. Clark, to be sold by Thomas Thornicroft, 1664. Rep. 28cm.
Wing C.3890   LP3   FEt   [I3]
                King 197 6A

CHIRINO DE SALAZAR (Fernando). *See* SALAZAR, F.Q.

CHISHULL (Edmund). Antiquitates Asiaticae Christianam aeram antecedentes; ex primariis monumentis Graecis descriptae, Latine versae,... commentariis illustratae. Accedit Monumentum Ancyranum. De nummo... dissertatio, (nunc correctior). *with* Inscriptio sigea antiquissima..., 1721. (two of three parts in one vol.)
Londini, typis Guil. Bowyer, 1728. Reb. 33cm.
LP17   [O4]
                King 541 6D

———Inscriptio sigea antiquissima [Greek.] exarata commentario eam... illustravit. *included with his* Antiquitates Asiaticae, 1728. (First of three parts)
Londini, prostant apud Guil. & Joan. Innys, 1721. Reb. 33cm
LP17   [O4]   King 541 6D

CHOQUET (François Hyacinthe).   De origine gratiae sanctificantis... libri tres. (3 parts in one vol.)
Duaci, ex officina Balthazaris Belleri, 1628. L reb. 21cm.
p:L1   bg   MS30   FEt   H2   King 291 9B

CHRYSOSTOM (John), *Saint.   See* JOHN CHRYSOSTOM, *Saint.*

CHYTRAEUS (David).   [Opera 4 vols.] Operum tomus secundus.   In Historiam Josue, Judicum, Ruth, in Prophetas... minores:... & onomasticon theologicum. (one vol. of four)
Lipsiae, impensis Henningi Grosii, Michael Lantzenberger, 1599. Rep. 30cm.
Adams C.1572   bg   BT19   PGL29   FEt   E4   King 177 11C

———*See also* SCHUBERT, C.

CICERO (Marcus Tullius).   De officiis lib.III cum copiosissimis viri... commentariis... a Petro Balduino... restituta *with his* Laelius, sive de amicitia dialogus *and his* Cato major, seu de senectute *also his* Paradoxa, ad M. Brutum. (4 parts in one)
Parisiis, apud Sebastianum Nivellium, 1556. former clasps German cy (roll signed CB 1556) BS rep. 24cm.
not in Adams   DU   FEt   [K2]   King 278 9B

CLAVIUS (Christophorus).   *See* EUCLID.

CLEMENT, *of Alexandria, Saint.*   Opera omnia ante annos quadraginta e Graeco in Latinum conversa, nunc vero recognita... a Gentiano Herveto.
Parisiis, apud Claudium Chappelet, 1612. Rep. 34cm.
bg   BT1   PGL32   FEt   A4   King 14 8E

CLUVER (Philip).   Introductio in universam geographiam tam veterem quam novam... tabulis... ac notis olim ornata a J. Bunone, (1697). Quibus in hac editione Londinensi accedunt additamenta plurima.
Londini, typis M. Jenour, impensis Joannis Nicholsoni, 1711. BS rep. 24cm.
donor's signature and date 1754   LP12   King 316 6A

COLEMAN (Thomas).   *See* Parliamentary Sermons.

COMBEFIS (François).   Bibliotheca patrum concionatoria, hoc est anni totius evangelia... omnia octo voluminibus comprehensa. (8 vols.)
Parisiis, sumptibus Antonii Bertier, 1662. Rep. 37cm.
LP8   (1706)   FEt   [O3]   King 449 3E

COMBER (Thomas).   The right of tithes re-asserted: wherein the proofs from divine institution,... and positive laws are further strengthened... from the objections taken out of Mr. Selden's History of Tithes. By the author of The right of tithes asserted, &c.
London, printed for H. Brome, and R. Clavel, 1680. Rep. 18cm.
Wing C.5489   probably LP12   King 411 7B

CONANT (John).　*See* Parliamentary Sermons.

CONTARINI (Gasparo), *Cardinal.*　Opera.
Parisiis, apud Sebastianum Nivellium, 1571. Rep. 33cm.

Adams C.2560　bg　BTI　FEt　L4　　　　　　　　　　　　　　　King 135 9D

CONRAD, *Abbot of Leichtenau, attrib.*　*See* BURCHARD, *Abbot of Ursperg.*

CORBET (Edward).　*See* Parliamentary Sermons.

CORNELIUS A LAPIDE　[STEEN (Cornelius van den).]　Commentaria in duodecim prophetas minores (in sex prophetas posteriores). (2 parts in one vol.)
Antverpiae, apud Martinum Nutium, 1625. Rep. 34cm.

crucifixion on tp inked over　bg　BT19　FEt　F4　　　　　　　　King 560 9E

———— Commentaria in Ezechielem Prophetam. *with his* Commentaria in Danielem Prophetam. (2 vols. in one)
Parisiis, apud Societatem Minimam, 1622. Rep. 34cm.

bg　BT19　FEt　F4　　　　　　　　　　　　　　　　　　　King 578 9E

———— Commentaria in omnes S. Pauli epistolas.
Antverpiae, apud Martinum Nutium, [1614–21]. Rep. 35cm.

lacks tp　bg　BT19　FEt　F4　　　　　　　　　　　　　　　　King 62 9D

———— Commentaria in quatuor prophetas maiores... *with* Commentaria in Jeremiam prophetam, Threnos, et Baruch. (2 vols. in one)
Parisiis, apud Societatem Minimam, 1622. Rep. 33cm.

bg　BT19　FEt　F4　　　　　　　　　　　　　　　　　　　King 57 9E

———— Commentarii in IV Evangelia, in duo volumina divisi. (2 vols. in one)
Lugduni, sumptib. Gabrielis Boissat & Sociorum, 1638. Reb. 35cm.

bg　BT19　FEt　F4　　　　　　　　　　　　　　　　　　　King 558 9E

———— In pentateuchum Mosis commentaria. Editio ultima, aucta & recognita.
Lutetiae Parisiorum, ex officina Edmundi Martini, 1626. Rep. 35cm.

bg　BT19　FEt　F4　　　　　　　　　　　　　　　　　　　King 577 9E

CORPUS JURIS CIVILIS.　*See* JUSTINIAN.

COTELIER (Jean-Baptiste)　SS. Patrum qui temporibus Apostolicis floruerunt; Barnabae, Clementis, Hermae, Ignatii, Polycarpi; opera edita et inedita vera et supposititia... ex MSS codicibus correxit, ac eruit;... (3 parts in 2 vols.)
Luteciae Parisiorum, typis Petri le Petit, 1672. Rep. 35cm.

UL22　FEt　[O2]　　　　　　　　　　　　　　　　　King 476 and 492 6D

COWPER (William), *Bp.*　The workes of Mr. Willia' Cowper late Bishop of Galloway. Now newly collected into one Volume...
London, imprinted for John Budge, 1623. Reb. 33cm.

STC.5909　bg　MS31　FEt　F3　　　　　　　　　　　　　　King 68 3E

CRAKANTHORP (Richard). Defensio Ecclesiae Anglicanae, contra Antonii de Dominis:... opus posthumum. Johanne Barkham in lucem editum.
Londini, ex typographia Bibliopolarum, 1625. Rep. 22cm.
STC.5975   p: 6s 6d   cp: g–e   LP4   [H3]   King 295 7D

————A treatise of the fift general councel held at Constantinople... Published by his brother Geo: Cracanthorp.
London, printed for R. M... for the benefit of the children of John Mynshew, deceased, 1634. Rep. 30cm.
STC.5984   LP4   [I4]   King 606 6A

CRANTZ (Albert).   *See* KRANTZ, A.

CRELLIUS (Johannes).   Opera omnia exegetica, duobus voluminibus comprehensa. (2 vols. in three)
Eleutheropoli/Irenopoli, sumptibus Irenici Philalethii, post 1656. Reb. 31cm.
UL22   [O2]   King 127 1C

CUDWORTH (Ralph).   The true intellectual system of the universe: the first part; wherein, all the reason and philosophy of atheism is confuted; and its impossibility demonstrated.
London, printed for Richard Royston, 1678. Rep. 30cm.
Wing C.7471   UL22   FEt   AEm   [N2]   King 218 6C

CURIEL (Joannes Alphonsus).   Lecturae seu quaestiones in Thomae Aquinatis primam secundae.
Antverpiae, apud Joannem Keerbergium, 1621. Rep. 38cm.
bg   KG10   FEt   L4   King 454 11F

CYPRIAN, *Bp., Saint.*   Opera... recognita, collatione facta editionum Pauli Manutii & Gulielmi Morelii... in tres tomos ad notationes Jacobi Pamelii... editio ultima prioribus emendiator: (3 vols. in one)
[Geneva], excudebat Joannes le Preux, 1593. Rep. 34cm.
Adams C.3167   bg   BT1   PGL32   FEt   A1   King 493 3C

CYRIL, *Bp. of Jerusalem, Saint.*   [Greek.] Catecheses, ex variis bibliothecis,... omnes nunc primum in lucem editae, cum Latina interpretatione Joannis Grodecii... aucta & emendata. Studio & opera Joan. Prevotii.
Parisiis, apud Claudium Morellum, 1609. Rep. 24cm.
bg   BT1   PGL32   FEt   B2   King 294 9B

CYRIL, *Patriarch of Alexandria, Saint.*   Opera quae hactenus haberi potuere, in tomos quinque digesta: nam quintus hac editione accessit. (5 vols. in one)
Basileae, per haeredes Joannis Hervagii et Eusebium Episcopium, 1566. prob. German 16th cent.   BS wooden boards rep. 36cm.
Adams C.3169   cp: a.f.h.   bg   BT1   PGL32   FEt   A4   King 505 11E

DANEAU (Lambert). Opuscula omnia theologica, ab ipso authore recognita, & in tres classes divisa.
Genevae, apud Eustathium Vignon, 1583. IPSWICH GS rep. 33cm.
Adams D.51   bg   BT10   FEt   D4   King 585 4E

DART (John).   The history and antiquities of the cathedral church of Canterbury, and the once-adjoining monastery: containing,... A survey... *and an* appendix of charters... (2 parts in one vol.)

London, printed and sold by J. Cole; J. Hoddle; J. Smith; and A. Johnson, 1726. Reb. 40cm.

LP12

DAVENANT (John), *Bp.*   Expositio epistolae Pauli ad Colossenses...iam primum edita: Olim ab eodem,... in Academia Cantabrigiensi... dictata.
Cantabrigiae, apud Thomam & Joannem Bucke, 1627. Rep. 28cm.

STC.6296   MS28   FEt   D4

———— Praelectiones de duobus in theologica controversis capitibus de judice controversiarum... de justitia habituali et actuali...
Cantabrigiae, ex Academiae typographeo, apud T. Buck 1631. BR rep. 29cm.

STC.6301   bg   DU(inscribed to BT35, but that entry deleted in the Book)   FEt   D4

DAVENPORT (Christopher).   *See* FRANCISCUS *a Sancta Clara.*

DAWSON (Thomas).   A treatise of loyalty and obedience; wherein the regal supremacy is asserted;...
London, printed by J. Leake, for R. Smith, 1710. BS panels rep. 20cm.

LP12

DE ANTIQUITATE BRITANNICAE ECCLESIAE.   *See* PARKER, M., *Abp.*

DE GORRAN (Nicholas).   *See* GORRANUS, N.

DE GROOT (Hugo).   *See* GROTIUS, H.

DESCARTES (René).   Principia philosophiae. Ultima editio collata (Editio quinta) *contains his* Specimina philosophiae seu dissertatio de methodo dioptrice et meteora. Ex Gallico translata. *and his* Passiones animae: nunc Latina donatae (ab H.D.M.) *also includes his* Meditationes de prima philosophia, *and* Appendix, 1670. (4 vols. in one)
Amstelodami, apud Danielem Elzevirium, 1672. Reb. 20cm.

UL31   [K2]

DESTRUCTORIUM VICIORUM.   *See* ALEXANDER *Carpentarius.*

DIODATE (Giovanni).   Pious and learned annotations upon the Holy Bible: plainly expounding the most difficult places thereof:... The second edition.
London, printed by Miles Flesher, for Nicholas Fussell, 1648. Reb. 23cm.

Wing D.1506   ms inscription by donor   UL8   [I2]

DIODORUS (Siculus).   Bibliothecae historicae libri XV. Hoc est, quotquot Graece extant de quadraginta,... Sebastiano Castalione totius operis correctore,... interprete. Interiecta est, Dictys Cretensis...
Basileae, [ex officina Henricpetrina], 1578. English early 17th cent. BS centre rep. 30cm.

Adams D.475   bg   ms owner's signature: Wm. Harrison   BP13   FEt   M1

DIONYSIUS 'The Areopagite', *Saint.*   Opera (quae quidem extent) omnia,... commentariis... editis elucidata. Quibus accessit Michaelis Syngeli... encomium... praeter appendices omnes editionis prioris.

Coloniae, ex officina haeredum Joannis Quentel, 1556. London mid 16th cent. roll signed NE O: RCb(4)883 and FPa(3)645 BS rep. 32cm.

Adams D.524   three vellum pastedowns 16 by 10cm., according to Paul Morgan: two with coloured initials from a treatise on canon law, the third from a theological commentary, all 14th/15th century.   LP4   FEt   [I4]   King 149 1B

———— Opera... cum scholiis S.Maximi et paraphrasi Pachymerae a Balthasare Corderio... Latine interpretam et notis theologicis illustrata. (2 vols.)
Antverpiae, ex officina Plantiniana Balthasaris Moreti, 1634. Rep. 35cm.

lacks tp to vol 1; ms owners: John Davenant, H. Henchman (see Ch. VII)   UL22   FEt   [N2]
King 498 2D

DODSWORTH (Roger).   *See* DUGDALE (*Sir* William).

DOMINIS (Marco Antonio de), *Abp.*   De republica ecclesiastica Libri X (5 parts in one – Vol.1 of two)
Londini, ex officina Nortoniana, apud Jo: Billium, 1617. Rep. 33cm.

STC.6994 (part)   bg   MS25   FEt   F3   King 69 8D

DORT (*Synod of*).   Acta synodi nationalis... ordinum generalium foederati Belgii provinciarum,...
MDCXVIII et MDCXIX *with* Judicia theologorum exterorum de quinque... articulis... MDCXIX. (2 parts in one vol.)
Lugduni Batavorum, typis Isaaci Elzeviri, 1620. GE rep. 34cm.

bg   MS38   FEt   E3   King 571 2D

DOWNHAM (George), *Bp.*   A treatise of justification: wherein is first set downe the true doctrine... then all objections... are answered and confuted,...and difficult places of holy Scriptures expounded and vindicated.
London, printed by E. Purslow, for Nicholas Bourne, and part... for the benefit of the children of... John Minshew,... 1639. Reb. 28cm.

STC.7123   p: 10s   MS47 (26 Oct 1641)   FEt   G2   King 174 6A

DOWNHAM (John).   Annotations upon all the books of the Old and New Testament: This second edition so enlarged,... by the labour of certain learned divines thereunto appointed,...as is expressed in the preface. (2 vols.)
London, printed by John Legatt, 1651. IPSWICH 1651 GS rep. 32cm.

Wing D.2063   BT44   FEt   G2   King 556 3C

DRAUD (George).   Bibliotheca classica, sive catalogus officinalis, in quo singuli singularum faculta-tum ac professionum libri,... in publicum prodierunt, secundum artes & disciplinas,... ordine alpha-betico recensentur:... supplementum, ab 1611 usque ad 1624... separatim editum. *also with* Bibliotheca exotica sive catalogus officinalis librorum peregrinis linguis... in officinis Bibliopolarum indagari potuerunt, & in Nundinis Francofurtensibus... habentur. *and with* La bibliotheque univer-sail... (1500–1624) (4 parts in two vols.)
Francofurti, impensis Balthasaris Ostern, 1625. L reb. 21cm.

MS28   FEt   H2   King 235 11B

DRUSIUS (Johannes), *elder.*   Ad loca difficiliora Josuae, Judicum, & Samuelem commentarius liber.

Franekerae Frisiorum, excudebat Fredericus Heynsius, 1618. Rep. 19cm.

bg   BT30   FEt   E2   King 690 11A

———— Ad voces Ebraicas Novi Testamenti commentarius duplex... item eiusdem annotationum in N. Testamentum pars altera. *also includes* Vitae operumque Joh. Drusii editorum et nondum editorum,... per Abelum Curiandrum.
Franekerae Frisiorum, excudebat Fredericus Heynsius, 1616. Rep. 19cm.

bg   BT30   FEt   E2   King 225 11A

———— Annotationum in totum J. C. Testamentum, sive Praeteritorum libri decem.
Franekerae, sumptib. Johannis Johannis, excudebat Aegidius Radaeus, 1612. Rep. 18cm.

bg   BT30   FEt   E2   King 242 11A

———— [Greek.] sive Ecclesiasticus Graece ad exemplar Romanum, & Latine *and his* Liber Hasmonaeorum qui vulgo prior Machabaeorum Graece... & Latine... cum notis sive commentario... *bound with* GENTILIS, A. Ad primum Macbaeorum disputatio, 1600.
Franekerae, excudebat Aegidius Radaeus [Veneunt in officina Zachariae Heyns], 1596–1600. Rep. 19cm

Adams B.1636 and 1646   cp: x under X of date   bg   BT30   FEt   E2   King 663 11A

———— Esthera. Ex interpretatione S.Pagnini... annotationes. Additiones Apocryphae... in Latinum conversae, & scholiis illustratae. *also includes his* Historia Ruth, 1586. *and his* In prophetam Amos & Hoseam, 1599–1600. (4 vols. in one)
Lugduni Batavorum, ex officina Johannis Paetsii, 1586. Rep. 16cm.

Adams D.927   bg   BT30   FEt   E2   King 391 11A

———— Historia Ruth,... ex Ebraeo Latine conversa... Tralatio Graeca ad exemplar Complutense. *bound with his* Esthera, 1586.
Franekerae, excudebat Aegidius Radaeus, 1586. Rep. 16cm.

Adams B.1332   bg   BT30   FEt   E2   King 391 11A

———— In prophetam Hoseam lectiones eiusdem in Graecam editionem ... quae extant fragmenta. *and his* In prophetam Amos lectiones *bound with his* Esthera, 1586.
[Antwerp], ex officina Plantiniana, apud Christophorum Raphelengium, 1599–1600. Rep. 16cm.

Adams B.1612   bg   BT30   FEt   E2   King 391 11A

———— Opuscula, quae ad grammaticam spectant, omnia, in unum volumen compacta; *includes his* De letteris Mosche Vechaleb. Editio tertia. *and his* Alphabetum Ebraicum vetus. Editio altera; *bound with his* Tobias Graece, 1591. *and also with* DRUSIUS, J., *younger,* Lachrymae J. Scaligeri, 1609. (3 vols. in one)
Franekerae, excudebat Aegidius Radaeus, 1609. Rep. 18cm.

bg   BT30   FEt   E2   King 231 11A

———— Tobias Graece. Emendante & recensente... ad usum scholarum. *in his* Opuscula, etc. 1608–09.
Franekerae (in Academia Franekerana), excudebat Aegidius Radaeus, 1591. Rep. 18cm.

Adams B.1632   bg   BT30   FEt   E2   King 231 11A

DRUSIUS (Johannes), *younger.*   Lachrymae Johannis Drusii junioris, tribus carminum generibus expressae, in obitum... Josephi Scaligeri *bound with* DRUSIUS,J., *elder,* Opuscula, 1609. (One of 3 vols. in one)
Franekerae, excudebat Aegidius Radaeus, 1609. Rep. 18cm.

bg   BT30   FEt   E2   King 231 11A

DUGDALE (*Sir* William).   The antiquities of Warwickshire illustrated; from records, lieger-books, manuscripts... beautified with maps, prospects and portraictures.
London, printed by Thomas Warren, 1656. Reb. 35cm.

Wing D.2479   hand coloured illns.   UL24   [N1]   King 623 6D

——— The baronage of England, or an historical account of the lives and ... actions of our English nobility. Tome the first(-second). (2 vols.)
London, printed by Tho. Newcomb for Abel Roper, John Martin and Henry Herringman, 1675–76. English, probably London late 17th cent. GF rep. 37cm.

Wing D.2480   from Caius in exchange for copy from UL24 (see Ch.VII)   AEm   [N3]
                                                                                        King 503 6D

——— The history of St Pauls Cathedral in London. From its foundation untill these times:... Beautified with sundry prospects of the church, figures of tombes, and monuments.
London, printed by Tho. Warren, 1658. Reb. 33cm.

Wing D.2482   LP12   King 6 6C

——— *and* DODSWORTH (Roger).   Monasticon Anglicanum, sive pandectae coenobiorum... ex MSS. Codd., Archivis, Bibliothecis. Volumen alterum (-tertium). (3 vols.)
1: *Londini, typis Richardi Hodgkinsonne, 1655.* 2: *Londini, typis Aliciae Warren, 1661.* 3: *[The] Savoy, excudebat Tho. Newcomb, 1673. Reb. 35cm.*

Wing D.2483, 2483A & 2484   hand coloured illns.   UL24   msGL   AEm   [N3]   King 552 6D

DU JON (Francois), *elder.*   Opera theologica... Editio postrema, prioribus auctior. Catalogum librorum,... Praefixa est vita auctoris. Tomus primus-secundus (2 vols.)
Genevae, apud Samuelem Crispinum, 1613. Reb. 33cm.

cp: a.k.   bg   BP8   PGL12 over PGL2 in both vols.   FEt   C4   King 559 3C

——— *See also* BIBLE – Latin, 1603 *and* TERTULLIAN, Q.S.F.

DUNS SCOTUS (John).   Quaestiones super IV libris sententiarum [Quaestiones 1 & 2, *ed.* Philip de Bagnacavallo] (2 vols. in one)
Venetiis, per Bonetum Locatellum, 1497. Reb. 31cm.

Goff D.383   cp: .i./m.   ms owner's name and many additions: Thomas Hichcock bg   BT1   FEt
L4   King 605(1) 9C

——— Quaestiones super IV libris sententiarum [Quaestiones 3 & 4 & quodlibets, *ed.* Mauritius de Portu Hibernicum] scripti Oxoniensis... Quaestiones quodlibetales... (3 vols. in one)
Venetiis, pro Andrea Torresani de Asula, per Simonem de Luere, 1506. Reb. 31cm.

Adams D.1121 & 1112   ms owner: Thomas Cahill Rect. de Slyndfolld   cp: qe/..   bg   BT1   FEt
L4   King 605(2) 9C

DURANDUS (Gulielmus) *of Saint-Pourçain.* In sententias theologicas Petri Lombardi commentariorum, libri quatuor,... Nunc vero denuo per alios... emendati,... una cum authoris vita,...
Lugduni, apud haeredes Gulielmi Rovillii, 1595. Reb. 35cm.

Adams D.1187   bg   KG14   FEt   L1   King 525 4D

DUREL (Jean).   A view of the government and publick worship of God in the reformed churches beyond ye seas. *includes his* Liturgy of the Church of England asserted, in a sermon. Translated by G.B. (2 vols. in one)
London, printed by J. G. for R. Royston, 1662. BR rep. 19cm.

Wing D.2695   ms owner: John Burrough 1662   LP4   FEt   [K2]   King 668 7C

DURY (John).　*See* Parliamentary Sermons.

DUVAL (Pierre).　*See* MAPS: Appendix H.

EIKON BASILIKE.　[Greek.] The pourtraicture of his sacred Majestie in his solitudes and sufferings.
[London], 1649. L reb. 21cm.

Wing E.306　lacks fp　LP2　FEg　[N2]　　　　　　　　　　　　　　　　King 262 9B

ELLIS (John).　*See* Parliamentary Sermons.

ELMENHORST (Gebhart).　*See* ARNOBIUS.

EPHRAEM (Syrus), *Saint.*　Opera omnia, quotquot in insignioribus Italiae bibliothecis, praecipue Romanis Graece inveniri potuerunt, in tres tomos digesta,... interprete & scholiaste Gerardo Vossio. Editio secunda. (3 vols. in one)
Coloniae, apud Arnoldum Quentelium, 1603. Rep. 31cm.

bg　BT1　PGL32　FEt　B2　　　　　　　　　　　　　　　　　　　King 562 3B

EPIPHANIUS, *Bp., Saint.*　[Greek.] Contra octoginta haereses. Opus eximium, panarium sive capsula medica appellatum, & in libros quidem tres tomos vero septem divisum. Omni graece conscripta nunc primum in lucem edita.
Basileae, [Johann Hervagen], 1544. Reb. 32cm.

Adams E.250　bg　ms additions on tp verso　BT1　FEp　A2　　　　　　　King 107 7E

————— Contra octoaginta haereses opus, Panarium,... aut capsula medica appellatum... Iano Cornario... interprete.
Basileae, ex officina Hervagiana per Eusebius Episcopum, 1578. Rep. 35cm.

Adams E.256　bg　BT1　PGL32　FEt　A2　　　　　　　　　　　　　　King 626 7E

EPISCOPIUS (Simon).　Opera Theologica. (4 parts in 2 vols.)
Amstelaedami, ex typographeio Joannis Blaeu (Apud viduam Johannis Henrici Boom), 1650–65. Rep. 35cm.
LP3　FEt　AEm　[N2]　　　　　　　　　　　　　　　　　　　　　King 59 3D

ERASMUS (Desiderius).　In Novum Testamentum annotationes, ab ipso autore iam quartum recognitae &... locupletatae.
Basileam, apud Inclytam Rauracorum, 1527. London 1550–70; O HMa(6), DIg(1) BS rep. 33cm.
Adams E.891　bg　MS2　FEt　C4　　　　　　　　　　　　　　　　King 640 10C

————— *See also* ATHANASIUS, AUGUSTINE, HILARY OF POITIERS, *and* JEROME, *Saints.*

ESTELLA (Diego de).　*See* STELLA, D.de.

ESTIENNE.　*See* STEPHANUS.

ESTIUS (Guilelmus).　*See* HESSELS, W.

EUCLID.　[Elementa] Euclidis elementorum libri XV. Accessit XVI de solidorum regularum... Nunc tertio editi,... auctore Christophoro Clavio. (2 parts in one vol.)
Coloniae, expensis Joh. Baptistae Ciotti, 1591. Rep. 30cm.

Adams E.968　LP1　FEt　[O2]　　　　　　　　　　　　　　　　　King 144 7E

EUISTOR (Franciscus), *pseud.*   *See* MORE, H.

EUSEBIUS, *Pamphili, Bp. of Caesarea,* and others.   [Greek.] Ecclesiasticae historiae.
Lutetiae Parisiorum, ex officina Roberti Stephani, 1544. Reb. 33cm.

Adams E.1093   ms on tp: 'Hoc age Tho. Scotte'   bg   MS3   FEt   A1   King 496 2D

———— Ecclesiastica historia, sex prope seculorum res gestas complectens... nunc ex fide Graecorum codicum per Joh. Jacobum Grynaeum... restituta.
Basileae, per Sebastianum Henricpetri, 1611. Reb. 33cm.

cp: m.f.   bg   BP13   FEt   A1   King 30 2D

———— [Greek.] Evangelicae praeparationis Lib. XV ex Bibliotheeca Regia *with* Evangelicae demonstrationis Lib. X. (2 vols. in one)
Lutetiae, ex officina Rob. Stephani, 1544–46. Reb. 33cm.

Adams E.1087   ms on tp: 'Hoc age Thos.Scotte'   bg   MS3   FEt   A1   King 694 2D

EVANCE (Daniel).   *See* Parliamentary Sermons.

F (E).   *See* FALKLAND (Henry Cary, *Visct.*).

FABRITIUS (Stephanus).   Sacrae conciones in... Psalmos Davidis et aliorum prophetarum in ecclesia Bernensi habitae... Nunc primum in lucem editae. (4 parts in one vol.)
Aureliae Allobrogum, apud Franciscum Nicolaum, 1622. Reb. 36cm.

p: 1^{li} bg   MS29 (1630)   FEt   D3   King 515 5E

FACIUS (Bartholomeus).   *See* GUICCIARDINI, F.

FAGIUS (Paulus).   Thargum, hoc est, paraphrasis Onkeli Chaldaica in Sacra Biblia, ex Chaldaeo in Latinum versa, additio... annotationibus... Pentateuchus... Tomus primus.
Argentorati, per Georgium Machaeropoeum, 1546. GS rep. 30cm.

Adams B.1274   p: 4fl[orins]   'Joh. Beaumonti' on tp   ms marginalia   MS45 (1634)   FEt   C3
King 212 11C

———— *See also* BUCER, M.

FAIRCLOUGH (Samuel).   *See* Parliamentary Sermons

FALKLAND (Henry Cary, *Visct.*).   The history of the life, reign and death of Edward II King of England, with the rise and fall of... Gaveston and the Spensers. Written by E. F. in 1627.
London, printed by J. C., for Charles Harper; Samuel Crouch; and Thomas Fox, 1680. Rep. 31cm.

Wing F.313   UL27   [N2]   King 88 6B

FERRARIUS (Philippus).   Lexicon geographicum, in quo universi orbis oppida, urbes, regiones... descripta recensentur; in duas partes divisum... Editio nova, accuratior. *with his* Tabula longitudinis ac latitudinis. (2 parts in one vol.)
Londini, ex officina Rogeri Danielis, 1657. Rep. 31cm.

Wing F.814   UL22   FEt   [N1]   King 641 6B

FERUS (Joannes).   *See* WILD, J.

FIDDES (Richard).   Life of Cardinal Wolsey... second edition, corrected by the author. (2 parts in one vol.)
London, printed by J. Barber for J. Knapton, R. Knaplock (and four others), 1726. BS panels rep. 33cm.
LP16
King 576 6D

FIELD (Richard).   Of the church, five bookes. (5 books & appendix in one vol.)
At London, imprinted (by Nicholas Okes) for Simon Waterson, 1606–10. Reb. 22cm.
STC².10857.5 and 10857.7   bg   KG4   FEt   G2
King 270 9B

FLACIUS (Matthias Illyricus).   Clavis scripturae S. seu de sermone sacrarum literatum... pars prima-altera pars. (2 parts in one vol.)
Basileae, ex officina Hervagiana per Eusebium Episcopium, 1580–81. Rep. 35cm.
Adams F.557   cp: xf   p: xiii³   bg   MS11   FEt   C3
King 154 1D
————— (ed.)   See also MAGDEBURG CENTURIATORS.

FLORENCE *of Worcester.*   (FLORENTIUS *Wigorniensis.*) *See* MATTHAEUS, *Westmonasteriensis.*

FORSTER (Johann).   Dictionarium Hebraicum.
Basileae, per Frobenium & Episcopium, 1564. Reb. 31cm.
Adams F.784   copious ms additions   MS27   FEp   K5
King 620 11C

FOX (John).   Actes and monuments of matters most speciall and memorable, happening in the Church, with an universall historie of the same... the sixth time newly imprinted. (2 vols.)
London, for the Company of Stationers, 1610. London cy; O: HEl(1), ?TCa(7) BS rep. 42cm.
STC.11227   bg   BT20   FEp   M2
King 437 6E

FRANCISCUS *a Sancta Clara.*   Deus, natura, gratia, sive tractatus de praedestinatione, de meritis & peccatorum remissione... Accessit paraphrastica expositio reliquorum articulorum confessionis Anglicae...
Lugduni, sumptibus Antonii Chard, 1634. Reb. 23cm.
LP4   FEt
King 359 9B

FREITAG (Arnold).   *See* MORNAY, P de.

FRITH (John).   *See* TYNDALE, W. *etc.*

FROST (John).   Select sermons, preached upon sundry occasions... now newly published.
Cambridge, printed for John Field, 1657. Rep. 27cm.
Wing F.2246   cp: w/oa   LP4   FEt   [I3]
King 312 6A

FULKE (William).   *See* BIBLE – N.T. – English.

FUNCK (Johann).   Chronologia. Hoc est, omnium temporum et annorum ab initio mundi, usque ad annum a nato Christo 1552. In prima editione ab autore deducta;... ad annum Christi 1601 producta. Item commentariorum libri decem (3 parts in one vol.)
Witebergae, impensis Andreae Hoffmanni, 1601. Reb. 35cm.
BP13   FEt   M2
King 536 3E

GAGUIN (Robert) *et al.*   Rerum Gallicarum annales, cum Huberti Velleii supplemento... usque ad Henricum II describuntur.
Francofurti, ex officina And. Wecheli, 1577. Rep. 32cm.
Adams G.25   bg   BP13   FEt   M1   King 138 4A

[GALE (Thomas), *ed.*]   Opuscula mythologica, ethica et physica. Graece & Latine... (9 vols. in one)
Cantabrigiae, ex officina J. Hayes, impensis Joann. Creed, 1671. BF rep. 17cm.
Wing G.156   DU   FEt   King 328 11A

GALLASIUS (Nicholas) *ed.*   *See* CALVIN, J., 1583 *and* IRENAEUS,

GAUDEN (John), *Bp.*   *See* EIKON BASILIKE (attrib. to Gauden) *and* Parliamentary Sermons.

GENTILIS (Albericus).   Ad primum Macbaeorum disputatio ad Tobiam Matthaeum Episcopum Dunelmensem. *bound with* DRUSIUS, J. [Greek.] sive Ecclesiasticus *and* Liber Hasmonaeorum, 1596–1600.
Franekerae, apud Aegidium Radaeum, 1600. Rep. 19cm.
Adams B.1646   BT30   FEt   E2   King 663 11A

GERHARD (Johann).   Harmoniae Evangelistarum Chemnitio-Lyserianae... commentario illustra-tae. Pars primo(-tertia). (3 vols.)
Jenae, typis & sumtibus Tobiae Steinmanni, 1626–27. Rep. 20cm.
MS30   FEt   F1   King 236 8A

———— In harmoniam historiae evangelicae de passione, crucifixione, morte et sepultura Christi... ex quatuor evangelistis contextam commentarius.
Francofurti, sumptibus Joannis Jacobi Porsii, 1622. Rep. 33cm.
bg   BT19   FEt   E4   King 15 8D

———— Locorum theologicorum cum pro adstruenda veritate,... copiose explicatorum... Tomus primus (-nonus & ultimus). (9 vols.)
Jenae, typis & sumtibus Tobiae Steinmanni, 1615–25. Reb. 20cm.
MS30   FEt   F1   King 240 8A

GERHARDUS (Andreas), *Hyperius.*   Commentarii in omnes Pauli Apostoli Epistolas, atque etiam in Epistolam Judae, nunc primum opera Joannis Mylii in lucem editi.
Tiguri, apud Christophorum Froschoverum, 1582–84. Rep. 31cm.
Adams H.1263   bg   BP10   PGL24   FEt   D3   King 597 10C

GESNER (Conrad).   Bibliotheca instituta et collecta primum... redacta recognita & in duplum post priores editiones aucta, per Josiam Simlerum.
Tiguri, apud Christophorum Froschoverum, 1574. Reb. 30cm.
Adams G.514   p: 10s 6d   deleted ms on tp and last leaf   BT1   FEp   K3   King 1 1B

———— Historiae animalium Lib.I De quadrupedibus viviparis.
Tiguri, apud Christ. Froschoverum, 1551. Reb. 38cm.
Adams G.532   hand coloured woodcut illustrations   BP15   FEp   H5   King 466 1D

———— Historiae animalium Lib.III ... De avium natura. *bound with* Historiae animalium Lib.II ... De quadripedibus oviparis. (2 vols. in one)

Francofurdi, ex officina Joannis Wecheli, 1585–6. Reb. 38cm.

Adams G.534 & 536   cp: II, b.f. III, q.   BP15   FEp   H5

King 465 1D

———— Historiae animalium Lib.IIII... de piscum & aquatilium animantium natura.
Tiguri, apud Christoph. Froschoverum, 1558. Reb. 38cm.

Adams G.538   cp: a.   BP15   FEp   H5

King 467 1D

———— *See also* CALEPINI, A.

GIBSON (Samuel).   *See* Parliamentary Sermons.

GILLESPIE (George).   *See* Parliamentary Sermons.

GIPPS (George).   *See* Parliamentary Sermons.

GLANVILL (Joseph).   Scepsis scientifica: or, confest ignorance, the way to science; *includes his*
Scire/i tuum nihil est: or, The authors defence of the vanity of dogmatizing;... (2 vols. in one)
London, printed by E. Cotes for Henry Eversden, 1665. Reb. 19cm.

Wing G.827 and 828   LP1   FEt   [H3]

King 691 10B

GLAREANUS (Henricus).   *See* LORITUS, H.

GLASS (Solomon).   Philologiae sacrae, qua totius... Veteris et Novi Testamenti... libri duo (-lib.
tertius & quartus)... editio secunda. (2 vols. of three)
Jenae, typis & sumtibus Ernesti Steinmanni, 1643–45. IPSWICH 1651 GS rep. 20cm.

BT43   FEt   K3

King 655–6 7B

———— Philologiae sacrae... liber quintus quo rhetorica sacra comprehensa. (3rd vol. of set)
Jenae, typis & sumtibus Ernesti Steinmanni, 1636. IPSWICH 1651 GS rep. 20cm.

BT43   FEt   K3

King 657 7B

GLOVER (Robert).   Nobilitas politica vel civilis.   Personas scilicet distinguendi, et ab origine inter
gentes, ex principum gratia nobilitandi forma... quo tandem & apud Anglos,... ostenditur. [com-
piled from Glover's ms by Thomas Milles]
Londini, typis Gulielmi Jaggard, 1608. Reb. 28cm.

STC.11922   lacks pp. 89–92 and all plates but Prince of Wales and Baron – these and all other
decorations hand coloured   UL24   [N1]

King 192 6B

GODEFROY (Denis), *ed.   See* JUSTINIAN, *Emperor of Rome, and* SENECA, L.A.

GODELEVAEUS (Wilhelmus), *ed.   See* LIVY, T.L.

GOLTZ (Hubert).   Fastos magistratuum et triumphorum Romanorum ab urbe condita ad Augusti
obitum ex antiquis tam numismatum quam marmorum monumentis restitutos...
Brugis Flandrorum, excudebat Hubertus Goltzius, 1566. English late 16th cent. GS rep. 29cm.

Adams G.833   ms owner and p: fitzhenry (Wm. Harrison) xiij^s iiij^d bg   BP13   FEt   M1

King 171 4A

GOODE (William).   *See* Parliamentary Sermons.

GOODWIN (Thomas).   *See* Parliamentary Sermons.

GORDON (James).   Theologia moralis universa octo libris comprehensa. Tomus prior.
Lutetiae Parisiorum, sumptibus Sebastiani & Gabrielis Cramoisy, 1634. GR reb. 35cm.
ms owner Palmerius?   DU   FEt   [I5]   King 542 7F

GORRANUS (Nicholas).   In omnes Pauli Epistolas elucidatio.
Antverpiae, prostant apud Joannem Keerbergium, 1617. Rep. 33cm.
bg   BT31   FEt   G3   King 41 2C

———— In quatuor Evangelia commentarius.
Antverpiae, prostant apud Joannem Keerbergium, 1617. Rep. 33cm.
bg   BT31   FEt   G3   King 40 2C

GOUGE (William).   A learned and very useful commentary on the whole epistle to the Hebrewes...
being the substance of thirty years Wednesdayes lectures at Black-fryers London. (4 parts in one
vol.)
London, printed by A. M., T. W. and S. G. for Joshua Kirton, 1655. IPSWICH GS reb. 29cm.
Wing G.1391   DU   FEt   [I3]   King 179 8C

———— *See also* Parliamentary Sermons.

GOWER (Stanley).   *See* Parliamentary Sermons.

GRABE (Johann Ernst), *ed.*   *See* BIBLE – Greek – O.T., 1707.

GRANION, *attrib.*   *See* MAJOR, J. *Scotus.*

GRATIANUS (Franciscus).   Decretum patrum sive concordia discordantium canonum cum suis
apparatibus.
Argentine, [J. Grüninger], 1490. Cambridge by W.G. (1478–1507) BS rep. 40cm.
Goff G.380   ms owners: Hugo Fraunce of Syon, Griffeth Trygary   KG1   PGL34   FEBLt   M4
                                                                             King 460 1A

———— Decretum Gratiani, emendatum, et notationibus illustratum: una cum glossis... Editio ultima.
(3 parts in one vol.)
Taurini, apud Nicolaum Bevilaquam, 1620. Reb. 37cm.
ms owner Alexr. Guthree   LP3   [N4]   King 486 1D

GRATIUS (Orthuinus).   Fasciculus rerum expetendarum & fugiendarum,... editus est Coloniae,
MDXXXV. ... Una cum appendice sive Tomo II. Scriptorum veterum... opera & studio Edwardi
Brown,... (2 vols.)
Londini, impensis Richardi Chiswell, 1690. Reb. 32cm.
Wing G.1583   UL31   FEt   [O2]   King 619 and 603 10C

GREENE (John).   *See* Parliamentary Sermons.

GREENHAM (Richard).   The workes... collected into one volume:... revised, corrected and published, for the further building of all such as love the truth,... (by Henry Holland). Fift and last
edition. (5 parts in one vol)

London, printed (by Thomas Creede) for William Welby, 1611–12. Prob. London cy GS rep. 29cm.

STC.12318   bg   BP14   FEt   F2   King 191 6C

GREENHILL (William).   *See* Parliamentary Sermons.

GREGORIUS *de Valentia*.   *See* VALENTIA, G. de.

GREGORY I, 'The Great', *Pope, Saint*.   ...Omnia, quae extant, opera:... repurgata & aucta... Jacobi
Pamelii... adpendici novae praefixa... (2 vols. in one)
Antverpiae, apud haeredes Arnoldi Birckmanni, 1572. Rep. 38cm.

Adams G.1173   cp: a.k.   bg   BT1   PGL32   FEt   B3   King 456 2E

GREGORY IX, *Pope*. Decretalium copiosum argumentum,...
[Paris], Uxoris defuncti Berthold Remboldt, 7 Octobris 1519. Reb. 36cm.

not in Adams (G.1210 dated 1510 closest) ms owners: Magister Patenson 'spes mea deus'   p: p'cim
x^σ Galfridi Trygary   Samuel Ward deletion of all refs. to Pope   KG1   PGL34   FEp   M4
                                                                                King 461 2E

———— Decretales... Ad exemplar Romanum diligenter recognitae. Editio ultima. *with* Liber sextus
decretalium D.Bonifacii Papae VIII. D.Joannis Papae XXII.   Tum communes... Editio ultima. (2
vols. in one)
Taurini, apud Nicolaum Bevilaquam, 1621–20. Reb. 35cm.

ms owner: Alexr. Guthree   LP3   [N4]   King 485 2E

GREGORY *of Nyssa, Saint*.   Opera... de Graeco in Latinum sermonem conversa... opera Laurentii
Sifani & Joannis Lewenklaii.   Quid hac secunda editione praestitum sit.
Basileae, per Eusebium Episcopium et Nicolai fratris haeredes, 1571. Rep. 32cm.

Adams G.1113   bg   BT1   PGL32   FEt   A2   King 206 8D

GREGORY *of Rimini*, 'Doctor Authenticus'.   In primum (-secundum) sententiarum nuperrime
impressus.   Et... diligentissime sue integritati restitutus.   Per... Petrum Garamanta... (2 vols. in
one)
Parrhisiis, a Claudio Chevallon, c. 1525. Reb. 28cm.

Adams G.1113   UL14   [I3]   King 164 8D

GREGORY, 'Thaumaturgus', *Saint*.   Opera omnia, quae reperiri potuerunt. Nunc primum Graece
et Latine coniunctim edita, cum indicibus necessariis. (5 parts in one vol.)
Parisiis, sumptibus Micaelis Sonnii, Claudii Morelli, et Sebastiani Cramoisy, 1622. Reb. 35cm.

BT36   FEt   A1   King 625 3E

GREW (Nehemiah).   Cosmologia Sacra: or a discourse of the universe as it is the creature and
kingdom of God... to demonstrate the truth and excellency of the Bible;... In five books.
London, printed for W. Rogers, S. Smith, and B. Walford, 1701. BP rep. 31cm.

probably LP12   King 98 6B

———— Musaeum regalis societatis.   Or a catalogue & description of the natural and artificial
rarities belonging to the Royal Society and preserved at Gresham Colledge... Whereunto is sub-
joyned The comparative anatomy of stomachs and guts... Lectures of 1676. (2 parts in one vol.)
London, printed by W. Rawlins, for the author, 1681. Rep. 32cm.

Wing G.1952   UL27   AEm   [N2]   King 90 6B

GRIMESTON (Edward), *trans.* *See* SERRE, J. de.

GROTIUS (Hugo). Annotata ad Vetus Testamentum Tomus I (–III). (3 vols. in one)
Lutetiae Parisiorum, sumptibus Sebastiani & Gabrielis Cramoisy, 1644. IPSWICH 1651 GS rep. 37cm.
BT43   FEt   K4   King 494 8E

———— Annotationes in acta Apostolorum et epistolas apostolicas... Cui subjuncti sunt... Pro veritate religionis Christianae... editio novissima. (3 vols. in one)
Parisiis, apud Thomam Jolly, [typis viduae Theod. Pepingu & Steph. Maucroy], 1648–50. Reb. 32cm.
BT43   FEt   K4   King 564 8D

———— Annotationes in libros Evangeliorum cum tribus tractatibus et appendice eo spectantibus. (First part of 3)
Amsterdami, apud Joh. & Cornelium Blaeu, 1641. Reb. 32cm.
BT43   FEt   K4   King 586 8D

———— De imperio summarum potestatum circa sacra.   Commentarius posthumus.
Lutetiae Parisiorum, 1647. Rep. 15cm.
ms additions p.312–5   LP4   King 338 7A

GRYNAEUS (Johann Jacob), *ed.*   Chronologia brevis Evangelicae historiae:.. in epistola Apostoli Pauli ad Romanos, declaratio: *with his* Aphoristica epistolae... Pauli ad Colossenses explanatio... anno 1585. (2 vols. in one)
Basileae, ex officina Sebastiani Henricpetri, 1580–86. L reb. 16cm.
Adams G.1331 (vol.1, second not in Adams)   bg   BT26   FEp   E2   King 388 9A

———— Disputationes theologicae, quae... habitae sunt in Basiliensi Academia...
Genevae, excudebat Eustathius Vignon, 1584. Rep. 23cm.
Adams G.1317   bg   BT26   FEt   E2   King 276 9A

———— Explanatio, epistolae primae et secundae Johannis Apostoli & Evangelistae:...
Basileae, per Sebastianum Henricpetri, 1591. L reb. 21cm.
not in Adams   bg   BT26   FEt   E2   King 653 9A

———— Monumenta S. Patrum Orthodoxographa. Hoc est, theologiae sacrosanctae ac syncerioris fidei Doctores numero c. LXXXV, Ecclesiae... (3 parts in two vols.)
Basileae, [ex officina Henricpetrina], [1569]. Rep. 30cm.
Adams M.1736   bg   BT1   PGL32   FEt   B2   King 217 9C

———— Pars altera theologicarum disputationum,... in Academia Heidelbergensi; & post reditum, in Basiliensi,... habuit.
Basileae, per Conradum Waldkirch, 1586. Rep. 23cm.
Adams G.1318   bg   BT26   FEt   E2   King 277 9A
———— *See also* EUSEBIUS, *Bishop of Caesarea.*

GUALTHERUS (Rudolphus).   *See* WALTHER, R.

GUICCIARDINI (Francisco).   Historiam sui temporis libri viginti, ex Italico in Latinum... nunc primum & conversi, & editi, Caelio Secundo Curione interprete. *also includes* FACIUS, B. Rerum gestarum Alphonsi... 1566. *and also* PONTANUS, J.J. De Ferdinando primo... 1566. (3 vols. in one)

Basileae, [excudebat Petrus Perna & Henrici Petri], 1566. BS rep. 32cm.

Adams G.1520   ms owner and p: Harrison 1570 11s   bm: α22.2   bg   BP13   FEt   M1

King 621 4A

GULIELMUS ARVERNUS, als. GUILLERMUS PARISIENSIS.   *See* WILLIAM OF AUVERGNE.

HACKET (John), *Bp.*   A century of sermons upon several remarkable subjects... published by Thomas Plume D.D.
London, printed by Andrew Clark for Robert Scott, 1675. Reb. 39cm.

Wing H.169   LP5   FEp   [N4]

King 440 7G

HAKEWILL (George).   An apologie or declaration of the power and providence of God in the government of the world. Third edition revised. (2 parts in one vol.)
Oxford, printed by William Turner, 1635. Reb. 29cm.

STC.12613   cp: b:q   DU   FEt   [I4]

King 608 6B

HALL (Anthony), *ed.*   *See* TRIVET, N.

HALL (Henry).   *See* Parliamentary Sermons.

HALL (Joseph), *Bp.*   The contemplations upon the history of the New Testament, now complete. The second tome. Together with divers treatises reduced to the greater volume. By Jos. Exon.
London, printed by James Flesher, 1661. Rep. 32cm.

Wing H.375   (part)   LP2   [I3]

King 563 9D

————— A recollection of such treatises as have been heretofore severally published, and are nowe revised,... with additions of some others.
London, printed for Samuel Macham, 1614–15. Rep. 29cm.

STC.12706   bg BT11   PGL22 with Samuel Ward's addition 'after he was a Portman'   FEt   F2

King 83 6C

HAMMOND (Henry).   A paraphrase, and annotations upon all the books of the New Testament, briefly explaining all the difficult places thereof. The second edition corrected and enlarged.
London, printed by J. Flesher for Richard Davis in Oxford, 1659. Rep. 36cm.

Wing H.573B   DU   FEt   [I5]

King 478 2A

————— A paraphrase and annotations upon the books of the Psalms, briefly explaining the difficulties thereof.
London, printed by R. Norton for Richard Royston, 1659. Rep. 32cm.

Wing H.578A   DU   FEt   [I5]

King 592 2A

————— A practical catechism. The eighth edition. Whereunto is added The reasonableness of Christian religion (5th ed.) (2 vols. in one)
London, printed by E. T. for R. Royston, 1668. Rep. 16cm.

Wing H.589   LP1   FEt   [I5]

King 362 7A

HARDWICK (Humphrey).   *See* Parliamentary Sermons.

HARMONY OF THE CONFESSIONS.   An harmony of the confessions of the faith of the Christian and reformed churches,... newly translated out of Latine into English. Also... is added The confession of the Church of Scotland (1581). (2 parts in one vol.)

London, printed by John Legatt, 1643. Reb. 20cm.
Wing H.802   LP4   [I2]   King 676 7C

HARRIS (Robert).   *See* Parliamentary Sermons.

HEGISIPPUS.   De rebus a Judaeorum principibus in obsidione fortiter gestis, decq, excidio Hiero-
solymorum, aliarumq, civitatum... libri V. Ambrosio interprete. Eiusdem Anacephaleosis fini
operis... adiecta est. [*Apud Sanctam Coloniam, excudebat Jaspar Gennepaeus*, 1544.] Thonged V rep.
30cm.
Adams H.149   at least half the pages defective   ms marginalia   BP0   FEBLt   A4   King 698 3A

HEINSIUS (Daniel).   Sacrarum exercitationum ad Novum Testamentum libri XX. In quibus...
Aristarchus Sacer, emendiator nec Paulo auctior, Indicesque... accedunt. (2 parts in one vol.)
Lugduni Batavorum, ex officina Elseviriorum, 1639. IPSWICH 1651 GS & F rep. 30cm.
BT43   FEt   K4   King 618 11C

HELVICUS (Christopher).   [Theatrum historicum: sive chronologiae systema novum... cum assig-
natione imperiorum, virorum celebrium... ad praesentem annum MDCXXIX.]
Marburg, 1628. V 46cm.
lacks tp and many more pages defective   UL24   msGL   [O3]   King '704' 6E

HEMMINGSEN (Niels).   Commentaria in omnes Epistolas apostolorum, Pauli, Petri, Judae,... ad
Hebraeos... summa doctrinae ecclesiarum Danicarum... indicatur.
Argentorati, excudebat apud Theodosius Rihelius, 1586. Rep. 32cm.
Adams B.1866   cp: m.f.   bg   BT19   PGL29   FEt   D4   King 44 4E

————Opuscula theologica, in unum volumen collecta.
Genevae, excudebat Eustathius Vignon, 1586. Rep. 33cm.
Adams H.209   bg   BT19   PGL29   FEt   D4   King 582 4E

HENDERSON (Alexander).   *See* Parliamentary Sermons.

HERLE (Charles).   *See* Parliamentary Sermons.

HERLINUS (Joannis Huldricus).   Analysis isagogica seu isagoge analytica ad lectionem primae et
secundae classis librorum Veteris Testamenti, qui Mosaici, & Historici appellantur: *with his* Isagoge
ad lectionem... Propheticorum omnium, (2 vols. in one)
Bernae Helveticorum, excudebat Joannes le Preux, 1607 (1604). Reb. 17cm.
cp: o-o   bg   BT1   FEt   E1   King 323 10A

HERMANS (Jakob).   *See* ARMINIUS, J.

[HEROLD (Johannes).]   Exempla virtutum et vitiorum, atque etiam aliarum rerum maxime mem-
orabilium, futura lectori supra modum magnus thesaurus,... per authores... iudicio, doctrina et fide
apud Graecos & Latinos praestantissimi habentur:...
Basileae, [per Henricum Petri], 1555. Rep. 30cm.
Adams E.1157   bg   BT1   FEt   E5   King 116 3B

HESSELS (Willem).   Absolutissima in omnes Beati Pauli et septem catholicas Apostolorum Epistolas commentaria tribus tomis distincta,... Accedunt huic novissimae editioni,... textus... annotationes... nec non index... studio & opera Jacobi Merlo Horstii. (3 vols. in one)
Coloniae Agrippinae, sumptibus Petri Henningii, 1631. IPSWICH 1651 GS rep. 35cm.

MS48   FEt   K4
                                                                              King 490 3D

———— ...Estii... in quatuor libros sententiarum commentaria: quibus pariter Thomae Summae
Theologicae partes omnes mirifice illustrantur. (4 vols. in one)
Parisiis, apud Jacobum Quesnel, 1647–8. IPSWICH 1651 GS rep. 37cm.

p: #15   MS48   FEt   K4
                                                                              King 483 3D

HESYCHIUS *of Jerusalem.*   In Leviticum commentaria,... pleraque sunt quibus haereses nostri temporis refutantur. (7 books in one vol.)
Parisiis, apud Nicolaum Chesneau, 1581. L reb. 17cm.

Adams H.511   bg   BT1   FEt   B2
                                                                              King 335 11A

HEYLYN (Peter).   Cosmographie, in four books: containing the chorographie and historie of the
whole world,... with an accurate and improved index... now annexed to this last impression, revised...
by the author... before his death. (6 parts in one vol.)
London, printed for Philip Chetwind, 1666. Rep. 35cm.

Wing H.1691A   LP1   FEt   [N2]
                                                                              King 60 5E

———— The stumbling-block of disobedience and rebellion, cunningly laid by Calvin.
London, printed by E. Cotes for Henry Seile, 1658. Reb. 15cm.

Wing H.1736   lacks tp   LP4   FEt   [H3]
                                                                              King 683 5B

HEYRICK (Richard).   *See* Parliamentary Sermons.

HICKES (Gaspar).   *See* Parliamentary Sermons.

HICKES (George).   The spirit of enthusiasm exorcised: in a sermon preach'd before the University
of Oxford,... Fourth edition. *with* Two discourses occasioned by the new prophets pretensions to
inspiration and miracles. (The history of Montanism, By a lay-gentleman. The new pretenders to
prophecy examined. By Nathaniel Spinckes, Presbyter...) (3 parts in one vol.)
London, printed for Richard Sare, 1709. Reb. 20cm.

LP12
                                                                              King 412 5B

HILARY *of Poitiers, Saint.*   Lucubrationes quotquot extant, olim per Des. Erasmum... mediocribus
sudoribus emendate, nunc denuo... per Martinum Lypsium collatae & recognitae.
Basileae, per Eusebium Episcopium et Nicolai fratris haeredes, 1570. Rep. 30cm.

Adams H.556   bg   BT1   PGL32   FEt   A2
                                                                              King 219 1B

HILL (Thomas), *of Trinity College, Cambridge.*   *See* Parliamentary Sermons.

HIMMEL (Johannes).   Memoriale Biblicum speciale continens librorum apocryphorum analysin
succinctam: Epitomen Biblicam... chronologiam Biblico-ecclesiasticam,... *bound with* SELMATTER,
A. A symphonia nova Evangelistarum, 1613. (2 vols. in one)
*Jenae, sumptibus Eliae Rehefeldi & Johan. Grosi, typis Johannis Beithmanni, 1624. Cambridge: Daniel
Boyse fl.1616–1630. BS rep. 19cm.*

p: 2:   DU   FEt   [I2]
                                                                              King 670 11B

HITTORPIUS (Melchior).   *See* AUCTARIUM BIBLIOTHECAE PATRUM.

HODGES (Thomas), *of Kensington.*   *See* Parliamentary Sermons.

HOPKINS (John).   *See* STERNHOLD, T. *and* HOPKINS, J.

HOSPINIAN (Rudolph).   ...De festis Judaeorum et ethnicorum,... De festis Christianorum... De origine, progressu, ceremoniis & ritibus... apud Christianos, tractatus. *with his* De templis, 1672. (3 vols. in one) *Genevae, sumptibus Samuelis de Tournes [& Joannis Antonii],* 1674. Rep. 34cm.

UL22   [N4]   King 574 5E

———— De monachis hoc est, De origine et progressu monachatus & ordinum monasticorum libri sex. *includes his* Historia Jesuitica, 1670. *Genevae, sumptibus Joannis Antonii & Samuelis De Tournes,* 1669. Rep. 34cm.

p: 17s 6d   UL22   King 573 5E

———— Historia Jesuitica.   *included with his* De monachis, 1669. *Tiguri, apud Johannem Rodolphum Wolphium,* 1670. Rep. 34cm.

UL22   [N4]   King 573 5E

HOWELL (William).   An institution of general history, or the history of the world. The second edition with large additions. (2 vols.)
London, printed for Henry Herringman, Thomas Bassett, William Crook, & William Cademan, 1680. Donor's GS (1681) rep. 37cm.

Wing H.3138   cp: f e/t #   UL26   AEm   [N3]   King 444 11F

HUGH *of Saint Victor.*   Opera omnia tribus tomis digesta. Studio et industria... Thomae Garzonii de Bagnacaballo postillis, annotatiunculis, scholiis, ac vita auctoris... nunc primum in Germania... in lucem edita. (3 vols. in one)
Moguntiae, sumptibus Antonii Heirat., excudebat Joannes Volmari, 1617. Rep. 35cm.

bg   MS0   FEt   G4   King 458 10F

HUGO *de Sancto Caro, Cardinal.*   *See* BIBLE – Latin – 1504.

HUMPHREYS (David).   An historical account of the Incorporated Society for the Propagation of the Gospel in foreign parts... their foundation... and the success of their missionaries in the British Colonies to... 1728.
London, printed by Joseph Downing, 1730. Reb. 20cm.

LP12   King 352 7D

HUNNIUS (Egidius), *the elder.*   Methodus concionandi, praeceptis et exemplis dominicalium quo-rundam Evangeliorum comprehensa.
Witebergae, typis M. Georgii Mullerii, 1595. Reb. 16cm.

not in Adams   cp: b.f.   UL19   FEp   [12]   King 336 7A

HYPERIUS (Andreas).   *See* GERHARDUS, A.

IRENAEUS, *Bp., Saint.*   Libri quinque adversus portentosas haereses Valentini & aliorum,... additis Graecis... opera & diligentia Nicolai Gallasii.
[Paris], apud Ioann. le Preux & Joannê Parvum, 1570. Rep. 35cm.

Adams I.157   cp:a–f and x under L of date   bg   BT1   PGL32 lost   FEt   A4   King 72 8E

JACKSON (Arthur).   A help for the understanding of the Holy Scripture... for the assistance and information of those that use... to reade some part of the Bible,... The first part (-the third part) (3 parts in two vols.)
[London], printed by Roger Daniel, [of Cambridge, for the author], 1643(–58). Reb. 23cm.
Wing J.67   LP1   [I2]   King 287 9B

JAMES I, *King.*   The workes of... James,... King of Great Britaine, France, and Ireland,... published by James [Montague], Bishop of Winton,...
London, printed by Robert Barker and John Bill, 1616. Reb. 35cm.
STC.14344   bg   MS17   FEt   F3   King 156 6D

JANSEN (Cornelius), *Bp. of Ghent.*   Commentariorum in suam concordiam, ac totam historiam Evangelicam partes IV. (4 parts in one vol.)
Moguntiae, apud Balthasarum Lippium, 1612. Rep. 35cm.
bg   BT17   PGL2   FEt   G4   King 537 3C

———— Paraphrasis in omnes Psalmos Davidicos cum argumentis... itemque in Proverbia, & Ecclesiasticum commentaria, Ecclesiae Cantica, ac in Sapientam notae.
Antverpiae, ex typographia Gisleni Jansenii, 1614. (2 vols. in one) Rep. 34cm.
bg   BT17   PGL2   FEt   G4   King 551 3C

JENKIN (Robert).   The reasonableness and certainty of the Christian religion. Third edition. (2 vols.)
London, printed by W. B. for Richard Sare, 1708. BP rep. 19cm.
probably LP12   King 415 11B

JENKYN (William).   *See* Parliamentary Sermons.

JEROME, *Saint.*   Lucubrationes omnes qua cum pseudepigraphis, & alienis admixtis in novem digestae tomos,... per Des. Erasmum R. emendatae. (9 vols. in six)
Basileae, apud Joan. Frobenium, 1524–26. London cy O:TP(1) & ?SW6(3) BS rep. 36cm.
Adams J.115   bg   BT41   PGL 31 (vols. 1–4)   BT42   PGL13 (vols. 5–6)   FEBLt   A4
                                                                                     King 477 10F

JEWEL (John) *Bp.*   The workes of... John Jewell,... newly set forth... and a brief discourse of his life. (4 vols. in one)
London, printed by John Norton, 1611. IPSWICH GS rep. 33cm.
STC.14580   bg   BT10   FEt   D4   King 631 4E

JOHN CHRYSOSTOM, *Saint.*   Opera,... recognita... ex editione Graeco-latina Frontonis Ducaei. (5 vols. in four)
Parisiis, [Grand Navire], 1614. Rep. 36cm.
bg   BT1   PGL32   FEt   B1   King 502 11E

———— SAVILE (*Sir* Henry), *ed.*   [Greek.] Opera Graeca, octo voluminibus. (8 vols.) *Etonae, excudebat Joannes Norton, in Collegio Regali, 1610–13. Rep. 35cm.*
STC.14629a   bg   BP5   PGL5   FEt   B1   King 500 7F

JOHN *of Damascus, Saint.*   [Greek.] Orthodoxae fidei accurata explicatio, IIII libris distincta, nuncque primum Graece & Latine simul,... gratiam edita: Jacobo Fabro interprete. *contains* Enarra-

tio Jodoci Clichtovei... De iis qui in fide obdormierunt... Historia duorum Christi militum. (2 vols. in one)
Basileae, per Henrichum Petri, 1548. Rep. 30cm.
Adams J.275   bg   BT1   PGL32   FEt   A4   King 194 11C

JOHN CLIMACUS, *Saint.*   [Greek.] Joannis Scholastici... Opera omnia: interprete Matthaeo Radero.
Lutetiae Parisiorum, sumptibus Sebastiani Cramoisy, 1633. Rep. 34cm.
BT36   FEt   A4   King 518 8E

JOHNSON (Thomas).   Novus Graecorum epigrammatum & poematicum delectus cum nova versione et notis... In usum scholae Etonensis. Editio quinta.
Londini, impensis Gul. & Joh. Innys, 1718. Reb. 17cm.
author was Usher of Ipswich School 1689–91   LP12   FEp   King 400 5A

JONES (William), *of East Bergholt.*   A commentary upon the Epistles of Saint Paul to Philemon, and to the Hebrewes, together with a compendious explication of the second and third epistles of Saint John.
London, printed by R. B. for Robert Allot, 1636. IPSWICH 1651 GS rep. 28cm.
STC^2.14739.5   MS48   FEt   E4   King 176 1B

JOSEPHUS (Flavius).   [Greek.] Opera quae extant,... Graecolatina editio... collatione castigatior facta est. (4 parts in one vol.)
Aureliae Allobrogum, excudebat Petrus de la Roviere, 1611. Rep. 34cm.
bg   BP13   msGL   FEt   M3   King 522 5E

JUNIUS (Franciscus).   *See* DU JON, F.

JUSTIN MARTYR, *Saint.*   Opera omnia, quae adhuc inveniri potuerunt, id est, quae ex regis Galliae prodierunt. Joachimo Perionio... interprete. (6 parts in one)
Parisiis, apud Jacobum Dupuys, 1554. Reb. 32cm.
Adams J.495   lacks 5th tp   cp: j.f.   bg   BT1   PGL32   FEt   A1   King 108 7E

JUSTINIAN, *Emperor of Rome.*   Corpus juris civilis a Dionysio Gothofredo recognitum, in quo, vice interpretationis, variae lectiones... necessariae adiectae. Tomus I–II (2 vols.)
Lugduni, sumptibus Syb. à Porta Gullielmus Laemarius, 1589. Reb. 20cm.
Adams C.2673   cp: k.   ms notes in vol.1   bg   KG1   PGL33   FEp   H2   King 229 5B

———— Corpus juris civilis Justinianei: cum commentariis accursii, scholiis contii, et D.Gothofredi lucubrationibus as accursium:...Tomus primus (– sextum et novum volumen... Editio postrema emendata) (6 vols.)
Aureliae, ex typographia Steph. Gamoneti, sumptibus Theodori de Juges, 1625. Donor's GS (vol. 3 only, formerly vol. 1) rep. 37cm.
ms owner: Wm. Cartright of Trinity Hall   LP3   [N4]   King 442 1D

KECKERMANN (Bartholomeus).   Operum omnium quae extant. Tomus primus (– secundus) (2 vols.)
Coloniae Allobrogum, apud Petrum Aubertum, 1614. Reb. 35cm.
cp: a.k.   bg   KG12   FEt   H5   King 499 9E

KIRBY (Joshua). Dr Brook Taylor's Method of perspective made easy, both in theory and practice. In two books... by Joshua Kirby, painter. Second edition. (2 parts in one vol.)
Ipswich, printed by W. Craighton, for the author, 1755. IPSWICH: LIBRARY: GS label rep. 26cm.
LP20 'The gift of the ingenious Authour' [N1]   King 320 6A

KIRCHER (Athanasius). Magnes sive de arte magnetica opus tripartitum,... eiusque in omnibus artibus & scientiis usus nova methodo explicetur... Editio secunda.. multo correctior. (3 books in one vol.)
Coloniae Agrippinae, apud Jodocum Kalcoven, 1643. French 1640s AGS (arms of the Abp. of Reims who d. 1651) rep. 20cm
LP1 FEt H5   King 661 7B

———— *See also* BIBLE – Concordance – Gk. Heb. & Latin, 1607.

KIS (Stephanus). Theologiae sincerae loci communes de Deo et homine, cum confessione de Trinitate... illustrati. Editio quinta. Cum... vita auctoris. *includes* Tabulae analyticae... sermonum de fide, charitate et patentia... fideliter declaratur, 1610. (2 vols. in one)
Basileae, per Conrad. Waldkirchium, 1608–10. Rep. 32cm.
bg BP7 PGL6 FEt C1   King 629 4B

KNIGHT (William). A concordance axiomaticall: containing a survey of theologicall propositions: with their reasons and uses in holie Scripture.
London, printed for John Bill, 1610. London cy GS rep. 29cm.
STC.15049 bg UL1 (who published the book) FEt K3   King 196 6A

KNOLLES (Richard). The generall historie of the Turkes, from the first beginning... to the rising of the Othonian Familie... with a new continuation from 1621 unto 1629 faithfully collected. Fourth edition.
[London], printed by Adam Islip, 1631. Rep. 34cm.
STC.15054 ms graffiti on fl DU [O3]   King 139 6D

KRANTZ (Albert). Regnorum Aquilonarium, Daniae, Sueciae, Norvagiae, Chronica. *includes his* Metropolis, 1576 *and* Saxonia, 1580 and Wandelia, 1580. (4 vols. in one)
Francofurti ad Moenum, apud haeredes Andreae Wecheli, 1583. London 17th cent. BP rep. (former clasps) 33cm.
Adams C.2874, 2877, 2887 and 2891 ms owner & p: Wm. Harrison 1593 20s portagium 4d
bm: α 12 on all four tp bg BP13 FEt M1   King 624 4A

LA BIGNE (Marguerin de),*ed.* Bibliothecae veterum patrum et auctorum ecclesiasticorum tomi octo... Editio tertia. (9 vols. in four)
Parisiis, [Grand Navire], 1609–10. Rep. 36cm.
bg BT1 PGL32 FEt A3   King 474 9F

LACTANTIUS FIRMIANUS (Lucius Caesilius). Opera, quae quidem extant omnia:... accesserunt Xysti Betuleii Augustani... commentaria...
Basileae, per Henricum Petri, [1563]. Rep. 31cm.
Adams L.27 bg BT1 PGL32 FEt A2   King 121 3B

LAMBARDE (William).   Dictionarium Angliae topographicum & historicum. An alphabetical description of the chief places in England and Wales; with an account of the most memorable events...
Now first publish'd from a manuscript under the author's own hand.
London, printed for Fletcher Gyles, 1730. GR rep. 25cm.

ms owner and donor's signature   LP12   King 317 6A

LANGLEY (John).   *See* Parliamentary Sermons.

LAUNOY (Jean de).   Epistolae omnes, octo partibus comprehensae, nunc demum simul editae...
cum praefatione apologetica, pro reformatione Ecclesiae Anglicanae.
Cantabrigiae, ex officina Joan. Hayes, impensis Edvardi Hall, 1689. BF rep. 36cm.

Wing L.621   UL31 (acc. to King)   [O2]   King 462 11F

LAVATER (Ludwig).   In libros Paralipomenon sive Chronicorum,... commentarius. Insertae sunt...
tabulae de genealogia Jesu Christi,... Editio secunda,... *bound with* In librum Josue, 1614. (One of 3
vols.) *Heidelbergae, impensis Andreae Cambierii,* 1599. Rep. 31cm.

(Adams L.310 has 1600)   bg   BP7   PGL6   FEt   C3   King 210 11C

———— In librum Josue... homiliae LXXIII... Accesserunt operi duo indices,... qui in his homiliis
explicantur. Editio tertia... *bound with* Liber Judicum, 1585. *and* In libros Paralipomenon..., 1599. (3
vols. in one)
Heidelbergae, typis Johannis Lancelloti, impensis Andraeae Cambieri, 1614. Rep. 31cm.

bg   BP7   PGL6   FEt   C3   King 210 11C

———— In librum Proverbiorum, sive Sententiarum Solomonis Regis... commentarii,... Accessit etiam
concio Solomonis de summo hominis bono, quam Ecclesiasten vocant... Editio tertia. *bound with*
Propheta Ezechiel, 1581.
Tiguri, apud Christophorum Froschoverum, 1586. Rep. 31cm.

Adams L.318   bg   BP7   PGL6   FEt   C3   King 141 11C

———— Liber Jobi, homiliis CXLI... Germanica lingua explicatus,... in lucem editus: ac recens ab
Hartmanno... Latinitate donatus. *with* Liber Hesterae homiliis XLVII... Germanica lingua expositus:
recens vero Joannis Pontisellae,... labore & industria, in linguam Latinam conversus. (2 vols. in one)
Tiguri, excudebat Christophorus Froschoverus, 1585. Rep. 30cm.

Adams L.314   bg   BP7   PGL6   FEt   C3   King 638 11C

———— Liber Judicum, homiliis CVII... opera atque labore expositus. Accessit exhortatio... ex Epistolae Jacobi *bound with* In librum Josue, 1614. (One of 3 vols.)
Tiguri, excudebat Christophorus Froschoverus, 1585. Rep. 31cm.

Adams L.307   bg   BP7   PGL6   FEt   C3   King 210 11C

———— Liber Nehemiae qui et secundus Ezrae dicitur, Homiliis LVIII... opera & labore expositus.
Tiguri, ex officina Froschoviana, 1586. L reb. 21cm.

Adams L.312   bg   BP7   PGL6   FEt   G2   King 672 11B

———— Propheta Ezechiel... homiliis seu potius Commentariis expositus... Editio secunda... *bound
with* In librum Proverbiorum, 1586.
Genevae, apud Eustathium Vignon, 1581. Rep. 31cm.

Adams L.320   bg   BP7   PGL6   FEt   C3   King 141 11C

LAZIUS (Wolfgang).   De gentium aliquot migrationibus, sedibus fixis, reliquiis, linguarumq;... libri
XII.

Basileae, per Joannem Oporinum, 1557. Rep. 36cm.

Adams L.347   UL24   FEt   AEm   [N2]   King 584 7E

LE GRAND (Antoine).   Institutio philosophiae, secundum principia... Renati Descartes: nova methodo adornata & explicata. In usum juventutis Academicae.
Londini: apud J. Martyn, 1672. Rep. 15cm.

Wing L.954   DU   AEm   [K2]   King 347 7A

LEICESTER (*Sir* Peter).   Historical antiquities, in two books. The first... of Great Brettain and Ireland. The second... concerning Cheshire. Faithfully collected... by Sir Peter Leycester whereunto is annexed a transcript of Doomsday-Book... as it concerneth Cheshire,....
London, printed by W. L. for Robert Clavell, 1673. Reb. 32cm.

Wing L.964   arms hand-coloured   UL24   FEt   AEm   [N2]   King 604 6C

LEIGH (Edward).   Annotations upon all the New Testament philologicall and theologicall:...
London, printed for W. W. and E. G. for William Lee, 1650 IPSWICH 1651 GS rep. 28cm.

Wing L.986   MS48   FEt   [I4]   King 611 6A

————— Critica sacra in two parts: The first... on all the radices, or primitive Hebrew words of the Old Testament;... second edition. The second philologicall and theologicall... upon all the Greek words of the New Testament... Third edition. (2 vols. in one)
London, printed by Abraham Miller and Roger Daniel for Thomas Underhill, 1650. IPSWICH 1651 GS rep. 27cm.

Wing L.991   MS48   FEt   [I4]   King 169 6A

LESSIUS (Leonhard).   De perfectionibus moribusque divinis libri XIV... *Antverpiae, ex officina Plantiniana, apud Balthasarem Moretum, & viduam Joannis Moreti, & Jo. Meursium, 1620. Rep. 24cm.*

LP4   [I2]   King 283 6A

LEY (John).   *See* Parliamentary Sermons.

LIGHTFOOT (John).   Horae Hebraicae et Talmudicae, impensae in Evangelium S. Johannis.
Londini, imprimebat Thomas Roycroft; prostant venales apud Benjamin Tooke, 1671. Reb. 19cm.

Wing L.2062   DU   FEt   [K2]   King 682 10B

————— *See also* Parliamentary Sermons.

LIPPOMANO (Aloysius), *Bp. of Bergamo*.   Catena in Exodum ex auctoribus ecclesiasticis plus minus sexaginta, iisque partim Graecis, partim Latinis, connexa...
Parisiis, apud Carolam Guillard, viduam Claudii Chevallonii, & Gulielmum Desboys, 1550. prob. English late 16th cent. BS rep. 36cm.

Adams L.750   cp: a.   bg   KG6   FEt   F5   King 504 9F

————— Catena in Genesim ex authoribus ecclesiaticis plus minus sexaginta, iisque partim Graecis, partim Latinis, connexa.
Parisiis, ex officina Carolae Guillard, 1546. Reb. 38cm.

Adams L.749   ms owner and additions: Nich. Gravelle Latin inscr: Matt.x.16   p: xx^s cp: a.e.   bg
KG6   FEp   F5   King 450 8F

LIVY (Titus Livius).   T. Livii Patavini Historiarum ab urbe condita decadis quartae(-quintae). *with* Chronologia *and with* In historiarum... libros, omnes,... ex variis... collectae. (4 parts in one vol.)

[London, impensis R. Watkins], 1589. Reb. 20cm.

STC.16612a   p: 2s 6d   probably   UL19   FEt   [K2]   King 372 7B

———— *ed.   See* LORITUS, H.

LLOYD (William), *Bp.*   An historical account of Church-government as it was in Great-Britain and Ireland, when they first received the Christian religion. By the Bishop of St. Asaph.
London, printed for Charles Brome, 1684. Rep. 19cm.

Wing L.2681   LP7   msGL   [N2]   King 374 7C

LOCKE (John).   The works, in three volumes. Vol. 1 third edition Vol. 2 third edition corrected. Vol. 3 (edition not specified)
London, printed for Arthur Bettesworth, Edmund Parker, John Pemberton, and Edward Symon, 1727. Reb. 31cm.

LP14   (Sept 1746)   King 612 6C

LOMBARD (Peter).   *See* DURANDUS *of Saint Pourain.*

LORINUS (Joannes).   Commentarii in Deuteronomium... Praecipue Graecis Latinisque traduntur. Nunc primum prodeunt. (2 vols.)
Lugduni, sumpt. Jacobi Cardon & Petri Cavellat, 1625–29. Rep. 36cm.

BT38   FEt   F4   King 501 2A

———— Commentarii in Ecclesiasten. Nunc denuo in Germania in lucem typis mandati.
Coloniae, sumptibus viduae Joannis Crithii, 1624. Rep. 35cm.

tp mutilated   BP2   FEt   F4   King 484 2A

———— Commentarii in Leviticum... Editio secunda castigatior...
Antverpiae, apud Petrum & Joannem Belleros, 1620. Rep. 35cm.

tp mutilated   BT37   FEt   F4   King 534 2A

———— Commentarii in librum Numeri... Editio recens, nunc primum luci donata.
Coloniae Agrippinae, sumptibus Antonii Hierati, 1623. Rep. 34cm.

BT39   FEt   F4   King 516 2A

———— Commentarii in librum Psalmorum, tribus tomis comprehensi... Editio postrema quae nunc primum in Germania lucem videt. (3 vols.)
Coloniae Agrippinae, sumptibus Antonii Hierati, 1619. Rep. 36cm.

bg   BP15   FEt   F4   King 469 2A

———— In Actus apostolorum commentaria: recognita, correcta, restituta, locupletata.
Lugduni, apud Horatium Cardon, 1609. Rep. 36cm.

merchant mark of donor on tp verso   bg   BP2   PGL8   FEt   F4   King 453 2A

———— In Catholicas Jacobi et Judae apostolorum Epistolas commentarii, nunc primum in lucem evvulgati, *with* In Catholicas tres B. Joannis et duas B. Petri Epistolas commentarii. Editio novissima... (2 vols. in one)
Lugduni, sumptibus Horatii Cardon (Jacobi Cardon & Petri Cavellat), 1619- 21. Rep. 36cm.

DU   FEt   F4   King 575 2A

LORITUS (Henricus), *Glareanus.*   In omneis, quae quidem extant, T. Livii Patavini clarissimi historici decadas, annotationes, cum eiusdem Chronologia... D. Erasmus cum Friburgi... degeret... Adiuncta autem est huic editioni Chronologia Henrichi Glareani...

Basileae, apud Mich. Isingrinium, 1540. Oxford or poss. London before 1573 BS rep. 32cm.
Adams L.767   ms owner: John Cardroler 1551?   bg   KG1   TEt   H4   King 87 1B

LOSS (Lucas), *ed.*   *See* BIBLE – N.T. – Latin, 1558–62, *and* 1571.

LUCAS (Franois).   In sacrosancta quatuor Jesu Christi Evangelia... commentarius. Alia eiusdem auctoris ad S. Scripturae lucem opuscula. *with* Commentariorum. Tomus tertius, 1612. (2 vols. in one)
Antverpiae, ex officina Plantiniana, apud Joannem Moretum (viduam & filios Joannis Moreti), 1606–12. IPSWICH 1651 GS rep. 34cm.
ms owner: Thomas Bedingfield   BT43   FEt   K4   King 519 10D

LUCENTIS (Xantis Pagnini).   *See* BIBLE – O.T. – Hebrew.

LUCIAN *of Samosata.*   [Greek.] Opera. Tomus I(–II) ex versione Joannis Benedicti. Cum notis integris Joannis Bourdelotti,... & selectis aliorum... ex Bibliotheca Isaaci Vossii. (2 vols.)
Amstelodami, ex typographia P. & J.Blaeu, 1687. L Reb. 20cm.
probably LP12   King 371 11B

LUDOLPH *of Saxony.*   Vita Jesu Christi e quatuor Evangeliis et scriptoribus orthodoxis concinnata... Editio nova... adiecta est ad calcem Matris Annae vita, per Petrum Dorlando...
Antverpiae, apud Joannem Keerbergium, 1618. Rep. 31cm.
ms inscription by donor   bg   MS36   FEt   G4   King 36 3B

LUTHER (Martin).   Tomus primus (-quartus) omnium operum... quorum Catalogum folio sequenti invenies. (4 vols.)
Jenae, excudebat Tobias Steinman, 1600–1612. Rep. 32cm.
Adams L.1744 (II only)   vol. 1 lacks tp   bg   BT8   PGL11   FEt   E4   King 117 3B
———— *See also* SIMONIUS, J.

LYNDEWODE (William), *Bp. of St David's.*   Provinciales seu Constitutiones Anglie *with* Constitutiones Othobonis. (2 parts in one vol.)
In inclita Parisiorum Academia impressum, cura Wolgangi Hopylii, impensis honesti mercatoris London. Wilhelmi Bretton, 1505. Reb. 33cm.
Adams L.2116 (part 1) and STC^2.17109   lacks tp starts Aii   p:viis   ms owners: John Thetford, canon of Butley whose ms on all blanks   woodblock stamp on fo.xii: a crowned R (see Ch.I) Nicholaus ..oung?   bg   BP0   FEp   M1   King 71 4A

LYRA (Nicholaus de).   *See* NICHOLAS *of Lyra.*

MAFFEIUS (Raphael), *Volaterranus.*   Commentariorum urbanorum... octo et triginta libri...
Basileae, [apud Frobenium et Episcopium], 1559. London cy BS O: ?HM a(6)775 rep. 32cm.
Adams M.104   ms owner: Wm. Harrison Ap'lis 7   bm: α 18. p: x^s bg   BP13   FEt   M2
                King 132 1B

MAGDEBURG CENTURIATORS. FLACCIUS (Matthias Illyricus) ed.   Ecclesiastica historia, integram Ecclesiae Christi ideam, quantum ad locum, propagationem, persecutionem... secundum singular centurias,... Per aliquot studiosos et pios viros in urbe Magdeburgica. (13 vols. in nine)

Basileae, per Joannem Oporinum, 1560–74. Rep. 31cm.

Adams M.110   bg   BT7   PGL15b   FEt   M3   King 220 1C

MAGISTRO (Symeone).   *See* BASIL *the Great, Saint.*

MAJOR (Johannes), *Scotus.*   Quartus sententiarum.
Paris, Philippe Pigouchet pour Johanne Granion, 1509. prob. cy Netherlandish BS rep. 27cm.

Adams M.251   ms owner: liber doctor astewyk   ms at incipit: Mr Blower 21 Ap'lis 1598   bg   BP0
H4   King 185 3A

MALDONADO (Juan).   Commentarii in quatuor evangelistas. In duos tomos... & nunc emendatius
in lucem editi. (2 vols. in one)
Moguntiae, sumptibus Arnoldi Mylii, excudebat Balthasar Lippius, 1602. Rep. 38cm.

crucifix on tp defaced in ink   MS4   FEt   G4   King 451 2E

MARBECKE (John).   A booke of notes and commonplaces, with their expositions, collected and
gathered out of the workes of divers singular writers... to those that desire the true understanding &
meaning of holy scripture.
London, imprinted by Thomas East, 1581. BS rep. 20cm.

STC.17299   ms donor's signature   MS45   FEt   [H3]   King 259 7D

MARCA (Pierre de), *Abp. of Paris.*   Dissertationum De concordia sacerdotii et imperii, seu de
libertatibus Ecclesiae gallicanae, libri octo. Stephanus Baluzius... hanc secundam editionem recog-
novit... (2 vols. in one)
Parisiis, apud Franciscum Muguet, 1669. Rep. 41cm.

UL22   FEt   [N4]   King 445 11E

MARCELLINUS (Ammianus).   Rerum gestarum qui de XXXI. supersunt, libri XVIII... emendati
ab Henrico Valesio... Editio posterior,... vitam Ammiani a Claudio Chiffletio... compositam. (3 parts
in one vol.)
Parisiis, ex officina Antonii Dezallier, 1681. Rep. 34cm.

ms owner: Tho: Baker Coll: Go: Socius ejectus   LP15 (1746)   King 523 10D

MARINETZ (Matthia), *trans.*   *See* BESSE, P. de.

MARLORAT (Augustin), *ed.*   *See* BIBLE - Latin - 1562–64.

MARSHALL (Stephen).   *See* Parliamentary Sermons.

MARTINI (Matthias).   Christianae doctrinae summa capita, quae continentur in symbolo apostoli-
co,... distincte explicata: item methodus S. theologiae, in quatuor libellos distributa: (2 vols. in one)
Herbornae Nassoviorum, [s.n.], 1603. Rep. 16cm.

bg   BT1   FEt   E1   King 368 10A

———— Institutio... De praesentia... Jesu Christi, Dei et hominis, in sacra coena, in ecclesia & in
medio inimicorum: pro confessione orthodoxa, contra Balthazaris Mentzeri vanas objectiones.
bound with his Demonstratio... quod conformi S. scripturis... contra... B. Mentzeri &S. calumnias. *and
his* De veritate divinae naturae Jesu Christi, veri et unici redemtoris nostri, Liber II. (3 vols. in one)
Bremae, typis Thomae de Villiers, apud Johannem Wesselium, 1617 (1612). Rep. 15cm.

bg   BT1   FEt   E1   King 361 10A

———— Summa operum, seu commentarius in legem duarum divinarum tabularum; in quo primo verba singulorum praeceptorum diligenter expenduntur,...
Bremae, apud Johannem Wesselium, 1612. Rep. 15cm.

bg BT1 FEt E1   **King 385 10A**

———— Theologia de unica... Jesu Christi persona,... ex scripturarum sanctarum apertis dictis,... contra blasphemias errores & calumnias haereticorum...
Bremae, typis Thomae Villeriani, scholae typographi, 1614. Rep. 15cm.

bg BT1 FEt E1   **King 360 10A**

———— Theologia popularis universa: Hoc est, Divini textus catechetici,... enarrati & explicati; *with his* Paraphrasis symboli apostolici ad institutionem sacri baptismi accommodata. (2 parts in one vol.)
Bremae, apud Thomam Villerianum, 1617. Rep. 16cm.

cp: a.f. bg BT1 FEt E1   **King 365 10A**

MARTINI (Jacob).   ...De tribus Elohim liber primus, photinianorum novorum et cum primis Georgi Eniedini blasphemiis oppositus. (2 vols. in one)
[Wittebergae], impensis Zachariae Schureri, typis Johannis Gormanni, 1614–15. Rep. 16cm.

bg BT1 FEt E1   **King 386 10A**

———— Partitiones theologicae, quadraginta titulis accurata methodo inclusae, & privatis exercitiis ad disputandum in incluta Wittenbergensi propositae. (2 vols.)
Wittebergae, impensis Clementis Bergeri Bibliopol., 1612. Rep. 18cm.

cp: q.n. bg BT1 FEt E1   **King 681 10A**

MARTYR (Peter).   *See* VERMIGLI, P.M.

MASON (Francis), *Rector of Sudbourne-cum-Orford.*   Vindiciae ecclesiae Anglicanae; sive De legitimo eiusdem ministerio, id est, de episcoporum successione,... editio secunda.
Londini, per Felicem Kyngstonum, 1625. Reb. 29cm.

STC.17598 UL25 FEt [I3]   **King 165 1B**

MATTHAEUS, *Westmonasteriensis and* FLORENTIUS, *Wigorniensis.*   Flores historiarum per Matthaeum Westmonasteriensem collecti: praecipue de rebus Britannicis:... usque ad MCCCVII. Et chronicon ex chronicis... ad MCXVIII. deductum: auctore Florentio Wigorniensi... cui accessit continuato ad MCXLI. (2 parts in one vol.)
Francofurti, typis Wechelianis apud Claudium Marnium & heredes Joannis Aubrii, 1601. Rep. 34cm.

bg BP13 FEt M2   **King 51 3C**

MAYNARD (John), *of Manfield.*   *See* Parliamentary Sermons.

MEDE (Joseph).   The works of the pious and profoundly-learned... corrected and enlarged according to the author's own manuscripts. (third to fifth books only - 3 books in one vol.)
London, printed for R. Royston, 1663–64. Rep. 30cm.

Wing M.1586 LP1 FEt [I3]   **King 101 6D**

MEDIA VILLA (Richardus de).   *See* RICHARD *of Middleton.*

MEDICES (Hieronymus).   Summae theologiae S. Thomae Aquinatis... explicatio formalis... & explanatur, auctore Hieronymo de Medices... Nunc primum... in Germania edita.

Coloniae, sumptibus Conradi Butgenii, 1622. Rep. 18cm.

bg   KG10   FEt   H2   King 380 5A

MEDINA (Bartolomeo).   Scholastica commentaria in Thomae Aquinatis Primam secundae (-tertiae) quaestiones... Post omnes omnium editiones... recognita. (2 vols. in one)
Coloniae Agrippinae, sumptibus Petri Henningii, 1618–19. Rep. 35cm.

bg   MS26   FEt   L4   King 526 5E

MEFFRETH.   Sermones Meffreth al's Ortulus regine de Sanctis. [Vol. 3 of Sermones de tempore et de sanctis] [*Basel, Nicholas Kesler, before 11 July 1486.*] Reb. 30cm.

Goff M.441 (part III)   lacks Ai   ms prayer of Wm. Smarte   names: Mr Toley John Griggs and others   ms index to 121 sermons probably in hand of Wm. Blower   bg   BP0   FEp   H4

                                                                  King 207 3A

MELANCTHON (Philipp).   Operum omnium... pars prima-quarta. (4 vols.) *Witebergae, excudebant haeredes Johannis Cratonis (Typis Simonis Gronenbergii), 1580–1601. Rep. 33cm.*

Adams M.1069   bg   BP7   PGL6   FEt   E4   King 56 2C

————— *See also* PEZEL, C.

MERCER (Jean).   ...Commentarii in librum Job. Adiecta est Theodori Bezae Epistola,... & istorum commentariorum utilate differitur. *bound with his* ...Commentarii in Salomonis Proverbia, Ecclesiasten, & Canticum canticorum. Adiecimus ad calcem horum commentariorum harmoniam... in Proverbia & Ecclesiasten. (2 vols. in one)
Genevae, excudebat Eustathius Vignon, 1573. English 1620–1630 BS rep. 32cm.

Adams M.1314   bg   BP6   FEt   C3   King 12 11D

————— ...Commentarii locupletiss. in Prophetas quinque priores inter eos qui minores vocantur. Quibus adiuncti sunt aliorum etiam & veterum... & recentium Commentarii, ab eodem excerpti. *Geneva, [Robert Estienne], n.d. Rep. 33cm.*

Adams M.1318   bg   BP6   PGL28 lost   FEt   C3   King 152 11D

————— ...In Genesin primum Mosis librum, sic a Graecis appellatum, commentarius nunc primum in lucem editus, addita Theodori Bezae praefatione.
[Geneva], ex typographia Matthaei Berjon, 1598. Rep. 32cm.

Adams M.1313   bg   BP6   PGL28   FEt   C3   King 11 11D

MESSANA (Franciscus a).   Lectura in Zachariam, cum paraphrasi in omnes duodecim Prophetas, quos minores nuncupant:
Antverpiae, ex officina Martini Nutii, 1597. L reb. 20cm.

Adams M.1364   bg   BT23   PGL17   FEt   G2   King 669 11A

MEWE (William).   *See* Parliamentary Sermons.

MIDDLETON (Conyers).   The history of the life of Marcus Tullius Cicero. Vols. 1–3 Second edition. (3 vols.)
London, printed for W. Innys and R. Manby, 1741. Reb. 20cm.

ms owner: Ipswich Socy. No.17   DU but possibly LP12   King 422 10B

MIDDLETON (Richard).   *See* RICHARD *of Middleton.*

MILLES (Thomas), *comp.*   *See* GLOVER, R.

MINSHEU (John).   [Greek.] – id est Ductor in linguas the guide into tongues,... in eleven languages, *with his* Vocabularium Hispanico-Latinum et Anglicum... a most copious Spanish dictionarie, with Latine and English... (2 parts in one)
Londini, sumptibus Johannis Minshaei, apud Joannem Browne, 1617. Rep. 38cm.
STC².17944   After 'And are to be sold at' on tp of second volume in hand of Silas Taylor: 'The Devil's Arse at Peak'   bg   MS17   PGL5 in error   FEt K5   King 473 7G

MINUCIUS FELIX.   Marci Minutii Felicis Octavius. Geverhartus Elmenhorstius recensuit   *bound with* ARNOBIUS Disputationum adversus gentes, 1610. (2 vols. in one)
Hamburgi, [s.n.], 1612. Rep. 31cm.
BT1   FEt   A4   King 39 9D

MOLLER (Heinrich).   Enarrationis Psalmorum Davidis, ex praelectionibus... in Academia Witebergensi exceptae, novissima editio, prioribus emendiator.
Genevae, apud Petrum & Jacobum Chouet, 1610. Rep. 33cm.
bg   MS10 (1616)   trompe l'oeil msGL   FEt   D3   King 33 2C

MONTAGU (Richard), *Bp.*   The acts and monuments of the Church before Christ incarnate.
London, printed by Miles Flesher and Robert Young, 1642. Rep. 28cm.
Wing M.2469   UL13   King 80 6B

MONTANUS (Beneditus Arias).   *See* ARIAS MONTANO, B.

MONTFAUCON (Bernard de).   The travels of the learned Father... from Paris thro' Italy... Made English from the Paris edition. Adorn'd with cuts.
London, printed by D. L. for E. Curll (& others), 1712. Reb. 20cm.
LP12   King 414 7B

MORE (Henry).   Apocalypsis apocalypseos; or the Revelation of St John the Divine unveiled,... a brief... exposition... of the whole Book of the Apocalypse.
London, printed by J. M. for J. Martyn, and W. Kettilby, 1680. Rep. 20cm.
Wing M.2641   DU   FEt   [H3]   King 686 10B

——— Divine dialogues, containing sundry disquisitions & instructions concerning the attributes and providence of God. The three... compiled by the care and industry of F. P. [Epistle to the reader signed Franciscus Euistor, More's pseudonym.]
London, printed by James Flesher, 1668. BF rep. 16cm.
Wing M.2650   DU   [I2]   King 348 10B

——— Enchiridion metaphysicum: sive, de rebus incorporeis succinta & luculenta dissertatio. Pars prima: De existentia & natura rerum incorporearum in genere.
Londini, typis E. Flesher. Prostat apud Guilielmum Morden, Bibliopolam Cantabrigiensem, 1671. Rep. 20cm.
Wing M.2654   DU   FEt   [H3]   King 688 10B

——— A plain and continued exposition of the several prophecies or divine visions of the Prophet Daniel, ...whereunto is annexed a threefold appendage.
London, printed by M. F. for Walter Kettilby, 1681. L reb. 20cm.
Wing M.2673   DU   FEt   [H3]   King 261 10B

———— The theological works of the most pious and learned... according to the author's improvements in his Latin edition.
London, printed and sold by Joseph Downing, 1708. GF rep. 36cm.

LP12   FEt   King 508 11F

MORERI (Louis).   Le grand dictionaire historique, ou le mélange curieux de l'histoire sacrée et profane... Huitèime édition où l'on a mis le supplément... corrigé les fautes censurées dans le Dictionaire critique de Mr. Bayle... (4 vols. in two)
A Amsterdam (La Haye), chez George Gallet [Henry Desbordes, Adrian Moetjens et al], 1698. Reb. 37cm.

LP12   King 507 10F

MORLAND (*Sir* Samuel).   The history of the Evangelical Churches of the valleys of Piemont, and... of the doctrine, life and persecutions of the ancient inhabitants... relation of the bloudy massacre, 1655... to the year 1658. (4 parts in one vol.)
London, by Henry Hills for Adoniram Byfield, 1658. Reb. 29cm.

Wing M.2779   UL15   [I3]   King 188 1C

MORNAY (Philippe de).   De sacra Eucharistia, in quatuor libros distinctum opus. In quo & eius institutio, celebratio, doctrina in primitiva ecclesia, quae fuerit;... sigillatim explicatur. (4 books in one vol.)
Hanoviae, typis Wechelianis apud Claudium Marnium & haeredes Johannis Aubrii, 1605. Rep. 34cm.

bg   BP6   PGL28   FEt   F3   King 650 11D

———— De veritate religionis Christianae liber; adversus atheos, epicureos... & caeteros infideles:... Gallice primum conscriptus, Latine versus... Accessit eiusdem authoris, vita mortisq. (interprete Arnoldo Freitagio). (2 vols. in one)
Herbornae Nassoviorum, [excudebat Christophorus Corvinus,] 1609. L reb. 17cm.

bg   BP6   PGL28 defective   FEt   F2   King 334 11B

———— Mysterium iniquitatis seu, historia Papatus. Quibus gradibus ad id fastigii enisus sit,... ubique a piis contra intercessum.
Salmurii, per Thomam Portaeum, 1611. Rep. 33cm.

bg   BP6   PGL28   FEt   F3   King 651 11D

———— Responsio ad librum Ebroicensis Episcopi de colloquio Fontisbellaquei anno MDC 4 maii habito... Nunc autem a Davide Licquaei... Latine versa.
Hanoviae, typis Wechelianis, apud Claud. Marnium & heredes Ioan. Aubrii, 1607. Rep. 21cm.

bg   BP6   PGL28   FEt   F2   King 275 11B

MORTON (Thomas), *Bp.*   Apologia catholica ex meris Jesuitarum contradictionibus conflata... eius libri duo de notis Ecclesiae. (2 parts in one vol.)
Londini, impensis Georgii Bishop, 1605–06. Reb. 21cm.

STC^2.18174 & 18174.5   bg   MS21   FEp   G1   King 675 7C

———— The encounter against M. Parsons by a review of his last sober reckoning... (2 books in one vol.)
London, printed for John Bill, 1610. Reb. 19cm.

STC.18183   bg   MS21   FEp   G1   King 667 7C

MULERIUS (Nicolaus).   Judaeorum annus lunae-solaris: et Turc-Arabum annus mere lunaris. Recens... deductus, & cum anno Romano facili methodo connexus. *bound with* SCHUBERT, C. De

scrupulis chronologorum, 1575. *and also* BIBLIANDER, T. Temporum a condito mundo, 1558. (3 vols. in one)
Groningae, excudebat Joannes Sassius, 1630. BS rep. 30cm.

p: 4 6   DU   FEt   [I3]   King 126 11C

MUSCULUS (Wolfgang).   Commentarii in Matthaeum evangelistam tribus tomis digesti... in hac novissima editione post ipsius authoris... recognita.
Basileae, per Sebastianum Henricpetri, [1611]. Rep. 32cm.

bg   BT2   PGL16   FEt   D2   King 24 4C

———— In Davidis Psalterium... commentarii:... Editio postrema.
Basileae, per Sebastianum Henricpetri, [1599]. Reb. 32cm.

Adams M.2013   bg   BT2   PGL16   FEt   D2   King 22 4C

———— In epistolam Pauli ad Romanos commentarii,... nunc demum magno studio recogniti... *with his* In Apostoli Pauli ambas Epistolas ad Corinthios commentarii... Editio ultima. (2 vols. in one)
Basileae, per Sebastianum Henricpetri, 1600–11. Rep. 32cm.

Adams M.2031   bg   BT2   PGL16   FEt   D2   King 26 4C

———— In Epistolas Pauli, ad Galatas & Ephesios commentarii; *with his* In Pauli Epistolas ad Philippenses, Colossenses, Thessalonicenses ambas, & primam ad Timotheum commentarii... nunc denuo... castigatius. (2 vols. in one)
Basileae, ex officina Hervagiana, per Eusebium Episcopium, 1569–70. Rep. 32cm.

Adams M.2038   cp in vol.2: x under A   bg   BT2   PGL16   FEt   D2   King 27 4C

———— In Esaiam prophetam commentarii... ac recens editi.
Basileae, ex officina Hervagiana, per Eusebium Episcopium, 1570. Reb. 32cm.

Adams M.2015   bg   BT2   PGL16   FEt   D2   King 23 4C

———— In Genesim Mosis commentarii plenissimi... nunc a multis mendis repurgati.
Basileae, per Sebastianum Henricpetri, [1600]. Rep. 32cm.

Adams M.2009   bg   BT2   PGL16   FEt   D2   King 21 4C

———— In Joannis Evangelium... commentarii in tres heptadas digesti... (3 parts in one vol.)
Basileae, ex officina Hervagiana, per Eusebium Episcopium, 1580. Reb. 32cm.

Adams M.2028   bg   BT2   PGL16   FEt   D2   King 25 4C

———— *See also* BASIL *the Great, Saint.*

MUSSO (Cornelio), *Bp.*   Delle prediche... parte seconda-quinta Di nuovo riordinate & in questa ultima editione da molti errori espurgate. (4 vols. in three)
Venetia, appresso i Gioliti, 1599. GR reb. 15cm.

Adams M.2062   UL32   [I1]   King 363 5A

———— Delle prediche quadragesimali... sopra l'Epistole & Evangeli correnti,... con la vita dell'autore,... seconda parte. (Second of 2 vols.)
Vinetia, stamperia de' Giunti, 1596. GR rep. 25cm.

not in Adams   UL32   [I1]   King 310 9B

MYLIUS (Johannus), *ed.*   *See* GERARDUS (Andreas).

NALTON (James). *See* Parliamentary Sermons.

NANNI (Petrus), *trans.* *See* ATHANASIUS, *Bp., Saint.*

NAUCLERUS (Joannes). Chronica, succinctim compraehendentia res memorabiles seculorum omnium... ab initio mundi... ad MCCCCC. Cum auctario Nicolai Baselii... et Appendice nova... in annum presentem. (3 parts in one vol.) Coloniae, ex officina Petri Quentel, 1544. Cloth reb. 32cm.

Adams N.72   ms owner: Gulielmus Cecilius & his marginalia   bg   BP3   FEp   M2

King 10 9C

NEUBRIGENSIS (Gulielmus). *See* WILLIAM OF NEWBURGH.

NEWCOMEN (Matthew), *of Dedham.* *See* Parliamentary Sermons.

NICEPHORUS CALLISTUS, *Xanthopoulos.* Ecclesiasticae historiae libri decem et octo. ...Opera vero ac studio Joannis Langi,... e Graeco in Latinum sermonem translati,... adiecimus... Magni Aurelii Cassiodori... Historiam. (2 vols. in one)
Francof., impensis Sigismundi Feyerabendii, 1588. Rep. 33cm.

Adams N.222   bg   BP13   FEt   M3

King 521 9D

NICHOLAS *de Lyra.* Postilla in universa Biblia Vol. IV. Postilla sup. Matheum fratris Nicolai de lira...
[*Cologne, Ulrich Zel, c.*1485]. Reb. 30cm.

Goff N.136 lacks last 2 fos. (I9 & 10)   ms marginalia and decorative pilcrows   bg   BP0   FEp   G5

King 4(4) 3A

————— See also BIBLE – O.T. – Latin

NORTH (*Sir* Thomas), *trans.* *See* PLUTARCH.

NUGNUS (Didacus). *See* NUNO CABEZUDO, D.

NUNO CABEZUDO (Diego). Commentarii, ac disputationes in tertiam partem summae theologiae Thomae Aquinatis cum additionibus eiusdem. Nunc primum accurate iuxta,... Tomus secundus. Hic accedunt quatuor insignes tractatus,... (2 vols. in one)
Venetiis, apud Petrum Dusinellum, 1612. Rep. 31cm.

cp: R6 N0 a.k.   bg   KG14   FEt   L1

King 124 4D

OECOLAMPADIUS (John). Commentaria omnes in libros prophetarum. In Jesaiam prophetam, hypomnematon, hoc est, commentariorum libri sex *bound with his* In librum Job exegemata... eiusdem in Danielem prophetam libri duo.
Genevae, apud Jo. Crispinum (e typographia Crispiniana), 1558–67. Reb. 31cm.

Adams B.1282   bg   BP10   PGL24   FEt   C4

King 649 8E

————— *See also* THEOPHYLACT, *Abp.*

OECUMENIUS, *Bp.* [Greek.]...Commentaria in hosce Novi Testamenti tractatus... accesserunt Arethae Caesareae Cappodociae Episcopi explanationes in Apocalypsin. Opus nunc primum Graece & Latine editum,... (2 vols.)
Lutetiae Parisiorum, sumptibus Claudii Sonnii, 1631. Reb. 35cm.

BT36   FEt   B3

King 488 10D

OGILBY (John).   America, being the latest and most accurate description of the New World;... the conquest of... Mexico and Peru and other... provinces with the European plantations in those parts;... an appendix containing a survey of the unknown South-Land and the Arctick Region. (3 parts and appendix in one vol.)
London, by the author, 1671. Reb. 40cm.

Wing O.165   lacks tp and Ai–iv   DU possibly UL21   FEp   [O3]   King 162 7G

———— Britannia, volume the first: or, an illustration of the Kingdom of England and Dominion of Wales: by a geographical and historical description of the principal roads...
London, printed by the Author, 1675. Rep. 42cm.

Wing O.168: the second version with London section reset   UL21   unique printed dedication leaf to Corporation of Ipswich   AEm   [O3]
                                                                                             King 162 1E

OLDENBURG (Henry), *ed.*   *See* ROYAL SOCIETY OF LONDON.

ORIGENES, *Adamantius.*   Opera quae quidem extant omnia... Translata & recognita:... cum vita auctoris (pars secunda) (2 vols. in one)
Basileae, per Eusebium Episcopium et Nicolai Fr. haeredes, 1571. Reb. 32cm.

Adams O.285   bg   BT1   PGL32   FEt   A1
                                                                                             King 92 11D

ORTELIUS (Abraham).   Theatrum orbis terrarum... denuo ab ipso auctore recognitum,... & quam plurimus novis tabulis atque commentariis auctum; *with* Parergon *and with* Nomenclator Ptolemaicus,... (3 parts in one vol.)
Antverpiae, ex officina Plantiniana, 1595. Reb. 44cm.

Koeman Ort 29 calls for 115 + 32 mapsheets: this has 109 + 26   ms scribbles on last leaf crucifixion scene cut from Terra Sancta map   maps pasted onto paper guards cut from two sources: a printed astrological calendar and a ms list of 1545 (see Ch. IV)   bg   MS16   FEp   [O3]
                                                                                             King 434 1E

OSIANDER (Andreae).   Harmoniae evangelicae libri IIII Graece et Latine,... item Annotationum liber unus Elenchus harmoniae. (5 parts in one vol.)
Basileae, [ex officina Frobeniana, per Hier. Frobenium et Nic. Episcopium], 1561. Rep. 29cm.

Adams O.359   bg   BT1   FEt   E5
                                                                                             King 2 6B

OSIANDER (Lucas), *elder.*   *See* BIBLE – Latin, 1608–09.

PAEZ (Balthasar).   Ad canticum Moysis Exodi XV commentarii cum annotationibus moralibus... Huic editione accesserunt tres indices:...
Antverpiae, apud Gulielmum a Tongris, 1619. Rep. 24cm.

MS43   FEt   G2
                                                                                             King 268 8B

———— Commentarii in canticum Ezechiae,... nunc primum in Galliis excusi.
Lugduni, sumptibus Ludovici Prost, 1623. Rep. 24cm.

MS43   FEt   G2
                                                                                             King 292 8B

———— Commentarii in canticum magnum Moysis, audite coeli quae loquor.
Antverpiae, apud Petrum, & Joannem Belleros, 1622. Rep. 22cm.

MS43   FEt   G2
                                                                                             King 298 8B

———— Commentarii in Epistolam Jacobi. Editio novissima suis indicibus illustrata.
Lugduni, sumptibus Horatii Cardon, 1617. Rep. 24cm.

cp: R1 N13+1   MS43   FEt   G2   King 289 8B

PALACIOS DE SALAZAR (Paulo).   In XII prophetas, quos minores vocant commentarius.
Coloniae, in officina Birckmannica, 1583. Rep. 16cm.

Adams P.59   cp: o a   bg   BT23   FEt   G1   King 349 7A

PALMER (Herbert).   *See* Parliamentary Sermons.

PAMELIUS (Jacob), *ed.   See* GREGORY I, *Pope and* TERTULLIAN, Q.S.F.

PAMPHILIUS (Eusebius).   *See* BIBLE – Latin, 1614.

PANVINIO (Onofrio).   Fasti et triumphi Roma Romulo Rege usque ad Carolum V. Caes. Aug...
Additae sunt... icones,... ex musaeo Jacobi Stradae, Romani, antiquarii.
Venetiis, impensis Jacobi Stradae Mantuani, 1557. English cy GS rep. 31cm.

Adams P.195   ms owner: fitzhenry (Wm. Harrison)   p: xii^s bg   BP13   FEt   M1
                                                               King 143 4A

PAPPUS (Johannes).   In omnes Prophetas, tam Maiores quatuor,.. quam Minores duodecim,
scholae breves et methodicae: propositae...
Francofurti ad Moenum, ex officina Johann. Spiessii, 1593. L Reb. 32cm.

Adams B.1287   bg   MS10   FEt   C3   King 216 2B

PAREUS (David).   Bellarmini... De amissione gratiae & statu peccati libri sex... *with his* De gratia &
libera arbitrio libri VI... (12 books in two vols.)
Heidelbergae, impensis Jonae Rosae, typis Johannis Lancelotti, 1613–14. Reb. 19cm.

bg   MS34   FEt   E3   King 381(3–4) 5C

———— Bellarmini... liber unus De gratia primi hominis... explicatus & castigatus... *with* ...De justificatione impii libri V... (6 books in two vols.)
Heidelbergae, impensis Jonae Rosae, typis Johan. Lancelotti, 1612–15. Reb. 19cm.

p: 2^{li} (prob. for 4 vols. of King 381)   bg   MS34   FEt   E3   King 381(1–2) 5C

———— Exercitationum philosophicarum & theologicarum libri IV. Cum praefatione Joh. Philippi
Parei. (4 books in one vol.)
Heidelbergae, impensis Jonae Rhodii, typis Johannis Lancelotti, 1610. Reb. 18cm.

bg   MS34   FEt   E3   King 339 5C

———— In divinam ad Galatas Pauli epistolam commentarius... nunc primum ab authore in lucem
editus.
Heidelbergae, impensis Jonae Rosae, typis Johannis Lancelotti, 1613. Rep. 24cm.

bg   MSI   PGL33   FEt   E3   King 272 5D

———— Hoseas propheta commentariis illustratus: cum translatione triplici;... adjectae sunt quator
orationes in Academia (1599–1600). (3 parts in one vol.)
Haidelbergae, typis Voegelinianis, [1605]. Reb. 25cm.

cp: 11.1   bg   MS1   PGL33   FEt   E3   King 293 5D

———— In Apocalypsin Johannis commentarius...
Heidelbergae, impensis Jonae Rosae,, typis Johannis Lancelotti, 1618.   Rep. 25cm.

bg   MS1   FEt   E3   King 290 5D

––––––– In divinam ad Corinthios priorem Pauli epistolam commentarius... extrema authoris opera diligenter recognitus... cum epistola dedicat; ad... senatum urbis Bremensis de origine coelibatus clericalis.
Heidelbergae, impensis Jonae Rhodii, typis Johannis Lancelotti, 1613. Rep. 25cm.

bg   MS1   PGL33   FEt   E3   King 303 5D

––––––– In divinam ad Hebraeos Pauli epistolam commentarius... extrema authoris opera diligenter recognitus & locupletatus. (2 parts in one vol.)
Heidelbergae, impensis Jonae Rosae, typis Johannis Lancelotti, 1613. Rep. 25cm.

bg   MS1   PGL33   FEt   E3   King 273 5D

––––––– In divinam ad Romanos Pauli epistolam commentarius... extrema authoris opera diligenter recognitus & auctus.
Heidelbergae, impensis Jonae Rosae, typis Johannis Lancelotti, 1613. Rep. 24cm.

bg   MS1   PGL33   FEt   E3   King 280 5D

––––––– In Genesin Mosis commentarius... quo praeter accuratam textus... atque interpretationem theoricam & practicam, controversiae & dubia fidei plurima perspicue explicantur...
Francofurti, impensis Jonae Rhodii, typis Johannis Lancelotti, 1609. Rep. 24cm.

bg   MS1   PGL33   FEt   E3   King 307 5D

––––––– *See also* URSINUS, Z.

PARKER (Matthew), *Abp.*   De antiquitate Britannicae ecclesiae, et nominatim de privilegiis ecclesiae Cantuariensis... historia... Londini... Joannis Daii 1572 excusa: nunc... recognita.
Hanoviae, typis Wechelianis, apud Claud. Marnium & haeredes Joannis Aubrii, 1605. Rep. 34cm.

bg   BP13   FEt   M2   King 16 6D

PARLIAMENTARY SERMONS (171 in all) bound in six volumes; all preached at Westminster between 1640 and 1646 and published in 4to. in London. Their first owner was William Dowsing of Coddenham, later of Stratford St Mary, who obtained a Commission from the Eastern Association to remove all traces of popery from the churches of East Anglia in 1643 and 1644. He annotated all the sermons with the date he read them, and with references and comments. For further details see Chapters IX and XII of the history of the Library. There is an important draft letter from Dowsing to Newcomen on the recto of the last leaf of sermon VI.2, (indicating the second sermon in the sixth volume) the first listed below. Numbers of sermons in each volume: I: 22; II: 31; III: 30; IV: 31; V: 30; VI: 27. V reb. 21cm.

LP9   King 654 6E

ARROWSMITH (John).   The Covenant-avenging sword brandished... 25 Jan 1642. *For Samuel Man,*
1643.   Wing A.3773   VI.2

———— Englands Eben-ezer or, stone of help... 12 March 1644. *By Robert Leyburn, for Samuel Man,*
1645.   Wing A.3775   II.23

ASHE (Simeon).   The best refuge for the most oppressed... 30 March 1642. *For Edward Brewster and*
John Burroughs, 1642.   Wing A.3949   IV.14

———— The church sinking, saved by Christ... 26 February 1644. *By G. M. for Edward Brewster,* 1645.
Wing A.3951   I.6

BAILLIE (Robert).   Errours and induration, are the great sins and the great judgements of the
time... 30 July 1645. *By R. Raworth, for Samuel Gellibrand,* 1645.   Wing B.459   I.12

———— Satan the leader in chief to all who resist the reparation of Sion... 28 February 1643. *For*
Samuel Gellibrand, 1644.   Wing B.468   V.3

BOLTON (Samuel).   [Greek.], or, the sinfulnes of sin... 25 March 1646. *By G. M. for Andrew Kemb,*
1646.   Wing B.3516   III.27

BOND (John).   Ortus occidentalis: or, a dawning in the West... 27 March 1644. *By J. D. for Fr.*
Eglesfield, 1645.   Wing B.3573   II.26
———— Salvation in a mystery: or a prospective glasse for Englands case... 27 March 1644. *By L. N. for*
Francis Eglesfield, 1644.   Wing B.3574   V.5

BOWLES (Oliver).   Zeale for Gods house quickned... 7 July 1643. *By Richard Bishop for Samuel*
Gellibrand, 1643.   Wing B.3884   VI.13

BRIDGE (William).   Babylons downfall... *By J. N. for John Rothwell,* 1641.   Wing B.4448   IV.4

———— A sermon preached... 29 November 1643. *For R. Dawlman,* 1643.   Wing B.4465   VI.25

BRIDGES (Walter).   Joabs counsell and King David's seasonable hearing it... 22 February 1642. *By*
R. Cotes for Andrew Crooke, 1643.   Wing B.4484A   VI.4

BURGESS (Anthony).   The Difficulty of, and the encouragements to a reformation... 27
September 1643. *By R. Bishop for Thomas Underhill,* 1643.   Wing B.5643   VI.21

———— Publick affections, pressed in a sermon... 25 February 1645. *By J. Y. for Thomas Underhill,* 1643.
Wing B.5653   III.25

———— The reformation of the church, to be endeavoured more than that of the common-wealth... 27 August 1645. *By G. M. for T. Underhill*, 1645.   Wing B.5654

I.13

———— Romes cruelty & Apostacie declared... 5 November 1645. *By George Miller for Tho. Underhill*, 1645.   Wing B.5655

II.21

BURGESS (Cornelius).   Another sermon preached... 5 November 1641. *By R. B. for P. Stephens and C. Meredith*, 1641.   Wing B.5668

II.4

———— The first sermon, preached... 17 November 1640. *By I. L. for Philemon Stephens and Christopher Meredith*, 1641.   Wing B 5671

IV.8

———— The necessity of agreement with God... 29 October 1645. *By G. Miller for Philemon Stephens*, 1645.   Wing B.5673

I.16

———— The second sermon, preached... 30 April 1645... discovering the vanity and mischief of the thoughts of a heart unwashed. *By J. R. for Philem. Stephens*, 1645.   Wing B.5680

III.9

———— Two sermons preached... the one 30 March 1642... the necessity and benefit of washing the heart... *By J. R. for Phil. Stephens*, 1645.   Wing B.5688

III.8

BURROUGHES (Jeremiah).   A Sermon preached... 26 November 1645. *For R. Dawlman*, 1646.   Wing B.6117

I.17

———— Sions joy... 7 September 1641. *By T. P. and M. S. for R. Dawlman, to be sold by Ben. Alline*, 1641.   Wing B.6119

II.2

BYFIELD (Richard).   Zion's answer to the nations ambassadors, according to instructions given to Isaiah from Gods mouth... 25 June 1645. *By John Field for Ralph Smith*, 1645.   Wing B.6395   III.11

CALAMY (Edmund), *the elder*.   England's antidote, against the plague of Civil Warre... 22 October 1644. *By I. L. for Christopher Meredith*, 1645.   Wing C.233

V.22

———— Englands looking glasse... 22 December 1641. *By J. Raworth for Chr. Meredith*, 1642.   Wing C.237

IV.11

———— Gods free mercy to England... 23 February 1641. *For Christopher Meredith*, 1642.   Wing C.253

IV.12

———— An indictment against England because of her self-murdering divisions... 25 December 1644. *By J. L. for Christopher Meredith*, 1645.   Wing C.256

I.5

———— The noble-mans patterne of true and reall thankfulnesse... 15 June 1643. 65p. *By G. M. for Christopher Meredith*, 1643.   Wing C.261

II.6

CARTER (Thomas).   Prayers prevalencie for Israels safety... 28 June 1643. *By Richard Cotes, and are to be sold by John Bellamie and Ralph Smith*, 1643.   Wing C.668

VI.12

CARTER (William).   Israels peace with God Benjamines overthrow... 31 August 1642. *For Giles Calvert, to be sold by Christopher Meredith*, 1642.   Wing C.679A

IV.23

CARYL (Joseph).   The arraignment of unbelief, as the grand cause of our nationall non-establishment... 28 May 1645. *By G. Miller for Giles Calvert*, 1645.   Wing C.749

III.10

————— England's plus ultra, both of hoped mercies and of required duties... 2 April 1646. *By G. M. for John Rothwell, and Giles Calvert,* 1646.   Wing C.752   II.29

————— Heaven and earth embracing; or, God and man approaching... 28 January 1645. *By G.M. for George Hurlock, and Giles Calvert,* 1646.   Wing C.779   III.22

————— Joy out-joyed: or joy in overcoming evil spirits and evil men, overcome by better joy... 19 February 1645. *By G. M. for John Rothwel, and Giles Calvert,* 1646.   Wing C.780   II.30

————— The nature, solemnity, grounds, property, and benefits of a sacred covenant. together with the duties of those who enter into such a covenant... 6 October 1643. *By E. G. for John Rothwell and Giles Calvert,* 1643.   Wing C.782   II.11

————— The saints thankfull acclamation at Christ's resumption of his great power and the initials of his kingdome... 23 April 1644. *By G. M. for Giles Calvert,* 1644.   Wing C.787   II.16

————— The workes of Ephesus explained... 27 April 1642. *For John Bartlet and William Bladen,* 1642. Wing C.790   IV.16

CASE (Thomas).   Deliverance-obstruction: or, the set-backs of Reformation ... 25 March 1646. *By Ruth Rowarth, for Luke Fawne,* 1646.   Wing C.827   I.21

————— Gods rising, his enemies scattering... 26 October 1642. *By J. R. for Luke Fawne,* 1644.   Wing C.830   IV.27

————— A model of true spiritual thankfulnesse... 19 February 1645. *By Ruth Raworth, for Luke Fawne,* 1646.   Wing C.833   III.30

————— The root of apostacy, and fountain of true fortitude... *By J. R., for Luke Fawne,* 1644.   Wing C.839   II.15

————— A sermon preached... 22 August 1645. *By Ruth Raworth, for Luke Fawne,* 1645.   Wing C.842   II.27

————— Two sermons lately preached... 2nd edition... 1642. *By J. Raworth for Luke Fawne,* 1642.   Wing C.846   IV.6 & 7

CAWDREY (Daniel).   The good man a publick good, 1. Passively, 2. Actively ... 31 January 1643. *By Tho. Harper, for Charles Greene, and P. W.,* 1643.   Wing C.1628   V.2

CHAMBERS (Humphry).   A divine ballance to weigh religious fasts in. Applyed to present use... 27 September 1643. *By M. F. for Samuel Man,* 1643.   Wing C.1915   VI.20

CHEYNELL (Francis).   The man of honour... 26 March 1645. *By J. R. for Samuel Gellibrand,* 1645. Wing C.3812   I.8

————— A plot for the good of posterity... 25 March 1646. *For Samuel Gellibrand,* 1646.   Wing C.3814   III.26

————— Sions memento, and Gods alarum... 31 May 1643. *For Samuel Gellibrand,* 1643.   Wing C.3816   VI.9

COLEMAN (Thomas).   The Christians course and complaint, both in the pursuit of Happinesse desired, and for advantages slipped in that pursuit... 30 August 1643. *By J. L. for Christopher Meredith,* 1643.   Wing C.5050   VI.18

Parliamentary Sermons (cont.)

———— Gods unusuall answer to a solemne fast. Or, some observations upon the late sad successe in the West... 12 September 1644. *For Christopher Meredith*, 1644.   Wing C.5051   V.19

———— The hearts ingagement... 29 September 1643. *For Christopher Meredith*, 1643.   Wing C.5052
                                                                                               II.10

———— Hopes deferred and dashed... 30 July 1645. *For Christopher Meredith*, 1645.   Wing C.5053
                                                                                               III.13

CONANT (John).   The woe and weale of Gods people... 26 July 1643. *By G. M. for Christopher Meredith*, 1643.   Wing C.5689   VI.17

CORBET (Edward).   Gods providence... 28 December 1642. *By Tho: Badger, for Robert Bostock*, 1642. Wing C.6241   IV.30

DURY (John).   Israels call to march out of Babylon unto Jerusalem... 26 November 1645. *By G. M. for Tho. Underhill*, 1646.   Wing D.2867   III.18

ELLIS (John).   The sole path to a sound peace... 22 February 1642. *By John Raworth, for George Latham, and John Rothwell*, 1643.   Wing E.592   VI.5

EVANCE (Daniel).   The noble order, or, the honour which God conferr's on them that honour Him... 28 January 1645. *By T. W. for Abel Roper*, 1646.   Wing E.3443   III.1

FAIRCLOUGH (Samuel).   The troublers troubled, or Achan condemned and executed... 4 April 1641. *By R. Cotes, for Henry Overton*, 1641.   Wing F.109   IV.1

GAUDEN (John), *Bp*.   The love of truth and peace... 29 November 1640. *By T. C. for Andrew Crooke*, 1641.   Wing G.362   lacks tp   II.1

GIBSON (Samuel).   The ruine of the authors and fomentors of civill warres... 24 September 1645. *By M. S. for John Hancock*, 1645.   Wing G.671   III.15

GILLESPIE (George).   A sermon preached... 27 March 1644. *For Robert Bostock*, 1644.   Wing G.756
                                                                                               V.6

———— A sermon preached... 27 August 1645. *By F. Neile for Robert Bostock*, 1645.   Wing G.758   I.1

GIPPS (George).   A sermon preached... 27 November 1644. *For Christopher Meredith*, 1645.   Wing G.779   V.28

GOODE (William).   The discoverie of a publique spirit... 26 March 1645. *By J. L. for Christopher Meredith*, 1645.   Wing G.1093   III.5

GOODWIN (Thomas).   The great interest of states & kingdomes... 26 February 1645. *For R. Dawlman, and are to be sold by Nath: Webb, and Will: Grantham*, 1646.   Wing G.1246   III.24

———— Zerubbabels encouragement to finish the temple... 27 April 1642. *For R. D. and are to be sold by Francis Eglesfield*, 1642.   Wing G.1267   IV.15

Parliamentary Sermons (cont.)

GOUGE (William).   The progresse of divine providence... 24 September 1645. *By G. M. for Joshua Kirton,* 1645.   Wing G.1393   I.15

————The saints support... 29 June 1642. *By G. M. for Joshua Kirton,* 1642.   Wing G.1397   IV.19

GOWER (Stanley).   Things now-a-doing... 31 July 1644. *By G. M. for Philemon Stephens,* 1644.   Wing
G.1462   V.13

GREENE (John).   Nehemiah's teares and prayers for Judah's affliction, and the ruines and repaire
of Jerusalem... 24 April 1644. *By G. M. for Philemon Stephens,* 1644.   Wing G.1822   V.8

GREENHILL (William).   [Greek.] The axe at the root... 26 April 1643. *By R. O. & G. D. for
Benjamin Allen,* 1643.   Wing G.1848   VI.7

HALL (Henry).   Heaven ravished: or a glorious prize, atchieved by an heroicall enterprize... 29
May 1644. *By J. Raworth, for Samuel Gellibrand,* 1644.   Wing H.340   V.10

HARDWICK (Humphrey).   The difficulty of Sions deliverance and reformation: together with the
activitie which he friends should manifest, during the time that her cause is an agitation... 26 June
1644. *By I. L. for Philemon Stephens,* 1644.   Wing H.704   V.11

HARRIS (Robert).   A Sermon preached... 25 May 1642. *By M. F. for John Bartlet,* 1642.   Wing H.875
                                                                                                                                                    IV.17

HENDERSON (Alexander).   A Sermon preached... 27 December 1643. *For Robert Bostock,* 1644.
Wing H.1439   VI.27

————A sermon preached... 18 July 1644. *For Robert Bostock,* 1644.   Wing H.1441   II.17

————A sermon preached... 28 May 1645. *By F. N. for Robert Bostock,* 1645.   Wing H.1443   I.9

HERLE (Charles).   Davids song of three parts... 15 June 1643. *By T. Brudenell for N. A.,* 1643.   Wing
H.1556   II.7

————A payre of compasses for church and state... 30 November 1642. *By G. M. for John Bartlet,*
1642.   Wing H.1561   IV.29

HEYRICK (Richard).   Queen Esthers resolves: or a princely pattern of Heaven-born resolution, for
all the lovers of God and their country... 27 May 1646. *For Luke Fawne, to be sold by Thomas Smith in
Manchester,* 1646.   Wing H.1749   III.29

HICKES (Gaspar).   The advantage of afflictions... 28 January 1645. *By G. M. for Christopher Meredith,*
1645.   Wing H.1837   I.19

————The glory and beauty of Gods portion... 26 June 1644. *By G. M. for Christopher Meredith,* 1644.
Wing H.1838   V.12

HILL (Thomas), *of Trinity College, Cambridge.*   The militant church, triumphant over the dragon
and his angels... 21 July 1643. *For John Bellamie and Ralph Smith,* 1643.   Wing H.2024   VI.15

————The right separation incouraged... 27 November 1644. *By R. Cotes, for John Bellamy, and
Philemon Stephens,* 1645.   Wing H.2026   I.4

———— The season for Englands selfe-reflection, and advancing temple-work... 13 August 1644. *By Richard Cotes, for John Bellamy, and Philemon Stephens*, 1644.   Wing H.2027   V.14

———— The trade of truth advanced... 27 July 1642. *By I. L. for John Bellamie, Philemon Stephens, and Ralph Smith*, 1642.   Wing H.2031   IV.21

HODGES (Thomas), *of Kensington.*   A glimpse of Gods glory...28 September 1642. *For John Bartlet,* 1642.   Wing H.2314   IV.25

JENKYN (William).   Reformation's remora: or, temporizing the stop of building the Temple... 25 February 1645. *By G. M. for Christopher Meredith*, 1646.   Wing J.650   I.20

LANGLEY (John).   Gemitus columbae: the mournfull note of the dove... 25 December 1644. *By Joh. Raworth for Philemon Stephens*, 1644.   Wing L.404   V.29

LEY (John).   The fury of warre, and folly of sin... 26 April 1643. *By G.M. for Christopher Meredith,* 1643.   Wing L.1879   VI.8

LIGHTFOOT (John).   Elias redivivus... 29 March 1643. *By R. Cotes, for Andrew Crooke,* 1643.   Wing L.2053   VI.6

———— A sermon preached... 26 August 1645. *By R. C. for Andrew Crook,* 1645.   Wing L.2068   III.14

MARSHALL (Stephen).   A divine project to save a kingdome... 22 April 1644. *By Richard Cotes, for Stephen Bowtell,* 1644.   Wing M.752   IV.5

———— Gods master-piece, a sermon tending to manifest Gods glorious appearing in the building up of Zion... 26 March 1645. *By Richard Cotes, for Stephen Bowtell,* 1645.   Wing M.756   I.7

———— Meroz cursed, or a sermon... 23 February 1641. *By R. Badger, for Samuel Gellibrand,* 1641.   Wing M.762   IV.13

———— A peace-offering to God... 7 September 1641. *By T. P. and M. S. for Samuel Man,* 1641.   Wing M.766   II.3

———— Reformation and desolation... 22 December 1641. *For Samuel Gellibrand,* 1642.   Wing M.770   IV.10

———— A sacred panegyrick, or a sermon... 18 January 1643. *For Stephen Bowtell,* 1644.   Wing.772   II.13

———— A sacred record to be made of Gods mercies to Zion... 19 June 1645. *By Rich. Cotes for Stephen Bowtell,* 1645.   Wing M.773   II.24

———— A sermon preached... 17 November 1640. *By J. Okes, for Samuel Man,* 1641.   Wing M.776   IV.9

———— The song of Moses, the servant of God, and the song of the Lambe... 5 June 1643. *For Sam: Man and Sam: Gellibrand,* 1643.   Wing M.789   II.9

———— The strong helper or the interest and power of the prayers of the destitute for the building up of Sion... 20 April 1645. *By Richard Cotes, for Stephen Bowtell,* 1645.   Wing M.790   III.7

———— [Greek.] The churches lamentation for the good mans losse... at the funeral of... John Pym. *For Stephen Bowtell,* 1644.   Wing M.793   II.12

Parliamentary Sermons (cont.)

MAYNARD (John), *of Manfield.*   A sermon preached... 26 February 1644. *By George Bishop for Samuel Gellibrand*, 1645.   Wing M.1452   III.4

MEWE (William).   The robbing and spoiling of Jacob and Israel considered and bewailed... 29 November 1643, *For Christopher Meredith*, 1643.   Wing M.1950   VI.24

NALTON (James).   Delay of reformation provoking Gods further indignation ... 29 April 1646. *For Samuel Gellibrand*, 1646.   Wing N.122   III.28

NEWCOMEN (Matthew), *of Dedham.*   The craft and cruelty of the churches adversaries... 5 November 1642. *For Peter Cole*, 1643.   Wing N.908B   II.5

———— Jerusalems watch-men, the Lords remembrancers... 7 July 1643. *By M. F. for Christopher Meredith*, 1643.   Wing N.911   VI.14

———— A sermon, tending to set forth the right use of the disasters that befall our armies... 12 September 1644. *By George Miller for Christopher Meredith*, 1644.   Wing N.913   V.18

PALMER (Herbert).   The glasse of Gods providence towards his faithful ones... 13 August 1644. *By G. M. for Th. Underhill*, 1644.   Wing P.235   V.15

———— The necessity and encouragement of utmost venturing for the churches help; together with the sin, folly and mischief of self-idolizing... 28 June 1643. *For John Bellamie*, 1643.   Wing P.243
                                                                                          VI.11

PERNE (Andrew).   Gospell courage, or christian resolution for God, and his truth... 31 May 1643. *By G. Dexter, for Stephen Bowtell*, 1643.   Wing P.1577   VI.10

PETERS (Hugh).   Gods doings, and mans duty... 2 April 1645. *By R. Raworth for G. Calvert*, 1646. Wing P.1703   II.28

PICKERING (Benjamin).   A firebrand pluckt out of the burning... 27 November 1644. *By I. L. for Philemon Stephens, and Samuel Gellibrand*, 1645.   Wing P.2150   V.27

PROFFET (Nicholas).   England impenitencie under smiting... 25 September 1644. *By George Miller for Christopher Meredith*, 1645.   Wing P.3647   V.20

REYNOLDS (Edward), *Bp.*   Israels portion in time of trouble... 27 July 1642. *By George Bishop, and Robert White, for Robert Bostock*, 1642.   Wing R.1256   IV.22

REYNOR (William).   Babylons ruining-earthquake and the restauration of Zion... 28 August 1644. *By T. B. for Samuel Enderby*, 1644.   Wing R.1324   V.17

RUTHERFORD (Samuel).   A sermon preached... 31 January 1643. *By Richard Cotes, for Richard Whittakers & Andrew Crooke*, 1644.   Wing R.2391   V.1

————A sermon preached... 25 June 1645. *By R. C. for Andrew Crook*, 1645.   Wing R.2393   lacks pp. 41–48   I.11

SALWEY (Arthur).   Halting stigmatiz'd in a sermon... 25 October 1643. *For Christopher Meredith*, 1644.   Wing S.522   VI.23

SCUDDER (Henry). Gods warning to England by the voyce of his rod... 30 October 1644. *By J. R. for Philemon Stephens and Edward Blackmore*, 1644. Wing S.2139   V.25

SEAMAN (Lazarus). Solomons choice, or a president for kings and princes... 25 September 1644. *By E. G. for J. Rothwell*, 1644. Wing S.2177   V.21

SEDGWICKE (Obadiah). An arke against a deluge, or safety in dangerous times... 22 October 1644. *By J. Raworth, fot [sic.] Samuel Gellibrand*, 1644. Wing S.2364   V.24

———— England's preservation... 25 May 1642. *By R. B. for Samuel Gellibrand*, 1642. Wing S.2372   IV.18

———— Haman's vanity, or, a sermon displaying the birthless issues of Church-destroying adversaries... 15 June 1643. *By R. Bishop for Samuel Gellibrand*, 1643. Wing S.2374   II.8

———— A thanksgiving-sermon... 9 April 1644. *By J. R. for Samuel Gelliband*, 1644. Wing S.2381   II.14

SEDGWICK (William). Zions deliverance and her friends duty: or the grounds of expecting, and meanes of procuring Jerusalem's restauration... The Second edition. *For John Bellamy & Ralph Smith*, 1643. Wing S.2393   IV.20

SIMPSON (Sidrach). Reformations preservation... 26 July 1643. *For Benjamin Allen*, 1643. Wing S.3825   VI.16

———— A sermon preached at Westminster. *For Peter Cole*, 1643. Wing S.3826   IV.3

SMITH (Peter). A sermon preached... 29 May 1644. *By J. L. for Christopher Meredith*, 1644. Wing S.4142   V.9

SPURSTOWE (William). England's eminent judgments, caus'd by the abuse of God's eminent mercies... 5 November 1644. *By E. G. for John Rothwell*, 1644. Wing S.5093   II.20

———— Englands patterne and duty in its monthly fasts... 21 July 1643. *For Peter Cole*, 1643. Wing S.5094   VI.1

STAUNTON (Edmund). Phinehas's zeal in execvtion of iudgement,... or, a divine remedy for Englands misery... 30 October 1644. *By J. L. for Christopher Meredith*, 1645. Wing S.5341   I.2

———— Rupes Israelis: the rock of Israel. A little part of its glory... 24 April 1644. *For Christopher Meredith*, 1644. Wing S.5342   V.7

STERRY (Peter). The spirit convincing of sinne... 26 November 1645. *By T. Forcet, for Henry Overton, and Benjamine Allen*, 1646. Wing S.5484   III.19

STRICKLAND (John). Gods work of mercy in Sions misery... 27 December 1643. *By J. Raworth, for L. Fawne*, 1644. Wing S.5970   VI.26

———— Immanuel, or the church triumphing in God with us... 5 November 1644. *By Matthew Simmons, for Henry Overton*, 1644. Wing S.5971   II.19

———— Mercy rejoycing against judgement: or, God waiting to be gracious to a sinfull nation... 29 October 1645. *By Matth. Simmons for Henry Overton*, 1645. Wing S.5973   III.16

STRONG (William). [Greek.] The Day of revelation of the righteous Judgement of God... 31 December 1645. *By T. H., and are to be sold by J. Benson, and J. Saywell*, 1645. Wing S.6003 III.20

SYMONDS (Joseph). A sermon lately preached at Westminster. *For Luke Fawn*, 1641. Wing S.6358 IV.2

TAYLOR (Francis). The danger of vowes neglected, and the necessite of Reformation... 27 May 1646. *By M. S. for Geo. Whitington, and Nath. Brookes*, 1646. Wing T.272 I.22

———— Gods covenant the Churches plea... 29 October 1645. *By R. Cotes for Stephen Bowtell*, 1645. Wing T.278 III.17

TEMPLE (Thomas). Christs government in and over his people... 26 October 1642. *For Samuel Gellibrand*, 1642. Wing T.634 IV.26

TESDALE (Christopher). Hierusalem, or a vision of peace... 28 August 1644. *By R. Cotes, for Phil. Stephens*, 1644. Wing T.792 V.16

THOROWGOOD (Thomas). Moderation justified, and the Lords being at hand emproved... 25 December 1644. *By I. L. for Christopher Meredith, and for Thomas Slater*, 1645. Wing T.1069 V.30

TUCKNEY (Anthony). The balme of Gilead, for the wounds of England... 30 August 1643. *By Richard Bishop for Samuel Gellibrand*, 1643. Wing T.3210 VI.19

VALENTINE (Thomas). A sermon preached... 28 December 1643. *For Samuel Man*, 1643. Wing V.26 IV.31

VINES (Richard). Calebs integrity in following the Lord fully... 30 November 1642. *By G. M. for Abel Roper*, 1642. Wing V.546 IV.28

———— The happinesse of Israel... 12 March 1644. *By G. M. for Abel Roper*, 1645. Wing V.551 II.22

———— Magnalia Dei ab aquilone; set forth in a sermon... 18 July 1644. *By G. M. for Abel Roper*, 1644... Wing V.559 II.18

———— The posture of Davids spirit when he was in a doubtfull condition... 22 October 1644. *By I. N. for Abel Roper*, 1644. Wing V.563 V.23

———— The purifying of unclean hearts and hands... 28 January 1645. *By G. M. for Abel Roper*, 1646. Wing V.565 III.23

WALKER (George), *of Watting Street*. A sermon preached... 29 January 1644. *By T. B. for Nathaniel Webb*, 1644. Wing W.364 III.3

WARD (John), *of Ipswich*. God judging among the gods... 26 March 1645. *By I. L. for Christopher Meredith*, 1645. Wing W.773 III.6

———— The good-will of him that dwelt in the bush; or, the extraordinary happinesse of living under an extraordinary providence... 22 July 1645. *By G. M. for Christopher Meredith*, 1645. Wing W.774 II.25

WHINCOP (John). Gods call to weeping and mourning... 29 January 1644. *By John Field for Nathanael Web and William Grantham*, 1646. Wing W.1663 III.2

———— Israels tears for distressed Zion... 24 September 1645. *By R. C. for Andrew Crooke,* 1645.   Wing W.1664   I.14

WHITAKER (Jeremiah).   The Christians hope triumphing in these glorious truths... 28 May 1645. *By G. Miller for John Bellamy,* 1645.   Wing W.1710   I.10

———— The danger of greatnesse: or, Uzziah, his exaltation and destruction... 14 January 1645. *By G. M. for John Bellamie,* 1646.   Wing W.1711   III.21

———— Ejrenopoios, Christ the settlement of unsettled times... 25 January 1642. *For John Rothwell,* 1642.   Wing W.1712   VI.3

WHITE (John).   The troubles of Jerusalems restauration, or, the churches reformation... 26 November 1645. *By M. Simmons for John Rothwel, and Luke Fawne,* 1646.   Wing W.1783   I.18

WILKINSON (Henry), *of Christchurch.*   Babylons ruine, Jerusalems rising... 25 October 1643. *For Christopher Meredith, and Sa. Gellibrand,* 1643.   Wing W.2220   VI.22

———— The gainefull cost... 27 November 1644. *For Chr. Meredith and Sa. Gellibrand,* 1644.   Wing W.2222   I.3

———— Miranda, stupenda. Or, the wonderfull and astonishing mercies which the Lord hath wrought for England... 21 July 1646. *By T. B. for Christopher Meredith and Samuel Gellibrand,* 1646. Wing W.2224   II.31

WILSON (Thomas), *of Kent.*   Jerichoes downfall... 28 September 1642. *By M. F. for John Bartlet,* 1643. Wing W.2948   IV.24

WOODCOCK (Francis).   Christ's warning-piece: giving notice to every one to watch, and keep their garments... 30 October 1644. *By J. R. for Christopher Meredith and Luke Fawne,* 1644.   Wing W.3429   V.26

———— Lex talionis: or, God paying everyman in his own coyn... 30 July 1645. *By G. M. for Christopher Meredith,* 1646.   Wing W.3431   III.12

YOUNG (Thomas), *of Stowmarket.*   Hopes incouragement pointed at in a sermon preached... 28 February 1643. *For Ralph Smith,* 1644.   Wing Y.92   V.4

PECK (Francis). Desiderata curiosa. Vol. the first (-second)... all now first published from original manuscripts. Adorned with cuts, (15 books in two vols.)
London, [s.n.], 1732–35. GR rep. 35cm.
UL24   King 511 6D

PELARGUS (Christopher). In Deuteronomium sacrum... commentarius.
Lipsiae, typis Abrahami Lambergi, sumpt. Joh. Franci, 1608–09. Rep. 20cm.
bg   BT30   FEt   F2   King 265 11B

————— In.. Exodum sacram, commentarius brevis.
Lipsiae, typis Abrahami Lambergi, sumpt. Johannis Franci, 1604. Rep. 20cm.
bg   BT30   FEt   F2   King 256 11B

————— In Leviticum sacrum Mosaicum commentarius... *bound with his* In Numeros sacros... commentarius brevis. (2 vols. in one)
Lipsiae, typis Abrahami Lambergi, sumpt. Joh. Franci, 1604–06. Rep. 20cm.
lacks tp to first vol.   bg   BT30   FEt   F2   King 257 11B

————— In Johannis Apostoli et evangelistae historiam evangelicam commentarius per quaesita & responsa...
Francofurti, sumpt. Joh. Thtmii, typis Nicolai Voltzii, [1615]. Rep. 20cm.
tp defective   bg   BT30   FEt   F2   King 258 11B

————— In Prophetarum omnium oceanum, sive Genesin... ex antiquitate puriore magna parte erutus commentarius.
Lipsiae, imprimebat Abraham Lamberg, imp. Joh. Franci, 1612. Rep. 20cm.
bg   BT30   FEt   F2   King 264 11B

————— *See also* BESODNER, P.

PELIKAN (Conrad). In libros, quos vocant Apocryphos, vel potius Ecclesiasticos,... commentarii. *with his* In quatuor evangelistas,... item in acta apostolorum commentarii. (2 vols. in one)
Tiguri, excudebat Christophorus Froschoverus, 1582. Reb. 33cm.
Adams P.600   bg   BT27   FEt   D3   King 55 1B

————— In Pentateuchum sive quinque libros Mosis,... Commentarii. Hic accessit narratio de ortu vita & obitu eiusdem, opera Ludovici Lavateri... *with his* In libros historicos... commentarii (2 vols. in one)
Tiguri, excudebat Christophorus Froschoverus, 1582. Reb. 33cm.
Adams P.596   bg   BT27   FEt   D3   King 38 1B

————— ...In prophetas maiores et minores, ut vulgo vocantur,... commentarii. *with his* In Job, Psalterium... commentarii. (2 vols. in one)
Tiguri, excudebat Christophorus Froschoverus, 1582. Reb. 33cm.
Adams P.598   bg   BT27   FEt   D3   King 599 1B

PELTANUS (Theodor). In proverbia Salomonis paraphrasis et scholia. Accedunt observationes e libris singularium Martini de Roa.
Antverpiae, ex typographeio Hieronymi Verdussi, 1606. Rep. 20cm.
cp: R1   BT13   FEt   G1   King 238 7D

PEMBLE (William). Vindicae gratiae. A plea for grace... certain lectures as touching the nature and properties of grace and faith:... second edition. (Bound with 5 other vols. in one)

148

London, printed by H. L. for J. Bartlet, 1629. Rep. 18cm.

STC.19592   LP4   FEt   [I2]

———— Five godly, and profitable sermons... preached in his lifetime in sundry places. *bound with his* Vindicae Gratiae, 1629.

Oxford, printed by John Lichfield for Edward Forrest, 1628.

STC.19576a   LP4   FEt   [I2]

———— An introduction to the worthy receiving the sacrament of the Lords supper. *bound with his* Vindicae Gratiae, 1629.

Printed by H. L. for James Boler, 1629.

STC.19580   LP4   FEt   [I2]

———— Salomons recantation and repentance: or the booke of Ecclesiastes briefly and fully explained. *bound with his* Vindicae Gratiae, 1629.

London, printed by J. H. for John Bartlet, 1628.

STC.19584   LP4   FEt   [I2]

———— A short and sweete exposition upon the first nine chapters of Zachary. *bound with his* Vindicae Gratiae, 1629.

London, printed by R. Young for John Bartlet, 1629.

STC.19586   LP4   FEt   [I2]

———— Vindiciae fidei, or a treatise of justification by faith,... delivered at Magdalen Hall in Oxford;... second edition. *Printed by John Lichfield for Edward Forrest, 1629. bound with his* Vindicae Gratiae, 1629.

STC.19590   LP4   FEt   [I2]

PEREIRA (Bento).   Secundus tomus selectarum disputationum in sacram scripturam,... super Epistola Pauli ad Romanos. (second of 2 vols.)
Lugduni, sumptibus Horatii Cardon, 1604. Reb. 26cm.

cp: a.   bg   BT1   FEt   G2

PERKINS (William).   The workes of that famous and worthie Minister of Christ, in the Universitie of Cambridge,... newly corrected... (3 vols.)
Cambridge, printed by John Legate [Cantrell Legge], 1608–09. Rep. 35cm.

STC.19649   BT5   FEp   [I4]

PERNE (Andrew).   *See* Parliamentary Sermons.

PETERS (Hugh).   *See* Parliamentary Sermons.

PETIT (Gulielmus).   *See* WILLIAM OF NEWBURGH.

PEZEL (Christoph).   De sacrosancta coena Domini. Tractatus propositus in Schola Bremensi, in explicatione examinis... Philippi Melancht...
[Bremae, excudebat Bernhardus Petri], 1590. Reb. 17cm.

(Adams P.948 is dated 1589)   bg   BT1   FEt   G1

———— In primum librum Mosis,... commentarius. Propositus in gymnasio scholae Bremensis, & nunc primum in lucem editus a Augusto Sagittario Dresdensi,...

Neostadii, apud haeredes Wilhelmi Harnisii, 1599. Reb. 17cm.

Adams P.953   bg   BT1   FEt   G1   King 356 5A

————— ,*ed.   See* THALMANN, B.

PHILIPOT (John).   Villare Cantianum: or Kent surveyed and illustrated... to which is added an
historical catalogue of the High-Sheriffs of Kent; collected by John Philipot Esq – father to the
authour [Thomas whose name appears as author on tp of this his father's work].
London, printed by William Godbid, 1664. Reb. 30cm.

Wing P.1989a   UL24   msGL   FEt   [N2]   King 166 6B

PHILO, *Judaeus.*   [Greek.]... Opera exegetica in libros Mosis, De mundi opificio, historicos &
legales, quae partim ab Adriano Turnebo... partim a Davide Hoeschelio... edita... Nunc Graece &
Latine... emissa ex accuratissima Sigismundi Gelenii interpretatione,...
Coloniae Allobrogum, excudebat Petrus de la Roviere, 1613. Rep. 33cm.

bg   BT1   PGL32   FEt   B2   King 569 1B

PHOTIUS.   [Greek.] Myriobiblon, sive bibliotheca librorum quos Photius legit & censuit. David
Hoeschelius... notis illustravit... Latine... reddidit... Andreas Schottus. (2 parts in one vol.)
[Geneva], Oliva Pauli Stephani, 1611. Reb. 35cm.

UL16   FEt   [O2]   King 157 5E

PICARDI (Jo.), *ed.   See* BERNARD, *Saint.*

PICKERING (Benjamin).   *See* Parliamentary Sermons.

PINEDA (Juan de).   Commentariorum in Job libri tredecim tomis duobus distincti. (2 vols.)
Antverpiae, apud Joannem Keerbergium, 1612. Rep. 30cm.

bg   BT17   PGL2   FEt   G3   King 123 3B

PINTO (Hector).   In Esaiam prophetam commentaria.
Antverpiae, in aedibus Petri Belleri, 1584. Rep. 17cm.

(Adams P.1268 is dated 1582)   bg   BT23   PGL17 lost   FEt   G1   King 395 11A

PISCATOR (Johann).   Commentarius in Exodum, id est, librum secundum Mosis:
Herbornae Nassoviorum, ex officina Christophori Corvini, 1615. Rep. 17cm.

bg   BT14   PGL23   FEt   E1   King 322 10A

————— Commentarius in Genesin, id est, librum primum Mosis: Editio secunda.
Herbornae Nassoviorum, ex officina Christophori Corvini, 1611. Rep. 17cm.

bg   BT14   PGL23   FEt   E1   King 373 10A

————— Commentarius in Leviticum: id est, librum tertium Mosis *with* Commentarius in Numeros:
and with Commentarius in Deuteronomium. (3 vols. in one)
Herbornae Nassoviorum, [Christophori Corvini], 1615. Reb. 17cm.

bg   BT14   FEt   E1   King 383 10A

————— Commentarius in libros duos Regem: quos vulgo duos posteriores Regum nominant,...
Herbornae Nassoviorum, excudebat Christophorus Corvinus, 1611.

BT14   PGL23   FEt   E1   King 369 10A

———— Commentarius in libros duos Samuelis: quos vulgo duos priores Regum nominant.
Herbornae Nassoviorum, ex off. Christophori Corvini, [1610]. Rep. 17cm.

bg　BT14　PGL23　FEt　E1

King 377 10A

———— Commentarius in librum Josuae: *with his* Commentarius in librum Judicum. *and with his* Commentarius in librum Ruthae. (3 vols. in one)
Herbornae Nassoviorum, ex off. Christophori Corvini, 1607–08. Reb. 17cm.

bg　BT14　PGL23 lost　FEt　E1

King 364 10A

———— In librum Psalmorum commentarius...
Herbornae Nassoviorum, ex officina Christophori Corvini, 1611. Reb. 19cm.

bg　BT14　PGL23 defective　FEt　E1

King 397 10A

———— In Prophetam Esaiam commentarius.
Herbornae Nassoviorum, [Christoph Corvini], 1612. Reb. 18cm.

bg　BT14　PGL23　FEt　E1

King 329 10A

———— In Prophetam Ezechielem commentarius. *with* In Prophetam Danielem commentarius. (2 vols. in one)
Herbornae Nassoviorum, [Christoph Corvini], 1614. Reb. 18cm.

bg　BT14　PGL23 defective　FEt　E1

King 384 10A

———— Commentarii in omnes libros Novi Testamenti: Antehac separatim editi: nunc vero in unum volumen collecti... ab authore recognita.
Herbornae Nassoviorum, [Christoph Corvini], 1613. Rep. 25cm.

bg　BT14　PGL23　FEt　E1

King 313 10A

———— Volumen primum (-secundum) thesium theologicarum; in illustri schola Nassovica, partim Herbornae, partim Sigenae disputatarum: praeside Johanne Piscatore. (2 vols. in one)
Herbornae Nassoviorum, ex officina Christophori Corvini, 1607. Reb. 17cm.

bg　BT14　PGL23 lost　FEt　E1

King 345 10A

PISTORIUS (Johann), *Nidanus.* Germanicorum scriptorum, qui rerum a Germanis... gestarum historias... reliquerunt, tomus alter... Ex bibliotheca Joannis Pistorii Nidani. (3 parts in one) [*See also* REUBER, J. Veterum scriptorum... Germanicorum (tomus unus), 1584. *and* WURSTISEN, C. Germaniae historicum (tomus unus *bound with* pars altera), 1585.]
Francofurti, apud haeredes Andreae Wecheli, 1584. Reb. 31cm.

Adams P.1318 (vol. 2)　tp hand cold.　UL24　AEm　[N2]

King 613(3) 3B

———— Polonicae historiae corpus: hoc est, Polonaricarum rerum Latini recentiores & veteres scriptores, ...uno volumine compraehensi omnes... Ex bibliotheca Joan. Pistorii Nidani. (3 vols. in one)
Basileae, per Sebastianum Henricpetri, (1582). English early 17th cent. BS rep. 33cm.

Adams P.1727　ms owner: Harrison p: xiii[s]　bm: τ 34.2　bg　BP13　FEt　M1　King 549 4A

PITISCUS (Bartholomeus) *and* SCULTETUS (Abraham).　Meletemata Psalmica: sive, idea concionum in psalmos Davidis confecta Joannis Adami, – Pars secunda – tertia. (3 parts in 3 vols.)
Francofurti, prostant Jonae Rosae, 1616–18–19. Reb. 27cm.

cp: h.f.　bg　MS33　FEt　E3

King 232, 3 & 4 9A

PIUS II, *Pope.* [Letters.] Familiares epistolae ad diversos in quadruplici vite eius statu transmisse: *Nuremberg, impensis Antonii Koburger, 1481.* Reb. 30cm.

Goff P.717 ms owner and annotations: f'ris Ric Bryngkeley bg BP13 FEp M3

King 130 9C

PLATINA (Bartholomeo). Historia... De vitis Pontificum Romanorum... usque ad Paulum II. Accessit supplementum... ad Pium V... & ad Paulum V. Accesserunt... omnium pontificum verae effigies...
Coloniae Agrippinae, sumptibus Petri Cholini, 1611. ½L reb. 25cm.

cp: g.f. BP13 FEt H2

King 302 6A

PLAUTUS (Titus Maccius). Opera Dionys. Lambini... emendatus: ab eodemque commentarius explicatus...
Aureliae Allobrogum, ex typis Vignonianis, 1605. Rep. 24cm.

ms owner and p: A Herne v^s LP4 AEm [K2]

King 281 5D

PLOT (Robert). The natural history of Oxford-shire, being an essay toward the natural history of England. By R. P.
Printed at the Theater in Oxford,...to be had there; and in London at S. Millers, 1677. Rep. 32cm.

Wing P.2586 UL24 FEt AEm [N2]

King 596 6C

PLUME (Thomas), *ed.* *See* HACKET, J., *Bp.*

PLUTARCH. The lives of the noble Grecians and Romaines, compared together by... Plutarke... out of French into English by Sir Thomas North.
London, printed by Richard Field, 1612. poss. London cy GS rep. 35cm.

STC.20069 ms donor signature Tobias Blosse bg BP7 PGL6 FEt H4

King 131 6C

POLANUS (Amandus). In librum Prophetiarum Ezechielis commentarii...
Basileae, typis Conradi Waldkirchii, 1608. IPSWICH GS rep. 21cm.

bg BT10 FEt G2

King 269 7D

———— Syntagma theologiae Christianae... iuxta leges ordinis methodici conformatum... Editio postrema,... correcta & emendata.
Hanoviae, typis Wechelianis, apud Danielem & Davidem Aubrios & Clementem Schleichium, 1625. Rep. 36cm.

bg MS40 FEt D4

King 580 4E

PONTANUS (Joannes Jovianus). *See* GUICCIARDINI, F.

POOLE (Matthew). Synopsis criticorum aliorumque S. Scripturae interpretum, vols. 1–4. (4 vols. in five)
Londini, typis J. Flesher & T. Roycroft, prostat apud Cornelius Bee, 1669–76. GF reb. 40cm.

Wing P.2853 UL28 AEg [N3]

King 438 1E

PRESTON (John). The breast-plate of faith and love. A treatise... delivered in 18 sermons upon three severall texts, by the late... Minister. The second edition, corrected. *with his* Life eternall second edition, 1631. *also with his* Three sermons, 1631. (3 vols. in one)
London, printed by W. J. for Nicolas Bourne, 1630. Rep. 20cm.

STC.20209 cp: .x2. LP2 FEt [H3]

King 251(1) 5B

———— The golden scepter held forth to the humble. With the churches dignitie by her marriage. And the churches dutie in her carriage. In three treatises... (2 vols. in one)
London, printed by R. B. for N. Bourne, A. Boler & R. Harford, 1638. Rep. 20cm.
STC.20226 p: 4^s LP2 FEt [H3] King 251(3) 5B

———— Life eternall or, a treatise of the knowledge of the divine essence and attributes. Delivered in 18 sermons. The second edition, corrected *bound with his* The breast-plate of faith, 1630.
London, printed by R. B. sold by Nicholas Bourne, and Rapha Harford, 1631. Rep. 20cm.
STC.20232 LP2 FEt [H3] King 251(1) 5B

———— The new covenant or the saints portion. A treatise... in fourteen sermons... The ninth edition.
London, printed by J. D. for Nicolas Bourne, 1639. Rep. 20cm.
STC.20247 LP2 FEt [H3] King 251(4) 5B

———— The saints qualification: or a treatise I. Of humiliation, in tenne sermons... II. Of sanctification, in nine sermons... whereunto is added a treatise of Communion with Christ... in three sermons. (3 vols. in one)
London, printed by R. B. for Nicolas Bourne, 1633. I.M. BS rep. 20cm.
STC.20262 LP2 FEt [H3] King 251(2) 5B

———— Three sermons upon the sacrament of the Lords supper. *bound with his* The breast-plate of faith, 1630.
London, printed by Thomas Cotes, for Michael Sparke, 1631. Rep. 20cm.
STC.20281 LP2 FEt [H3] King 251(1) 5B

PRIDEAUX (John), *Bp.* Viginti-duae lectiones de totidem religionis capitibus, praecipue hoc tempore controversis, pro ut publice habebantur Oxoniae in Vesperiis... Editio tertia. (3 vols. in one)
Oxoniae, excudebat Hen. Hall, Hen. Cripps, Hen. Curteyn (L. Lichfield vol.3) & Thom. Robinson, 1648. IPSWICH GS rep. 29cm.
Wing P.3438 MS49 FEt [I4] King 128 1B

PROFFET (Nicholas). *See* Parliamentary Sermons.

PROSPER OF AQUITAINE, *Saint.* Opera. Accurata exemplarium vetustorum... repurgata.
Coloniae Agrippinae, excudebat Arnoldus Kempensis, sumptibus Joannis Crithii, 1609. Rep. 16cm.
bg BT1 PGL32 FEt B2 King 392 7A

PRUDENTIUS CLEMENS (Aurelius). Opera,... noviter ad MSC. fidem recensita,... a Johanne Weitzio. Accesserunt omnium doctorum virorum,... notae, scholia atque observationes... (2 parts in one vol.)
Hanoviae, typis Wechelianis apud haeredes Johannis Aubrii, 1613. Reb. 19cm.
bg BT1 PGL32 FEt B2 King 382 8B

PURCHAS (Samuel). Purchas his pilgrimage. Or relations of the world and the religions observed in all ages and places discovered,... unto this present. Second edition. (9 books in one vol.)
London, printed by William Stansby for Henrie Fetherstone, 1614. London cy GS rep. 30cm.
STC.20506 marks of clasps bg BT31 FEt H4 King 89 6C

———— Purchas his pilgrimes. A history of the world, in sea voyages & lande travells... The first-fourth part. (20 books in four vols.)

London, printed by William Stansby, for Henrie Fetherstone, 1625. Rep. 34cm.

STC.20509   lacks engr. tp   BT32   FEt   H4

QUIRINO DE SALAZAR (Fernando).   *See* SALAZAR, F.Q.

RADA (Juan de).   Controversiae theologicae S. Thomam & Scotum, super quatuor libros sententiarum... (4 parts in 2 vols.)
Coloniae Agrippinae, apud Joannem Crithium, 1620. Rep. 23cm.

cp: q.i.   bg   KG14   FEt   H2

King 299 9B

RAINERIUS *de Pisis.*   Pantheologia, sive summa universae theologiae.
Nuremberg, Anton Koberger, 1474. (Second of 2 vols.) English early 18th cent. BR GS rep. 48cm. with clasps
Goff R.7   begins at fo. 22 and lacks fo. 172   ms annotations and on last leaf: 'M^d q' hoc volumen pertinet conve'tu' Cantab'ggie per p[ro]curacion' frat'is Galfrid' Jullys' all illuminated initials cut out except N of Negligentia on fo. 131   MS16 – whose executors never delivered the first vol. to the Library

King '706' 6E

RAINOLDS (John).   The summe of the conference betweene John Rainoldes and John Hart: touching the head and faith of the Church,...
London, printed by W. Hall for Thomas Adames, 1609. IPSWICH GS rep. 20cm.

STC.20629   bg   BT10   FEt   G2

King 222 7C

RALEIGH (*Sir* Walter).   The history of the world. (4 books in one vol.)
London, printed for H. Lownes, G. Lathum and R. Young, 1628 (but engr. tp for Walter Burre, 1614). Rep. 34cm.

STC.20640   lacks first leaf   BT34   FEt   H4

King 158 6C

RAVANELLUS (Petrus).   Bibliotheca sacra, seu, Thesaurus scripturae canonicae amplissimus... in duas partes divisum cum additamentis... (2 vols. in one)
Genevae, sumptibus Petri Chouet, 1650–51. IPSWICH 1651 GS rep. 33cm.

BT43   FEt   [I5]

King 74 2C

RAWLEY (William), *ed.*   *See* BACON, F.

REMONSTRANTS/ISM.   Censura in Confessionem sive Declarationem sententiae eorum qui in foederato Belgio Remonstrantes vocantur,... a professoribus Academiae Leidensis instituta. *bound with* Apologia, 1622 *and* Confessio, 1629. (3 vols. in one)
Lugduni Batavorum, ex officina Bonaventurae & Abrahami Elzevir, 1626–29. Reb. 20cm.

DU   [I2]   AE coloured: Censura and Confessio blue, Apologia red

King 221 5B

———— Apologia pro confessione sive declaratione sententiae eorum,... *contra* censuram quatuor professorum Leidensium. *bound with* Censura in Confessionem, 1626–29.
[Leyden?], impressa, 1629. Reb. 20cm.

DU   [I2]   AE coloured red

King 221 5B

———— Confessio sive Declaratio sententiae Pastorum, qui in foederato Belgio Remonstrantes vocantur, super praecipuis articulis religionis Christianae. *bound with* Censura in Confessionem, 1626–29.
Herder-wiici, apud Theodorum Danielis, 1622. Reb. 20cm.

DU   [I2]   AE coloured blue

King 221 5B

REUBER (Justus).   Veterum scriptorum, qui Caesarum et Imperatorum Germanicorum res per aliquot secula gestas, literis mandarunt. Tomus unus. Ex bibliotheca Justi Reuberi. [*See also* PISTO-RIUS, J. Germanicorum scriptorum, 1584. *and* WURSTISEN, C. Germaniae historicum, 1585.]
Francofurti, apud haeredes Andreae Wecheli, 1584. ABS (donor's arms) reb. 31cm.

Adams R.376   tp device hand coloured   ms on tp: L.M.T.   UL24   AEm   [N2]

King 613(2) 3B

REYNOLDS (Edward), *Bp*.   Twenty five sermons preached upon several occasions by... Edward, now Lord Bishop of Norwich, the second volume. (Twelve sermons: nos. XIV-XXV)
London, printed by Tho. Ratcliffe, for George Thomason, 1659–63. Reb. 20cm.

Wing R.1245A (part only)   XXIV is Ipswich visitation sermon of 10 Oct 1662   LP2   FEt   [H3]

King 689 7C

——— The works... corrected and amended. (4 parts in one vol.)
London, printed by Tho. Newcomb for George Thomason, 1658. Rep. 30cm.

Wing R.1234   LP2   FEt   [I4]

King 591 6B

——— *See also* Parliamentary Sermons.

REYNOR (William).   *See* Parliamentary Sermons.

RHODOGINUS (Ludovicus Coelius).   *See* RICHERIUS, L.C.

RIBERA (Francisco de).   In librum duodecim Prophetarum commentarii, ... persaepe etiam allegoricum complectentes.
Coloniae Agrippinae, in officina Birckmannica, sumptibus Arnoldi Mylii, 1593. English early 17th cent BS rep. 32cm.

Adams R.473   BS boss as on Wm. Harrison books   ms initials: T.B.   MS8   FEt   G4

King 125 11C

RICHARD *of Middleton*.   In tertium (– quartum) sententiarum.. quaestiones. *with his* Tria quodlibeta. (3 parts in one vol.)
Venetiis, per Lazarum Soardum, 1509. Reb. 32cm.

Adams M.1421, 1422 & 1425   ms owners: liber doctor astewyk   W^s Smarte Gippi'   bg   BP0   FEp
L4

King 5 3A

RICHERIUS (Ludovicus Coelius).   Rhodogini lectionum antiquarum libri triginta, recogniti ab auctore... cornucopiae seu thesaurus utriusque linguae appellandi. Postrema editio.
Coloniae Allobrogum, excudebat Philippus Albertus, 1620. Reb. 34cm.

ms owner: Johannes Burrough   LP4   FEt   [I3]

King 595 2C

RIPA (Raphael), *Bp*.   Ad Thomae Aquinatis totam primam partem notationes, et dubitationes scholasticae,... defenditur.
Venetiis, apud Marcum Antonium Somaschum, 1609. Rep. 31cm.

cp: R5 N12 deleted,   R4 a.   bg   KG14   FEt   L1

King 96 4D

RIVET (André).   Commentarius in Hoseam prophetam. In quo, praeter scholia, textus enarrationem,... hoc tempore agitatae discutiuntur: Accessit explicatio cap. LIII Esaiae prophetae. *Lugduni Batavorum, ex Isaaci & Jacobi Commelini, typis Petri Mulleri,* 1625. L reb. 21cm.

MS30   FEt   F2

King 358 11B

───── Commentarius in Psalmorum propheticorum, de mysteriis Evangelicis, decadem selectam. In quo, praeter scholia, textus accuratam enarrationem... & controversiae non paucae, hoc tempore agitatae, discutiuntur.
Lugduni Batavorum, Isaaci & Jacobi Commelini, ex officina Arnoldi Hoogenackeri, 1626. L reb. 21cm.

bg   MS30   FEt   F2   King 296 11B

───── ...Operum theologicorum quae Latine edidit, Tomus Primus... in Genesin... in Exodum.
Roterodami, Arnold Leers, 1651. IPSWICH 1651 GS rep. 37cm.

DU   FEt   [I5]   King 480 1A

ROBERTSON (William).   [Hebrew.] The Hebrew text of the Psalmes and Lamentations but published (for to encourage... beginners in their way) with the reading thereof in known English letters,... (2 parts in one vol.)
London, printed for the author; to be sold by H. Robinson, A. Crook, L. Fawn and S. Thomson, 1656. L Reb. 18cm.

Wing R.1613 (part only)   ms donor's signature   UL19   [K2]   King 340 5A

ROLLOCK (Robert).   In epistolam S. Pauli... ad Romanos commentarius, analytica methodo conscriptus. Altera editio emendatior... *with his* In epistolam S.Pauli... ad Colossenses, commentarius. (2 vols. in one)
Genevae, apud Jacobum Stoer (Samuelem Crispinum), 1608/02. Rep. 15cm.

bg   MS19   FEt   E1   King 346 10A

───── In evangelium... secundum S.Johannem commentarius... nunc denuo in lucem editus.
[Geneva], apud Jacobum Stoer, 1608. L reb. 16cm.

bg   MS19   FEt   E1   King 390 10A

ROSINUS (Joannes).   Romanorum antiquitatum libri decem ex variis scriptoribus summa... diligentia collecti.
Basileae, typis Conrad Waldkirch, ex officina haeredum Petri Pernae, 1583. English early 17th cent. BS rep. 31cm.

Adams R.799   ms notes (Wm. Harrison)   bm: α 15   bg   BP13   FEt   M1   King 214 4A

ROYAL SOCIETY OF LONDON.   Philosophical Transactions: giving some accompt of the present undertakings, studies, and labours of the ingenious in many... parts of the world. Vol.1... 1665–1666.
In the Savoy, printed by T. N. for John Martyn, and James Allestry, [1667]. Reb. 23cm.

LP1   FEt   [H3]   King 255 7D

───── *See also* SPRAT, T. *Bp.*

RUFINUS (Tyrannius).   Opera quae extant, partim antehac nunquam in lucem edita, partim... castigata, & in duos tomos divisa. Tomus primus. *with* In LXXV Davidis Psalmos commentarius. Tomus secundus. (2 vols. in one)
Parisiis, apud Michaelem Sonnium, 1580. Rep. 33cm.

Adams R.880 & 881   bg   BT1   PGL32   lost   FEt   B2   King 63 2C

RUPERT, *Abbot of Deutz.*   Opera omnia (-tomus secundus). (2 vols.)
Coloniae Agrippinae, in officina Birckmannica, sumptibus Arnoldi Mylii, 1602. Rep. 34cm.

cp: a.k.   bg   MS0   FEt   G4   King 554 8E

RUTHERFORD (Samuel).   *See* Parliamentary Sermons.

SACCHI (Bartholomaeus). *See* PLATINA, B.

SALAZAR (Ferdinandus Quirinus).   Expositio in proverbia Salomonis. Nunc primum in Germania edita. (2 vols.)
Coloniae Agrippinae, apud Joannem Kinckium, 1621–22. Reb. 34cm.
BT13   FEt   G4   King 153 and 570 3E

SALEMON, *Bp. of Constance.*   Glosse ex illustrissimis collecte auctoribus incipiunt... *with* Ab acti magistrato... (2 parts in one vol.)
Augsburg, monastery of SS Ulrich & Affa, 1474–76. Reb. 37cm.
Goff S.21   ms owner: W^s Smarte Gippi' & marginalia   bg   BP0   [O3]   King '705' 3A

SALMERON (Alphonse).   Commentarii in Evangelicam historiam, et in acta Apostolorum: nunc primum in lucem editi. Additi est auctoris vita, per Petrum Ribadeneiram conscripta. (12 vols. in five)
Coloniae Agrippinae, apud Antonium Hierat, et Joan. Gymni, 1612–14. Rep. 30cm.
bg   BT16   PGL4   FEt   G3   King 201 2B

———— Commentarii in omnes Epistolas Pauli, & Canonicas; in quatuor tomos... in ordine autem tomus decimus tertius. (4 vols. in two)
Coloniae Agrippinae, apud Antonium Hierat, & Joannem Gymnicum, 1614–15. Rep. 30cm.
crucifix on tp excised   bg   BT16   PGL4   FEt   G3   King 202 2B

SALWEY (Arthur).   *See* Parliamentary Sermons.

SANCTIUS (Gaspar).   Commentarii in Actus Apostolorum Accessit Disputatio de SS. Jacobi & Pauli Apostolorum Hispaniam adventu. In lucem nunc primum editi,... (2 parts in one vol.)
Lugduni, apud Horatium Cardon, 1616. IPSWICH 1651 GS rep. 24cm.
BT43   FEt   K4   King 306 11B

———— In duodecim Prophetas minores & Baruch Commentarii cum paraphrasi. Nunc primum prodeunt... (2 parts in one vol.)
Lugduni, sumpt. Jacobi Cardon et Petri Cavellat, 1621.   ½L reb. 36cm.
BT43   FEt   K4   King 527 9E

———— In Ezechielem & Danielem prophetas commentarii cum paraphrasi. Nunc primum prodeunt... (2 parts in one vol.)
Lugduni, sumptibus Horatii Cardon, 1619.   ½L reb. 36cm.
BT43   FEt and label   K4   King 530 9E

———— In Isaiam prophetam commentarii cum paraphrasi. Nunc primum evvulgati.
Lugduni, sumptibus Horatii Cardon, 1615.   ½L reb. 36cm.
BT43   FEt   K4   King 529 9E

———— In Jeremiam prophetam commentarii cum paraphrasi. Accessit explicatio Psalmi CXXXVI. Paraphrasi item poetica ad Threnos, & eundem Psalmum. Haec omnia nunc primum prodeunt.
Lugduni, sumptibus Horatii Cardon, 1618.   ½L reb. 36cm.
BT43   FEt   K4   King 532 9E

———— In libros Ruth, Esdrae, Nehemiae, Tobiae, Judith, Esther, Machabeorum commentarii. Nunc primum prodeunt.

Lugduni, sumptibus Jacobi Cardon, 1628.   ½L reb. 36cm.

BT43   FEt and label   K4   King 531 9E

———— In librum Job Commentarii cum paraphrasi. Nunc primum prodeunt.
Lugduni, sumptibus Jacobi Cardon et Petri Cavellat, 1625.   ½L reb. 36cm.

BT43   FEt   K4   King 528 9E

———— In quatuor libros Regum, & duos Paralipomenon, commentarii. Nunc primum prodeunt.
Lugduni, sumpt. Jacobi Cardon et Petri Cavellat, 1623.   ½L reb. 36cm.

BT43   FEt   K4   King 517 9E

———— In Zachariam Prophetam commentarii cum paraphrasi.
(Lugduni, Horatio Cardon, 1616.) IPSWICH 1651 GS rep. 24cm.

lacks tp   BT43   FEt   K4   King 305 11B

SANDERSON (Robert), *Bp.*   XXXIV sermons.. ad aulam, ad clerum, ad magistratum, ad populum.
To which is prefixed a large preface. *also with his* XIV sermons... fifth impression. (2 vols. in one)
London, printed by E. Cotes for A. Seile, 1664. Rep. 32cm.

Wing S.606 and S.634   DU   FEt   [I3]   King 103 6C

SANSON (Nicholas).   *See* MAPS: Appendix H.

SANSOVINO (Francesco).   Del Secretario... libri VII... il modo di scriver lettere acconciamente &
con arte,... & in diverse occasioni. (7 books in one vol.)
Venetia, appresso Bartolomeo Carampello, 1596. Reb. 15cm.

not in Adams   ms pasted on rear fl   UL32   FEp   [I1]   King 353 5A

[SAUMUR. Four theses in Latin.]   Syntagma thesium theologicarum in academia Salmuriensi.
Second edition. (4 parts in one vol.)
Salmurii, apud Joannem Lesnerium, 1665. Rep. 23cm.

LP2   FEt   [I2]   King 288 8B

SAVILE (*Sir* Henry), *ed.*   Rerum Anglicarum scriptores post Bedam praecipui, ex vetustissimi
codicibus manuscriptis nunc primum in lucem editi. Adiecta ...chronologia.
Londini, excudebant G. Bishop, R. Nuberie, & R. Barker, 1596. English early 17th cent. GS rep. 35cm.

STC.21783   ms ½t by Henry Tracey   bg   KG11   PGL21   FEt   M2   King 53 5F

———— *See also* BRADWARDINE, T.*Abp. and* JOHN CHRYSOSTOM, *Saint.*

SAYRE (Gregory).   Clavis regia sacerdotum, casuum conscientiae sive theologiae moralis... copios-
issime explicans.
Monasterii Westfaliae, sumptibus Michaelii Dalii & Bernardi Raesfelt, 1628. Reb. 36cm.

bg   KG10   FEt   L2   King 70 3E

SCAPULA (Johannes).   Lexicon Graecolatinum novum... Editio ultima, priori locupletior & correctior... Dialectorum omnium a Jacobo Zvingero... redactarum. (3 parts in one vol.)
Genevae, apud Philippum Albertum, 1619. Reb. 33cm.

bg   MS41   FEp   K3   King 520 9D

SCHARPIUS (Joannes).   Cursus theologicus, in quo controversiae omnes de fidei dogmatibus,...
pertractantur. In duos tomos divisus. (2 vols. in one)

Genevae, apud Petrum & Jacobum Chouet, 1618. Rep. 24cm.
p: 10 6   bg   MS39   FEt   G2   King 271 8B

SCHINDLER (Valentin).   Lexicon pentaglotton, Hebraicum, Chaldaicum, Syriacum, Talmudico-Rabbinicum, & Arabicum:... collectum et concinnatum... cum triplice indice:
Hanoviae, typis Joannis Jacobi Hennei, 1612. Rep. 34cm.
LP1   FEt   [I5]
                                                                                     King 546 1B

SCHLICHTING (Jonas).   *See* SZLICHTING, J.

SCHOTT (Gaspar).   Cursus mathematicus, sive absoluta omnium mathematicarum disciplinarum Encyclopaedia, in libros XXVIII digesta,... accesserunt in fine theorese mechanicae novae.
Herbipoli, sumptibus haeredum Joannis Godefridi, excudebat Jobus Hertz, 1661. Rep. 35cm.
DU   [O2]
                                                                                     King 61 9E

SCHUBERT (Clemens).   Libri quatuor De scrupulis chronologor. in quibus non solum calculus... cum serie quatuor Monarchiarum & Olympiadibus Graecorum, ... Nunc primum editi. *Bound with* MULERIUS, N. Judaeorum annus lunae- solaris, 1630.
Argentorati, excusum apud Bernhardum Jobinum, 1575. BS rep. 30cm.
Adams S.735   cp: d.f.   DU   FEt   [I3]
                                                                                     King 126 11C

SCOTT (John).   The Christian life, from its beginning to its consummation in glory. With proper and useful indexes. The ninth edition. (3 parts in one vol.)
London, printed for James and John Knapton, John Darby et al, 1729. BP rep. 35cm.
LP15 (1746)
                                                                                     King 524 8E

SCUDDER (Henry).   *See* Parliamentary Sermons.

SCULTETUS (Abraham).   Concionum in Jesaiam prophetam, ad populum Haidelbergensem habitarum,... studio & opera Balthasaris Tilesii. (2 parts in one vol.)
Genevae, Excudebat Petrus Aubertus, 1610. Rep. 18cm.
bg   KG7   FEt   E3
                                                                                     King 370 9A

———— Medullae theologiae patrum Pars prima... Editio quarta (– pars secunda) (2 parts in one vol.)
Ambergae, prostat in officina Abrahami Vetteri, (typis Michaelis Forsteri), 1613 (1606). Reb. 22cm.
bg   KG7   FEt   E3
                                                                                     King 230(1) 9A

———— Medulla theologiae patrum Pars tertia – pars IV (2 parts in one vol.)
Heidelbergae, typis Gotthardi Voegelini (impensis Jonae Rosae, typis Johannis Lancelloti), 1609–1613. Reb. 22cm.
bg   KG7   FEt   E3
                                                                                     King 230(2) 9A

———— *and* BOCKSTADIUS (Joannes). Concionatorum Heidelbergensium In epistolam ad Romanos concionum ideae, confectae studio & opera Nicolai Eccii Leobergensis.
Heidelbergae, sumptibus Jonae Rosae, excudebat Johannes Lancellotus, 1619. Reb. 20cm.
bg   MS33   FEt   E3
                                                                                     King 237 9A

———— *See also* PITISCUS, B. *and* SCULTETUS, A.

SEAMAN (Lazarus).   *See* Parliamentary Sermons.

SEDGWICK (William).   *See* Parliamentary Sermons.

SEDGWICKE (Obadiah).   *See* Parliamentary Sermons.

SELMATTER (Andraeus).   A symphonia nova Evangelistarum,... qua per oracularium textuum quatuor divisim novam concinnationem,... breviter, & perspicue, enarratur. *bound with* HIMMEL, J. Memoriale Biblicum, 1624. (2 vols. in one)
Basileae, excudebat Johannes Schroterus, sumptibus Abrahami Vetteri, 1613. BS rep. 19cm.
cp: e.f.   DU   FEt   [I2]   King 670 11B

SELNECCER (Nicolaus).   In omnes Epistolas Pauli commentarius plenissimus,... nunc primum in lucem editus, studio filii Georgii Selnecceri. (2 parts in one vol.)
Lipsiae, sumtibus Jacobi Apelii, ex officina Abrahami Lambergi, 1595. L reb. 31cm.
Adams B.1870   bg   BT12   PGL18 over PGL15a   FEt   E4   King 93 8D

SENECA (Lucius Annaeus).   Quae extant opera, ad veterum exemplarium fidem nunc recens castigata... commentariis selectioribus... auctore D. Gothofredo *with his* Rhetoris... excerpta... N. Fabri, A. Schotti *et al.* (2 vols. in one)
Parisiis, excudebat Petrus Chevalier, 1607. Rep. 34cm.
bg   MS5 (1613)   FEt   H5   King 545 5E

SERARIUS (Nicolaus).   Commentarium in librum Josue, liber primus (-tomus posterior). (2 vols. in one)
Moguntiae, ex officina typographica Joannis Albini, 1609–10.   ½L reb. 32cm.
lacks tp to vol.1   bg   KG7   FEt   G3   King 129 3B

———— Judices et Ruth explanati. (2 parts in one vol.)
Moguntiae, e Balthasaris Lippii typographeo, 1609. Reb. 30cm.
bg   KG7   FEt   G3   King 65 3B

SERRANUS (Petrus).   In Levitici lib. commentaria. *bound with* Commentaria in Ezechielem Prophetam: (2 vols. in one)
Antverpiae, ex officina Christophori Plantini, 1572. Reb. 32cm.
Adams S.994   bg   BT1   FEt   G3   King 42 9D

SERRES (Jean de).   A general inventorie of the history of France, from the beginning of that monarchie,... continued unto these times, out off the best authors... Translated out of French into English by Edward Grimeston.
London, imprinted by George Eld, 1607. English cy AGS rep. 31cm.
STC.22244   LP4   FEt   [I4]   King 587 10D

SEXTUS (Empiricus).   [Greek.] ...Opera quae extant... quibus in tres Philosophiae partes... Henrico Stephano interprete: Adversu mathematicos,... Gentiano Herveto Aurelio interprete, Graece nunc primum editi. (2 parts in one vol.)
Genevae [printed above obliterated place name], typis ac sumptibus Petri & Jacobi Chouet, 1621. Rep. 33cm.
LP4   FEt   [I4]   King 155 10D

SIBBES (Richard)   Beames of divine light, breaking forth from severall places of holy scripture,... in XXI sermons. *with* The spirituall jubile. *also includes his* Light from heaven,... in four treatises *with* The churches riches, by Christs poverty... (4 vols. in two)

London, printed by G. M. (E. P., R. Badger) for N. Bourne and R. Harford, 1638–39. Rep. 19cm.
STC.22475, 22498 and 22489   LP2   King 389(2–3) 5C

———— Evangelicall sacrifices in XIX sermons: – The third tome (2 vols. in one)
London, printed by T. for N. Bourne, (E. Purslow) and R. Harford, 1639–40. Rep. 14cm.
STC.22491   lacks tp   LP2   King 389(4) 5C

———— An exposition of the third chapter of the epistle of Paul to the Philippians: also two sermons
of Christian watchfulnesse; an exposition of... the second chapter... and A sermon upon Malachi. (2
parts in one vol.)
London, printed by T. Cotes for Peter Coles, 1639. Reb. 19cm.
STC.22493   LP2   King 389(5) 5C

———— A learned commentary or exposition upon the first chapter of the second epistle of Paul to
the Corinthians. Being the substance of many sermons... at Grayes-Inne, ...published... by Tho.
Manton.
London, printed by J. L. for N. B., sold by Tho. Parkhurst, 1655.   ½L reb. 30cm.
Wing S.3738   LP2   [H3]   King 170(1) 6A

———— The returning backslider, or a commentarie upon...XIIII chapter... of... preached... and
published by his owne permission, *includes his* The Saints priviledge orm a Christians constant
advocate, 1638. (2 parts in one vol.)
London, printed by G. M. for George Edwards, 1639. Rep. 19cm.
STC.22500   LP2   King 389(1) 5C

———— The saints cordialls,... delivered in sundry sermons, at Graies-Inne... and at Cambridge.
London, printed by M. S. for Henry Cripps, 1658. Rep. 28cm.
Wing S.3743   LP2   [H3]   King 170(2) 6A

———— The soule's conflict with it selfe, and victory over it selfe by faith... fourth edition.
London, printed by M. F. for R. Dawlman, 1638. Rep. 17cm.
STC.22511   cp: i/p   LP2   King 389(6) 5C

SIGONIO (Carlo).   De antiquo iure civium Romanorum, Italiae Provinciarum, ac Romanae iuris
prudentiae iudiciis, libri XI.
Francofurti, apud heredes Andreae Wecheli, Claudium Marnium, & Joan. Aubrium, 1593. Rep. 31cm.
Adams S.1101   ?bm: 11   BP13   FEt   M3   King 145 2B

SIMLER (Josia), *ed.   See* GESNER, C.

SIMONIUS (Joannes).   Triumphus secularis. Oratio: qua; ob divinitus, ...Martini Lutheri,... a V
Novembris 1617... panegyri. *bound with* TARNOVIUS, J. In Psalmos commentarius, 1628.
Rostochi, typis suis Joachimus Pedanus descripsit, sumptus Johannes Hallervordius fecit, 1618. IPSWICH 1651
GS rep. 18cm.
MS48   FEt   E2   King 224 10B

SIMPSON (Sidrach).   *See* Parliamentary Sermons.

SLEIDAN (Johannes).   De statu religionis ac reipublicae continuatio... ad nostra usque tempora,
non ex superiori editione Alemannica,... concinnata per Michaelem Casparum.
Francofurti, ex officina viduae Matthiae Beckeri, 1614. Rep. 19cm.
bg   BP13   FEt   H2   King 226 5B

SMITH (Peter).   *See* Parliamentary Sermons.

SOCINO (Fausto).   Opera omnia in duos tomos distincta. ...Opera exegetica & didactica... opera polemica. (2 vols.)
Irenopoli, [Bibliotheca Fratrum Polonorum], 1656-. Reb. 31cm.
UL22   FEt   [O2]   King 617 1C

SPAIN – History.   Rerum Hispanicarum Scriptores aliquot,... ex bibliotheca Roberti Beli Angli... in duos tomos digesti,... Tomus prior – posterior. (2 vols. in one)
Francofurti, ex officina Andreae Wecheli, 1579. Cambridge cy O: HMg(2) IN(9) BS rep. 32cm.
Adams S.821   ms owner and p: Harrison 13s 4d   former clasps   bg   BP13   FEt   M1
                                                                                          King 48 4A

SPANHEIM (Friedrich).   Dubia Evangelica discussa & vindicata tum a cavillis atheorum, tum a corruptelis sectariorum... (3 parts in two vols.)
Genevae, sumptibus Jacobi Chouet, 1634–39. L reb. 24cm.
BT43   FEt   K3   King 304 8B

SPELMAN (*Sir* Henry).   Concilia, decreta, leges, constitutiones, in re ecclesiarum orbis Britannici... ad nostram aetatem... primus hic tomus (ad 1066). (First vol. of three)
Londini, excudebat Richardus Badger, impensis Ph. Stephani & Ch. Meredith, 1639. Rep. 33cm.
STC.23066 (part)   UL5 (who published the book)   FEt   M2   King 17 6B

SPINCKES (Nathaniel).   *See* HICKES, G.

SPRAT (Thomas), *Bp.*   The history of the Royal-Society of London, for the improving of natural knowledge.
London, printed by T. R. for J. Martyn and J. Allestry, 1667. Rep. 19cm.
Wing S.5032   LP1   [H3]   King 687 7D

SPURSTOWE (William).   *See* Parliamentary Sermons.

STACKHOUSE (Thomas).   A new history of the Holy Bible, from the beginning of the World, to the establishment of Christianity... The second edition carefully revised,... by the Author. (2 vols.)
London, printed for Stephen Austen, 1742–44. Reb. 37cm.
prob. LP12   King 510 11E

STAUNTON (Edmund).   *See* Parliamentary Sermons.

STEBBING (Henry).   Polemical Tracts; or a collection of papers written in defence of the doctrines and discipline of the Church of England. To which are added a short exposition... and a sermon.
Cambridge, printed at the University Press, by Corn. Crownfield, sold by C. Bowyer in London, 1727. Reb. 34cm.
ms donor's signature   LP18 (1748)   King 540 8E

STEEN (Cornelius van den).   *See* CORNELIUS A LAPIDE.

STELLA (Diego de).   Eximii verbi divini concionatoris, in... Evangelium secundum Lucam enarrationum. Tomus primus (-secundus: Editio ultima ab authore recognita).

Antverpiae, sumptibus vidueae & haeredum Petri Belleri, 1612. (2 vols. in one) IPSWICH GS rep. 30cm.

bg   BT10   FEt   G4   King 34 11C

STEPHANUS (Carolus).   Dictionarium historicum, geographicum, poeticum. Authore Carolo Stephano... huic postremae editioni accessit collium, sylvarum... diligenter ac fideliter excerptus. *Genevae, apud Samuelem Crispinum,* 1621. English cy 1668 BS rep. 24cm.

cp: e.   DU   FEt   K2   King 309 9B

STEPHANUS (Henricus).   [Greek.] Thesaurus Graecae linguae, ab Henrico Stephano constructus. (5 vols. in four)
Geneva, Henr. Stephani Oliva, [1572]. Reb. 38cm.

Adams S.1790   UL12   FEt   [I5]   King 448 2E

─────── *See also* BIBLE – Concordance – Greek and Latin, 1600 and 1624, *and* SEXTUS, E.

STERNHOLD (Thomas) *and* HOPKINS (John).   The whole book of Psalmes: collected into English meeter... with apt notes to sing them withall. *bound with* BIBLE - Hebrew, 1574.
London, printed by G. M. for the Companie of Stationers, 1633. Rep. 16cm

STC.2642   UL19   K2   King 332 5A

STERRY (Peter).   *See* Parliamentary Sermons.

STILLINGFLEET (Edward), *Bp.*   Irenicum. A weapon-salve for the churches wounds, or the divine right of particular forms of Church-government: Second edition. *bound with his* Origines Sacrae, 1666. *(2 books in one vol.)*
London, printed for Henry Mortlock, 1662. Reb. 19cm.

Wing S.5597   LP4   FEt   [H3]   King 260 11A

─────── Origines sacrae, or a rational account of... the Christian faith, as to the truth... of the Scriptures,... Third edition.
London, printed by R. W. for Henry Mortlock, 1666. Reb. 19cm.

Wing S.5618   LP4   FEt   [H3]   King 260 11A

─────── A rational account of the grounds of Protestant religion: ...wherein the... Church of England vindicated from the imputation of schism; and... controversies between us and those of the Church of Rome throughly examined. (3 parts in one vol.)
London, printed by Rob. White for Henry Mortlock, 1665. Rep. 32cm.

Wing S.5624   LP4   FEt   [I4]   King 588 6B

STRICKLAND (John).   *See* Parliamentary Sermons.

STRIGELIUS (Victor).   [Greek.] Hypomnemata. In omnes libros Novi Testamenti, quibus et genus sermonis explicatur,... edita a Victorino Strigelio. *with his* Hypomnemata in omnes Epistolas Pauli et aliorum Apostolorum et in Apocalypsin. (2 vols. in one)
Lipsiae, [in officina Voegelini], c. 1565. Rep. 23cm.

Adams S.1934   bg   BT26   FEt   G2   King 244 9B

STRONG (WILLIAM).   *See* Parliamentary Sermons.

STUCKI (Johann Wilhelm).   Antiquitatum convivialium libri III. Editio secunda,... emendiator:. (3 parts in one vol.)

Tiguri, apud Johannem Wolphium typis Frosch., 1597. Reb. 32cm.

Adams S.1961   ms owner Joannes Watson, Christ. Coll. and Latin inscription on tp   bm: τ 27.

UL22   FEp   [O3]   King 602 6B

———— *See also* VERMIGLI, P.M.

SUAREZ (Francisco).   ...Opera omnia (24 parts in 10 vols.)

Moguntiae, sumptibus Hermanni Mylii Birckmanni, excudebat Balthasar Lippius, 1616–1630. IPSWICH in cartouche GS rep. 36cm.

KG15   FEt   L3   King 495 10E

SYMONDS (Joseph).   *See* Parliamentary Sermons.

SZEGEDINUS (Stephanus).   *See* KIS, S.

SZLICHTING (Jonasz).   Commentaria posthuma, in pleroque Novi Testamenti libros... In duos tomos. (2 books in one)

Irenopoli, sumptibus Irenici Philalethii, 1656. Rep. 31cm.

UL22   FEt   [O2]   King 147 1C

TACQUET (Andrew).   Opera mathematica... a Simone Laurentio Veterani. (7 parts in three vols.)

Antverpiae, apud Jacobum Meusium, 1669. Reb. 32cm.

p: 25#   LP3   FEp   [O2]   King 140 7E

TANNER (Thomas), *Bp.*   Bibliotheca Britannico-Hibernica: sive, de scriptoribus, qui in Anglia, Scotia, et Hibernia ad saeculi XVII initium floruerunt,... commentariis:... Praefatio, historiam literariam Britannorum Bibliothecae... Bostonum Buriensem...

Londini, excudit Gulielmus Bowyer, 1748. Reb. 35cm.

LP19   msGL   [N1]   King 512 6D

———— Notitia Monastica; or, an account of all the abbies, priories, and houses of friers, heretofore in England and Wales; and... colleges and hospitals founded before 1540. Published by John Tanner, Vicar of Lowestoft, etc.

London, printed by William Bowyer... sold by John Whiston, John Osborn, and Francis Changuion, 1744. Rep. 34cm.

LP19   [N1]   King 513 6D

TARNOVIUS (Joannes).   [Exercitationes Biblicae], libri quatuor, quorum III Miscellaneorum et IV Dissertationum... diligentius inquiritur ac defenditur. (2 vols. of four)

Lipsiae, typis Gregorii Ritzschii & impensis Johannis Hallervordi, 1640. Reb. 17cm.

MS48   inscription to BT40 in error   FEt   E2   King 367 10B

———— In prophetas minores commentarii. (Eleven parts in 2 vols.)

Rostochi, literis Joachimi Pedani, impensis Joh. Hallefordii, 1623–29. Reb. 20cm.

BT40   FEt   E2   King 241 & 677 10B

———— In Psalmos poenitentiales septem commentarius brevis:... ex ipsa scripturam natis ac probatis indicatur. *with his* Tres Eliae. Hos est, comparatiotrium... reformatorum Eliae Thesbitae, Johannis Baptistae, Martini Lutheri,... 1618. *his* Quaestio num et quae foedera cum diversae religionis hominibus, 1618. *also contains* TARNOVIUS, P. Panegyricus... recitatus in solemni Academiae, 1618. *and also* SIMONIUS, J. Triumphus secularis, 1618. (5 vols. in one)

Rostochi, literis Joachimi Pedani, 1628. IPSWICH 1651 GS rep. 18cm.

p: 1 6 on first tp   MS48   inscription to BT40 in error   FEt   E2   King 224 10B

——— In threnos Jeremiae commentarius:... ex ipsa scripturam natios ac probatis indicatur.
Rostochi, sumptu Johannis Hallervordii, 1642. Reb. 18cm.

MS48   inscription to BT40 in error   FEp   E2   King 684 10B

TARNOVIUS (Paulus).   Panegyricus.. in quo occasione jubilaei Lutherani... recitatus in solemni Academiae... *with* TARNOVIUS, J. In Psalmos commentaria, 1628.
Rostochi, typis suis Joachimi Pedani descripsit, sumptus Johannes Hallervordius fecit, 1618. IPSWICH 1651 GS rep. 18cm.

MS48   inscription to BT40 in error   FEt   E2   King 224 10B

TAYLOR (Brook).   *See* KIRBY, J.

TAYLOR (Francis).   *See* Parliamentary Sermons.

TAYLOR (Jeremy), *Bp.*   Ductor dubitantium, or the rule of conscience in all her general measures;... for the determination of cases of conscience. In four books.
London, printed by James Flesher, for Richard Royston, 1660.   ½L Reb. 31cm.

Wing T.324   cp: g#   LP1   FEt   [I4]   King 148 9D

TAYLOR (John).   Marmor Sandvicense cum commentario et notis. *with his* Commentarius ad legem Decemviralem de inope debitore in partis dissecando:... in Cantabrigiae... 1741 recitavit.
Cantabrigiae, excudebat Jos. Bentham, prostant apud G. Thurlbourn et al., 1743–42. IPSWICH LIBRARY GS on red label rep. 26cm.

LP13   (1748)   [N1]   King 318 6A

TAYLOR (Silas).   The history of gavel-kind, with the etymology thereof,... remarks upon many occurrences of British and English history... to which is added a short history of William the Conqueror. (2 parts in one)
Printed for John Starkey... sold at his shop, 1663. Reb. 19cm.

Wing T.553   ms donor inscription by author on tp verso   UL18   (1677)   [I2]   King 685 7C

TESDALE (Christopher).   *See* Parliamentary Sermons.

TEMPLE (Thomas).   *See* Parliamentary Sermons.

TEMPORARIUS (Joannes).   Chronologicarum demonstrationum libri tres. (3 parts in one vol.)
Rupellae, ex officina Hieronymi Haultini, 1600. Reb. 26cm.

Adams T.299   lacks tp   DU   FEp   [I3]   King 77 6A

TENA (Ludovicus de), *Bp.*   Commentaria, et disputationes in epistolam D.Pauli ad Hebraeos.
Toleti, Petro Rodriguez, [1611–12]. IPSWICH GS rep. 29cm.

BT43   FEt   K4   King 175 1C

TERENCE (Publius).   Comoediae ad optimorum exemplarium fidem recensitae. Accesserunt variae lectiones, quae in Libris MSS. & eruditorum commentariis notatu digniores occurrunt. (2 vols.)

London, impensis J. and P. Knapton, et G. Sandby, 1751. ½L reb. 23cm.

LP12 King 431 9B

TERTULLIAN (Quintus Septimus Florens). Opera quae adhuc reperiri potuerunt omnia: ex editione Jacobi Pamelii Brugensis... annotationes Beati Rhenani,... notae breves... Francisci Junii. (3 parts in one vol.)
Franekerae, excudebat Aegidius Radaeus, 1597. Rep. 30cm.

Adams T.416   bg   BT1   PGL32   FEt   A1 King 110 1B

THALMANN (Benedict).   Assertio verae et orthodoxae doctrinae de unitate personae & distinctione duarum naturarum in Christo: et refutatio dogmatis de ubiquitate,... sanctorum... scriptis collecta, a Benedicto Thalmanno... ac... recognita a Christophoro Pezelio.
Heydelbergae, apud Josuam Harnisium, 1589. Rep. 16cm.

Adams T.441   bg   BT1   FEt   G1 King 343 5A

THEODORET, *Bp.*   Opera omnia quae ad hunc diem Latine versa sparsim extiterunt. (2 vols. in one)
Parisiis, apud Michaelem Sonnium, 1608. Reb. 34cm.

cp: a.h.d.   bg   BT1   PGL32   FEt   B2 King 598 10D

THEOPHYLACT, *Abp. of Ochrida.*   [Greek.] Commentarii in quatuor Evangelia... opus nunc primum Graece et Latine editum.
Lutetiae Parisiorum, apud Carolum Morellum, 1631. Reb. 36 cm.

BT36   FEt   B3 King 489 2D

———— Tomus primus, enarrationes in quatuor Evangelia continens. Joanne Oecolampadio interprete. *with* In omnes Pauli.. Epistolas enarrationes,... per Joannes Lonicerum... in Latinum conversae. Ad haec, eiusdem... in aliquot Prophetas minores compendiaria explanatio,... (2 vols. in one)
Basileae, [apud haeredes Andr. Cratandri], 1541–40. Rep. 30cm.

T.592   bg   BT1   PGL32   FEt   B3 King 589 1B

THOMAS AQUINAS, *Saint.*   ...Commentaria in omnes epistolas beati Pauli... profundiora theologie accurate dilucidantia... correcta per me Petrum de Bergamo.
Basilee, Michaelis Furter, impensis Wolfgangi Lachner, 1495. Reb. 29cm.

Goff T.234   ms owners: Richard Nykke (1506), John Meyne, W^s Smarte Gippi'   bg   BP0   FEp
G5 King 3 3A

———— Summa totius theologiae... per quaestiones & responses explicatur; in tres partes ab auctore suo distributa. Editio novissima. (3 vols. in one)
Parisiis, sumptibus Petrii Chevalier, 1615. Rep. 34cm.

bg   MS18   FEt   L1 King 20 4D

———— Tomus XV. complectens Catenam auream in Mattheum, Marcum, Lucam, et Joannem... Editio nova... per Cosmam Morellus.
Antverpiae, apud Joannem Keerbergium, 1612. Rep. 34cm.

bg   BT1   FEt   G4 King 535 2C

———— *See also* CURIEL, J.A., MEDICES, H., MEDINA, B., ROPA, R., *Bp. and* VALENTIA, G.de.

THORESBY (Ralph). Ducatus Leodiensis: or the topography of the.. town and parish of Leedes, and parts adjacent... To which is added... a catalogue of his Musaeum,... of manuscripts... with an account of some unusual accidents, after the method of Dr. Plot.
London, printed for Maurice Atkins, 1715. Reb. 32cm.

LP12   King 18 6C

THOROTON (Robert). The antiquities of Nottinghamshire, extracted out of records, original evidences,... and other authorities. Beautified with maps, prospects and portraictures.
London, printed by Robert White, for Henry Mortlock, 1677. Reb. 32cm.

Wing T.1053   hand coloured engravings   UL24   FEp   [N2]   King 644 6D

THOROWGOOD (Thomas). *See* Parliamentary Sermons.

THOU (Jacques Auguste de). Histoire de M. de Thou, des choses arrivées de son temps. Mise en François par P. Du Ryer... Historiographe du Roy. Tome premier – Tome troisième.
A Paris, chez Augustin Courbé, 1659. Reb. 35cm.

DU   [N2]   King 482 3D

THURMAIR (Johann). *See* AVENTINUS, J.

TOSSANUS (Daniel). Operum theologicorum volumen I–II. (2 vols.)
Hanoviae, typis Wechelianis, apud Claudium Marnium & haeredes Johannis Aubrii, 1604. IPSWICH GS rep. 20cm.

cp: m.f.   bg   BT10   FEt   F2   King 245 11A

TOSTADO (Alphonso), *Bp.* Opera omnia quotquot in scripture sacrae expositionem et alia,... nunc primum in Germania post Venetas impressiones... in lucem edita, (12 vols. and index)
Coloniae Agrippinae, sumptibus Joannis Gymnici et Antonii Hierati, 1613. BR rep. 37cm.

some tp crucifixes excised   bg   BT33   FEt   F5   King 443 11F

TREMELLIUS (Joannes Immanuele). *See* BIBLE – Latin, 1603 *and* BUCER, M.

TRIVET (Nicholas). Annales sex Regum Angliae... nunc primum... edidit Antonius Hall.
Oxonii, e Theatro Sheldoniano, 1719–22. BP rep. 19cm.

donor's signature   LP12   King 423 10B

TUCKNEY (Anthony)   *See* Parliamentary Sermons.

TWISSE (William). Vindiciae gratiae, potestatis, ac providentiae Dei: Hoc est, ad examen... Perkinsiani... a Jacobo Arminio, responsio.
Amstelodami, apud Joannem Janssonium, 1632. Rep. 35cm.

DU unless deletion of BT35 in Book an error   FEt   D4   King 581 4E

TYNDALE (William), FRITH (John), *and* BARNES (Robert). The whole workes of..., three worthy martyrs,... beyng before scattered, & now in print here exhibited to the Church... (3 vols. in one)
London, John Daye, 1572–73. probably London cy (rolls not in O) BS rep. 30cm.

STC.24436   bg   MS2   FEt   K3   King 178 6B

TYPOTIUS (Jacob). Symbola varia diversorum principum Sacrosanc. Ecclesiae & sacri Imperii Romani. Cum uberrima Isagoge ... Ex museo Octavii de Strade. (3 vols. in one)

Praga, Aegidius Sadeler, 1601–03. Rep. 29cm.

MS30   FEt   H5   King 86 11C

URSINUS (Zacharias).   Corpus doctrinae orthodoxae sive, Catecheticarum explicationum... D. Parei opera... recognitum... adiuncta sunt miscellania catechetica seorsum excusa. (2 vols. in one)
Genevae, sumptibus Samuelis Crispini, 1616. Reb. 17cm.

ms marginalia   LP13   FEp   D3   King 396 5A

———— Opera theologica... partim antehac non edita, partim ex Germanica in Latinam... conversa... tributa in tomos tres... studio et opera Quirini Reuteri. (3 vols. in two)
Heidelbergae, typis Johannis Lancelloti, impensis Jonae Rosae, 1612. Reb. 32cm.

bg   BP9   PGL14   FEt   D3   King 79 3C

USSHER (James), *Abp.*   Annales Veteris Testamenti, a prima mundi origine deducti: una cum rerum Asiaticarum et Aegyptiacarum chronico,...
Londini, ex officina J. Flesher, & prostant apud J. Crook & J. Baker, 1650. IPSWICH 1651 GS rep. 29cm.

Wing U.147A   MS48   FEt   [I4]   King 610 2B

VALENTIA (Gregorius de).   Commentariorum theologicorum tomi quatuor in quibus omnes quaestiones... in summa Thomae Aquinatis, ordine explicantur;... Nunc primum in Gallia... ex editione Ingolstadiensi... ab auctore recognita,.... (4 vols.)
Lutetiae Parisiorum, Rolini Theoderici & Petri Chevalerii, 1609. Rep. 35cm.

donor's merchant mark on tp verso in first three vols.   bg   BP2   PGL8   FEt   L1   King 533 4D

VALENTINE (Thomas).   *See* Parliamentary Sermons.

VALERIANO BOLZANI (Giovanni Pierio).   Hieroglyphica, sive de sacris Aegyptiorum aliarumq. gentium literis, commentariorum libri LVIII... editio novissima. (3 vols. in one)
Francofurti ad Moenum, sumptibus Antonii Hierati, excudebat Erasmus Kempffer, 1614–13. Rep. 25cm.

bg   BT1   FEt   H2   King 696 8B

VATABLI (Francisci).   *See* BIBLE – Polyglot, 1599.

VAZQUEZ (Gabriel).   Opera omnia... (Commentariorum ac disputationum... Sancti Thomae). (8 vols.)
Antverpiae, apud Petrum & Joannem Belleros, 1620–21. Rep. 35cm.

BP16   FEt   L2   King 553 5F

VELAZQUEZ (Juan Antonio).   In Epistolam Pauli ad Philippenses, commentarii & adnotationes,... (2 vols.)
Lugduni (Parisiis), sumptibus Laurentii Durand (apud Societatem), 1628 (1632). Rep. 34cm.

bg   BT40   FEt   G4   King 497 3D

VERMIGLI (Pietro Martire).   Defensio doctrinae veteris et Apostolicae de ... Eucharistiae Sacramento... in quatuor distincta partes, adversus Stephani Gardineri,... cui accesserat... dialogus de utraque in Christo natura. Omnia nunc primum in unum corpus collecta... (5 parts in one vol.)
Basileae, ex officina Petri Pernae, 1581. Reb. 31cm.

Adams M.762   bg   BT3   PGL20   FEt   C2   King 142 10C

——— In Epistolam Pauli ad Romanos... commentarii doctissimi. *bound with his* In selectissimam Pauli... ad Corinthios, 1579. (2 vols. in one)
Heidelbergae, typis Iohannis Lancelloti, impensis Andreae Cambieri, 1618. Rep. 31cm.

bg   BT3   PGL20   FEt   C2   King 645 10C

——— In Samuelis prophetae libros duos... commentarii... denuo editi. His auctarii loco accessit, Palaestinorum, Tyriorum ac Sidoniorum... ex sacris et profanis monumentis... historia... tractatus: per Johan. Guilhel. Stuckium.
Tiguri, apud Joannem Wolphium typis Frosch., 1595. Reb. 31cm.

Adams M.779   bg   BT3   PGL20   FEt   C2   King 639 10C

——— In primum librum Mosis, qui vulgo Genesis dicitur, commentarii,... Editio secunda... vita eiusdem a Josia Simlero... descripta. *with his* In librum Judicum... commentarii doctissimi cum tractione... (2 vols. in one)
Heidelbergae, e typographeio Johannis Lancelloti, impensis Andreae Cambieri, 1606–09. Rep. 31cm.

bg   BT3   PGL20   FEt   C2   King 632 10C

——— In selectissimam Pauli priorem ad Corinthios Epistolam,... ad sereniss. Regem Angliae, &c. Edvardum VI commentarii doctissimi. Editio tertia. *bound with his* In epistolam Pauli ad Romanos, 1618. (2 vols. in one)
Tiguri, apud Christophorum Froschoverum, 1579. Rep. 31cm.

Adams M.790   cp: x over t   BT3   PGL20   FEt   C2   King 645 10C

——— Loci communes... ex variis ipsius auctoris scriptis in unum volumen collecti, & in quatuor classes iuxta veram methodum distributi... theses, orationes, epistolae... scriptae.
Heidelbergae, sumptibus Danielis & Davidis Aubriorum & Clementis Schleichii, 1622. Rep. 32cm.

MS30   FEt   C2   King 634 10C

——— Melachim id est, Regum libri duo posteriores cum commentariis... in primum totum & secundi priora XI Capita, et Joannis Wolphii in secundi quatuordecim ultima capita.
Heidelbergae, ex officina Andreae Cambieri, 1599. Reb. 31cm.

Adams M.783   bg   BT3   PGL20   FEt   C2   King 209 10C

VINES (Richard).   *See* Parliamentary Sermons.

VITALIS (Joannis).   Speculum morale totius sacrae scripturae... in quo universa fere loca, & figurae veteris, ac Novi Testamenti... explanantur.
Venetiis, apud Societatem Minimam, 1603. Rep. 21cm.

ms gift inscr by donor   bg   MS7   (1615)   FEt   G2   King 671 11B

VITRINGA (Campegius).   Commentarius in librum prophetiarum Jesaiae, quo sensus orationis eius sedulo investigatur;... Editio nova. (2 vols.)
Leovardiae, excudit Henricus Halma, 1724. Reb. 39cm.

LP3   (1746)   [O3]   King 439 2E

VOLATERRANO (Rafaello).   *See* MAFFEIUS, R.

VOSSIUS (Gerhard Jan).   De arte grammatica libri septem. (4 parts in one vol.)
Amsterdami, apud Guilielmum Blaeu, 1635. Reb. 19cm.

LP4   [K2]   King 665 11B

——— *See also* EPHRAEM, Syrus, *Saint.*

WAENGLER (David).   *See* PAREUS, D.

WALAEUS (Balduinus).   Novi Testamenti libri historici, Greac. & Lat. perpetuo commentario ex antiquitate...
Lugduni Batavorum, ex officina & typographia Adriani Wyngaerden, 1653. Reb. 25cm.
DU   [I3]   King 308 8B

WALKER (George).   *See* Parliamentary Sermons.

WALTHER (Rudolph).   In Acta apostolorum per... Lucam descripta, homiliae CLXXIIII.
Tiguri, apud Christoph. Frosch., 1557. Reb. 30cm.
Adams G.1385   ms owners: erased   bg   BP1   FEt   PGL19   D1   King 99 8C

———— In Pauli apostoli Epistolam ad Galatas homiliae LXI.
Tiguri, excudebat Christophorus Froschoverus, 1576. London cy BS rep. 30cm.
Adams G.1399   ms marginalia   former clasps   BP1   FEt   PGL19   D1   King 91 8C

———— In Pauli Apostoli Epistolam ad Romanos homiliae.
Tiguri, excudebat Christophorus Froschoverus, 1566. Reb. 30cm.
Adams G.1392   bg   BP1   FEt   PGL19   D1   King 627 8C

———— In priorem (-posteriorem) Pauli ad Corinthios epistolam homiliae. (2 vols. in one)
Tiguri, excudebat Christophorus Froschoverus, 1572. London cy BS rep. 32cm
Adams G.1396   former clasps   p: Prec' x^s witnes Jhon Pack   ms owner & prophetic Latin inscr:
Nicholaus Yong   bg   BP1   FEt   PGL19   D1   King 607 8C

———— In prophetas duodecim, quos vocant minores,... homiliae. Editio secunda priori longe emendiator.
Tiguri, excudebat Christophorus Froschoverus, 1566. Reb. 32cm.
not in Adams   ms inits: R N   bg   BP1   FEp   PGL19   D1   King 568 8C

———— Isaias. In Isaiam prophetam.. homiliae CCCXXVII.
Tiguri, excudebat Christophorus Froschoverus, 1583. Reb. 32cm.
Adams G.1361   ms marginalia   bg   BP1   FEp   PGL19   D1   King 32 8C

———— Joannes Evangelista... in evangelium secundum Joannem homiliae CLXXX. *with his* In Joannis Epistolam canonicam, homiliae XXXVII. (2 vols. in one)
Tiguri, excudebat Christophorus Froschoverus, 1565. Reb. 32cm.
Adams G.1380   bg   BP1   FEp   PGL19   D1   King 102 8C

———— Lucas Evangelista. In Evangelium secundum Lucam homiliae CCXV.
Tiguri, excudebat Christophorus Froschoverus, 1570. BS rep. 32cm.
Adams G.1376   cp: g.f.   former clasps   bg   BP1   FEt   PGL19   D1   King 111 8C

———— Marcus Evangelista... in Evangelium secundum Marcum homiliae CXXXIX. Editio secunda priori locupletior et emendatior.
Tiguri, excudebat Christophorus Froschoverus, 1564. London cy BS rep. 32cm.
Adams G.1372   p: 6 6   ms marginalia and paste-in   bg   BP1   FEt   PGL19   D1   King 97 8C

———— Matthaeus evangelista... homiliarum in Evangeliium secundum Matthaeum. Pars prima - pars altera. (2 vols.)
Tiguri, excudebat Christophorus Froschoverus, 1583–84. Reb. 30cm.
vol. 1 not in Adams vol 2 G.1371   cp: k.f.   bg   BP1   FEp   PGL19   D1   King 106 & 114 8C

WALTON (Brian), *ed.*   *See* BIBLE – Polyglot, 1655–57.

WARD (John), *of Ipswich.*   *See* Parliamentary Sermons.

WEINRICH (Georg).   Explicatio Epistolae Paulinae, quam Apostolus in primis Ecclesiae Philippensium inscripsit & nuncupavit. *with his* Explicatio Epistolae Paulinae, quam Apostolus in primis Ecclesiae Colossensium inscripsit & nuncupavit. (2 vols. in one)
Lipsiae, impensis Thomae Schüreri, 1615. Rep. 18cm.

bg   MS33   FEt   Gl   King 674 11B

WELLS (Edward).   A new sett of maps both of antient and present geography... [maps only without geographical treatise.]
Oxford, printed at the Theater, 1700. BP rep. 42cm.

Wing W.1288   DU   King '703' 1E

WHINCOP (John).   *See* Parliamentary Sermons.

WHITAKER (Jeremiah).   *See* Parliamentary Sermons.

WHITAKER (William).   Opera theologica, duobus tomis nunc primum collecta... subiuncta... est de auctoris vita & morte descriptio. (2 vols. in one)
Genevae, sumptibus Samuelis Crispini, 1610. Reb. 35cm.

cp: a.e.   bg   KG2   PGL7b over PGL7a   FEt   D4   King 583 4E

WHITE (Francis), *Bp.*   A replie to Jesuit Fishers answere to certain questions propounded... Hereunto is annexed a conference... with the same Jesuit. (2 parts in one vol.)
London, printed by Adam Islip, 1624. Rep. 29cm.

STC.25382   bg   KG9   FEt   K3   King 180 6A

WHITE (John).   *See* Parliamentary Sermons.

WILD (Johann).   Annotationes in Exodum, Numeros, Deuteronomium, Lib. Josue, Lib. Judicum.
Coloniae Agrippinae, apud haeredes Arnoldi Birckmanni, 1574. L reb. 16cm.

Adams F.348   bg   BT23   FEt   Gl   King 379 11A

——— In... Evangelium secundum Joannem, ... enarrationes.
Lugduni, apud Guliel. Rovillium, 1562. Reb. 16cm.

as Adams F.376 (but that dated 1557)   tp defective   bg   BT23   FEt   Gl   King 324 11A

——— In... Evangelium secundum Matthaeum... enarrationes. Per fratrum Joannem Ferum. (Two parts in one vol.)
Lugduni, apud Ioannem à S. Paulo, 1609. Rep. 17cm.

bg   BT23   FEt   Gl   King 393 11A

——— ...In totam Genesim, non minus eruditae quam catholicae enarrationes. Tertia aeditio.
Coloniae Agrippinae, apud haeredes Arnoldi Birckmanni, 1572. Rep. 17cm.

Adams F.345   bg   BT23   PGL17   FEt   Gl   King 366 11A

——— Jobi historiae,... explicatio in CXIIII conciones eleganter distributa,... ante annos XXII per Joannem Ferum... enarrata. Nunc vero... repurgata interprete Tilmanno Bredenbachio.

Coloniae Agrippinae, apud haeredes Arnoldi Birckmanni, 1574. Rep. 17cm.

Adams F.350   bg   BT23   PGL17   FEt   G1   King 331 11A

———— Opuscula varia: quorum catalogum sequens pagina fusissime docebit. (9 parts in one vol.)
Lugduni, apud Guliel. Rovillium, 1567. I.H. BS rep. 16cm.

Adams F.330   owner's initials or cp: f b   LP13   King 344 11A

———— Postillae sive conciones... in Evangelia & Epistolas, que a die Paschae, ad adventum usque,... in... Ecclesia recitantur, iam primum latinitati... per Ioannem Guntherum... Pars secunda.
Lugduni, apud haeredes Jacobi Juntae, 1558. L reb.17cm.

not in Adams   bg   BT23   PGL17   FEt   G1   King 394 11A

WILKINSON (Henry), *of Christchurch.*   *See* Parliamentary Sermons.

WILLET (Andrew).   Hexapla in Danielem: that is, a six-fold commentarie upon the most divine prophesie of Daniel,... divided into two bookes: (2 books in one vol.)
[London], printed by Cantrell Legge for L. Greene, 1610. Rep. 30cm.

STC^2.25689.3   bg   KG13 = BT15   msGL (for William read Jeremy) over PGL2   FEt   F3
                                                           King 82 6B

———— Hexapla in Genesin, that is, a six-fold commentary upon Genesis:... divided into two tomes... now the second time revised, corrected,... and enlarged. (2 tomes in one vol.)
London, printed by Tho. Creede, for John Norton (for Thomas Man), 1608. Rep. 30cm.

STC.25683a   bg   BT15   msGL with error over PGL2 torn out   FEt   F3   King 85 6B

———— Hexapla in Leviticum. That is, a six-fold commentarie upon the third booke of Moses, called Leviticus... by the same author of Hexapla... perused and finished by P[eter] S[mith].
London, printed by Aug. Matthewes, for Robert Milbourne, 1631. Reb. 29cm.

STC.25688   cp: Ko   UL10   FEt   F3   King 81 6B

———— Hexapla: that is, a six-fold commentarie upon the... Epistle of Saint Paul to the Romans:... divided into two bookes. (2 books in one vol.)
[London], printed for Leonard Greene [by Cantrell Legge], 1611. Rep. 29cm.

STC.25690   bg   BT15   msGL with error over PGL2 torn out   FEt   F3   King 84 6B

———— Synopsis Papismi, that is, a generall view of Papistrie: wherein... the summe of antichristian doctrine is set downe,... the fourth time... published... and augmented. *includes his* Tetrastylon Papismi... the fourth time published. 1613. (2 vols. in one)
London, imprinted by Felix Kyngston for Thomas Man, 1613–14. Rep. 34cm.

STC.25699   bg   BT15   labels lost   FEt   F3   King 58 8E

WILLIAM *of Auvergne.*   Postilla sive expositio epistolarum et evangeliorum dominicalium: necnon de sanctis et eorum communi: una cum ferialibus tam de toto tempore anni & etiam eorundum sanctorum.
Lugduni, Jean de Vingle pour Stephan Gueynard, 1500/01. Reb. 19cm.

Goff G.707   ms owner & p: Powle Wythypoll 11s   KG1   FEp   King 253 11A

———— Opera omnia. Tomis duobus contenta,... in hac posteriori editione... ad authoris sensum recognita,... per Joannem Traianum. (2 parts in one vol.)
Venetiis, ex officina Damiani Zenari, 1591. Rep. 34cm.

Adams G.1595   bg   BT19   FEt   G4   King 579 9D

WILLIAM OF NEWBURGH.   De rebus Anglicis sui temporis, libri quinque... nunc primum auctiores XI. capitulis... & notis Joannis Picardi.
Parisiis, apud Carolum Sevestre & Davidem Gillium et Joannem Petit-pas, 1610. Reb. 18cm.

bg BP13 FEt H2
King 376 5A

WILLIS (Browne).   A survey of the cathedrals of York, Durham, Carlisle (etc.)... containing an history of their foundations, builders, antient monuments and inscriptions;... With an exact account of all the churches and chapels... illustrated with 32 curious draughts... (3 vols. in two)
London, printed for T. Osborne; and for T. Bacon in Dublin, 1742. Reb. 24cm.

LP12 FEp
King 311 6A

WILSON (Thomas).   A Christian dictionarie opening the signification of the chiefe wordes dispersed generally through Holie Scriptures... whereunto is annexed: a particular dictionary for the Revelation of St. John, etc. (2 parts in one vol.)
London, printed by W. Jaggard, 1612. Reb. 18cm.

STC.25786   owner & donor's signature   bg MS13 FEp K3
King 673 7C

WILSON (Thomas), *of Kent.*   *See* Parliamentary Sermons.

WINCKELMANN (Johannes).   Commentaria in sex prophetas minores: Oseam- Michaem (Nahum-Malachiam:) brevi et perspicua paraphrasi. (2 vols. in one)
Francofurti, typis Matthiae Beckeri (ex typographeio Nicolai Hofmanni), impensis Georgii Eberii & consortum, 1603. Rep. 16cm.

cp: c.   bg BT1 FEt G1
King 333 11A

WOLF (John).   *See* WOLPHIUS, J.

WOLLASTON (William).   The religion of nature delineated.
London, printed by Samuel Palmer, sold by B. Lintot, W. & J. Innys, J. Osborn et al., 1726. Reb. 30cm.
LP11 (1734)   msGL (whole page)   [N2]
King 321 6B

WOLPHIUS (Joannes).   [Sermons.] Deuteronomium in Mosis librum V... sermonum libri IIII. Nunc primum opera et studio... in lucem editi. *also contains his* Josua... sermonum liber unus... in lucem editus, 1592. *and his* Historia Judicum... accessit Ruthae historia, 1598. (3 vols. in one)
Tiguri, in officina Froschoviana (apud Joannem Wolphium, F.), 1585. Rep. 32cm.

Adams W.238 & 239   vol. 3 not in Adams   bg   BP10   PGL3 over PGL24 (the latter correct)   FEt D3
King 115 11C

———— *See also* VERMIGLI, P.M.

WOLSEY (Thomas), *Cardinal.*   *See* FIDDES, R.

WOLZOGEN (Johannes Ludovicus).   ...Opera omnia, exegetica, didactica, et polemica. (2 vols.)
Irenopoli, (Bibliotheca Fratrum Polonorum), 1656-. Reb. 31cm.
UL22 FEt [O2]
King 600 1C

WOODCOCK (Francis).   *See* Parliamentary Sermons.

WURSTISEN (Christian), *ed.*   Germaniae historicorum illustrium quorum plerique; ab Henrico IIII ad MCCCC,... Tomus unus.   *and his* Germaniae historicorum,... post Henrici IIII... Pars altera.
bound with REUBER, J. Veterum scriptorum Germanicorum, 1584. (2 vols. in one)

Francofurdi, apud heredes Andreae Wecheli, 1585. Reb. 31cm.
Adams G.494   UL24   AEm   [N2]   King 613(1) 3B

YOUNG (Thomas), *of Stowmarket.*   *See* Parliamentary Sermons.

ZACHARIAS, *Bp.*   ...In unum ex quatuor sive de concordia evangelistarum, libri quatuor, iam nunc primum typis excusi... ab Ammonio redacta,... *included with* BRUNFELS, O. Annotationes, 1535.
[Cologne], excudebat Eucharius Cervicornus, 1535. BS rep. 32cm.
Adams Z.20   owner's mark and date 1547 on tp   bg   BP0   FEt   D2   King 112 4C

ZANCHI (Jerome).   Operum theologicorum, Tomus primus-octavus.
[Heidelbergae], excudebat Stephanus Gamonetus [Petrus Aubertus], 1613. (8 vols. in four) L reb. 35cm.
bg   KG3   PGL3   FEt   D2   King 160 4C

ZEPPER (Wilhelm).   Sylva... in textus ex quatuor Evangelistis dominicales. Ubi quaelibet dominica duas ad minimum conciones,...
Herbornae Nassoviorum, [Christoph Corvini], 1608. Rep. 19cm.
bg   KG3   FEt   E2   King 250 10B

ZOSIMUS *the historian.*   Historiae novae libri VI, numquam hactenus editi:... historiae Procopii..., Agathiae..., Iornandis..., ...Leonardi Aretini commentariis.
Basileae, Petri Pernae, 1576. Reb. 33cm.
Adams Z.188   ms owner and p: Harrison 13s 4d   bg   BP13   FEp   M3   King 150 3E

ZWINGER (Jacobus).   *See* SCAPULA, J.

ZWINGER (Theodor), *elder.*   Theatrum humanae vitae... tertiatione novem voluminibus locupletatum... renovatum Jacobi Zvingeri Fil. recognitione. (29 parts in 5 vols.)
Basileae, per Sebastianum Henricpetri, [1604]. Reb. 35cm.
bg   BP11   FEt   H5   King 555 3D

ZWINGLI (Ulrich).   Operum... conscriptorum, partim... in Latinum translatorum. Pars prima (–secunda). *with his* Annotationes in Genesim, Exodum etc...una cum Psalterio per eundem Latinitate donato. (3 vols.)
Tiguri, excudebat Christophorus Froschoverus, 1581. Rep. 30cm.
Adams Z.217   bg   BP10   PGL24   FEt   C2   King 200(1–2) & 215 1C

Cum gratia & priuilegio Imp.
ad Quadriennium.   1547.
Eucharius Ceruicornus excudebat,anno 1535.

From ZACHARIAS, *Bp.*

BRIEF DETAILS OF THE TEN MANUSCRIPTS IN THE LIBRARY

These are drawn from M.R. James' and N.R. Ker's accounts[11], all using Westhorp's numbering. On vellum, except numbers 5 and 10. The bindings are all 19th or 20th century.

1   14th/15th century CONCORDANTIAE BIBLIORUM. fos. 301 (several others missing) written in three cols. (73 lines) in 31 x 19cm. Each letter originally had a handsome initial in gold on a ground quarterly pink and blue with white foliage.   BP0   M4

2   12th/13th century BEDA, IN LUCAM. 130 fos. written in two cols. (40 lines) in 24 x 17cm. Coloured initials. Chain mark at end. Possibly from Bury.   BP0   G5

3   Mid-12th century EXODUS GLOSATUS. 130 fos. written in three cols. in 18 x 18.5cm. Opening letter H and first verse magnificently illuminated in style of Canterbury books of the period. Foliage inhabited by white lion–dogs.   BP0   E5

4   Mid-14th century MARIALE. 133 fos. written in two cols. (44 lines) in 22 x 14cm. Partial borders in gold and colour on the first two folios. The gift of Abbot John to Bury; probably John de Brinkele (1361–1379).   BP0   H4

5   Mid-15th century PABULUM VITE (fos. 1–81) and Jacobus de Voragine, SERMONES quad-ragesimales (fos. 82–191). On paper, written in 21.5 x 14.5cm. Incomplete.   BP0   H4

6   13th century (but first six fos. added in 15th cent.) COMPILATIONES THEOLOGICAE. fos. 6 + 182. Until the 15th cent. fos. 1–93 of Pembroke College MS 101 (now in C.U.L.) together with this manuscript made up one book with the Bury Abbey pressmark S.65. Evidence of former chaining at front.   BP0   H4

7   Early 16th century HORAE and other devotions. fos. 290 on 19 lines in 14 x 10.5cm. London work in English. Decorated initials (no gold) and marginal decorations. Hand changes at fo. 97 where ownership by Anne Withipoll indicated (*see* Chapter XIII).   BP0   FEt: ORATIO'ES   H2 King 274

8   Early 13th century 1) RICARDUS SUPER PSALMOS and 2) JOSUE ET JUDICES GLOSATI. The two parts bound together in 15th century. 1: fos. 4–135 Two cols. of 40 lines with at least 80 lines in margins in 12 x 7.5cm. 2: fos. 137–229 15.5 x 11.5cm. Bury Abbey pressmarks B.240 and B.55 and donor inscription dated 20 Julii 1596 to Collegium [name erased] (Magdalene in fact, see Chapter I).   BP0   H2

9   Early 13th century BIBLIA and at end INTERPRETATIONES NOMINUM (fos. 339- 355). Two cols. of 55 lines in 14 x 8.5cm. First folio has elaborate coloured partial border with dragon and faces; initials to the Catholic Epistles also fine. Copious marginalia added from the 1560s to 1711. *See* Chapter XIII. No donor after Robert Sallowes presented it to the Corporation in about 1565. AE blue, gauffered [I2]

10   1637, on paper: CATECHETICAE VERSIONES VARIAE by G.S. Catechisms in English, Latin, Hebrew and Greek. Licensed for the Press on page 55 by John Oliver on 26 January 1637. The manuscript original for a published octavo of 1638 (STC.4806). The manuscript continues with verse catechisms which presumably were never published. G.S. was probably George, son of Edwin Sandys, Archbishop of York.   *See* Chapter XIII.   UL32   [I1]   King 355

A

MASTERS, USHERS and TOWN PREACHERS

In the first two lists, complete for the dates they cover, the names of those who played a part in the care or growth of the Library collection are shown in capitals. Only those Ushers involved are listed.

Masters

1586	John Berkeley
1604	James Leman
1608	George Downing
1611	JOHN COTTESFORD
1612	ALEXANDER READ
1613	JOHN COTTESFORD
1616	NICHOLAS EASTON
1630	WILLIAM CLARKE
1645	Christopher Glascock
1650	CAVE BECK
1657	Robert Woodside
1659	Henry Wickham
1663	Jeremy Collier
1664	Robert Stephenson
1695	ROBERT CONINGSBY
1712	EDWARD LEEDES
1737	Thomas Bolton
1743	ROBERT HINGESTON
1767	JOHN KING
1798	Rowland Ingram
1800	William Howorth

Town Preachers

1591	JOHN BURGES
1602	– Reeves
1604	John Askewe
1605	SAMUEL WARD
1640	NATHANIEL SMART
1643	MATTHEW LAWRENCE
1652	STEPHEN MARSHALL
1655	CAVE BECK
1656	Benjamin Bruning to 1663

After Bruning only JOSEPH CUTLOVE
and Dr THOMAS BISHOP, both also
Tower Church incumbents, were donors.

Ushers

JAMES LEMAN   1594–1604
JOHN COTTESFORD   1612–13 and 1616–18
JOHN CONEY   1613–16
SAMUEL BUTLER   1668–73 (as donor)

B

DONORS TO THE TOWN LIBRARY

Donors are listed in the order in which their names appear in the Benefactors' Book. Some are entered twice, but duplicate entries in the same list are ignored. A line is drawn in each list to divide those giving before and after about 1618. Parishes in Ipswich are given by dedication only, elsewhere by name.

BAYLIFFS & PORTMEN

BP		£	s	ob.	born/buried	PGL	PCC will
0	WILLIAM SMARTE			1599	Tower		
1	Robert Cutler	10		1619	Nicholas/Sproughton	19	77 Parker
2	Matthew Brownrigg	5		1635	Quay	8	39 Sadler
3	Thomas Sicklemore	4		1620	Lawrence		15 Soame
4	Robert Snelling	10		1627	Peter	ms#	
5	William Bloyse	9		1622	Nicholas/Grundisburgh	5	
6	Richard Martin	3		1622	Westerfield	28	9 Swanne
7	Tobias Blosse	5		1631	Belstead	6	24 St John
8	William Cage	2	10	1645	Clement/Burstall	12	37 Twisse
9	Richard Cock	3		1629	Matthew	14	
10	Michael Goodeere	3		c1626	Tower	24	
11	William Acton	10		1616	Mary Elms		20 Meade
12	Thomas Johnson	3	6	1618	Mary Elms	26	53 Meade
13	John Acton	10		1662	Bramford		
14	Martha, widow of John Knapp	1		1604	Peter		
15	Thomas Eldred	5		1624	Clement	22	53 Byrde
16	Robert Sparrowe	5	2	1642	Lawrence		
17	John Carnaby	3		c1631	Quay		

ms gift labels written by John Coney

KNIGHTS & GENTLEMEN

KG		£	s	ob.	lived	PGL
1	Sir Edmund Withipoll	2		1619	Margaret	34
2	Francis Brewster Esq	1		1644	Wrentham	7a & b
3	Edward Bacon Esq	3		1618	Barham	3
4	John Lany Esq	1		1633	Margaret	
5	Nicholas Rivett	1	10	1643	Brandeston	
6	Thomas Cornwallis	2		1627	Soham and Ipswich	
7	Leonard Caston	2		1618	Tower	
8	Sir Clypesby Gaudy	2		1619	Wenham parva	
9	John Burrell	1			Ipswich	
10	Sir Isaac Jermy	2		1634	Stutton	
11	Mrs Catherine Dod				Ipswich	21
12	Thomas Ungle	(1	10)	1618	Ipswich see also BT29	
13	Jeremy Hubbard	(2	5)	1622	Ipswich see also BT15	
14	John Hodges	10		1651	London Woodbridge Layham	
15	Robert Leman	10		1637	Brightwell and Stephen	

MINISTERS & SCHOLLERS

MS		£	s	parishes served	ob.
0	John Burges DD	3		*Town Preacher* 1591–1602	
1	Samuel Ward BD PGL33	2	10	*Town Preacher* 1605–40 Tower 24–7, 32–5	1640
2	John Carter		13	*Bramford* 1583 Belstead 1617 (see *D.N.B.*)	1635
3	Thomas Scott	1	10	*Clement* 1612–1623 to Utrecht (see *D.N.B.*)	1626
4	Thomas Garthwaite	1		Copdock 1616 Lawrence 1617 Blaxhall 1621	
5	Alexander Read	1		Fellow of Pembroke Master 1612–3	
6	John Cottesford	1	10	Usher and Master 1612–18 Helen? Bedingfield	1622
7	John Coney	1		Usher 1613–16	1617
8	Thomas Nuttall		10	*Tower* 1615–16 *to Saxmundham* 1616	
9	William Smith		12	*Freston* and Wherstead 1587–	
10	Robert Steffe	1		*Tuddenham* Martin 1610–	
11	Richard Leaver	1		Belstead 1594–17	
12	William Ashton	1		Whitton 1593 *Blakenham parva* 1596	
13	John Daye		5	*Nicholas* 1612–16	
14	Ralph Brownrigg DD	1		*Fellow Pembroke Hall* (see *D.N.B.*)	1659
15	Thomas Drax		–	*Harwich* 1611–1618 (see *D.N.B.*)	1618
16	John Caston	5		*Otley* 1598– *Clopton* 1606–31	1631
17	John Brunning MD	2	10	*Semer* 1622 (as Minister)	1663
18	Thomas Southabie	1		*Combs* 1615	
19	John Sherwood MD	1		(see *Venn*, Pemb. 1621) practised at Brome	
20	John Chaplin	1		*Capel St Mary* 1598–	
21	Daniel Hearne		10	*Henley* 1607 Bramford 1623 Hemingstone 1630	
22	Henry Frogge	1		Walton 1600 *Trimley* Martin 1600 Mary 1606	1620
23	Henry North		10	*Easton* 1603	1619
24	John Watson	1		*Woolpit* 1611–43 (ejected)	1646
25	John Anthony MD	1		practised in Ipswich 1619– (see *D.N.B.*)	1655
26	George Turnbull	1	6	*Creeting* 1611 *Margaret* 1624 Easton 1633	1648
27	Alexander Rainold		6	*Tattingstone*	
28	Robert Wickes	1		*Erwarton* 1622–	
29	Jonathan Skinner	1		*Tower* 1627–30 susp. from Woolverstone 1636	
30	John Webbe	9	5	*Falkenham* 1598–	
31	Richard Raymond		13	*Tower* 1630–2	
32	William Harborne		15		
33	Nathaniel Smart senior	1		Nicholas 1617–25	1632
34	Nicholas Beard		10	Peter 1630–6 resigned to Wren	
35	John Fenton		8	*Lawrence* 1621–31 or longer	
36	Richard Rainsford		10	*Helen* 1625–32	
37	John Allen	1	10	*Mary Quay* 1620 to New England 1637	
38	Gilbert Rany		15	*Mary Stoke* 1626–37	1637
39	William Clarke		15	*Master* 1630–45 Nicholas 1646–53	1653
40	Jude Allen	1		*Stephen* 1625	1631
41	Nicholas Easton	2		*Master* 1616–30	
42	William Hubbard		10	*Stephen* 1631–9 or longer	
43	Thomas Sherman	1	10	Tuddenham Martin 1609 *Hintlesham* 1610	
44	Thomas Warren		15	Lawrence 1633–5 resigned to Wren	
45	John Suckerman			Akenham 1621	
46	Jeremy Cateline senior			Peter 1617 Barham 1629 then to Wickham Market	
47	Peter Witham			Peter 1638–47	
48	Nicholas Stanton	5		*Margaret* 1641–9	1649
49	William Garlate		8	*Monk Soham* 1646–74	1674

The parish or post named in the donors' list given above in *Italic*

179

BT		£	s	PGL
1	Elizabeth Walter – legacy 1588	50		32
2	Robert Cole tanner	6		16
3	Edmund Day dyer	4		20
4	Henry Buckenham mercer	5		10
5	Roger Cutler	2		
6	John Bruning shipcarpenter	5		9
7	Peter Cole grocer	4		15a & 15b
8	Richard Burlingham mariner	2		11
9	Richard Jennings draper	1		
10	Robert Benham	4		
11	Thomas Eldred	1		22 but see also BP15
12	George Copping draper	1		18
13	Robert Knapp merchant	1	10	27
14	Richard Fisher	2		23
15	Jeremy Hubbard	2	5	but see also KG13
16	Jeremy Barber	5	5	4
17	Christopher Algate		3	2
18	Thomas Hayles	2	3	25
19	Benjamin Osmond	8	12	29 and £10 in will?
20	William Clyatt	2	14	
21	George Acton	2	6	1
22	Edward Baldry	1		
23	William Cole	2		17
24	John Randes	2		30
25	Richard Wasse		10	
26	Richard Smyth shearman	3		
27	George Raymond	5	5	
28	Thomas Lane 'gave ye caraidge of most of ye bookes'.			
29	Thomas Ungle	1	10	but see also KG12
30	Joseph Parkhurst	2		

31	John Sicklemore			
32	John Smythier merchant	3	5	
33	William Cutler	10		
34	John Catcher vintener	6		
35	Edmund Allen chamberlain	5		
36	Robert Shawe merchant	5		
37	John Warner fishmonger	5		
38	John Reynolds	1		
39	Thomas Cleere	1		
40	Benjamin Cutler			
41	James Tomson glover	2		31
42	Mabel Clemetson his executrix	1		13
43	Susan Penning	20		
44	Edmund Holton	2	5	

DONORS UNLISTED (UL) AND LISTED POST-1660 (LP)

UL	LP			date of gift
1		John Bill	Printer of London	c1612
2		Bazeleel Sherman	Grocer of St Lawrence	1618*
3		Thomas Foster	Minister St Matthew	1630*
4		Simon Pettewade	Minister St Lawrence	1636*
5		Christopher Meredith	Stationer of London	c1640
6		John Blomefeild the elder	Ironmonger of St Mary Quay	1640*
7		Samuel Hudson	Minister Capel St Mary	1644
8		Robert Stansby	Minister St Helen	c1650
9		Matthew Lawrence	Town Preacher	1651 & 6
10		Jeremy Cateline the younger	Minister St Peter then Barham	1651
11		Stephen Marshall	Town Preacher	1655*
12		John Gipps Esq		c1655
13		Thomas Gibbes	of Norwich	c1655
14		– Ironside		c1655
15		Thomas Wade		c1660
16		Hamon Le Strange	of Pakenham	c1660
17		Sir Henry Felton Bt	of Playford	1661
	4	Edward Reynolds	Bishop of Norwich	1662
	3	John Robinson	Portman St Mary le Tower	1666
	1	Nicholas Phillips	Portman St Margaret	1666
	2	John Colman		1668
18		Silas Taylor	Keeper of Harwich Naval Stores	1668
19		Samuel Butler Usher		1672
20		Nathaniell Sorrell	son of Sir Manuell (money)	1673
	5	Sir Andrew Hackett	Master in Chancery	1675
21		John Ogilby	Cosmographer Royal	1675
22		Mrs Dorothy Seckford	of Seckford Hall	c1676
23		Dr John Eachard	Master of Katherine Hall	c1676
24		Dr John Knight	Serjeant Surgeon to Chas. II	1680
25		John Lambe Esq	of Barham	1681
26		Sir John Barker Bt	Member for Ipswich	1681
27		– Vandeere		c1681
28		Henry Whiting Portman		1686
29		Sir Nicholas Bacon KB	of Shrubland Hall	c1687*
30		Capt Nicholas Kerrington	of Wapping Middx.	c1687*
31		Nathaniel Acton Esq	of Bramford	1690
32		John Wallace MD	of St Nicholas	c1690
33		John Burroughes	Portman	c1690*
	6	Capt Devereux Edgar	Grimston House	1695

181

UL	LP			date of gift
34		Thomas Bright	Portman St Matthew	1697*
	7	Miles Wallis (II)	Portman	1705 & 6
	8	Joseph Cutlove	Minister St Mary le Tower	1706
	9	William Matthews	Minister St Margaret	1725
	10	Thomas Bishop DD	Minister St Mary le Tower	1727
	11	William Wollaston Esq	Member for Ipswich	1734
35		Thomas Coggeshall (if not a former owner of Hewett books)		1737*
	12	Thomas Hewett	Minister Bucklesham	1745 & 73
	13	Robert Hingeston	Master	1745 & 49
	14	Henry Hubbard	Fellow of Emanuel	1746
	15	Thomas Stisted	Fellow of Caius	1746
	16	Peter Hingeston senior	Minister St Peter and Capel	1746
	17	Charles Beaumont	Minister Witnesham	1747
	18	Francis Folkard	Minister Clopton	1748
	19	John Tanner	Minister Lowestoft	1748 & 59
	20	Joshua Kirby	Artist and author	1756
36		Thomas Bishop junior	Minister St Mary le Tower	1767

* indicates no books remaining from those given by this donor

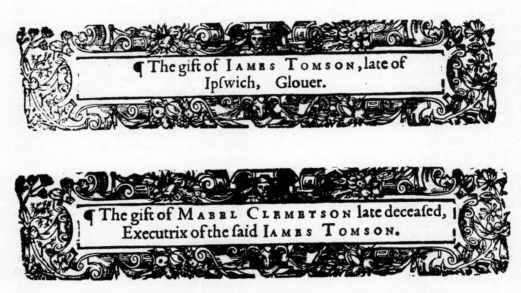

Figure 11a. Gift labels printed with factotums, perhaps by John Bill.

C

PRINTED GIFT LABELS

Labels were specially printed between 1613 and 1617 for at least 34 donors. For Francis Brewster and Peter Cole, two versions were prepared, and those of James Tomson and Mabel Clemetson are decorated with factotums. Robert Knapp's label is only known from the impression it left on the title page of King 561. One for Richard Jennings, Draper (BT9) has been lost from the Hebrew Concordance of 1581 (King 455).

PM   Portman. All except William Bloise (or Bloyse) have 'Master'
CCM Common Council Man
FB   Free Burgess

1	Acton, George, CCM	BT21
2	Algate, Christopher, CCM	BT17
3	Bacon, Edward, Esquier	KG3
4	Barber, Jeremy, CCM	BT16
5	Bloise, William, PM	BP5
6	Blosse, Tobias, PM	BP7
7	Brewster, Francis, (a) Esquier; (b) and Master	KG2
8	Brownrigg, Matthew, PM	BP2
9	Bruning, John, Shipcarpenter	BT6
10	Buckenham, Henry, CCM, Mercer	BT4
11	Burlingham, Richard, FB, Mariner	BT8
12	Cage, William, PM	BP8
13	Clemetson, Mabel	BT42
14	Cock, Richard, PM	BP9
15	Cole, Peter, (a) FB, Grocer; (b) FB only	BT7
16	Cole, Robert, CCM, Tanner	BT2
17	Cole, William, FB	BT23
18	Coppin, George, FB	BT12
19	Cutler, Robert, PM	BP1
20	Day, Edmond, CCM, Dyer	BT3
21	Dod, Catherine, Widow	KG11
22	Eldred, Thomas, CCM	BT11 & BP15
23	Fisher, Richard, FB	BT14
24	Goodeere, Michael, PM	BP10
25	Hayles, Thomas, CCM	BT18
26	Johnson, Thomas, PM	BP12
27	Knapp, Robert, FB	BT13
28	Martin, Richard, PM	BP6
29	Osmond, Benjamin, CCM	BT19
30	Randes, John, CCM	BT24
31	Tomson, James, Glover	BT41
32	Walter, Elizabeth, Widow	BT1
33	Ward, Samuel, Town Preacher	MS1
34	Withipole, Sir Edmond, Knight	KG1

Labels 10, 11, 15a and 20 are dated Feb.1613; label 16 is dated August 1613 and the remainder are undated.

All the labels, with the exception of PGL7a (not discovered in time) have been listed under STC^2.3368.5 in the *Addenda* and *Corrigenda* to the revised *S.T.C.*, Vol. 1, pp. 615–6.

The gift of Master Edward Bacon, Esquier.

The gift of William Bloise Port-man of Ipswich.

The gift of Master Tobias Blosse, Portman of Ipswich.

The gift of F R A N C I S B R E W S T E R Esquier.

The gift of Master Francis Brewster, Esquier.

The gift of Master Matthew Brownrig, Portman of Ipswich.

Feb. 1613. The gift of Richard Burlingham Mariner, *and a free Burgis of Ipswich.*

The gift of Master William Cage, Portman of Ipswich.

The gift of Master Richard Cock, Portman of Ipswich.

The gift of Peter Cole, Free-burgesse in Ipswich.

August 1613. The gift of R O B E R T C O L E Tanner, late one of the Common Counsell of Ipswich.

The gift of William Cole, Free-burgesse in Ipswich.

The gift of Master Robert Cutler, Portman of Ipswich.

The gift of Mistris C A T H E R I N E D O D Widowe.

The gift of Master Michael Goodeere, Portman of Ipswich.

The gift of Master Thomas Iohnson, Portman of Ipswich.

The gift of Master Richard Martin, Portman of Ipswich.

The gift of Mistresse Walter, Widdow.

The gift of Master Samuel Warde, Town-Preacher in Ipswich.

The gift of Sir Edmond Withepole, Knight.

Figure 11b. Printed gift labels set in 14pt. (English).

The gift of George Acton, one of
the Common Counsell of Ipswich.

The gift of Christopher Algate, one of
the Common Counsell of Ipswich.

The gift of Ieremy Barber, one of
the Common Counsell of Ipwich.

The gift of Iohn Bruning,
Shipcarpenter of Ipswich.

Feb. 1613. The gift of *Henry Buckenham Mercer,*
and one of the Common Counsell of Ipswich.

Feb. 1613. The gift of Peter Cole Grocer,
and a free Burgis of Ipswich.

The gift of George Coppin,
free Burgesse of Ipswich.

Febr. 1613.   The gift of *Edmond Day* Dier,
and one of the Common Counsell of Ipswich.

The gift of Thomas Eldred, one of
the Common Counsell of Ipswich.

The gift of Richard Fisher,
free Burgesse of Ipswich.

The gift of Thomas Hayles, one of
the Common Counsell of Ipswich.

The gift of Beniamin Osmond, one of
the Common Counsell of Ipswich.

The gift of Iohn Randes, one of the
Common Counsell of Ipswich.

Figure 11c. Printed gift labels set in 18pt. (Great Primer).

D

BOOKS BOUGHT FROM THE WALTER BEQUEST

Books provided for the Library with £50 from bequests made by Mrs Elizabeth Walter, widow, daughter of John Moore, Portman, in 1588. Despite the heading of the list there is of course no question that she gave them. The list on pages B4 and B5 in the Benefactors' Book is in John Coney's hand (where Samuel Ward makes additions they are in Italics in this transcript). Authors' names are copied from the list; except where indicated, the title is *Opera*; here the number of volumes only is stated, with price paid, and, where it is to be found on the title page, the bookseller's coded price. Where printed gift labels are lost, the original number is in brackets. GL = Greek and Latin.

page B4

M^res. Walter gave these bookes viz:

King	Author	No. of vols.	£	s	d	coded price	No. of PGL
67	Ambrosii	2	1	5		a.k.	2
31	Anselmii	1	0	17			1
13	Athanasii GL	1	1	7	0		1
39	Arnobii	1		8			(1)
50	Bernardii	1	1	1	6		1
119	Basilii Magni	1		12	6		1
474–5	Bibliotheca Patru'	6	5	12	6		5 (1)
502	Chrysostomi	4	3	12			4
14	Clemens Alexandrinus	1		15			1
505	Cyrilli Alex:	1	1	5		a.f.h.	1
493	Cypriani	1			9		1
294	Cyrilli Hieros:	1		6	6		1
lost	Chrysologi	1		2	6		(1)
194	Damasceni	1		6			1
107 & 626	Epiphanii GL	2		13	10		1
562	Ephra'e Syri	1		11			1
lost	Fulgentii Basiliae 1587	1		2			(1)
lost	Grego: Nazian: GL	2	2	6	0		(1)
206	Gregorii Nyssen:	1		7	6		1
456	Gregorii Magni	1	1	5	8	a.k.	1
219	Hillarii	1		7	6		1
108	Justini Martyris	1		7	6	j.f.	1
335	Isychii Presbyt.	1		4			1
72	Irenaeii	1		5	6	f.	(1)
121	Lactantii	2		5	6		1
217	Orthodoxographia Patru'	2	1	0	0		2
92	Origenis	1		15	0		1
lost	Optati	1		2			(1)
569	Philonis Judaei	1		13	4		1
382	Prudentii	1		6	6		1
392	Prosperi	1		3	4		1
lost	Pet. Lombardi Sent'	1		3			(1)
63	Ruffini	1		11			(1)
598	Theodereti	1	1	6	6	a.h.d.	1
589	Theophylacti	1		11			1
110	Tertulliani	1		16	6		1

2 globes celestiall & terrestrial   *4 10 0*

		£	s	d
594	*Bradwardini Cantuariensis* Archiepisc. [erasure] opera *edita ab Henr. Savilio*	00	15	0
535	Aquinatis Aurea catena	00	9	0
105	Borrhaeus in Job & Eccle'm	00	6	6
544	*Basiliɔ graecolat: 2 vols:*	3	10	0
2	Andr: Osiandri Harmonia Evang: GL	00	6	0
116	Hanapi Exempla virtutu' & vitiorɔ	00	10	
696	Pierii Hieroglph:	00	13	
135	Gaspar Contaren	00	9	
163	Pererius Jesuit.' in Ep'lam ad Roman:	00	8	
301	Arias Montanus in Prophetas minores	00	7	
333	Wincklemann in 6 Proph. minores	00	5	
42	Petrus Serranus in Levit: et Ezech:	00	8	
1 & 263	*Simleri, Besodneri, oxon: bibliothecae*	00	13	8
326	Pezelii opera 3 vol.	00	6	
lost	Tileni opera in 2 vol.	00	7	
323	Huldric. Herlinus	00	4	
+	Ja: Martinus in 3 vol: ⎫	1	8	
*	Mat: Martinus in 8 vol: ⎭			
605	Scotus in 2 vol:	00	17	
		[Total £47	15	10]

+ 386 and 681 (1 and 2).

* 360, 361, 365 (c.p. a.f., for the set?), 368 and 385.

Books Bequeathed by Thomas Hewett

'Decr. 5th 1745:
The Revd Mr Thomas Hewett, Rector of Bucklesham, gave a fair edition of Pausanias.'
(Entry in the Book in the hand of Robert Hingeston.)

King numbered the Pausanias 94; it was indeed a fair edition – an Aldine. Hewett entered another gift of his in the manuscript Catalogue of Robert Coningsby: Cavendish's Life of Wolsey. Both of these works are lost.

Many other books came to Ipswich after Hewett's death in 1773, as provided for in the instructions he left. They were apparently not listed as he requested nor were they accessioned properly, merely placed on the shelves (in the Sacristy and Schoolroom, presumably), according to size and wherever there was space. Hingeston died in 1767 so that Hewett's are the only books without 'Ipswich Library' in Hingeston's hand on the title pages; this identifies them. In Coningsby's manuscript Catalogue of 1705 they were entered (about 1798) in a hand as yet unidentified: that of the assistant who numbered the Library for King's first *List*. King attributed to Hewett only those 19 works with a Hewett ownership inscription; they are marked K below. It is suggested that all of the following are Hewett gifts; those with m have been lost:

6K	Dugdale	History of St Pauls Cathedral, 1658.
18K	Thoresby	Ducatus Leodiensis, 1715.
75K	Dart	History of... Canterbury, 1726.
94Km	Pausanius	Graecio descriptio. Venice, 1516.
98	Grew	Cosmologia sacra, 1701.
126	Bibliander	Temporum a condito..., 1588.
243Km	Spenser	The Faerie Queene, 1590.
311	Willis	A survey of the cathedrals, 1742, 2 vols.
314 m	Boyer	The Royal Dictionary Fr.-English and Eng.-French, 1729.
315 m	Petit	The Hebrew Guide, 1752 & Joseph Beaumont's poems, 1749.
316K	Cluver	Introductio in universam geographiam, 1711.
317K	Lambarde	Dictionarium Angliae, 1730.
342 m	Udall	History, life and death of Mary Stuart, 1636.
350	Baron	Metaphysica generalis, 1658.
351K	Dawson	Treatise on loyalty and obedience, 1710.
352	Humphreys	Historical account of the I.S.P.G. 1730.
371	Lucian	Opera, 1687.
398Km	Bacon	De... augmentis scientiarum, 1662.
399 m	Kirby	Suffolk Traveller, 1735.
400K	Johnson	Epigrams, 1718.
401 m		Life of Charles II, 1686.
402Km	Petty	Political Arithmetick, 1691.
403	Alciatus	Emblemata, 1591.
404	Cheke	De pronuntiatione Graecae, 1555.
405Km	Clarke	An essay on Study, 1731.
406	Child	New discourse of trade, 1694.
407 m	Cicero	Tully's Offices, *ed.* Cockman, 1714.
408Km	Hildrop	Miscellaneous works. 2 vols. 1754.
409 m	Ward T.	England's Reformation. 2 vols. 1747.
410 m	Gondi	Memoires of Cardinal de Retz. 4 vols. 1723.
411	Comber	Right of tithes re-asserted, 1680.
412K	Hickes	The spirit of enthusiasm exorcised, 1709.
413Km	Mapletoft	Principle and duties of the Christian Religion, 1712.
414K	Montfaucon	Travels... from Paris thro' Italy, 1712.
415	Jenkyn	Reasonableness of the Christian Religion. 2 vols. 1708.
419 m	Collins	Peerage of England 4 vols. 1714
423K	Trivet	Annales. 2 vols. 1719, 1722

424	Bible	O.T. Gk. *ed.* Grabe. Septuagint. 8 vols. 1707, 1720.
425 m	Willis	An historie of Abbies and Cathedrals. 2 vols. 1718–19.
426 m	John Chrysostom	Of the Priesthood, 1759.
427 m	Long	Boyle's Lectures, 1730.
428 m	Narborough	Voyages.
429 m	Kirby	Suffolk Traveller. Second edition, 1764.
430 m	Horatius	Opera *ed.* Sandby, 1749.
431	Terence	Comediae. 2 vols. 1751.
432 m	Hume	History of England. 8 vols. 1767.
507K	Moreri	Le Grande Dictionaire Historique. 2 vols. 1698.
508	More	Theological Works, 1708.
509	Bayle	Dictionary. 5 vols. 1734.
510	Stackhouse	History of the Bible. 2 vols. 1742.
511	Peck	Desiderata Curiosa. 2 vols. 1732.
592	Hammond	A paraphrase on the Psalms, 1659.
608	Hakewill	An apologie, 1675.
630	Bible	Concordance Gk/Lat *ed.* Stephanus, 1624.
695Km	Macknight	Harmony of the Gospels, 1756.
697	Boys	Sixteen sermons, 1672.
420 m	Poellnitz	Memoirs, 1737.
421 m	unknown	Lives, etc., 1712.

Mr Coggeshall (the donor, according to King), may have been a former owner of these books; if Hewett acquired them later they would be part of his bequest.

422	Middleton	Life of Cicero. 3 vols. 1741.

This set is marked 'Ipswich Socy. No 17' – perhaps a Hewett acquisition left to the Library.

[416 and 417: King gives Hewett as donor, but the Bishops, father and son, gave the books.]

LOSSES FROM THE LIBRARY

A list of all works known to have been lost or withdrawn from the Library from the earliest days.

KEY TO DATES AT WHICH LOSSES WERE NOTICED:

JC etc   Shelf and number in John Coney's lists, *c.*1615.

RSW   Removed by Samuel Ward in the early years of the Library's existence.

M1630   Missing at Ward's stock-check on 8 February 1630.

M1651   Listed in the Book, but not present to be fore-edge marked on 12 April 1651 (and therefore not missed in 1705).

M1705   Robert Coningsby took stock preparatory to writing his Catalogue, and found these titles wanting.

M1799   John King listed two titles and overlooked the Cavendish, all missing from the Coningsby Catalogue, before sending the latter to the printer.

M1860   The three-man subcommittee of the Corporation mustered the books and submitted a list of losses with their report, including a number of books which were not in fact lost. Only those books which *were* missing (i.e. did not appear in 1903) are listed here.

M1903   Henry Ogle listed further losses sustained since 1860.

1989:   There have been no further losses since 1903.

ANDREWES (Lancelot), *Bp.* XCVI sermons. *London,* [prob. 1629 edition STC.606] BT34 [replaced 1662 by LP4 1631 King 151]

ARIAS MONTANO (Benedito). In Proph. minores. [other than existing 1583 edition given by BT1] MS46 M1651

B. (R.) [BOYLE (Robert).] Occasional reflections on several subjects... *London, W. Wilson for Henry Herringman,* 1665. Wing B.4005 LP1 [H3] King 325 M1860

BABINGTON (Gervase), *Bp.* Works. *London,* 1615 [STC.1077 or 1078] MS9 M1630 [and replaced by BT34 1622 edition King 64]

BACON (Francis). De dignitate et augmentis scientiarum. *Amstelaedami, sumptibus Joannis Ravesteinii,* 1662. LP12 King 398 M1860

BARTHOLOMAEUS, *Anglicus de Glanvilla.* Liber de proprietatibus rerum. [several possible editions] BP0 RSW

BEAUMONT (*Dr.* Joseph). Original poems in English and Latin. *Cambridge,* 1749. (*bound with* PETIT, P., Hebrew Guide, 1752.) LP12 King 315 M1860

BELLANTIUS (Lucius). De astrologica veritate liber quaestionum. *Basileae, [per Jacobum Parcum impensis Joannis Hervagii],* 1554. Adams B.488 BP13 H5 King 184 M1860

BEZA (Theodore). In Canticum Canticorum homiliae. *[Geneva], excudebat Jo. le Preux,* 1587. Adams B.922 (*bound with* SERARIUS, N., 1580) BP8 JC:A.12 M1651

BIBLE. Vulgate, with glosses. [not identifiable] BP0 RSW

BIBLE Concordance – English *ed.* Clement Cotton. *London,* prob.1627 STC.5843 BT35 I3 M1705

BONNER (Edmund), *Bp.* Articles [Doctrine or Homilies.] *London,* 1555. STC.3282–3285] MS35 M1651

BOYER (Abel). The Royal Dictionary, French and English, and English and French. (2 vols.) *London, J. & J. Knapton, etc.,* 1729. LP12 King 314 M1860

BOYS (John). Anglicanae Homiliae. [prob. Expositions of all the principall scriptures used in our English liturgie, *London,* 1609–1622. STC.3455, 3456 or 3457] KG9 M1630

BUCANUS (Gulielmus). Loci communes. [prob. Institutiones theologicae... *Genevae,* J. le Preux, 1609.] MS17 M1630

CAMERERIUS (Joachimus) *the Younger.* Symbolorum & emblematum... [many editions] MS30 M1651

CARTWRIGHT (Thomas). In librum Salomonis, qui inscribitur Ecclesiastes homiliae. *Londini* [though Coney stated Marpurgi], *impensis Tho. Man,* 1604. STC.4710 MS25 JC:A.11 RSW [and replaced by 1617 edition King 223]

CAVENDISH (George). Life of Cardinal Thomas Wolsey. ?1761 edition. LP12 M1799

CHARLES II. Life of Charles II. [prob. Augustus Anglicus: a compendious view... *London, [printed for Samuel Holford],* 1686. Wing A.4215] LP12 King 401 M1860 or 1903

CICERO (Marcus Tullius). Tully's Offices, trans. Mr T. Cockman, the third edition, revised and corrected. *London, Samuel Buckley,* 1714. LP12 King 407 M1860

CLARKE (John) *of Hull.* An essay on Study. *London,* 1731. LP12 King 405 M1860

COLLINS (Arthur), *compiler.* The Peerage of England. 3rd edition. London, 1714. (4 vols.) LP12 King 419 M1860

DESCARTES (René). De principia philosophia (3 parts) Meditationes. *Amsterodami, apud L. & D. Elsevirios,* 1664. UL19 [K2] King 354 M1860

DRAXE (Thomas), *of Harwich.* Works. (2 vols.) [Any of STC.7173–7188] MS15 M1651

DUGDALE (*Sir* William). The antiquities of Warwickshire illustrated. *London,* 1656. Wing D.2479 UL24 [duplicate copy] [N1] King 643 M1903

ERASMUS (Desiderius). Annotationes in novum testamentum. [several 16th century editions] BP0 RSW [replaced by MS2 King 640]

FULGENTIUS, *Bp. of Ruspa, Saint.* Opera quae extant omnis... *Basileae, Sebastianum Henricpetri,* 1587. JC:A.1 M1651

GARDNER (Thomas). Historical account of Dunwich. *London,* 1754. LP19 King 319 M1860

GONDI (Jean Francois Paul de), *Cardinal de Retz, Abp. of Paris.* Memoires de Cardinal de Retz. (4 vols.) *Amsterdam,* 1723. LP12 King 410 M1860

GREGORY *of Nazianzus, Saint, ed.* J. Lewenklaius. Opera omnia in tomi tres... (in 1 vol.) *Basileae, ex officina Hervagiana, per Eusebium Episcopium,* 1571. [Replaced by 2 vol. edition, Gk & Lat, 1609, 1611.] BT1 gave first on JC:B1.2; second on A2 M1860 or 1903

HARRIS (Robert?). Works, [perhaps 24 sermons, 1635. STC.12816] MS42 M1651

HERNE. Works (2 vols.) Given by Thomas Eldred as BT11 [No Herne identified. Could it be that Daniel Hearne of Henley published 2 vols. of which no copies in STC?] M1651

HIGDEN (Ranulphus). Polychronicon. [prob. STC.13438, 39 or 40] BP0 RSW

HILDROP (John). Miscellaneous works. (2 vols.) *London,* 1754. LP12 King 408 M1860

HORATIUS FLACCIUS, *Quintus.* Opera, ed. Sandby. *London,* 1749. LP12 King 430 M1860

HUGH *of St. Victor.* Opera. (2 vols.) BP0 RSW [replaced by MS6 King 458]

HUME (David). History of England. (8 vols.) *London,* 1767. [BM Cat. has 1763 or 1770] LP12 King 432 M1860

JENKYN (William). An exposition of the Epistle of Jude. Pt. 1, 2nd edition. *London,* 1656. Wing J.641 DU [I4] King 173 M1903

JOHN CHRYSOSTOM, *Saint.* ...Of the priesthood, (6 books) trans. from Gk. by J. Bunce. *London,* 1759. LP12 King 426 M1860

———— Homiliae quaedam Gk & Latin. *Basileae,* 1585. BP0 JC:A.10 M1651

KING (Daniel) *of Chester.* The Vale-Royall of England, or, The County-Palatine of Chester illustrated by W. Smith and W. Webb. *London, by John Streater,* 1656. Wing K.488 UL24 [N2] King 186 M1860

KIRBY (John). The Suffolk Traveller. *Ipswich,* 1735. LP12 King 399 M1860

———— The Suffolk Traveller. 2nd edition. *London,* 1764. LP12 King 429 M1799

LA CERDA (Joannes Ludovicus de). Adversaria sacra. *Lugduni,* 1626. LP1 [I5] King 539 M1903

LAKE (Arthur), *Bp.* Works. [prob. Sermons with some meditations. *London,* 1629. STC.15134] BT34 M1705

LAMBARD (William). The perambulation of Kent [prob. *London,* 1656. Wing L.216] UL24 M1705 if in fact it ever came to the Library.

LIVES etc. 1712. UL35 or LP12 King 421 [Identification impossible]

LONG, (perhaps Roger, astronomer). Boyle's Lectures, 1730. [Unidentified] LP12 King 427 M1860

LORINUS (Joannes). In Ecclesiasten et Psalmos. *Lugduni,* 1606. [Not in BM Cat.] BP2 JC:A2.15 RSW

LUDOVICUS. In acta apostolorum tomus alter. *Irenopoli,* 1656. [not identified] UL22 King 100 M1860

MACKNIGHT (James). A Harmony of the four Gospels. *London,* 1756. LP12 King 695 M1860

MAPLETOFT (John). The principles and duties of the Christian Religion. Second Edition, 1712. LP12 King 413 M1860

MASSON (Jean Papire). Gesta Collationis Carthaginiensis. [Council of Carthage] *Heidelburg, ex typog. H. Commelini,* 1596. Adams C.792 (*bound with* OPTATUS) M1705

MORTON (Thomas), *Bp.* 'Against the Romish church.' [If MS21 was the donor as King states, this might be

STC.18184 or 85, but if given later STC.18172: Antidotum adversus ecclesiae Romanae..., *Cambridge*, 1637, may have been in the Library] King 700 M1860

NANNINI (Remigio), *Fiorentino*. Considerationi civili sopra l'Historie di Francesco Guicciardini, 1588. [BM Cat. has *Venetia*, 1582, but no 1588 edition] UL32 King 699 M1860

NARBOROUGH (*Sir* John). Voyages. [many editions] LP12 King 428 M1799

OPTATUS, *Bp. of Mela, Saint.* Altri libri sex de Donatistiarum schismate. *[Heidelberg], ex bibliopolio Commeliniano*, 1599. Adams O.216 *bound with* MASSON, J.P., Gesta Collationis... 1596. BT1 JC:A.4B2 M1705

PAGNINUS (Santes). Lexicon Latino-Hebraicum, 1575. [prob. Thesaurus linguae sanctae. *Lugduni, apud Bartholomaeum Vincentium*, 1575.] MS14 King 693 M1903

PAREUS (David). [MS1 gave 9 vols. of which 7 remain. One was missing from E3] M1705

PAUSANIAS *the Traveller.* Commentarii in Graeciam describentes. *Venetiis, in aed. Aldi, et Andreae soc.,* 1516. LP12 [O3] King 94 M1860

PETER *Chrysologus, Saint.* Sermones. *Moguntiae*, 1607. [This edition not in BM Cat.] JC:A.9 M1630

PETIT (Peter), *Vicar of Royston.* The Hebrew Guide. *London*, 1752, *bound with* BEAUMONT, J. Original Poems, 1749.. LP12 King 315 M1860

PETRUS *Comestor*, Historia Scholastica. [many editions] BP0 M1651

PETRUS *Lombardus, Bishop of Paris.* Sententiarum... [many works include this word in the title] BT1 M1651

PETTY (*Sir* William). Political Arithmetick. *London*, 1691. Wing P.1933 LP12 King 402 M1860

POELLNITZ (*Baron* Carl Ludwig von). Memoires, 2 vols. [of 5?] *Amsterdam*, 1737. UL35 or LP12 King 420 M1860

POLANUS (Amandus). Syntagma theologiae Christianae. *Geneva*, 1612. BT2 [replaced by MS40 in 1625 edition] King 580 M1630

RIVET (André). [3 vols left, but Coningsby noted one lost on F2 in 1705]

ROLLOCK (Robert). 6 vols. given by MS19 [see STC.21267–86] now 2 vols. only M1651

SCHWENTER (Daniel). Manipulus linguae, 1628. [Not in BM Cat.] [K2] King 337 M1860

SEGAR (*Sir* William). Honour Military and Civill. *London*, 1602. STC.22164 UL24 [N1] King 193 M1860

SERARIUS (Nicolaus). In Ecclesiasten Solomonis. *Genevae*, 1580. [Not in BM Cat. or Adams] (*bound with* BEZA, T, In canticum.., 1587.) M1651

SPEED (John). The Historie of Great Britaine. [many editions] UL2 M2 M1705

SPENSER (Edmund). The faerie queene. *London, [R.Field] for W.Ponsonbie*, 1590. STC.23080 LP12 King 243 M1903

TILENUS (Daniel). Opera (2 vols.) [not identified in BM Cat.; just possibly Adams T.710] BT1 M1651

TUCCIUS. In cantica Cant. Solomonis. *Lugduni*, 1606. [not identified] MS7 JC:A2.9 M1651

TURNBULL (Richard). Works. [prob. Exposition upon James and Jude, 1591–1606 STC.24339, 40 or 41] MS26 M1651

UDALL (William). The history of the life and death of Mary Stuart. *London*, 1636. [STC.24510 or 11] LP12 King 342 M1903

USSHER (James), *Abp.* 'On Kingly power.' [prob. The Power communicated by God to the Princes. *London*, 1661. Wing U.196] LP4 M1705

VERMIGLI (Pietro Martire). Loci communes. [perhaps London, 1576 or 1583] BT3 M1630 [and replaced by MS30 King 634]

VINCENTIUS *Bellovacensis.* Speculum Morale Vincentii. [prob. *Venetiis*, 1493] BP0 RSW

WARD (Thomas). England's Reformation. (2 vols.) *London*, 1747 LP12 King 409 M1903

WILLET (Andrew). [KG13 = BT15 gave 5 vols. There are now 5 but one from a different donor.]

WILLIS (Browne). An Historie of the... Abbies and... Cathedral Churches... *London*, 1718–19. LP12 King 425 M1860

ZEPPER (Wilhelm). 3 lost of 4 vols. 1603 [BM Cat. has Ars habendi, 1604.] KG3 E2 King 250 M1705

A LIST OF FORMER OWNERS OF THE BOOKS AND MANUSCRIPTS.

Donors to the Library are listed as owners here only if their marks of ownership are clear on the books themselves. Three donors, William Smarte (BP0), John Knight (UL24) and Thomas Hewett (LP12) bequeathed books of their own which are listed elsewhere; they do not appear here. Books are indicated by King numbers and principal names of authors. Names marked * are indexed in N.R. Ker's *Medieval Libraries of Great Britain*, 1964 or A.G.Watson's *Supplement* of 1987.

Owner	King	Author
Allen, John	182(1)	Alexander Carpentarius
Astewyk, Thomas	185	Major
do.	5	Richard of Middleton
Bacon, Edward	472	Beza
Baker, Thomas	523	Marcellinus
Beaumont, John	212	Fagius
Bedingfield, Thomas	519	Lucas
Blosse, Tobias	131	Plutarch
*Brinkele, J. de	ms 4	
Broke, Christopher	133	Latin Bible
Brownrigg, Matthew	646	Brenz
do.	453	Lorinus
do.	533	Valentia
*Bryngkeley, Richard, *fr.*	130	Pius II
Burrough, John	297	Birckbek
do.	668	Durel
do.	595	Richerius
Butler, Samuel	340	Robertson
Cahill, Thomas	605(2)	Duns Scotus
Cardroler, John	87	Loritus
Carew, Robert	678	Carew
Cartwright, William	442	Justinian
Causton, John	434	Ortelius
do.	'706'	Rainerius
Cecil, William	10	Nauclerus
Coney, John	671	Vitalis
Cottesford, John	8	Latin Bible
Davenant, John, *Bp.*	498	Dionysius
Daye, John	673	Wilson
Denton, Thos	182(1)	Alexander Carpentarius
Dowe, Baroniah	284	Biblia Hebraica
Dowsing, William	654	Parliamentary Sermons
Folkard, Francis	540	Stebbing
*Fraunce, Hugo	460	Gratianus
Gardiner, –	652	Alexander
Gibbon, John	181	Becon
Glemham, Henry	341	Castiglione
Gravelle, Nich.	450	Lippomano
Guthree, Alexander	486	Gratianus
do.	485	Gregory IX
Harrison, William	136	Agricola
do.	146	Appian
do.	118	Diodorus
do.	138	Gaguin

Owner	King	Author
do.	171	Goltz
do.	621	Guicciardini
do.	624	Krantz
do.	132	Maffeius
do.	143	Panvinio
do.	549	Pistorius
do.	214	Rosinus
do.	48	Spain (Bell)
do.	150	Zosimus
Henchman, Humphrey, *Bp.*	498	Dionysius
Herne, A.	281	Plautus
Hichkock, Thomas	605 (1)	Duns Scotus
Hollins, John	205	Beroaldus
*J., abbas	ms 4	(Brinkele, Abbot John de)
Jullys, Geoffrey, *fr.*	'706'	Rainerius
Lenn, Andrew	678	Carew
Meyne, John	3	Thomas Aquinas
Nykke, Richard, *Bp.*	3	Thomas Aquinas
Pack, John	607	Walther
Palmerius?	542	Gordon
Patenson, *Magister*	461	Gregory IX
Rainold, Alexander	620	Forster
Rainsford, Richard	36	Ludolph
Reddrich, Thos	452	Latin Bible
Scotte, Tho.	496	Eusebius
do.	694	Eusebius
Stansby, Robert	282	Diodate
Suckermann, John	286	Beza
	259	Marbecke
*Thetford, John, *fr.*	71	Lyndewode
Toppclyff, Thomas, D.C.L.	133	Latin Bible
Trygary, Griffeth	460	Gratianus
do.	461	Gregory IX
Wallace, John	341	Castiglione
do.	ms 10	Catecheticae
Watson, John	468	Aristotle
do.	602	Stucki
Wythypoll, Anne	ms 7	Horae
Wythypoll, Paul	253	William of Auvergne
Young Nicholaus	607	Walther

THE MAPS IN DR JOHN KNIGHT'S ATLASES

Index to the two bound volumes of maps: King '701' and King '702', each 43 by 60cm. (rebound), into which all but the first map fit without folding. They were bequeathed to the Library by Dr John Knight (UL24) and arrived in July 1680; the first volume has one of the elaborate calligraphic gift labels which are to be found in most Knight books (fig. 5). Most of the maps are from the *Cartes générales de toute les parties du monde...* of Nicholas (and Guillaume) Sanson (s), the second largest group is by Pierre Duval (v), and the latest date on a map 1671. The maps are numbered consecutively (starting from 1 in each volume) in Knight's hand. Only the Tyne River map seems to have been coloured by Knight himself. At least ten maps have been lost from the end of Vol. II. To keep the index as short as possible, map titles here are mostly abbreviated. The dates given are those shown on the maps.

Reference numbers from *Les Atlas Français XVIe.–XVIIe. siècles*, by Mireille Pastoureau (Paris 1984), are those given there in square brackets under N. et G. Sanson and P. Duval respectively. Those maps not found in Pastoureau but in the B. L. *Map Catalogue* are given longer references to that work; those in neither are marked -; + indicates a footnote. In some cases Mme. Pastoureau has suggested that only the date has been changed on a reissued map; then the entry takes the form: [00 dated 16—].

VOLUME I

fo.		date	Sanson	Duval
1 +	Le carte de L'Europe (53.5 by 75cm.)	v 1669		–
2	Orbis vetus et orbis veteris	s 1657	98	
3	Mappe-monde du globe terrestre	s 1669	209	
4	L'Hydrographie	s 1652	2	
5	Les deux poles, arctique et antarctique	s 1657	97	
6	Planisphere ou carte generale du monde	v 1666		11
7	missing			
8 +	La France etc. Ocean Septentrional	v 1668		–
9 +	La mer Mediterrannée vers l'Orient	v		
10+	La mer Mediterrannée vers l'Occident	v		17 bis
11+	Moscovie dit... Grande et Blanche Russie	v		17
12	Table alphabetique des Lieux	v		10
13	Tabula geog. locorum... concilia	v		
14	Geog. Synodica... Tabula prima	s 1667	206	43
15	Geog. Patriarchialis	s 1669	–	
16	Geog. Synodica... Tabula secunda	s 1667	207	
17	Iesu Christi...Petri...Pauli...itinera	s 1665	171	
18	Geog. Sacrae... Tabula prima	s 1662	169	
19	Geog. Sacrae... Tabula secunda	s 1662	170	
20	Britannicae Insulae	s 1641	104	
21	Les Isles Britannicques	s 1665	116	
22	Le royaume d'Angleterre	s 1665	117	
23+	The River of Tyne Ralph Gardner	[1655]		
24	Ancien royaume de Northumberland	s 1658	23	
25	Anciens royaumes de Mercie et East-Angles	s 1654	25	
26	Anciens royaumes de Kent, d'Essex, etc.	s 1654	24	
27	Provinces d'West	s 1654	26	
28	Principauté de Galles	s 1658	27	
29	L'Escosse royaume	s 1665	118	
30	L'Escosse delà le Tay	s 1665	119	
31	L'Escosse deçà le Tay	s 1665	120	
32	Les isles Orcadney Schetland et de Faro	s 1665	121	
33	Irlande royaume	s 1665	122	

fo.		date	Sanson	Duval
34	Partie meridionale ...d'Irlande	s 1665	123	
35	Partie septentrionale d'Irlande	s 1665	124	
36	Royaume de Danemarq	s 1658	29	
37	Nort-Iutlande	s 1659	30	
38	Royaume de Norwege	s 1668	173	
39	Gouvernement de Bahus	s 1668	174	
40	Gouvernement d'Aggerhus	s 1668	175	
41	Partie merid. du G. de Dronthemus	s 1668	177	
42	Partie septent. du G. de Dronthemus	s 1668	178	
43	Gouvernement de Bergenhus	s 1668	176	
44	Gouvernement de Wardhus	s 1668	179	
45	Atlantis insula	s 1669	208	
46	Royaume se Suede	s 1669	180	
47	Helsinge, Medelpadie, Angermannie etc.	s 1666	184	
48	Cajanie, ou Bothnie orientale	s 1666	187	
49	Sud-Gotlande	s 1659	31	
50	Westro-Gothlande	s 1666	181	
51	Ostro-Gothlande	s 1666	182	
52	Sueonie ou Suede	s 1666	183	
53	Finlande, Nylande et Tavasthus	s 1666	188	
54	Partie occ. de la Lapponie Suedoise	s 1666	185	
55	Partie orient. de la Lapponie Suedoise	s 1666	186	
56	Amerique septentrionale	s 1669	213	
57	Amerique meridionale	s 1669	214	
58	Le Canada, ou Nouvelle France	s 1656	86	
59	Le Nouveau Mexique, et la Floride	s 1656	87	
60	Mexique, ou Nouvelle Espagne	s 1656	88	
61	Les Isles Antilles etc.	s 1656	89	
62	Le Perou et... la riviere Amazone	s 1656	93	
63	Terre Ferme etc.	s 1656	91	
64	Part. de Terre Ferme: Guyane et Caribane	s 1656	92	
65	Le Bresil	s 1656	95	
66	Le Paragayr, le Chili etc.	s 1668	216	
67	Le Chili	s 1669	215	
68	La Terre et les Isles Magellaniques	s 1668	217	
69	Asia vetus	s 1667	202	
70	L'Asie	s 1669	211	
71	Les estats de l'empire des Turqs en Asie	s	5	
72	Estats... du Grand Seigneur des Turqs	s 1654	83	
73	Estats... des Turqs en Europe	s 1655	84	
74	Coste de Dalmacie	s 1664	152	
75	Anaplus Bophori	s 1666	165	
76	Illyricum occidentis	s	162	
77	Illyricum orientis	s	163	
78	Pamphilia & Pisidia by Guillaume Sanson	s 1670	–	
79	Germano-Sarmatia	s 1655	110	
80	Sarmartia	s 1654	106	
81	Cimmeria	s 1665	160	
82	Colchis, Iberia, Albania	s 1667	156	
83	...l'empire du Sophi des Perses	s	7	
84	Carte des trois Arabies	s 1654	6	
85	Les isles Philippines	s 1654	K.116.29	
86	Partie meridionale de l'Inde	s 1654	9	
87	L'Inde deçà et delà le Gange	s 1654	8	
88	La Chine royaume	s 1656	10	

fo.		date	Sanson	Duval
89	Tartarie europeene ou Petite Tartarie	s 1665	154	
90	Description de la Tartarie	s 1665	11	
91+	Royaume de Iapon Ph. Briet		K.116.55	
92	Africa vetus	s 1667	203	
93	Afrique	s 1669	[212 dated 1668]	
94	Estats et royaumes de Fez et Maroc	s 1655	14	
95	Partie de la Barbarie, roy. d' Alger	s 1655	15	
96	Roy. et desert de Barca et l'Egypte	s 1655	17	
97	Partie de la coste de Barbarie	s 1655	16	
98	L'Afrique, ou Lybie, Saara, etc.	s 1655	18	
99	Haute Ethiopie	s 1655	19	
100	Basse Aethiopie	s 1655	20	

VOLUME II

fo.		date	Sanson	Duval
1	Galliae antiquae	s 1641	108	
2	Le royaume de France	s 1665	126	
3 +	Le Royaume d'Aquitaine	v 1671		—
4 +	Les Royaumes de Bourgogne et d'Arles	v 1671		—
5 +	Le Roy. de la France Occidentale	v 1671		—
6 +	Le Roy. de la France Orientale	v 1671		—
7	Le Comté de Haynaut	s 1673		—
8	missing			
9	Provinces Unies de Pays Bas	s 166–		
10	Picardie et les Pays Bas Catholiques s 1667		[51 dated 1648]	
11	Duché, et Gouvernement de Normandie	s 1667	[50 dated 1648]	
12	Duché, et Gouvernement de Bretagne	s 1650	[37 dated 1650]	
13	Champagne and Brie	s	39	
14	Diocese, Prevoste et Eslection de Paris	s	128	
			45 under Cartes particulières	
15	Gouvt. Generale de l'Isle de France	s 1651	127	
16	Gouvt. Generale d'Orleans	s 1650	40	
17	Gouvt. Generale de Guienne et Guascogne	s 1650	43	
18	Duché d'Aiguillon	v 1654	K.63.18	
19	Royaume de Navarre	s 1652	68	
20	Sardones	s 1660	131	
21	Gouvt. General du Languedoc	s 1667	[44 dated 1651]	
22	Comté, et Gouvt. de Provence	s 1667	[46 dated 1652]	
23	Gouvt. General du Lyonnois	s	[42 dated 1651]	
24	Le Gouvt. General du Dauphiné	s 1667	[45 dated 1652]	
25	Les deux Bourgognes, Duché et Comté	s 1648	41	
26	La Lorraine	s 1661	[129 is not dated]	
27	L'Alsace	s 1666	130	
28	Haute Lombardie	s 1648	75	
29	Basse Lombardie	s 1648	77	
30	Le Piemont et le Montferrat	v		31
31	Partie septent. des estats de Savoye	s 1663	145	
32	Partie merid. des estats de Savoye	s 1663	146	
33	Italia Antiqua cum insulis Sicilia	s 1641	112	
34	L'Italie et les Isles circomvoisines	s 1665	144	
35+	Ducato di Bracciano olim Sabatia Daniel Widman	c.1600		
36	Estats de l'Eglise et de Toscane	s 1648	78	
37+	Desc. dello Stato della Chiesa e della Toscana G.G. Rossi	1669		
38	Royaume de Naples	s 1662	—	

fo.			date	Sanson	Duval
39	Calabre		s 1648	80	
40	Sicile		s 1663	–	
41+	Pozzuolo et Iuochi	Mario Cartaro	1588		
42+	Ischia	Mario Cartaro	1586		
43	Isle de Corse Isle de Sardaigne		s	82	
44	Isle et Royaume de Candie		s	201	
45	Hispaniae Antiquae		s 1641	111	
46	L'Espagne		s 1665	141	
47	Parte meridional do Reyno de Portugal		s 1654	73	
48	Parte septentrional do Reyno de Portugal		s 1654	72	
49	Les estats... de Portugal en Espagne		s 1653	71	
50	Toletani Archiepiscopatus	?Widman as 35	c.1600		
51	Les estats de Castille merid. Espagne		s 1652	69	
52	Les estats de Castille septent. Espagne		s 1652	67	
53	Royaume d'Arragon		s 1663	142	
54	Les estats d'Arragon en Espagne		s 1663	70	
55	Principauté de Catalogne		s 1660	143	
56	Germania antiqua		s 1641	109	
57	Cercle de Franconie		s 1669	192	
58	La Souabe		s 1669	193	
59	Palatinat du Rhein, Alsace etc.		s 1648	48	
60	Konigreich Boheim		s 1654	58	
61	Provinces unies – Boheme, Silesie, etc.		s 1654	59	
62	Les Suisses, les allies etc.		s 1667	[53 dated 1648]	
63	Bayern Baviere		s 1655	55	
64	Le Tirol		s 1654	54	
65	Hertzogthumber Steyer, etc.		s 1657	57	
66	Ertz-Herzogthumb Osterreich		s 1657	56	
67	Hongrie, Transilvanie, etc.		s 1665	148	
68	Cours du Danube		s 1665	149	
69	Empire d'Allemagne Royaume de Boheme		s 1665	191	
70	La Flandres Gallicane		v		25
71	Estats Cleves et Juliers		s 1648	49	
72	Cercle de Westphalie		s 1659	52	
73	Haute partie de la Basse Saxe		s 1657	63	
74	Basse partie de la Basse Saxe		s 1657	64	
75	Haute Saxe		s 1655	60	
76	Churfurstenthum, und March Brandenburg		s 1654	61	
77	Hertzogthumb Pommern		s 1654	62	
78	La Prusse duché		s 1659	134	
79	La Curlande duché		s 1659	135	
80	Masovie duché, et Polaquie		s 1665	196	
81	La Livonie duché		s 1663	125	
82	La Carelie et l'Ingrie		s 1666	189	
83	Estats de la couronne de Pologne		s 1663	[65 dated 1655]	
?	Partie de Lithuanie		s 1666	199	
95	Basse Podolie ou Palatinat de Braclaw		s 1665	140	

Notes

I.1 A two sheet map with, unusually, a vertical join.

I.8–11 A four-sheet map of Europe if cropped and joined up.

I.23 Gardner's Tyne engraved by Hollar for Stent, is the only English map in the atlases. It was intended to illustrate *England's grievance discovered in relation to the coal-trade*, London, 1655, but copies of the map were still being offered for sale by Stent's successor John Overton as late as 1672 according to his catalogues published in various editions of Fage's *Cosmographie* (Wing F.82).

I.91   Briet's Iapon *c.*1650 in B.M. K.116.55 is an earlier state with fewer alternative names for features to the south of the islands.

II.3–6   A four-sheet map of France if cropped and joined.

II.35   B.M. 23835(7) is an earlier state with no detail beyond the boundaries of the Duché, no cartouche, and without the name of Daniel Widman, who may have been the engraver; one Georgio Widman engraved for Rossi much later, *c.*1685. II.50 seems to be from the same set.

II.37   Possibly intended for the Rossis' *Mercurio Geographico*.

II.41 & 42   Probably from Cartaro's 13 map Atlas of the Provinces of Naples.